Norms and Gender Discrimination
in the Arab World

Norms and Gender Discrimination in the Arab World

Adel SZ Abadeer

NORMS AND GENDER DISCRIMINATION IN THE ARAB WORLD
Copyright © Adel SZ Abadeer, 2015.

First published in 2015 by
PALGRAVE MACMILLAN®
in the United States—a division of St. Martin's Press LLC,
175 Fifth Avenue, New York, NY 10010.

Where this book is distributed in the UK, Europe and the rest of the world,
this is by Palgrave Macmillan, a division of Macmillan Publishers Limited,
registered in England, company number 785998, of Houndmills,
Basingstoke, Hampshire RG21 6XS.

Palgrave Macmillan is the global academic imprint of the above companies
and has companies and representatives throughout the world.

Palgrave® and Macmillan® are registered trademarks in the United States,
the United Kingdom, Europe and other countries.

ISBN: 978–1–137–39854–3

Library of Congress Cataloging-in-Publication Data

Abadeer, Adel SZ, 1954–
    Norms and gender discrimination in the Arab world / Adel SZ Abadeer.
        pages cm
    Includes bibliographical references and index.
    ISBN 978–1–137–39854–3 (hardback : alk. paper)
        1. Women—Arab countries. 2. Sex discrimination against women—
    Arab countries. 3. Women's rights—Arab countries. 4. Arab countries—
    Social life and customs. I. Title.

HQ1784.A623 2015
305.40917'4927—dc23   2015012232

A catalogue record of the book is available from the British Library.

Design by Newgen Knowledge Works (P) Ltd., Chennai, India.

First edition: October 2015

10 9 8 7 6 5 4 3 2 1

To all women in the Arab World

Contents

Part IV Summary and Conclusion

Figures and Tables

Figures

Tables

Acknowledgments

I am grateful for valuable comments from an anonymous reviewer, ideas from my colleagues in the Economics Department at Calvin College, and feedback from conference presentations. I would like to thank Calvin College for granting me a time release to finish the book, and the Economics Department for funding a research assistance work.

I also would like to express my special appreciation to my research assistant, Lauren De Haan, for her insights and editorial assistance.

PART I

Introduction

CHAPTER 1

Introduction

Gender bias and discrimination against women are appalling practices that exist as a manifestation of humanity's fall from grace. Such
practices illustrate the victimization of women in private and public
spheres. In both these spheres, gender roles and reward-punishment schemes
are designed to protect and sustain collective norms and traditions in favor of
the collective community, mostly dominated by men, at the expense of wom-
en's well-being. According to the declaration of the United Nations Committee
on the Elimination of Discrimination against Women (CEDAW), "[T]he term
'discrimination against women' shall mean any distinction, exclusion or restriction made on the basis of sex which has the effect or purpose of impairing or
nullifying the recognition, enjoyment or exercise by women, irrespective of
their marital status, on a basis of equality of men and women, of human rights
and fundamental freedoms in the political, economic, social, cultural, civil or
any other field" (UN 1993: article 1).

In his book *Masculine Domination* (1998), Pierre Bourdieu underscores the
principle of women's inferiority and exclusion, which is related to the principle
of division and dissymmetry of the universe where men and women are considered subjects and objects, agents and instruments, and are treated as such.
In the domain of symbolic exchanges, women only appear as objects or sym-
bols whose meaning is determined by their environment (by men), and whose
function is to contribute to the expansion or perpetuation of the symbolic
capital held by men (Bourdieu 1998). Bourdieu contrasts women's negative
virtue and negative honor (virginity and fidelity) against men's positive virtue
and honors—which can be translated to mean negative and positive freedoms,
respectively. A "real" man feels the need to rise to any challenge as an opportunity to increase his honor by "pursuing glory and distinction in the public
sphere" (Bourdieu 1998: 51).

Accordingly, a woman's honor resides in her body and her reputation, the lat-
ter of which cannot be fully controlled by her, especially in the case of women

with active public lives or active public presence. To sustain their "negative honor" (to use Pierre Bourdieu's term), women should lower their exposure to all incidents that may cause their reputation and their honor to be tarnished. Consequently, women are likely to confine themselves to their private sphere and do their best to reduce any interaction that may damage their honor—such as contact with strangers or exposing their bodies to them—by covering their bodies (wearing sanctioned clothes such as *hijab*, *niqab*, or *burqa*) and ceasing communication with strangers (the non-direct blood relatives). The man upholds or restores honor by guiding or forcing women to behave according to the collective traditions and expectations.

Social markers of female submissiveness include bending, stooping, lowering oneself; submitting, curved, supple postures; docility, and directing the gaze at one's feet and not making eye contact (Bourdieu 1998). Other social markers include women's exclusion or separation in public spheres. An example of this is dress codes, such as requirements that women wear *hijab* (head and neck covering), *abaya* (a loose garment that covers a woman's body except her face and hands),[1] *niqab* (body and face covering, except the eye), or *burqa* (a full body cover; the most strict veil) in public spheres. Female submissiveness is instilled at a young age. This imposed submissiveness exists in many societies, with greater prevalence in gender-discriminating collectivist societies (Bourdieu 1998). In this setting, men also become insidious victims of the dominant representation of honor. The desire to claim honor directs men's perspective and practices like a force—"It guides his actions like a logical necessity . . . but without imposing itself as a rule, or as the implacable logical verdict of a kind of rational calculation" (Bourdieu 1998: 50). This force can lead the man of honor to accept certain actions—like killing his beloved wife, sister, daughter, or even mother—as inevitable and self-evident, which others would view as inconceivable or impossible.

According to Bourdieu, collective expectations or collective privileges place male and female spheres in opposition. The female's sphere is one of fragility and frivolity while the male sphere is one of machismo and virility (1998: 57). Such socially constructed norms and expectations can lead to permanent gender discrimination in societies that sanction such behaviors and expectations. Bourdieu underscores the role of family, religious institutions, the educational system, and the state in continuing the objective and subjective structure of male dominance and female submissiveness. He criticizes religious institutions since "they explicitly inculcate (or used to inculcate) a familialist morality, entirely dominated by patriarchal values, with, in particular, the dogma of the radical inferiority of women" (Bourdieu 1998: 87). The educational system continues to transmit patriarchal notions. These Aristotelian notions are also relayed by the state, "which ratified the prescriptions and proscriptions of private patriarchy with those of public patriarchy" (Bourdieu 1998: 87).

Different aspects of gender discrimination against women are prevalent in almost all countries. The primary purpose of this book is to analyze how informal norms contribute to prevalent gender discrimination in collectivist societies. Members of these societies are taught to conform and subordinate their needs to collective needs, resulting in forced obedience and collective punishment. In contrast, in individualist societies, people are more independent and are usually not locked into traditionally prescribed social norms and rules (Dayan et al., 2001; Howard-Hassmann 1993; Sedikides and Brewer 2001).

Norms refer to socially constructed rules regarding how people should behave in various situations. According to James Coleman, "Norms are expectations— about one's own action, that of others, or both—which express what action is right or what action in wrong" (1987: 135). According to Elinor Ostrom, "Social norms are shared understandings about actions that are obligatory, permitted, or forbidden" (2002: 143–144). Hausman and McPherson underscore that "[norms] are somehow created, modified, sustained, and enforced by people and sometimes they breakdown" (Hausman and McPherson 2006: 85). Jon Elster underscores the influence of punishment on obedience toward norms, "When people obey norms, they often have a particular outcome in mind: they want to avoid the disapproval—ranging from raised eyebrows to social ostracism—of other people" (1989: 104). Social norms are shared by other people and are partly enforced by the members of society. This is in contrast to private norms, which are self-imposed and are not sustained by the approval or disapproval of other individuals (Elster 1989).

Examples of social norms include consumption norms that regulate things such as one's manners of dress, movie viewings, reading habits, and so on; norms against behaviors "contrary to nature," which may differ across different societies, for example, norms against incest, homosexuality (e.g., the Arab world and other societies, in contrast to the West and other societies that accept homosexuality as natural behavior, or at least not contrary to nature), female genital mutilation/cutting (FGM/C) in many societies, and polygyny (Western societies, among others, oppose polygyny as contrary to nature, in contrast to the Arab world, except Tunisia); norms of reciprocity; norms of retribution, which enjoin to return harm done by others; norms of cooperation; work norms, which include norms against living off other people, or norms against participation of women in certain jobs in certain societies, especially gender-discriminating societies; and norms of distribution, which may explain why women, especially individualist women in gender-discriminating societies, may be willing to oppose unfair gender-discriminating norms and rules and expose themselves to social/collective retribution for their behavior/choice rather than accepting these societal norms (Elster 1989).[2]

Certain religious and social norms overlap, especially in collectivist societies. Examples include fasting, attending prayer, adhering to dress codes, and behaving according to socially sacred norms and values.

Norms can be explicit—written or spoken—or implicit, where an individual knows when he/she transgress them. Norms can be classified into prescriptive or descriptive. Prescriptive norms refer to behaviors that are approved by other people, for example, women covering their heads or wearing *niqab* or *burqa* in some parts in the Arab world because they are modest and respectful. Descriptive norms describe typical behaviors without imposing a judgment on them, for example, more women in the Arab world cover their heads or wear the *niqab* or *burqa*.

Norms should be distinguished from habits since habits are private, not enforced by others, and "their violation does not generate self-blame or guilt" (Elster 1989: 106). Some economists, who argue for the collective rationality of norms, claim that these social norms have good social consequences that explain the existence of such norms, for example, norms of hospitality and fairness (Elster 1989). However, not all social norms have good social consequences, due to the negative effects of certain prevalent norms on potential victims because of these victims' exclusion or reduced weights in the initiation and practice of these norms. Examples of such norms include FGM/C, "honor killing," and constraints on women's freedom of choice of wardrobe, movement, education, employment, and social and political activities and participation in gender-discriminating societies. Thus, some followers of certain social norms are influenced by fear of collective punishment and ostracism, such that social norms "create powerful incentives that guide people's behaviors—as spouses, parents, and citizens and workers—and behavior outside the accepted boundaries can unleash formal and informal systems of sanction" (The World Bank 2001: 109).

Informal norms, such as customs,[3] taboos,[4] mores,[5] religions, traditions, and codes of conduct, play important roles in sustaining and perpetuating gender discrimination and can dominate or supersede political, social, and economic interests in some collectivist societies. Many of those placed at an advantage by these informal norms unknowingly benefit from them while others make deliberate use of these norms to exploit others through institutional power structures (Hausman and McPherson 1993).

The definition of a norm is very close to the definition of culture. Culture encompasses the range of human worldviews, beliefs, ideas, and behaviors that are not attributed to genetic inheritance. It also refers to various activities and attributes such as moral standards, and norms of individuals, groups, or societies (Smith 2001; Williams 1976; Kroeber and Kluckhohn 1952; Storey 2009). The United Nations Educational, Scientific, and Cultural Organization (UNESCO) defines culture as "the set of distinctive spiritual, material, intellectual, and emotional features of society or a social group, and it encompasses, in addition to art and literature, lifestyle, ways of living together, value systems, tradition and beliefs" (2009: 9). According to Arnold Toynbee, culture consists of "regularities in the behavior, internal and external, of the members of the society, excluding those regularities that are purely hereditary" (Quoted in Akerlof 1976: 600).[6] Popular culture refers to the culture that is widely accepted or favored by many people. It also refers to hegemony, which is the way the dominant group in society seeks to win the consent of subordinate groups, through the process of manipulating intellectual and moral leaderships (Storey 2009: 10), propagating its norms and values, and forcing the subordinate groups to assimilate their norms and values with those of the dominant group. Moral standards and norms are among the major domains of the cultural system (Storey 2009: 27). This book uses "culture" to designate the entire way of life (activities, beliefs, and customs of people, groups, or societies) (Smith 2001).[7] Cultural practices and exchanges that represent the nondiscriminatory artistic features of the intellectual, spiritual, and aesthetic development of a group or a society should be welcomed as a manifestation of society's heritage and beliefs. However, in many societies, especially the collectivist ones, certain aspects of culture may represent the worldview of the dominant and elite group(s) at the expense of marginalizing and sometimes excluding subordinate groups from participating in the formation and practices of such beliefs and customs. Karl Marx emphasized the role of dominant ideology that reflects the interests of the ruling elites—for example, the bourgeois in capitalist societies—which makes conventional and socially constructed norms and roles seem natural. Dominant ideology engages a mistaken or distorted view of reality, which allows people remain content with their miserable life. Jack Knight defines ideology as "the beliefs and values—the cognitive map—according to which social actors interpret and give meaning to the world" (Knight 1992).

Ideology refers to a worldview shaped in part by existing social institutions, including what others do and what they are expected to do. Accordingly, "a women's ideological perspective regarding the proper role of women is formed by the existing conventions and norms of her society" (Knight 1992: 81). According to Denzau and North, ideologies are "the shared framework of mental models that groups of individuals possess that provide both an interpretation of the environment and a prescription as to how that environment should be structured" (Denzau and North 1993: para 3). Ideology also refers to a certain articulated ideas by specific group of people (Storey 2009). Ideology may indicate how some texts and practices present distorted images of reality, producing false consciousness. These distortions serve the interest of the powerful against the interests of the powerless, for example, the capitalist ideology according to Karl Marx. The dominant class or group do not see themselves as exploiters or oppressors. More importantly, the powerless—the subordinate groups—do not see themselves as oppressed or exploited (Storey 2009). Ideology also refers to the power relation outside of the center of dominance/power, for example the feminists' notion of how the patriarchal ideology tries to conceal, mask, and distort gender relation in society (Storey 2009). Roland Barthes underscores the role of connotation when referring to ideology or myth, in which the society refers to its values and norms positively, while views others' norms and values negatively (in Storey 2009). For example, in the Arab world, women's freedom connotes lack of morality and modesty, while collectivist norms and values that constrain women's freedom connote respect, discipline, and modesty. Other examples from the Arab world include the following: secularism connotes atheism; women's freedom connotes profanity, lack of morality, and the breaking down of families and societies; and, adherence to prayers, *jihad*, and other religious rituals connotes solidarity and faithfulness. In addition, Valentine's Day connotes adultery and immoral relations, and mimicking unwelcome foreign practices and norms.

Ideology also refers to the power relation outside of the power center, for instance, feminists speak against patriarchal ideology and how it distorts gender relations in society, whereas specific elements of the victim groups speak of the majority or oppressors' ideology. Media, texts, films, and so on can be exploited to represent the particular image of the world chosen by the elite/winners.

Certain aspects of culture discriminate, marginalize, and exclude population groups on the basis of ethnicity, race, religion, gender, and so on. Such discriminating cultural practices or values should be opposed, confronted, and repealed since they violate basic human rights.

Some norms are inclusive and moral since they contribute to the advancement of all individuals, groups, and societies. Other norms are converted to formal rules by the state or the collective leadership in the community, who impose them on other members or groups. Gender-discriminating norms (FGM/C, discrimination in education and employment, restrictions on women's movement, under-age marriage, violence against women, spousal rape, and excluding women from certain spheres such as the legislative, executive, and judicial branches of government) in certain collectivist societies are examples of norms and norm-based-laws[8] and regulations. These norms are associated with gender distributional effect, benefiting certain members or group(s)—mostly men—in leadership roles at the expense of others—mostly women.

Gender-discriminating norms and rules that inflict pain on women, marginalize them, and/or exclude them from certain spheres and functions raise questions about their morality. However, morality is a very complex term. It is in large part a human construct, where individuals can determine right and wrong in their societies based on personal feelings and beliefs (Hausman and McPherson 2006). Not all norms are morally defensible. Amrtya Sen (1990) highlights some norms of intrafamilial inequality that discourage women from objecting to the unequal distribution of food between boys and girls, and to the millions of premature female deaths. More established "in groups" may benefit from norms at the expense of other disadvantaged groups (Hausman and McPherson 2006). What is considered immoral practice of gender-discriminating norms according the universal human rights may not be immoral in societies that sanction or condone these norms or rules. Examples include the violation of women's bodily integrity in the case of FGM/C, domestic violence, and "honor killing" norms and rules in certain countries in the Arab world (U.S. DOSa 2014).

Moral norms are a subclass of social norms. They are marked by their subject matters, "interpersonal interaction where significant benefits and harms are at stake," the weights of moral norms "typically override other considerations," and the internal (inner guilt and feeling shame) and external (blame, shame and other forms of collective punishments) sanctions attached to the violations of these norms (Hausman and McPherson 2006: 81). Internal and external sanctions influence compliance with norms. Individuals comply with norms in part because their net benefit (individual and collective benefits minus individual and collective costs) warrants such compliance. It is in their best interests to do so. Allan Gibbard, a renowned ethical theorist, underscores the difference between accepting a norm and "being in the grip" of a norm (Hausman and McPherson 2006). Acceptance of norms reflects a deliberative judgment and a conscious endorsement of the norm. In contrast, "being in the grip" reflects the involuntary state in which one finds oneself moved by the demand of a norm while believing it to be pointless or improper (Hausman and McPherson 2006).

It is important to distinguish between conventional morality and critical morality. Conventional morality is what society, especially the dominant group(s) and elite leadership, believe to be morally correct. Critical morality refers to what is actually morally correct (Karayiannis and Hatzis 2010). The norm of reciprocity, which is considered as an "indispensable norm for social justice, political stability, and social harmony" (Aristotle, in Karayiannis and Hatzis 2010: 6) plays an important role in gender equality. However, many customs and traditions in gender-discriminating societies lack reciprocity, generating significant distributional effect in which some groups, intentionally or unintentionally, enjoy significant gains at the expense of others. In many societies, the norm of reciprocity is not honored due to the skewed distribution of power. In gender-discriminating societies, the act of opposing certain gender-discriminating practices may generate negative reciprocity, since opposing such practices provokes collectively based retaliations against these attacks on collective moral norms. As early as in Ancient Athenian society, stigma and punishment have been used as social control mechanisms to reinforce moral norms (Karayiannis and Hatzis 2010). Collective control over education and media serves to impose such moral norms on individuals and/or internalize them in people's minds, the winners and victims of skewed moral norms, men and women in the case of gender "moral" norms respectively. In addition, collective shame and punishment are used to deter any behavior contrary to prevailing moral norms (Karayiannis and Hatzis 2010). In these societies, anonymity is usually not protected where individual behavior is a common knowledge. This also explains the crucial role of individuals' reputations in these societies in avoiding potential collective shame and punishment. Reputation, in many societies, per se, is a good enough reason to initiate collective reaction in terms of punishing dissenters or rewarding adherents of moral norms.

Some social scientists doubt the influence of moral norms on people's behaviors, claiming that people follow norms because such norms serve their interests. Others assert the influence of moral norms on people's behaviors (Hausman and McPherson 2006). Collective control over education and media imposes such moral norms on individuals and internalizes them within the mindset of the society.

This book focuses on how informal norms influence the structure of formal rules on people's behaviors. The compound effects of informal institutions and formal rules limit and sometimes prohibit women's participation in certain practices, for example, certain jobs and political and judicial positions (Nussbaum 1988, 2000, 2011; Sen 1985a, b, 1992, 1999, 2002; U.S. DOSa 2014).

Gender Discrimination in Less Developed Countries (LDCs)

Although varying degrees of gender discrimination exist in almost all countries, it is more widespread in collectivist LDCs, where restrictions are imposed on women to deprive them from certain liberties. The prevalence of discriminating informal norms and traditions provoke, encourage, and even reward gender discrimination in many LDCs. The absence or ineffective presence of formal rules (e.g., statutory laws, common laws and regulations, and their enforcements) that protect women's rights, invites male dominant collectivist units (or groups) to exploit women's vulnerability. Furthermore, gender discriminatory practices, regardless of how appalling, may be of less significance to LDC governments, given other urgent problems that LDC governments face. Governments' limited resources, skewed priorities, and the prevalence of corruption in many LDCs play their role, as well.

In some LDC societies, governments use gender-discriminating norms and rules as political instruments to settle certain disputes with rival groups or respond to internal pressure, usually from powerful religious groups, at the expense of further victimization of women.

Examples of such practices include the ill-fated death of thirteen schoolgirls in Mecca, Saudi Arabia, after a fire in their school dorm, because the *Mutawe'en* (the virtue police in Saudi Arabia; formally, the Commission for the Promotion of Virtue and Prevention of Vice) kept the girls inside, and even beat girls who tried to escape the fire because the girls were not wearing the headscarves and *Abayas* (loose black robes) according to the *Mutawe'en's* strict interpretation of Islamic sanctioned dress code (BBC 2002; Al Banna 2013). An Afghani presidential decree, in March 2009, permits spousal rape and the husband's right to confine his wife or wives to their home—such that women cannot leave home except with the permission of their husbands—is another example of the influence of gender-discriminating norms on formal rules and laws (USCIRF 2011: 220). The truce between the Pakistani government and the *Taliban,* allows the *Taliban* to close girls' schools in regions under their control (USA Today 2009). In 2009, the Sudanese police arrested thirteen women for wearing trousers instead of the Islamic sanctioned *hijab*, according to the authority's interpretation of Islamic *shari'ah*/law (NBC News 2009). In March 2013, Hamas, the ruling group in Gaza (part of the Occupied Palestinian Territories) imposed a law separating sexes in schools starting at the age of nine, in accordance with its strict interpretation of sacred Islamic norms/teachings, effective from September 2013 in all schools, including private and Christian schools. Furthermore, in March 2013, Hamas banned women from participating in Gaza's UNRWA-organized marathon because it contradicts Islamic norms and traditions. The ban prompted UNRWA to cancel the event (Al Jazeera 2013).[9] In Egypt, the 2012 Constitution (before the toppling of the government in 2013) removed a clause that specifically guaranteed equality for women, leaving room for discriminatory interpretations (USA Today 2013). In March 2013, the Muslim Brotherhood, which came to power in Egypt after the parliamentary and presidential elections in Egypt in 2011/12, issued a statement against a proposed UN declaration to condemn violence against women. The statement rejected the UN declaration since it contradicts the principles of Islam, and claimed that the declaration aims to destroy both the family and society (Washington Times 2013).

The Case Studies: The Arab World

The Arab world is an excellent case study for analyzing how gender-discriminating norms marginalize women in LDCs. The Arab world's countries have long histories of cultural norms and traditions that can be traced back many centuries and even millennia (see Appendix 1.1 for lists of countries in the Arab world according to the Leagues of Arab States, United Nations Development Programme (UNDP), and the World Bank). Unfortunately, women are among the main victims of the discriminating norms and traditions that have been inherited and perpetuated. Certain understandings, interpretations, and practices of sacred norms, which are embedded in traditions, codes of conduct, and formal laws, are used or exploited to discriminate against women in both private and public spheres.[10] Moreover, these discriminating norms can be exploited as political instruments by the "winners" of such institutional settings to perpetuate their dominance and to sustain their inherited gains at the expense of the victims. Even though gender discrimination is not limited to certain aspects of Arab or Islamic dominant cultures, there are strikingly prominent features in these cultures (at varying levels) that are exploited to discriminate against women.

Most Arab countries have objected to and have had reservations about many important articles in international conventions and treaties on the human rights for women because they are at odds with well-established sacred norms and formal rules and practices in these countries/societies (Burch 2004 U.S. DOSa, 2010; UN 2010).

International socioeconomic indicators provide clear signs of gender discrimination in most Arab countries. For example, The UNDP's Gender Inequality Index (GII)[11] shows the Arab world with a GII of 0.546 to be among the group of countries with the highest gender inequality index compared with the world average of 0.450, as shown in figure 1.1.

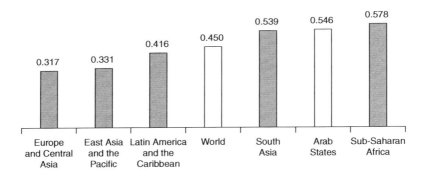

Figure 1.1 Gender inequality index, developing countries regions, 2013.
Source: UNDP (2014) table 4: 172–175.

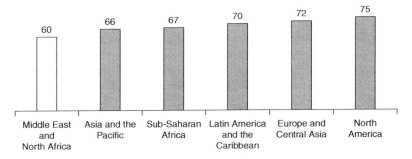

Figure 1.2   Global Gender Gap Index, regional performance, 2014 (%).

The MENA region includes 15 Arab countries and Israel. Taking Israel out of this group would lower the index of this region further, since Israel ranked 65th with GGGI of 70 percent.

Source: Data compiled from Global Gender Gap Report (2014).

The 2013 Global Gender Gap Report also ranks the Middle East and North Africa (MENA) region at the bottom in terms of the global gender gap index (GGGI), compared to other regions in the world as shown in figure 1.2. GGGI was introduced by the World Economic Forum in 2006 to measure the gaps (rather than the levels, since levels of available resource and opportunities differ among countries) in four sub-indices: economic participation and opportunity, education, political empowerment, and health (Global Gender Gap Report 2014). Furthermore, GGGI measures the gaps in outcome rather than the gaps in means, since the means may not be transformed into actual functioning due to various constraints against using such means. A higher score means lower gender gap, and vice versa. The fourteen Arab countries in the report rank near or at the bottom of 142 countries. None of the Arab countries ranks in the top 100 countries.

Figure 1.3 takes a closer look at the Arab countries' global gender gap index, and their ranking at or near the bottom of the 142 surveyed countries. Twelve of the Arab countries were among the bottom 20 countries.

The MENA region ranked lowest, with significant gaps in economic participation and political empowerment (Global Gender Gap Report 2014).

Similarly, the UNDP's Gender Empowerment Measure[12] points to the prevalence of gender discrimination in the Arab world, which contains five of the six worst ranks: Morocco, Algeria, Saudi Arabia, Egypt, Bangladesh, and Yemen, respectively (UNDP 2009 table K: 186–190). The Arab world also ranks last in categories such as female participation rate in labor force, percentage of seats held by females in national parliament (UNDP 2014 table 4), and satisfaction with freedom of choice (UNDP 2014 table 9). Most Arab countries rank near the bottom of the world rankings with regard to the ratio of estimated female-to-male earned income, holding fourteen of the eighteen lowest ranks. The other four countries are Iran, India, Afghanistan, and Pakistan (UNDP 2009 table K). The above trends and records of gender inequality and discrimination warrant further research of the causes of such dismal records of women's capabilities.

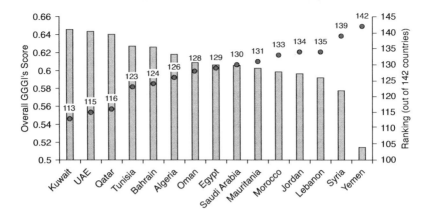

Figure 1.3 Global Gender Gap Index (GGGI), and ranking of the Arab countries (out of 142 countries), 2014.

Source: Data compiled from Global Gender Gap Report (2014) table 5: 12.

There are, however, growing indications of positive changes that are taking place in some Arab and Middle-Eastern countries with regard to repealing gender-discriminating formal laws, especially in less collectivist societies and countries such as Tunisia. Recently, some small steps in the Kingdom of Saudi Arabia took place when King Abdullah granted women the right to vote and run in municipal elections for the first time, starting in 2015 (MacFarquhar 2011), and allowed two Saudi female athletes to participate in the 2012 London Olympics for the first time in history (Pilon 2012). These small steps could be a signal of significant policy change.

Gender Discrimination Statistics Do Not Tell the Whole Story

Estimates of cases of discrimination against women vary significantly due to the complexity and the formal "illegality" of such practices. Discrimination against women is considered illegal in almost all countries in which governments have signed international and regional treaties and conventions regarding the protection of human rights including women's rights. Such treaties include the Universal Declaration of Human Rights (UDHR) in 1948, The Convention of the Elimination of all Forms of Discrimination against Women (CEDAW) in 1979, and The Declaration on the Elimination of Violence against Women in 1993, inter alia. Nonetheless, many governments often deny or obscure the presence of gender-discriminating practices in their countries, or downplay their extent, for fear of losing trade privileges, foreign assistance, foreign investment, or for the sake of preserving national pride. Statistics on gender discrimination, especially on violence against women, are difficult to find, especially in collectivist societies, where claims and reports of gender discrimination and abuse are usually obscured or denied. Many incidences go unreported, and the reported incidences are typically considered minor and are usually dismissed (Ghanim 2009). "One of the most common forms of violence against women is that performed by a husband or male partner. This type of violence is frequently invisible since it happened behind closed doors, and effectively, when legal systems and cultural norms do not treat domestic violence as a crime, but rather as a 'private' family matter, or a normal part of life" (WHO 2012). Many victims of gender violence do not volunteer to share information because they feel shame; they fear they will be blamed for such violence, and they fear reprisal (CHANGE 1999). Chapter 11 will explain the issue of violence against women in more detail.

Many victimized women may not recognize their marginalized status since they inherit and are taught to accept their "inferior" status. Others may not have the notion that they have been wronged. Consequently, women tend to accept the prevailing norms and practices in their surrounding communities that make them ignorant about the violations of their basic human rights and capabilities (Nussbaum 2000: 140). In a study on violence against women in Qatar, Kaltam Al-Ghanem highlights the ignorance of some victims about their own victimization, "The essence of this workshop [violence against women in Qatar] is to create awareness that there is violence within the family here, because most females are not even aware that they are victims of domestic violence. We want them to know and speak out" (2008).

Even when women recognize the violation of their rights, personal shame and stigma associated with being victimized may deter many of them from identifying themselves as abused or victimized (El Saadawi 1980; de Bary 1998; UN 2006; Ghanim 2009; UNICEF 2012). Only a small fraction of gender discrimination or incidences of violence are reported, usually when such incidences are so severe that they satisfy the collective thresholds of discrimination or violence. Such collective thresholds are much higher than those in individualist societies, or those used in international human rights conventions, declarations, and protocols. Bassam Kadi, a human rights activist in Syria, states, "A woman needs to have her nose broken before she can really do anything. The laws do not deal with all types of violence, like mere beating. There should be details on the role of the laws in promoting violence. They needed to ask for new laws that protect women from all types of violence" (Roumani 2006).

The application of different criteria and procedures by international organizations, NGOs, and governments adds to the difficulty of identifying and counting cases of gender discrimination accurately and objectively. The credibility, methods, and the motives of organizations or agents that make such estimates may tempt these organizations and agents to overstate or understate the number of cases of gender discrimination in the Arab world.

Prevalence of Gender Discrimination in LDCs: Example from the Arab World

The following data, statistics, and practices highlight the prevalence of gender discrimination against women in the Arab world. These examples are used

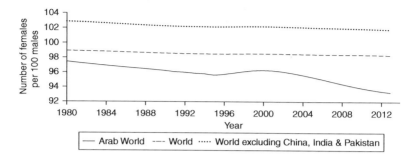

Figure 1.4 Number of females per 100 males in total population, 1980–2013.

Source: Data collected from the World Bank (2014) World Development Indicators 2014. Last updated September 24, 2014. http://data.worldbank.org/data-catalog/world-development-indicators.

throughout the book to untangle the role of discriminating informal norms in marginalizing women and depriving them of basic human rights.

A. Low female-male population ratio: most countries in the Arab world have a female-male ratio of less than 100 females per 100 males, which is lower than the world ratio.[13] Figure 1.4 shows the low female-male ratio in total population in the Arab world for the period of 1980–2013. The number of females per 100 males—in terms of the total population of the Arab world in 2013—was about 93.3, compared to almost 98.4 females per 100 males in the world. However, the number of females per 100 males in the world, excluding China, India, and Pakistan in 2013, was 101.8 (the ratios in China, India, and Pakistan are 92.9, 93.4, and 94.7 respectively in these heavy populated countries with a history of gender discrimination).[14]

Many studies[15] underscore the disturbing phenomena of low female-male ratios in China, South Asia, and the Middle East. Estimates of missing women are about 6.7 percent in China, 7.9 percent in India, 7.8 in Pakistan, 4.2 percent in Bangladesh, 4.2 percent in West Asia (3.1% in Syria and 2.4% in Turkey), 9.3 percent in Afghanistan, 3.7 percent in Iran, 4.6 percent in Egypt, 1.2 percent in Algeria, and 2.1 percent in Tunisia (Klasen 2008). These countries account for about 94 percent of the more than 100 million women missing from around the world (Klasen 2004 table 1: 24).[16]

B. Gender selective feticide: Research shows evidence of selective abortion of female fetuses (whose sex is detected by ultrasound and amniocentesis) and of female infanticide (Heise et al. 1994) in many LDCs. There are no comparable statistics on gender selective feticide in the Arab world; however, the low female-male population ratio in most of the Arab countries sheds some light on the presence of female feticide in this region (Yount 2001; Yount et al. 2000). Research in Egypt shows a preference for sons among couples in terms of fertility behaviors and their uses of contraceptives (Yount et al. 2000). A World Bank study on fertility decisions shows strong preference for sons in the Arab world and South Asia, compared to the rest of the world (Filmer et al. 2008).

C. Discriminatory childcare: In societies where boys are more highly valued than girls, boys receive more preventive care and more timely attention when they fall ill. In some societies, girls receive less food or less nutritious food than boys, which may lead to malnutrition and impaired physical development among girls (Ravindran 1986; Tandon and Sharma 2008; Yount 2003). These are factors of the unusually high mortality rate among young girls in many countries in the Middle East, among other countries. The relatively high mortality among young girls is due to the fact that they enjoy much lower odds of visiting doctors than boys do, the widespread familial bias against young girls with regard to nutrition and investment on girls' access to curative care and professional management of illness episodes, and girls receiving less access to immunization. Discriminatory childcare with regards to young girls is due in part to inherited discriminatory norms, women's lack of financial independence, and their dependency on their husbands, which are all symptoms and outcomes of gender-discriminating norms in many countries (Yount 2003).

D. Female genital mutilation/cutting (FGM/C): FGM/C is widespread in many countries in the Arab world, especially in poor rural areas. Recent statistics from UNICEF show that the percentage of women aged 15–49 who have been subject to FGM/C is 98 percent in Somalia in 2006, 93 percent in Djibouti in 2006, 91 percent in Egypt in 2008, 88 percent in Sudan in 2010, 69 percent in Mauritania in 2011, and 19 percent in Yemen in 2013 (UNICEF 2014). Remarkably, there are no formal laws against FGM/C in many countries (U.S. DOSa, 2011), which leave the continuation of FGM/C practices to the widespread belief in inherited norms and traditions that promote FGM/C. An estimated two million young girls are victims of FGM/C each year. FGM/C is often performed under unsterile conditions. Such an invasive procedure can lead to death, acute pain, recurrent urinary tract infections, mental trauma, painful intercourse, complications during childbirth, and death (WHO 2001, 2008, 2013; Yoder et al. 2004). Chapter 10 analyzes FGM/C in detail, focusing on the role of informal norms in sustaining FGM/C in some societies/countries in the Arab world.

E. Female under-age and forced marriage: Female under-age marriage is widespread in the Arab World and other regions in the world, especially among the poor and rural regions. 45 percent of girls younger than eighteen years are married in Somalia, 35 percent in Mauritania, 33 percent in Sudan, 32 percent in Yemen, 17 in Egypt, 16 in Morocco, and 13 percent in Syria (UNICEF 2013c). The practice of female underage marriage in the Arab world is mostly practiced with the consent of a male guardian (usually the father), according to inherited informal norms (Jamjoom, 2009). Studies also show a rise in the phenomenon of temporary marriage—also known as summer marriage or tourism marriage—in Egypt, and other Arab countries, where much older wealthy tourists from the Arabian Gulf (mostly from Saudi Arabia, Kuwait and United Arab Emirates) marry underage girls for a temporary period ranging from two weeks to two months (in some cases for a few hours) through marriage brokers who share the dowry with the parents of the underage brides

(Al-Aharam 2009; McGrath 2013; Mansouri 2013; U.S. DOSa 2014). Further analysis is covered in chapter 11.

F. Discrimination against women in labor markets and economic participation: the influence of informal norms on formal rules and governance structures of transactions impose significant constraints to female participation in the labor force and the unemployment rates among women in gender-discriminating collective societies.

The 2014 Human Development Report shows the striking gap between the Arab world's female labor-force participation rates (the percentage of female population ages 15–64 who are members of the labor force) and the world rates. In 2012, the female labor-force participation in the Arab world was 24.7 percent, which is lower than half the world rate of 50.6 percent. This significant gap reveals the acceptance of gender-discriminating informal norms and the existence of formal restrictions and more costly governance structures of transactions against female employment and entry into the labor force in the Arab world. The World Bank's statistics show that the ratio of female-male labor-force participation in the Arab world was 33.7 percent in 2012, about half of the world ratio of 66 percent, highlighting gender segregation, societal pressures, and formal laws and government regulations that ban women from participating in certain sectors or jobs (U.S. DOSa: Saudi Arabi 2014; Human Rights Watch 2014a). The Arab countries make up 14 of the bottom 20 ranked counties in terms of the ratio of female-male labor-force participation. The other six countries include five West- and South-Asian countries: Turkey, India, Pakistan, Iran, and Afghanistan (UNDP 2014 table 4: 172–175).

Moreover, the Arab world ranked last compared to other regions in the world in economic participation and opportunity index. This includes the gaps in labor-force participation rates, the remuneration and advancement gaps, ratios of women to men among legislators, senior officials, and managers, and ratio of women to men among professional and technical workers (Global Gender Gap Report 2014: 5) as seen in figure 1.5. The MENA region (includes fourteen Arab countries and Israel) ranks significantly lower than the rest of the world (the index should be lower if Israel is removed from this

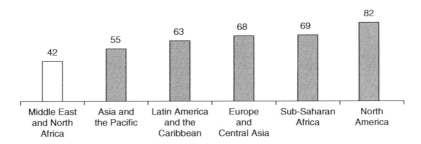

Figure 1.5 Global Gender Gap Index: Economic Participation and Opportunity Index, Regional Performance, 2014 (%).

Source: Data collected from Global Gender Gap Report (2014). Geneva, Switzerland.

list, since Israel's index is 64 percent; much higher than the region's index of 42%). The report also shows that 11 Arab countries are among the bottom 15 countries in the ranking of labor force participation rate gap (the other countries are Pakistan, Iran, India, and Turkey), 14 Arab countries are among the bottom 17 countries in terms of estimated earned income gap (the other countries are Iran, Pakistan, and India), and 10 Arab countries were among the bottom 12 countries in the ratio of women to men in legislators, senior officials and managers (the other countries are Pakistan, and Bangladesh) (Global Gender Gap Report 2014).

G. **Excessive constraints and limitations on women's political rights:** Gender-discriminating norms play an important role in curtailing women's leadership and political rights and representation. According to widely accepted religious norms in the Arab world and other similar countries, women should not have leadership over men, especially in high-level roles in judicial, legislative, and executive branches. Figure 1.6 shows the percentage of seats held by women in national parliaments in the Arab world compared to other regions in the world.

This may in part be explained by the imposed restrictions on female participation in political affairs and in high-level decision-making processes. In certain countries, women are completely excluded from running for a political office.[17] Further analysis is covered in chapter 13.

Figure 1.7 shows a comprehensive index of gender gap in political empowerment published by the World Economic Forum. It measures, "the gap between men and women at the highest level of political decision-making through the ratio of women to men in minister-level positions and the ratio of women to men in parliamentary positions" (Global Gender Gap Report (2014: 5).

H. **Violence against women:** Inherited norms and traditions condone and even encourage violence against women in many societies. Violence against women exacerbates in countries where there is no law against domestic violence, or where this is a lack of effective enforcement of laws against offenders

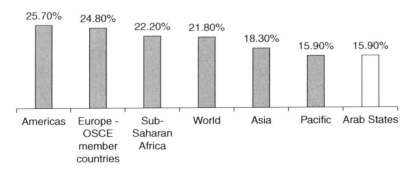

Figure 1.6 Percentage of women in National Parliaments (Both Lower and Upper Combined), World Regions, 2014.

Source: Inter-Parliamentary Union (2014), http://ipu.org/wmn-e/arc/world010914.htm. As of September 1, 2014. OSCE: Organization for Security and Co-operation in Europe.

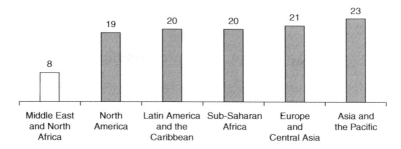

Figure 1.7 Global Gender Gap Index: Political Empowerment, Regional Performance, 2014 (%).
Source: Data collected from Global Gender Gap Report (2014). Geneva, Switzerland.

(U.S. DOSa 2014; Kassem et al. 2012). There are also excessive legal, financial, and cultural barriers that prevent women from reporting domestic violence. A 2008 survey by the Egyptian Center for Women's Rights (ECWR) shows that 83 percent of Egyptian women have been sexually harassed, 50 percent of women faced harassment (U.S. DOSa: Egypt 2010), and 50 percent of female victims of domestic violence were beaten by their husbands (US-DOSa: Egypt 2008). A more recent survey in 2011 shows that 81 percent of Egyptian men think they have the right to beat their wives and daughters (U.S. DOSa: Egypt 2014). In Morocco, more than 50 percent of women agree that a husband is justified in beating his wife if she goes out without his permission, neglects the children, or argues with him (Kishor and Subaiya 2008).

I. Other constraints and discriminating norms against women's choices: In many Arab countries, women lack viable alternatives with regards to marriage, divorce, inheritance, child custody, traveling, and access to the judicial system. Such constraints on choices are rooted in cultural and religious norms and interpretation of sacred texts or teachings (U.S. DOSa 2014).

J. Honor killing: Honor killing refers to the killing of an individual, mostly girls or women, for committing acts that bring dishonor to the family or the collective group according to existing honor/shame norms and traditions. In Egypt, the law does not specifically address "honor" crimes, and there are no reliable statistics of such; these crimes do occur, however, especially in rural areas (U.S. DOSa: Egypt 2014). A study on female homicide in Alexandria, Egypt, shows that 47 percent of all women killed were murdered by a relative after being raped (CHANGE 1999).[18] In Jordan, The Cassation Court generally cuts the Supreme Criminal Court's judgment against the honor killing perpetrators by half. Based on the general Amnesty Law in Jordan, the government drops charges against a perpetrator as soon as the family does. Customs in Jordan and other countries too, dictate the rape victim's family may spare the rape victim's life if the perpetrator (rapist) marries her (U. S. DOSa: Jordan 2014). In Algeria, laws provide a "crime of passion" provision with less punishment for the perpetrators of honor crimes (U. S. DOSa: Algeria 2014). The majority of Arab women killed in Israel and the occupied territories were killed because of alleged inappropriate relationships (U. S. DOSa: Israel and the Occupied Territories 2014). In Iraq, honor crimes are sometimes arranged to appear as suicide, and the sentences against the perpetrators of honor crimes are mitigated to a maximum of three years in prison (U. S. DOSa: Iraq 2014). In Kuwait, honor crimes are considered misdemeanors with a maximum punishment of three years in prison and a small fine (U.S. DOSa: Kuwait 2014).[19] A female's disobedience with regard to immoral, especially sexual, behavior is the most common reason given to justify honor killings, even if this behavior is only rumored (U.S. DOSa 2014; UN 2006). Further analysis of honor killing is covered in chapter 11.

In the Arab world, Middle East, and other collectivist societies in the world, the honor of a family or a man is connected to the chastity of the women in their family. Sexually dishonored women who are victims of rape or who engage in sex outside the marriage disgrace the honor of their families, and therefore are punished accordingly, sometimes with death.

K. Excessive reservations to international human rights conventions/treaties: Almost all Arab states that ratified The Convention on Elimination of all Forms of Discrimination against Women (CEDAW) submitted reservations to certain articles, compared to 26 percent of the non-Arab states that ratified CEDAW (this ratio would be lower if South Asian states were excluded). Most reservations were based on the incompatibility between the articles and the formalized sacred norms in the laws of many Arab countries. A more detailed analysis of the rationale of many Arab states' reservations to articles in conventions on women's human rights will be covered in chapter 2.

Contents of the Book

In addition to the introduction in Part I, the contents of the book are divided into three parts. Part II is the heart of the book, covering the theoretical foundations required to understand the role of norms in institutions and their influence on gender relationships and discrimination against women, especially in collectivist societies in less developed countries. Part II is comprised of eight chapters. Chapter 2 highlights the importance of institutions and how informal norms influence institutions. Chapter 3 Analyses the relation between norms, cultural relativism, and gender discrimination. Chapter 4 highlights the capability approach and its crucial role in understanding how discriminating norms constrain and distort women's capabilities. Chapter 5 illustrates the characteristics of collectivist societies (in contrast to individualist societies) in the Arab World and other less developed countries. Chapter 6 highlights how metanorms enforce and advance gender-discriminating norms in collectivist societies. Chapter 7 explains how women internalize and even justify gender discrimination. Chapter 8 highlights how discriminating norms skew the distribution of *status goods* between men and women in collectivist societies and the effects of the skewed distribution of status goods on women. Chapter 9 concludes part II with an analysis of how the high thresholds of measuring gender discrimination, injury, and violence against women tend to underscore and obscure the prevalence of gender discrimination, and aid in sustaining such practices in many collectivist societies.

Part III covers some case studies of gender-discriminating norms and practices in the Arab World. Chapter 10 analyzes FGM/C, and the role of norms in sustaining FGM/C in the Arab World. Chapter 11 highlights how prevalent norms are exploited to condone or justify domestic violence against women. Chapter 12 covers the influence of discriminating norms in restricting women's economic rights. Chapter 13 illustrates how discriminating norms restrict and exclude women from specific aspects of the legal and political rights, power, and representation. The book ends with a summary and conclusion in part IV.

Appendix 1.1: Lists of Countries in the Arab World

Due to applying different criteria, the list of Arab countries may differ from one international organization to another. Table A1.1 provides lists of countries in the Arab world according to their membership in the League of Arab States, the UNDP's (United Nations Development Programme) list of the Arab States, the World Bank's list of the Arab World, the World Bank's list of countries in MENA, and the World Economic Forum's list of countries in MENA.

Table A1.1 List of Arab countries

Country	League of Arab States	UNDP's Arab States	World Bank's Arab Word	World Bank's MENA[a]	World Economic Forum's MENA
Algeria	Yes	Yes	Yes	Yes	Yes
Bahrain	Yes	Yes	Yes	No	Yes
Comoros	Yes	No	Yes	No	No
Djibouti	Yes	Yes	Yes	Yes	No
Egypt	Yes	Yes	Yes	Yes	Yes
Iraq	Yes	Yes	Yes	Yes	No
Jordan	Yes	Yes	Yes	Yes	Yes
Kuwait	Yes	Yes	Yes	No	Yes
Lebanon	Yes	Yes	Yes	Yes	Yes
Libya	Yes	Yes	Yes	Yes	No
Mauritania	Yes	No	Yes	No	Yes
Morocco	Yes	Yes	Yes	Yes	Yes
Oman	Yes	Yes	Yes	No	Yes
Palestine (West Bank and Gaza)	Yes	Yes	Yes	Yes	No
Qatar	Yes	Yes	Yes	No	Yes
Saudi Arabia	Yes	Yes	Yes	No	Yes

Continued

Table A1.1 Continued

Country	League of Arab States	UNDP's Arab States	World Bank's Arab Word	World Bank's MENA[a]	World Economic Forum's MENA
Somali	Yes	Yes	Yes	No	No
Sudan	Yes	Yes	Yes	No	No
Syria[b]	N0	Yes	Yes	Yes	Yes
Tunisia	Yes	Yes	Yes	Yes	Yes
United Arab Emirates	Yes	Yes	Yes	No	Yes
Yemen	Yes	Yes	Yes	Yes	Yes
Iran	No	No	No	Yes	No
Israel	No	No	No	No	Yes

[a] MENA: Middle East and North Africa.
[b] Syria was suspended from the League of Arab States in November 2011.

Sources: Arab League Online: http://www.arableagueonline.org/hello-world/#more-1; the UNDP's (United Nations Development Programme) list of Arab States: http://www.undp.org/content/dam/undp/library/corporate/HDR/2014HDR/HDR-2014-English.pdf; The World Bank's list of the Arab States http://data.worldbank.org/region/ARB; and, The World Bank List of MENA (includes 12 Arab States and Iran): http://data.worldbank.org/region/MNA; and, World Economic Forum's Global Gender Gap Report 2014: http://reports.weforum.org/global-gender-gap-report-2014/.

PART II

Analysis of Norms and Gender Discrimination

CHAPTER 2

Institutions and Gender Discrimination

Institutions are social constructs fashioned by collective human choices. They embody the generally accepted way of thinking and behaving. They are humanly devised constraints that structure human interactions. According to Crawford and Ostrom, "An institution...is a regular behavior pattern sustained by mutual expectations about the actions that others will take...The grounds for looking at institutions as norms rest on an assumption that many observed patterns of interaction are based on the shared perceptions among a group of individuals of proper and improper behavior in particular situations"(1995: 583).

Institutions serve the interest of those who intentionally, or unintentionally, win bargaining power. Thus, the "winners" influence the rules that govern a society with regards to justice, inclusion, efficiency, and so on (Denzau and North 1993; Rutherford 2001). According to Douglass North, "Institutions are not necessarily or even usually created to be socially efficient; rather they, or at least the formal rules, are created to serve the interests of those with the bargaining power to create new rules" (1998: 20). Jack Knight affirms the influence of institutions on women's perspectives and roles: "[A] woman's ideological perspective regarding the proper role of women is formed by the existing conventions and norms of her society" (1992: 81).

Institutions emerge whenever individuals attempt to live and work together. They are the basic networks of the convention, norms, rights, and rules on which a society is based (Knight 1992). Institutions structure social interactions by "establishing rules to guide future action with which social actors comply in making their strategic choices" (Knight 1992: 54). They do this through combinations of information about the choices of other individuals or groups, and threats or sanctions imposed on dissenters who do not comply with these norms or rules, which are utilized to ensure compliance with such institutional norms or rules. Norms differs from rules in that rules are subsets of norms that have been formalized and are accompanied with punishments when broken (Ostrom 2012). According to Geoffrey

Marshall, rules may "'penalize, prohibit, require, obligate, prescribe, inform, guide, empower, permit, license, enable, facilitate, entitle, command, define, designate, constitute, distribute, describe, exempt, and identify' future courses of action" (Marshall 1983: 188 in Knight 1992: 67). Formal rules occur when informal norms become explicit laws sanctioned by governments of other ruling groups (Knight 1992; Karayiannis and Hatzis 2010). Norms and rules are not inherently benevolent or efficient (North 1990, 1998, 2000, 20002; Elster 1989; Knight 1992). Some economists argue that social norms exist as a result of their collective positive influence on society. Others, including Jon Elster, argue against this notion, saying that not all norms are "win-win" situations; not all people benefit from them. Some gender-discriminating norms such as FGM/C, 'honor crimes', and socially sanctioned female dress codes make women worse off. Some norms that should make everybody, especially individualist's members, better off, such as women's freedom of movement, work, marriage, travel, and choice of wardrobe, are not observed in gender-discriminating societies (Elster 1989: 107–109). The complexity of certain norms/rules serves in "keeping outsiders out and upstarts down" (Elster 1989: 109). Consequently, norms can function as methods of inclusion and exclusion, in which the insiders enjoy higher and more commanding levels of social capital (Ogilvie 2004a, b), external capabilities (Foster and Handy 2008), and cultural capital (Storey 2009). The insiders can develop "negative solidarity" toward the outsiders (Elster 1989: 109). This partly accounts for the hostility of the ruling majority in discriminating societies toward outsider women's human rights groups, individualists, and international organizations.

Consequently, these shared norms and rules are usually embraced by the unintended and intended "winners." Meanwhile, the unintended and intended losers, or victims of such norms or rules, oppose or at least endure these rules that do not reflect their preference or aspirations. While these rules treat all members of the same group similarly, they do not treat every group similarly. These rules are known to be applicable to all men and women who choose to engage in interpersonal activities (Knight 1992: 68).

The Syntax of Institutions

Crawford and Ostrom (1995) highlight five main components of the institutional syntax that help to understand institutions and institutional analysis:

1. The attributes, which refer to the values that distinguish each member of the institution.
2. The deontic logic referring to what is permitted, obliged, and forbidden. In general, behaviors that do not conform to the prescription are punished.
3. The aim describes particular actions or obligations of the assigned deontic.
4. The conditions that describe how, when, and where the aim is permitted, required, or forbidden.
5. The "or else" or the sanctions imposed for noncompliance.

Once deontic operators assign a certain action to a member, that action becomes obligatory under specific conditions for certain members of that society, for example, when a female is assigned the action of wearing a headscarf or *hijab* in the public sphere or in the presence of a nonrelative male. The insufficiency of most rule systems leads to different interpretations of the deontic rules and punishment for the violators of institutional norms (Crawford and Ostrom 1995). This may explain the different forms and levels of gender discrimination in different countries in the Arab world.

For example, women in many Arab countries are obliged to adhere to collectively sanctioned dress codes whenever they are in public. If they do not adhere to this obligation, they will be directly punished by the virtue police or other collectivist members and indirectly through shaming or harassing their male relatives, because of the shame they have brought their families, especially their male relatives/guardians. Women are the attributes; the deontic is women's obligation; the aim is their response to the deontic of adhering to dress code or not; the conditions refer to where women are obliged to adhere to the dress code; and "or else" refers to the punishment imposed on women who do not adhere to the obligation of the collective dress code by the virtue police or other collectivist members.

Norms can also be classified as passive and active. Passive norms cause people to refrain from committing prohibited acts, for example, the norm of not dating or having relations with a male before marriage, as it is socially forbidden. In contrast, FGM/C is an example of an active norm that is performed on young girls.

To be effective, the threat of sanctions must be backed by a rule or norm that changes the "deontic" assigned to a certain "aim." "The rule or norm backing an OR ELSE [the sanctions] establishes both a range of punishments available and assign the authority and procedures for imposing an OR ELSE" (Crawford and Ostrom 1995: 586). In addition, the specialized individuals (for example, the virtue police in some Arab countries/communities) or all participants who monitor people's conformance to the collective norms are potential enforcers of "or else" punishment. Sanctions are usually imposed for doing what is forbidden and, to a lesser extent, for not doing what is obligatory (Crawford and Ostrom 1995). In many societies, or communities within a given society, the difference between what is forbidden and what is permitted can be vague, such that the same act can be permitted in one area and forbidden in another. The magnitude of forbidden acts is expected to be much higher in a collectivist society than in an individualist society. In general, collectivist societies tend to have more forbidding and less permitting norms than individualist societies, which in turn leads to higher levels of collective punishments against unsanctioned individualist acts/behaviors.

Crawford and Ostrom (1995) use a "delta" parameter of the costs or benefits of the inducements and deterrents for any particular deontic. Delta's value should reflect the importance of the deontic in a given society or community. "Honor killing" is an example of a higher external "delta" value in certain societies in the Arab world, while a public admonishment of women by the virtue police for violating the dress code in public spheres has a lower "external delta" value. The internal value of delta refers to the costs and benefits, such as personal guilt and/or shame when violating social norms, and the feeling of pride when conforming to them. This is amplified when the cost of following the norms is high (Crawford and Ostrom 1995: 587; Ostrom 2000).

Individuals or groups that treat certain acts as forbidden will incur costs when living in societies in which such acts are permissible. For example, in societies where women have the freedom to choose their attire and their beliefs and make major life decisions, individuals who forbid these freedoms will face higher costs. This explains, in part, the tendency of individuals with shared norms to build communities with shared deontic logics that do not correspond with those of the larger society. These individuals may reward each other for breaking the larger society's norms and rules (Crawford and Ostrom 1995), especially when there is lack of (or less severe) punishment for violating the individualist society's norms. However, in certain collectivist societies, such behavior can be forbidden and punished accordingly, especially in societies with mandated membership, lack of anonymity, higher levels of monitoring of individuals' behaviors, severe punishment imposed against violators of norms, and the elevation of certain norms into metanorms, in which not only the deviants (first-order violators), but also the shirkers (second-order violators) are punished.

Kenneth Boulding (1956) underscores the subjective knowledge structure, or "image," which consists of both images of "fact" and images of "value." According to Boulding, "the image of value is concerned with the rating of the various parts of our image of the world according to some scale of better-ness or worseness" (1956: 11).[1] Subtle or weak messages are less likely to influence the image. However, repeated messages or those with strong authority can penetrate people's resistance and alter their image. For example, religious people with strict observance to the precepts of their sacred books are likely to resist any doubt around the authority of such sacred norms and beliefs. They may either ignore the message or their resistance may take the form of emotive response such as anger and hostility (Boulding 1956). Therefore, "If the resistances are very strong, it may take very strong, or often repeated messages to penetrate them, the effect is realignment or reorganization of the whole knowledge structure" (Boulding 1956: 12). This may explain the influence and distribution of certain ingrained norms in peoples' and societies' image of the world. This is especially true for public images that are shared by members of the ruling/dominant group, for example, the image regarding gender relations and roles in gender-discriminating societies (Boulding 1956). Messages that align with existing images of the world in a given society are welcomed, while messages that oppose the existing societal image are met with strong resistance and/or rejection.

The difference/dispute between supporting and opposing messages reflects the dispute between the winners and losers/victims of the status quo, and explains why the winners invest significantly to perpetuate their gain against the losers/victims of the existing societal image of the world. The winners of the status quo of institutional setting and image aim to "lock in" their distributional gain, leading to a path dependence problem where women and other subordinate groups suffer varying practices of marginalization and exclusion (Ostrom 2012).

The Institutional Economic Approach

The institutional economic approach involves the study of the general ethical system that influences institutions. This is an approach that takes into account analysis and ideology from interdisciplinary fields (Dugger 1995; Rutherford 2001). In institutional economics, past, present, and future are linked through the study of the institution and its development (Mayhew 2009; Hausman and McPherson 1993). It is particularly relevant to women in gender-discriminating societies where a dominant group imposes certain morals and norms (Rutherford 2001; Knight 1992).

The institutional approach accentuates the bounded rationality that can result from information and cognitive constraints (North 1990; Rutherford 2001). An individual's behavior reflects the balance between the "homo economicus" and "homo sociologicus." Homo economicus is governed by instrumental rationality that adapts to changing circumstances and future rewards. In contrast, "socio economicus" is governed by social traditions that dictate behaviors. Jon Elster states that the ideal homo economicus "is easily caricatured as a self-constrained, asocial atom," while the ideal homo sociologicus is caricatured as "the mindless plaything of social forces" (1989: 99).

The original institutional economic approach studies how economies and societies vary regularly through time and space (Mayhew 2009). The new institutional economic approach offers explanation as to why the evolutions of individual countries, or groups within each country, differ from one another (Harris et al. 1998). According to Douglass North, "The new institutional economics is an attempt to incorporate a theory of institutions into economics" (1998: 17). This approach builds on the neoclassical theory and works to stimulate discussion of formal rules and structures as well as informal norms and social networks (North 1998; Rutherford 2001). In general, the new institutional approach focuses more on the evolution of norms and rules, transaction cost analysis, and the assumption of non-anonymity of individuals (Rutherford 2001: 173). In addition, the new institutional economic approach is not ethically neutral. It is more suspicious of certain collective actions as a way to achieve ethical outcomes (Mayhew 2009). The original institutional economic approach accepts cultural relativism, which faces criticism concerning its indifference to human suffering and abuse (Mayhew 2009).

Judith Butler, in her book "Undoing Gender" (2004), highlights the double edged nature of certain norms and normativity, "[A]lthough we need norms in order to live and to live well, and to know in what direction to transform our social world, we are also constrained by norms in ways that sometimes do violence to us and which, for reasons of social justice, we must oppose" (Butler 2004: 206).

On the other hand, economic and social institutions may influence social interactions, and therefore the evolution of institutional norms and rules by altering returns on relationships, the nature of sanctions, and the likelihood and outcomes of interactions between different types of people (Bowles 1998). For example, the adverse effects of gender discrimination and female marginalization may distort the social preference of women, making them more likely to internalize abuse and discrimination, and therefore less likely to oppose or reject such discrimination. Irrational behavior by marginalized or abused women can be explained, in part, using cognitive and social psychological theory, which aims to explain individual behavior in different social situations.

Therefore, economic analysis should attempt to incorporate observations of individuals who do not behave as economists assume they will; a concept well stated by Akerlof and Dickens: "[W]e must translate psychological theory into concepts amenable to incorporation into an economic model" (1982: 307). Likewise, proper policies and interventions that succeed in improving women's status can influence informal norms through gradual changes in perception and perspectives. These changes will lead to a better understanding of women's rights, capabilities, and actions. Malcolm Rutherford illustrates the interdependent relationship between individuals and societies, "Society is created out of actions of individuals, but it can also be argued that the individual, to some significant extent, is the creation of his social situation" (1994: 6).

Therefore, a tension in the power structures of a society exists between those who wish to perpetuate a situation for their benefit and those who wish to change it. What makes common sense for a certain generation or a certain society may not appeal to another generation or society, depending on this tension between static and dynamic forces, as stated by Anne Mayhew, "[I]t is naïve to fancy that what is common sense to us will appeal as common sense to later generations" (2009: 279). Kenneth Boulding supports this notion, "the image not only makes society, society continually remakes the image" (1956: 64). In most collectivist societies, the balance of power and status favor the supporters and winners of the status quo, since they can impose inherited/existing norms and rules on the whole society. Jack Knight (1992) explains the role of power in institutional settings and its distributional effect on the wellbeing of individuals or groups in this way: power refers to the ability of someone (or a group, or the community) to affect one's (an individual or a group, for example, women) feasible set of options. Men or society in general, especially in collectivist societies, can exercise power over women in the following ways: first, constrain women's choices, preventing or prohibiting women's rights, such as voting rights, rights of movement and travel, and/or women's rights to choose certain individualist goods such as attire. Second, expand women's choices by adding alternatives that suit women's subjective interests but are contrary to women's real interests, such as substituting collectivist goods—sanctioned by the collectivist ruling group/elite—for individualist goods. Third, control the availability of women's feasible set of preferred choices, especially of individualist goods. Fourth, alter women's valuation of the available alternatives by threatening a retaliatory action against women. Fifth, manipulate women's preferences through media, education, and propaganda.

In summary, society can get women to adopt institutional norms and rules that distributionally favor men, even in the light of better alternatives (Knight 1992).

Classification of Institutions and Gender Discrimination

Institutions typically fall into three major categories: informal institutions, formal institutions, and the governing structure of transactions. Informal institutions include embedded norms, customs, mores, religions, and self-imposed codes of conduct in each society. Formal institutions include statute laws, common laws, and regulations that determine the distribution of power across different levels of government. The governing structure of transactions refers to the "play of the game" where contracts and their governance costs become the status quo, rather than the exceptions (Denzau and North 1993; North 1994, 1998, 2000, 2002; Williamson 1993, 2000; Dugger 1995). "A country's social norms, customs, legal frameworks, markets, and hierarchies—the elements of its institutional framework—often reinforce one another, so it is difficult to effect societal change by changing only one part of the framework" (The World Bank 2001: 108).

Informal Institutions (or Norms or Constraints)

Informal institutions are prevailing norms, culture, customs, traditions, religions, myths, and taboos, in addition to self-imposed codes of conduct that provide for the continuity of culture (North 1998, 2000, 2002). These institutions are especially influential in collectivist societies. Many informal institutions develop through evolutionary processes of gradual feedback and adjustment, and tend to change slowly over time (Williamson 2000; Kasper and Streit 1998). Informal institutions reveal the formation and gradual acceptance, or power structure and the strengthening conviction in such norms, regardless of their ethics or fairness.

Informal norms play a crucial role in explaining the status of women in different societies, in different historic times, and in different geographic regions. They help explain the different costs and benefits of relationships between people and their surrounding physical and social environments. "The grounds for looking at institutions as norms rest on an assumption that many observed patterns of interaction are based on the shared perceptions among a group of individuals of proper and improper behavior in particular situations" (Crawford and Ostrom 1995: 583).

Prevailing informal institutions influence individuals' mental models with regard to their shared perceptions, expectations, and interpretation of the world around them, "...People act in part upon the basis of myths, dogmas, ideologies, and 'half-baked' theories" (Denzau and North 1993: para 1). Informal institutions that victimize a certain population group (for example women) not only distort their mental models, but also, offer another group, men, the opportunity to gain at the expense of women. The winners, exploiting their societal power, can extract "distributional" rent when transacting or contracting with the victims of such institutions (Abadeer 2008).

Informal institutions highlight the importance of understanding the presence of embedded norms and traditions that perpetuate prejudice such as gender discrimination and the marginalization of women. As stated by Douglass North, "History demonstrates that ideas, ideologies,[2] myths, dogmas, and prejudices matter; and an understanding of the way they evolve is necessary for further progress in developing a framework to understand societal changes" (1994: 363).

The role of informal norms in gender discrimination against women is visibly entrenched, especially in many collectivist societies. Moreover, the prevalence of metanorms,[3] in which the society punishes both the deviants and shirkers of the norms, especially in collectivist societies, heightens gender discrimination in these societies. Metanorms act as intractable instruments against policies or interventions to eliminate gender discrimination in LDCs.

Gender discrimination in collectivist countries, even those with higher standards of living (for example, the oil rich Arab states of the Persian / Arabian Gulf), provides a classic example of how informal institutions assert the social, political, and economic rights and superiority of men. Under these circumstances, women become marginalized and largely excluded from certain activities, transactions, and decision-making processes. Women are expected, and sometimes forced, to act according to collectivist decisions and norms that are collectively imposed on them, such as the prevalence of female genital mutilation (FGM/C) in some Middle Eastern and sub-Saharan African countries; honor killing and violence against women for committing—or for being the subject of rumor/doubt/fear of committing—acts considered immoral or unsanctioned by the collectivist group; *devadasis* (temple prostitutes or dancers in India); *dowry* payments (a payment by the bride's parents to the groom's family for marrying the bride in South Asia); *dowry* death (the killing of brides by her in-laws for dowry money in some states in in India); and *sati* (widows' burning at the funeral pyres of their deceased husbands in India), especially in rural regions (Abadeer 2008). Such informal traditions explain, in part, why the majority of women in many countries think that a husband is justified in hitting his wife under certain circumstances, and why the majority of domestic violence and rapes are rarely reported or prosecuted (Amnesty International 2005a,b; de Bary 1998; UNICEF 2012; U.S. DOS 2014a; Human Rights Watch 2014a). Such informal environments tend to distort the structure of the victims' mental models, so they become more likely to accept and internalize such informal discriminating norms and constraints, perpetuating their victimization.

Certain informal norms are deeply rooted and undisputed in societies, such as certain sacred/religious norms. The longevity of these norms explains the limited success of short-term interventions, since the informal roots of gender discrimination may outlast these short-lived interventions. An example is the recurrence of polygyny in the Arab world (and some other Islamic states).

These norms also emphasize the importance of long-term, ongoing interventions and commitments to initiate and continue the process of breaking down these discriminating informal norms. Norms that are disputable or subject to re-interpretation can be changed or modified according to the deontic criteria assigned to certain acts, for example, from forbidden acts to permitted acts, or from required acts to permitted acts, and vice versa (Crawford and Ostrom 1995). A striking example of a changing norm is FGM/C in some Arab countries, which for centuries was informally obligatory, but is increasingly being frowned upon, and even formally forbidden in some Arab countries. Also, the norm of condoning or tolerating domestic violence is being challenged in many Arab countries, especially with more media coverage of women's rights violations and the growing national and international pressures to change this practice. Examples of such changes include the adaption of a law against domestic abuse by the Council of Ministers in Saudi Arabia in 2013, and doubling the penalties against domestic violence perpetrators in Tunisia (U.S. DOSa 2014).

Cultural differences play a crucial role in explaining the influence of norms on the state of women in different societies. They help explain the different costs and benefits of certain relationships between people and their surrounding physical and social environments. Chapter 5 highlights the attributes of individualist versus collectivist societies and the crucial influence of norms in collectivist societies, especially norms that discriminate against certain population groups—such as gender-discriminating norms and how they influence people's behaviors in inter- and intra-societies, or in in-group and out-group settings.[4]

Governments are less likely to initiate policies to intervene with prevalent discriminating informal institutions, since the success of such interventions in transforming long-term informal institutions is difficult to materialize, or even measure, given the short-term structure and duration of governments. Governments may therefore perpetuate such norms and codes of conduct, if such practices are collectively popular and sanctioned. International interventions by states, formal organizations (global or regional), and nongovernment and civil society organizations should play an increasing role in addressing gender discrimination practices in collectivist societies, especially in supporting national movements and calls for reform.

Many governments in collectivist societies subscribe to international conventions and treaties of human rights, including the rights of women, but they do so with formal reservations to specific articles in these conventions and treaties. For example, many Arab nations do not uphold Articles 2, 9, 15, 16, and 29 in CEDAW (Convention on the Elimination of All Forms of Discrimination Against Women), because of the incompatibility between the provisions of these articles and the provisions of sacred norms (mainly Islamic *shari'ah*, or Islamic law) in these states (Mayer 2000; UN 2010; UN n.d.-b; U.S. DOSa 2014; Human Rights Watch 2014a). Other countries may overlook the effective enforcement of some articles and requirements in these international conventions and treaties, sustaining gender discrimination norms and practices, along with the victimization of women in their societies. Further analysis of these articles, the rationale behind the Arab states' reservations, and the influence of sacred norms, mostly religious norms, in making such reservations, is covered in the last part of this chapter.

Gender Identity and Gender Discrimination

Abraham and Platteau (2001) illustrate the vulnerability of the victims of discrimination: "In these encounters, the elite provides an authority structure which imposes its rule or its interpretation of the traditions on the lower people who have no choice but to comply" (14). Women are less likely to violate or voice opposition to existing social norms, fearing retribution, because these societies have histories of credible threats. The elite groups—men supported by formal institutions—use their power and privilege to appropriate, deflect, or exploit resources belonging to the vulnerable members of their communities—women. Meanwhile, women are entrapped in these communities; forced to act in accordance with an a priori set of social rules defining their social identity (Platteau 1994a,b). A woman's identity, especially in collectivist societies, is socially constructed to suit the aspirations of the surrounding community. Violating attributes attached to identity can induce external anxiety to other members and can invoke strong and sometimes detrimental responses, as explained by Akerlof and Kranton: "Following the behavioral prescriptions for one's gender affirms one's self-image, or identity, as a 'man' or as a 'woman.' Violating the prescriptions evokes anxiety and discomfort in oneself and in others. Gender identity, then, changes the 'pay-offs' from different actions" (2000: 716–717). Identity also partially explains detrimental behaviors like FGM/C, certain forms of domestic violence, and "honor killing" (Akerlof and Kranton 2000). FGM/C is linked to feminine identity as it relates to beauty, cleanliness, and fidelity. It is performed on younger girls to force them into the community's constructed identity and force the valued attributes of women in the society upon them. FGM/C transforms the girl's physical characteristics creating a physical marker to match a required ideal. The relationship of FGM/C to expected rewards and societal interactions like marriage will be covered in detail in chapter 10. Domestic violence, including spousal rape, is condoned in certain societies and can be exploited as a punishment when a woman deviates from her socially assigned identity of obedience and submission. Honor killing is an example of extreme collective responses to a woman's violation of her social identity as virtuous and the holder of her family and community's honor with regard to their obedience and sexual behavior or just rumors of it. Anxiety rooted in rumors can cause a man and/or the entire community to defend this constructed identity even at the cost of harming the lives of women.

Akerlof and Kranton also highlight the importance of identity-related payoffs from women's behaviors, or the externalities associated with a woman's personal behavior. Adherence to assigned identity will lead to positive externalities for the collective society while women behaving individualistically will be seen as an insult on men's masculinity and social norms leading to negative externalities. Such individualistic behavior causes anxiety and loss of utility to other collectivist members in society, especially men and close relatives. Therefore, such behavior should be confronted accordingly to defend men's identity, reduce social disruptions, and maintain sense of unity in society (2000).

Women's entrapment in gender-discriminating societies is heightened by their involuntary membership in collectivist in-groups, such that their departure brings shame and disgrace to the collectivist unit that must be punished accordingly, increasing the risk and cost associated with exiting. Entrapment is also heightened due to the lack of other viable options, especially in light of severe collective restrictions and punishments on women's capabilities, such as the freedom to move or associate with (or belong to) other (or out-group) communities. Women's lack of voice also heightens their vulnerability, since, oftentimes, women's identity in gender-discriminating societies is associated with obedience and submissiveness. The call for female human rights in gender-discriminating societies may be understood as violation of women's assigned identity and a call for social disorder, heightening the collective opposition. Only a few people, mostly affluent and educated individualists, can exit this society and voice their dissent against gender-discriminating practices; however, the vast majority of women and other individualists in these collectivist societies can neither exist nor voice grievances. The vast majority either accepts their collectively assigned identity, or internalizes such discrimination and adapts to them, and in the process tolerates lower levels of self-image, wellbeing, and violations of women's human rights (Hirschman 1970). Violating the assigned identity exposes dissenters to ridicule, ostracism, exclusion, and even severe physical punishment.

Judith Butler underscores the difference between the true identity and socially assigned identity. True identity belongs to an individual free from social or collectively assigned roles or identities. The socially assigned identity is enforced by the community of women, and other individualists, and exposes them to risk to if they choose to live the lives they value according to their true identity: "[W]e continue to live in a world in which one can risk serious disenfranchisement and physical violence for the pleasure one seeks, the fantasy one embodies, the gender one performs" (2004: 214). Moreover, Butler says power and knowledge play a role in forming people's perceptions on what is true and real. Power and knowledge are not separable, they work together to create a subtle or explicit criteria for worldview, creating a power-knowledge nexus that establishes what is acceptable, and what fits the identity assigned to each person or group. "The way in which women are said to 'know' or to 'be known' are already orchestrated by power precisely at that moment in which the terms of 'acceptable' categorization are instituted" (Butler 2004: 215). Masculinity is a form of cultural capital located at the center of the circular power field in gender-discriminating societies.[5] Women are forced to compete for a place closer to the center. They perpetuate gender discrimination through condoning masculine cultural traits. Women do this in order to gain a higher position in the hierarchy of the cultural capital exchange.

This may explain the behavior of certain women who exchange the cultural capital of their gender background with that of the male gender, for the sake of gaining higher position in the hierarchy, through endorsing or condoning masculine cultural traits, even though such acts perpetuate gender discrimination (Bourdieu 1986).

Women in many collectivist societies do not participate, are not invited to participate, or are banned from participating, in the formulation of social norms or rules. Therefore, they are forced to abide by imposed external norms and rules. This banned participation violates women's rights, reduces their capabilities, and further limits their functionings. Such norms and formal rules are imposed on women through varying forms of coercion. Spousal rape, condoned domestic violence, other forms of sexual coercions, and denied access to unsanctioned individualist goods further discriminate against women (Alkire 2002; CHANGE 1999). Gender violence and coercion norms sanction violence against women, which in turns enforces upholding of such norms. This creates a vicious cycle of norms sanctioning discrimination, and discriminatory acts becoming norms (Myrdal 1944).

Women who violate (or deviate from) such imposed norms, are considered deviants or dissenters and are punished accordingly. The societal response varies depending on how stringent these laws and norms are, the degree of collectivism, and the degree and instruments of coercing women to abide by such norms and laws in these societies. Collective punishments range from verbal rebuking to physical violence and death, for example, honor killing (see chapter 11). However, actual use of violence is not required; implicit or explicit threats are usually sufficient to constrain and distort women's capabilities and functionings (Fafchamps 2004).

Even though informal rules are constraint in the short run, corrective institutions may influence the evolution of such norms over the long run (Bowles 1998). For example, the adverse effects of gender discrimination and marginalization of women influence women's preferences in a negative way, and make them lower their outlooks, especially in case of the perpetuated history of gender discrimination and marginalization. Conversely, the usually gradual influence of corrective interventions and gender-neutral economic, social, and political institutions, on the evolution of informal norms, stresses the need for immediate interventions by governments, international organization, and domestic and international nongovernment and civil society organizations. Such interventions can mitigate the effects of existing inefficient and unfair informal institutions. The pressure from the International Olympic Committee on the government of Saudi Arabia, for example, led to the royal decree of King Abdullah to allow the participation of the two Saudi female athletes in the 2012 London Olympic Games for the first time in the history of Saudi Arabia (Pilon 2012).

Informal norms tend to stabilize social expectations and structure social life. They provide information about the anticipated behavior of members of society. It follows that in the case of dissenting, or a noncompliance with these informal norms, the stability of the informal institutions will be threatened.

In such a case, other measures take place to sustain these informal institutions, such as their formalization, the structuring of collective decision making, and the introduction of external enforcement mechanisms (Knight 1992). Informal norms influence the distribution of resources such as status goods, collectivist goods, and individualist goods among different groups and members in each society. The resulting distribution in turn affects the power distribution and asymmetries in formal institutions, which can favor certain population groups, for example collectivist units and men in general, at the expense of others, such as women in gender-discriminating societies. This may explain how informal norms can persist even when efforts are made to change them with formal rules (Knight 1992).

The distributional effect of informal norms determines the cost-benefit structure among the members of a society. Men and women who have the same expectations about these rules will gain from the interactions. This does not mean that all men and women in the community will be satisfied with the existing set of gender rules. It merely means that because of the existence of such rules, they cannot do better for themselves in the interaction by choosing another action (Knight 1992). Noncompliance with these rules may expose the dissenters to collective punishments. When the collective punishment is too severe (outweighing the benefits of noncompliance), members may resign to internalizing the resulting cognitive dissonance due to their inability to change such rules or norms. That being said, these members (women, for example), always have an incentive to change the status quo to fix the skewed distribution of existing informal rules (Knight 1992). The "winners" of existing informal rules will prefer the status (staticism), while the victims or "losers" will prefer changing the status quo (dynamism). The tension between staticism and dynamism will determine the stability of the informal institutions.

Informal norms should be shared by the members of a given society to establish consistent and expected behavioral patterns. Lack of shared information may expose certain members to unexpected responses or behaviors from other members. In such cases, the process of expectation formation breaks down. Jack Knight underscores two major causes of this breakdown: the ambiguity of the informal rules (and the incorrect interpretation of informal rules) and the size of the society or community. The ambiguity of informal rules can be applied to gender relationships. Even if the rule is known, the interpretation of the anticipated actions may differ (1992). This plays a crucial role in different levels and scopes of gender discrimination in varying communities. As the size of community increases, interactions with strangers become more likely and the probability that individuals will be confronted by someone who will discipline their behavior decreases, ceteris paribus (Knight 1992). Individuals who favor certain informal rules are more likely to confront noncompliance if the long-term benefit is higher than the cost of punishment. Thus, the incentive to sanction noncompliance depends on the benefit and cost of sanctioning, "The greater is the distributional advantage produced by the status quo, the greater will be the incentive for informal sanctions" (Knight 1992: 180).

Second, Formal Institutions

Formal institutions refer to the polity, judiciary, laws, regulations, and their implementation. Formal institutions mirror the societal power structure (Kasper and Streit 1998; North 1990, 1994, 1998; Williamson 2000; Knight 1992; Crawford and Ostrom 1995; Ostrom 2012). According to Elinor Ostrom, "[Formal] rules are linguistic statements similar to norms but rules carry an additional, assigned sanction if forbidden actions are taken and observed by a monitor" (2012: par 10). They are designed and formally enforced to reflect the distribution of power across different levels of government. Factors such as recognition and implementation lags, and other specific circumstances influence the length of time to change a formal rule.[6]

Formal rules in many less developed countries sanction various inherited norms that discriminate against women in terms of what these rules allow, require, or forbid, and the various mechanisms to employ these rules (Crawford and Ostrom 1995). Consequently, they oppose (or have explicit reservations against) certain articles in international conventions and declarations on human rights that give women certain capabilities and functionings that violate widespread cultural and religious norms and formal laws and legislations in these countries.

Formal institutions are also created as a way of stabilizing or changing informal conventions and norms. "When the efficacy of informal institutions is threatened, social actors try to invoke the external-enforcement mechanism of the state to establish institutional constraints that give them a distributional advantage . . . The logic of formal institutionalization is to constrain the actions of others through the actions of a third party" (Knight 1992: 188). Moreover, formal institutions can be used to structure social interactions that lack prior institutional framework.

"The compliance with formal rules is reinforced by the sanction of an external-enforcement mechanism" (Knight 1992: 171). External enforcement mechanisms include the state and other forms of collective power, laws, regulations, and the accompanying punishment against noncompliant members of society. The distributional effect of the intentional mechanism of formal rules differs from the unintentional mechanism of informal norms (Knight 1992). Formal laws and regulations that favor certain group(s) of people (for example, based on gender, race, religion, ethnicity, caste) typically have negative distributional effects on other groups, often, those groups that are overlooked, marginalized, or excluded. Gender-discriminating laws and regulations have negative distributive effects that exclude or marginalize women in these collectivist societies. Formal rules and laws serve, in part, to affirm the strength of social norms and conventional morality and/or to counteract the decay of such social norms and morality. In such cases, violating such rules and laws exposes dissenters to harsh punishments, and this has been from as early as in the ancient Athenian society, where such punishments can be applied as "substitutes for the lack of strong social norms and the waning power of conventional morality in the fourth century" (Karayiannis and Hatzis 2010: 16).

Winners of collectivist norms and rules take advantage of such formal rules to uphold their gained status and power. This lowers their transactional costs and maximizes their gain from contracts or transactions at the expense of women who are deprived of significant cultural and social capital (CHANGE 1999). In such cases, the outcomes of these contracts or transactions are likely to be socially inefficient. Women, in addition to being deprived of most institutional rent, are worse off due to physical, mental, and emotional discrimination and abuse.

Third, Governance Structure of Transactions

The governance structure of transactions refers to the cost of transactions and the lack anonymity among the participants of such transactions. Accordingly, contracts and the costs of governing them become the rules rather than the exceptions. These costs lead to remarkable and rather complex sets of ex-post outcomes of such contracts, due to the built–in contractual hazards and the lack of sufficient safeguards (Williamson 2000).

Incomplete and asymmetric information are both examples of distorted governance structure of transactions. The inferior level of women's information relates to women's lack of human and social capital. This is especially true in collectivist, discriminating societies where women lack well-organized social networks and closures (Ogilvie 2004a, b). Other examples include discriminating constraints on women's movements, their inability to acquire their preferred individualist goods and services, limitations on education, limitations on labor market access, limited access to credit, finance, property, and other legal rights such as divorce and custody of children. The above examples heighten women's costs of making transactions, and limit and distort their capabilities and functionings.

Incomplete/asymmetric information plays a crucial role in the governance structure of the game. Male members and other collectivist units (typically controlled by male members) in these societies usually have a superior position they can utilize to extract information and other transactional gains at the expense of those with inferior positions (wives, daughters, other female relatives—female members of society in general). Incomplete contracts or transaction processes reflect men's well-designed set of ex-post responses to women's reactions, given the societal collective limitations on women's capabilities and functionings. Furthermore, husbands, male relatives, and other collectivist units (families, clans, and tribes), can enforce the terms that suit their interests and disregard the ones protecting women's individualist preferences or needs since women lack the ability to enforce or are uninformed about their interests or rights to start with. Men can also impose and enforce noncontractual terms, as long as the terms increase men's payoff. Oliver Williamson summarizes the above behaviors, "contract as mere promise, unsupported by credible commitments, will not be self-enforcing" (2000: 601).

The interaction among the above three levels of institutions—informal institutions, formal institutions, and the governance structure of transactions—is dominated by the influence of the longevity of institutions, especially in collectivist societies: the informal norms influence the structure of formal rules, which in turn, influence the governance of transactions, or rules of the game.

The feedback between the three levels of institutions is generally weak and at best slow, especially in the short run. This is true unless radical societal changes take place introducing different sets of formal rules and a different perspective toward changing the existing informal norms. The successful deviant behaviors of certain individuals or groups may develop new trends (Bowles 1998; Butler 2004). The tension between sustaining the status quo and transforming it is stated clearly by Michal Foucault: "schematically speaking, we have perpetual mobility, essential fragility or rather the complex interplay between what replicates the same process and what transforms it" (2002: 203). Judith Butler affirms the importance of tracing the roots of gender discrimination and identity to be able to transform them: "It is important not only to understand how the terms of gender are instituted, naturalized and established as pre-suppositional but to trace the moment where that binary system of gender is disputed and challenged, where the coherence of the categories are put into questions, and where the very social life of gender turns out to be malleable and transformable" (Butler 2004: 216).

The Arab World's Dilemma of Signing/Ratifying Universal Conventions and Treaties on Human Rights

A 2003 United Nations report on the integration of women's human rights focusing on violence against women in the Middle East shows significant progress with regard to the promotion and protection of human rights in the last decade of the 20th century. It highlights February 1 as the first Women's Day in the Arab world, the dedication of 2001 as the Year of Arab Women, the launch of the Arab Women's Organization by the League of Arab States, and the establishment of an Arab Women's Council (United Nations 2003). However, several challenges still hinder the improvement of women's status in the Arab world.

Discriminating informal norms, especially those rooted in sacred religious texts and teachings, are deeply ingrained in everyday living for millions who live in the Arab world, and in similar states. In these regions, sacred norms penetrate individual behaviors, social relationships, the distribution of status and power, and socially sanctioned codes of conduct. Socially sanctioned constraints and prohibitions limit and distort people's capabilities and functioning; the heavy burden of such discriminating norms are imposed on women. Various forms of discriminating norms are tolerated, endorsed, or even enforced. Some are elevated to the status of formal rules and laws, which expose the deviant members of society not only to informal reprimands, but also to formal punishments.

Levels of punishment can greatly vary. In general, individualist people and individualist societies are likely to accept, or at least respect, the choices and preferences of deviants from informal norms, even though they may disagree with such choices (Butler 2004). More importantly, punishing such deviants is itself punishable in individualist societies, since it violates the deviants' freedom to choose and distorts their capabilities and functionings. In contrast to individualist societies, collectivist societies adhere to and obey the collectively accepted and imposed norms, regardless of whether or not these norms are efficient, ethical, just, or inclusive, and regardless of the detrimental effects on the victims of these norms. Most, if not all, of the norms in collectivist societies correspond to the preferences and choices of strong, elite, and dominant group(s). In exceptional cases, a powerful and dominant minority group may impose their preferences and choices on the rest of the given society. Unfortunately, women belong to the weak and dominated group in many societies, where they are the victims of gender-discriminating norms sanctioned by the elite, dominant, and strong group(s) in their societies (U.S. DOSa 2014; Human Rights Watch 2014a).

The following case study of Arab countries' relationship with CEDAW explains the influence of discriminating informal norms (or informal institutions) on formal institutions in the Arab world.

CEDAW is considered the beacon of universal conventions on women's rights. It was adopted by the United Nations General Assembly in December 1979 following 33 years of preparation by the United Nations Commission on the Status of Women. CEDAW took effect in September 1981. It includes a preamble and six parts that cover 30 articles (UN, n.d.-b).

The most common challenges cited by Arab countries are their reservations to articles 2, 9, 15, 16, and 29 of CEDAW. Most Arab states expressed reservations about any provisions that might run counter to Islam or Islamic *shari'ah*[7] (The Islamic law), and Arab values and traditions (UN 2003). These reservations underline the crucial role of informal norms and codes of conduct in most of the collectivist Arab world. As of November 2014, 188 states have ratified CEDAW, including 19 members of the League of Arab States.[8] Seventeen of the 19 Arab states have outstanding reservations on certain parts/articles of CEDAW. Djibouti and Comoros are the only two Arab states that ratified CEDAW without reservations. They are the newest countries to join the Arab League, and they share more of traditional African informal norms and traditions than those norms of the Arab world. Article number 2 of CEDAW calls on all states to condemn, eliminate, and prohibit all forms of discrimination against women, and to establish legal protection of the right of women on an equal basis with men. It also calls for effective protection of women against all forms of discrimination, including abolishing existing discriminating laws, regulations, customs, and practices.

Article number 9 states that all countries should grant women all rights given to men regarding acquiring, changing, or retaining their nationality and the nationality of husbands and children.

Article number 15 calls for equal treatment of men and women in civil matters, before the law, and equal rights to movement and freedom. Women and men should accord the same legal capacity and the opportunities to exercise that capacity.

Article number 16 calls for the elimination of all forms of discrimination against women in marriage and familial relationships, and for equality of men and women in their right to enter into marriage, their rights during marriage, and at its dissolution. It gives same rights and responsibilities with regard to children (number and spacing of children), and same rights and responsibilities with regard to guardianship, trusteeship, and adoption of children. Additionally, it calls for setting a minimum age for marriage in order to prevent under-age marriages.

Finally, article number 29 provides proper arbitration for potential disputes between two or more state parties concerning the interpretation or application of CEDAW that cannot be settled by negotiation, upon the request of one party.

Of these, articles 2 and 16 are most central to CEDAW's purpose, "Articles 2 and 16 are considered by the Committee to be core provisions of the Convention. Although some States parties have withdrawn reservations to those articles, the Committee is particularly concerned at the number and extent of reservations entered to those articles" (UN 2009).

Table 2.1 and figure 2.1 illustrate the influence of norms (informal institutions) on the formal rules and laws (formal institutions), which in turn, influence the governance of transactions (or play of the game) in such a way as to instill such discriminating norms, formalize them, and heighten their influence on women's capabilities and functionings in the Arab world, similar societies, and countries.

Table 2.1 illustrates the formal reservations made by the Arab states to the above CEDAW articles (See appendix 2.1 for more detailed information).

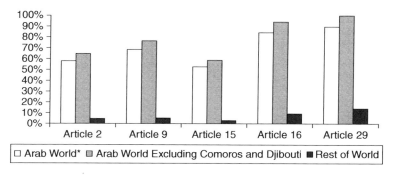

Figure 2.1   Relative reservations (#reservations/#countries) to selected CEDAW's articles (%).
*Mauritania and Saudi Arabia made general reservations to CEDAW without specific reservations to certain articles.

Source: Data collected from United Nations (2010) Convention on the Elimination of All Forms of Discrimination against Women (CEDAW): Declarations, reservations, objections, and notifications of withdrawal of reservations. http://www2.ohchr.org/english/bodies/cedaw/docs/AdvanceVersions/CEDAW-SP-2010-2.pdf and from (UN n.d.-b) https://treaties.un.org/Pages/ViewDetails.aspx?src=TREATY&mtdsg_no=IV-8&chapter=4&lang=en#39. Last accessed November 13, 2014.

Table 2.1 Total and comparison of reservations of Arab States to reservations of non-Arab States to CEDAW, as of March 1, 2010

(1) CEDAW's Article Number	(2) Number of Total Reservations	(3) Number of Reservations of Arab States, including Mauritania and Saudi Arabia*	(4) Number of Reservations of Non-Arab States	(5) Percentage of Reservations of Arab States to Number of Arab States that have Ratified CEDAW (19 states)	(6) Percentage of Reservations of Non-Arab States to Number of Non-Arab States that have Ratified CEDAW (169 states)	(7) = (5) / (6) Relative Reservations of Arab States to non-Arab States	Percentage of Reservations of Arab States to Number of Arab States that have Ratified CEDAW (17 states), Excluding Comoros
2	19	11	8	58	5	12.2	65
9	21	13	8	68	5	14.5	76
15	15	10	5	53	3	17.8	59
16	32	16	16	84	9	8.9	94
29	41	17	24	89	14	6.3	100

*Mauritania and Saudi Arabia made general reservations to CEDAW without specific reservations to certain articles. Column (3) includes Mauritania and Saudi Arabia in the total numbers of the reservations.

Source: Date collected from United Nations (2010). Convention on the Elimination of All Forms of Discrimination against Women (CEDAW): Declarations, reservations, objections and notifications of withdrawal of reservations. http://www2.ohchr.org/english/bodies/cedaw/docs/AdvanceVersions/CEDAW-SP-2010-2.pdf. Last accessed November 14, 2014.

The percentage of reservations by Arab states to the number of all Arab states that ratified CEDAW is very high, ranging from forty-two percent on article 15 to eighty-nine percent on article 19, compared to three percent and fourteen percent for all non-Arab countries, respectively. The Arab states' high rate of reservations to CEDAW articles underscores the influence of the gen-der-discriminating informal norms that are elevated to formal rules or laws. Table 2.1 shows that relative Arab states' reservations are 6 to 18 times the non-Arab states' reservations to CEDAW's articles.

How Sacred Norms Influence the Arab States' Reservations to CEDAW

The 1981 Universal Islamic Declaration of Human Rights (UIDHR) adopted by the Islamic Council of Europe and the 1990 Cairo Declaration on Human Rights in Islam (CDHRI), adopted by the Organization of Islamic Cooperation (OIC), distinguish human rights in Islam from the United Nations' 1948 Universal Declaration of Human Rights (UDHR). Both UIDHR and CDHRI emphasize that human rights are decreed by the divine *shari'ah*, *Allah* is the source of all *shari'ah*, and Prophet Muhammad conveyed the culmination of the divine guidance to all humanity. Muslims "believe that that rationality by itself without the light of revelation from God can neither be a sure guide in the affairs of mankind nor provide spiritual nourishment to the human soul, and, knowing that the teachings of Islam represent the quintessence of Divine guidance in its final and perfect form, feel duty-bound to remind man of the high status and dignity bestowed on him by God" (Islamic Council 1981: Preamble). CDHRI affirms the divine nature of the Islamic human rights, such that no one has the right to suspend or violate them due to their divine nature,

> *Believing that fundamental rights and universal freedoms in Islam are an integral part of the Islamic religion and that no one as a matter of principle has the right to sus-pend them in whole or in part or violate or ignore them in as much as they are binding divine commandments, which are contained in the Revealed Books of God and were sent through the last of His Prophets to complete the preceding divine messages thereby making their observance an act of worship and their neglect or violation an abomi-nable sin, and accordingly every person is individually responsible—and the Ummah [nation/state of Islam]collectively responsible—for their safeguard.* (OIC 1990).

The importance of religious norms and values is underscored in many articles in UIDHR and CDHRI, where many rights and obligations are conditioned in accordance with the framework, tenets, norms, provisions, principles, and authority of *shari'ah* (Islamic Council 1981; OIC 1990). Such modifications can restrict individual rights of participation in public affairs, conditioned on enjoining what is rights and preventing what is wrong, which is subject to the interpretations of *shari'ah*, for example, restrictions on or exclusion of non-Muslims and on Muslim women according to various interpretations and practices of *shari'ah*, individuals freedom, education, free movement, inheri-tance, legal rights, and freedom of expression.[9]

Many articles in UIDHR and CDHRI underscore exclusive rights to the Islamic *ummah* (Islamic state or community), which confer certain rights only to believers. Both declarations emphasize the family as the foundation of society, and women's equality to men in dignity. Both declarations, however, do not specify rights or duties, thus leaving them to the interpretation of ruling leaders in Islamic *ummah*, according to their interpretations of *shari'ah*. Both declarations also affirm the husband's responsibility to support his wife and children. Article XIX in UIDHR echoed the husband's responsibility and adds, "Within the family, men and women are to share in their obligations and responsibilities according to their sex, their natural endowments, talents and inclinations" (Islamic Council 1981), without further explanation. Articles 24 and 25 in CHDRI summarize the central role of divine/religious norms and rules, "All the rights and freedoms stipulated in this Declaration are subject to the Islamic Shari'ah," and, "The Islamic *shari'ah* is the only source of reference for the explanation or clarification of any of the articles of this Declaration," respectively (OIC 1990). Furthermore, Article IV of UIDHR states, "It is the right and duty of every Muslim to refuse to obey any command which is contrary to the Law [*shari'ah*], no matter by whom it may be issued." Consequently, Muslims must follow the Islamic interpretation of human rights since it comes from *Allah*. Due to the divine nature of Islamic human rights, they are irrevocable and unchangeable. In general, Islamic human rights constrain such rights that may contradict the collective interest of the Islamic *ummah*, according to the interpretations of Islamic *shari'ah*. Opinions, behaviors, and acts that may harm Islam, Muslims, or Islamic *ummah*, for example, blasphemy against *Allah* or the Messenger (Prophet Muhammad), and denying *Allah*, the Messenger, or the Book (the *Qur'an*), are punished according to interpretation of Islamic *shari'ah*. In some cases, this may even result in death.

Based on the above, some Arab countries opted to express a general rejection to all articles or provisions of CEDAW that contradict the norms of Islamic law. Mauritania offers a blanket reservation on any articles that contradicts the essence of Islamic *shari'ah*: "The Government of Mauritania, . . . , has approved and does approve it[CEDAW] in each and every one of its parts which are not contrary to Islamic sharia and are in accordance with our Constitution" (UN 2010: 32).[10] Likewise, the government of Oman states its general reservation to, "All provisions of the Convention not in accordance with the provisions of the Islamic sharia and legislation in force in the Sultanate of Oman" (UN 2010: 43). The government of Saudi Arabia's reservation asserts the value and influence of the sacred norms of Islamic laws in a way that empties CEDAW of its core purpose, "In case of contradiction between any term of the Convention and norms of Islamic law, the Kingdom of Saudi Arabia is not under obligation to observe the contradictory terms of the Convention" (UN 2010: 47–48). CEDAW's purpose of eliminating all forms of discrimination against women is outweighed or dwarfed by the strong influence of informal norms that discriminate against women in many collectivist societies. Therefore, further analysis of the roots of these norms, their authenticity, their prevalence, their enforcement, and their elevated status into formal rules and laws is warranted to shed light on the well-being of women.

A detailed analysis of the Arab States' reservations to selected CEDAW's articles would underscore the crucial role of norms in justifying such reservations. The common thread of the Arab states' (and other Islamic countries) reservations to Article 2 in CEDAW is the application of provisions that do conflict with existing family codes (Algeria), the provisions that are bound within the provisions of the Islamic *shari'ah* (Bahrain, Egypt, Iraq, Libya, Morocco, Oman, and United Arab Emirates), and the inconsistency of this article with existing provisions of the constitution (Qatar). Similar reservations were made by other non-Arab Islamic states such as Bangladesh, Malaysia, and Pakistan.

The rationale of the Arab states' reservations to Article 9 is the incompatibility of paragraph 2 of this article with the provisions of Islamic *shari'ah* (Bahrain, Iraq), and the tradition and custom of a child taking the nationality of the father (Egypt, Kuwait, Morocco, Oman, Qatar, Saudi Arabia, Tunisia, and UAE). This is true in the case of Algeria and Qatar. Other states (Jordan, Lebanon, and Syria) did not offer any explanation for their objections. Egypt's reservation states that it is more suitable for children to acquire the father's nationality, "It is clear that the child's acquisition of his father's nationality is the procedure most suitable for the child and that this does not infringe upon the principle of equality between men and women, since it is customary for a woman to agree, upon marrying an alien, that her children shall be of the father's nationality" (UN n.d.-b: 11). The tone of Egypt's reservation reflects deep-seated gender-discriminating norms, such that a clear example of gender discrimination is not even considered as such. These countries deny the prevalence of many forms of gender discrimination in their societies, since they do not accept that such discriminating practices discriminate against women. Rather, they view these as default practices of gender equality, regardless of their violation of universal conventions and treaties on women's human rights.[11]

The common thread of the Arab States' reservations to Article 15 is the incompatibility of certain provisions of Islamic law, family laws, and/or established practices with regard to women's legal capacity, testimony, right to conclude contracts, and freedom of movement, residence, and domicile in Arab states (UN 2010). Such reservations are based on inherited norms, especially sacred religious norms embedded in the provisions of Islamic *shari'ah*.

Reservations to Article 16 are also based on the incompatibility of the provisions of Article 16 to formalized sacred norms regarding marriage and familial relations.

Egypt's reservation to Article 16 is a good example of the incompatibility between the provisions of Article 16 and the embedded sacred norms rooted in the Islamic *shari'ah*. Such religious norms are invoked to justify a sense of "equivalency" of rights and duties rather than "equality" between a husband and his wife. The reservation did not refer to what constitutes a "just balance" or the "equivalent" rights and duties,

[The] reservation to the text of article 16 concerning the equality of men and women in all matters relating to marriage and family relations during the marriage and

upon its dissolution, without prejudice to the Islamic sharia provisions whereby women are accorded rights equivalent to those of their spouses so as to ensure a just balance between them. This is out of respect for the sacrosanct nature of the firm religious beliefs which govern marital relations in Egypt and which may not be called in question and in view of the fact that one of the most important bases of these relations is an equivalency of rights and duties so as to ensure complementarity which guarantees true equality between the spouses, not a quasi-equality that renders the marriage a burden on the wife. The provisions of the sharia lay down that the husband shall pay bridal money to the wife and maintain her fully and shall also make a payment to her upon divorce, whereas the wife retains full rights over her property and is not obliged to spend anything on her keep. The sharia therefore restricts the wife's rights to divorce by making it contingent on a judge's ruling, whereas no such restriction is laid down in the case of the husband. (UN 2010: 15–16)

The reservation stresses the "sacrosanct nature of the firm religious beliefs that govern marital relations," with little room for compromise, even when such beliefs discriminate against wives and impose on them unfavorable and non-negotiable customs and rules. Under these circumstances, women are forced to abide by the existing laws and customs that are rooted in the society's collective belief and enforcement of such sacrosanct teachings. Given the nature of this reservation, women's capabilities and functionings to enter into a marriage, their rights and duties with regard to their relationships with their husbands, and rearing children, their right to seek to divorce and collect alimony, and their right to child custody, are based on the ill-defined use of ambiguous terms like "equivalency" and "complementarity" between wives and husbands. Egypt's reservation endorses the use of formal rules rooted in sacred informal norms as instruments to guarantee "true" equality between spouses, criticizing CEDAW's article 16 for its call for a distorted "quasi-equality" that imposes a greater burden on the wife.

Informal norms, which are elevated to formal rules and enforced in collectivist societies by the winners of such norms and rules, summarize the intent of this book. Women and other individualist members of society must obey and follow these norms and rules, due to the high cost of deviating from these discriminating norms in collectivist societies. In a nutshell, the essence of Egypt's reservation to Article 16 is to rationalize, using sacred norms, certain forms of discrimination against women, as integral to everyday life in Egypt.

The reservations of Arab states to CEDAW highlight the uncertainty of their (and other similar states that use sacred norms, such as Islamic *shari'ah*, as a rationale for their reservations) intentions and respect for the object and purpose of CEDAW. France's objection to Saudi Arabia's general reservation to CEDAW underscores the uncertainty with regard to the commitment and compliance of the Arab States to the object and purpose of CEDAW, "By stating that in case of contradiction between any term of the Convention and the norms of Islamic laws, it is not under obligation to observe the terms of the Convention, the Kingdom of Saudi Arabia formulates a reservation of general, indeterminate scope that gives the other States parties absolutely no idea which provision of the Conventions are affected or might be affected in future" (UN n.d.-b). The common thread of the reservations of Arab States makes it very difficult to ascertain the scope of each state's compliance, and could make the provisions of CEDAW ineffective, as Mounira Charrad summarizes, "Women's basic personal rights have been among the most contested issues of the law in the history of the Islamic world in the contemporary period in the MENA [Middle East and North Africa] region" (2007: 242).

The above analysis accentuates the immense influence of informal norms on formal rules and laws, and therefore on the daily life of women in collectivist societies, mostly in the Arab world.

Appendix 2.1

Table A2.1 The years of Arab States' ratification of CEDAW and the outstanding reservations to selected articles in CEDAW as of November 13, 2014.

Country	Ratification Year	Outstanding Reservations to CEDAW's Articles as of March 1, 2010					
		General Reservations	Article 2	Article 9	Article 15	Article 16	Article 9
Algeria	1996		2		15.4	16	29.1
Bahrain	2002		2	9.2	15.4	16	29.1
Comoros	1994						
Djibouti	1998						
Egypt	1981		2	9.2		16	29.1
Iraq	1986	Yes	2 (f, g)	9.1, 9.2		16	29.1
Jordan	1992			9.2		16.1(c, d, g)	29.1
Kuwait	1994			9.2		16.1(f)	29.1
Lebanon	1997			9.2		16.1(c, d, f, g)	29.1
Libya	1989		2			16.1(c, d)	29.1
Mauritania*	2001	Yes					
Morocco	1993		2	9.2	15.4	16	29.1
Oman	2006	Yes		9.2	15.4	16.1(a, c, f)	29.1
Qatar	2009		2 (a)	9.2	15.1,2,4	16.1(a, c, f)	29.1
Saudi Arabia	2000	Yes		9.2			29.1

continued

Table A2.1　Continued

Country	Ratification Year	Outstanding Reservations to CEDAW's Articles as of March 1, 2010					
		General Reservations	Article 2	Article 9	Article 15	Article 16	Article 9
Syria	2003		2	9.2	15.4	16.1 (c, d, f, g), 16.2	29.1
Tunisia	1985	Yes		9.2	15.4	16.1 (c, d, f, g, h)	29.1
United Arab	2004		2(f)	9	15.2	16	29.1
Yemen	1984						29.1

*Mauritania partially withdrew it general reservation on July 25, 2014.

Sources: Date collected from United Nations (2010). Convention on the Elimination of All Forms of Discrimination against Women (CEDAW): Declarations, reservations, objections, and notifications of withdrawal of reservations relating to the Convention on the Elimination of All Forms of Discrimination against Women. http://www2.ohchr.org/english/bodies/cedaw/docs/AdvanceVersions/CEDAW-SP-2010-2.pdf.

Also see (UN n.d.-b) Treaty Collection: Chapter IV. 8. Convention on the Elimination of All Forms of Discrimination against Women. https://treaties.un.org/PagesNiewDetails.aspx?src=TREATY&mtdsg no=IV8&chapter=4&lang=en. Accessed November 13, 2014.

CHAPTER 3

Cultural Relativism and Gender-Discriminating Norms

Cultural relativism and feminism represent unique yet different and opposing views on the universality of human rights described in the UDHR (the 1948 Universal Declaration of Human Rights) and CEDAW (the 1979 Convention on the Elimination of All Forms of Discriminations against Women). In general, cultural relativists consider meanings, values, freedoms, capabilities, and functionings to be defined only within a cultural context. In contrast, feminists seek to widen the applications of universal human rights to affirm gender equality in all practices pertaining to human capabilities and functionings.

Cultural Relativism, Norms, and Gender

Cultural relativism is the principle that people's beliefs, identities, roles, and acts should be understood and evaluated within the context of their culture. Under this principle, universal or international human rights provisions that undermine cultural tenets and traditions in societies should be rejected or modified to fit the cultural foundations in these societies. Universal human rights that contradict the cultural tenets in different societies should be considered intrusive into matters that belong to these societies.

Cultural relativists seek to protect and maintain the cultural context in which people are forming or accepting their sense of worth and identity (Mayer 1995, 1999). Culture-specific values and norms should not be compared to those in other cultures. Thus, there is no one common universal set of values and norms on which human rights are constructed. Cultural relativists oppose certain articles, specific claims in certain articles (or specific interpretations of such articles) in universal human rights conventions and declarations. They claim that these articles reflect Western values and norms that do not encompass or align with the values of the non-Western world (Brems 1997; Nayak 2013). Cultural relativists underscore collective and group rights, rather than individual rights (the main focus in Western societies).

Cultural relativism states that norms and values are culturally produced. Normative senses are applicable within each culture, and do not need to synchronize with the norms, meanings, and values of other cultures. Since each culture defines the values and norms of its members, "cultures must respect each other's autonomy" (Singer 1999). Societal meanings and values should not be compared or ranked globally, since each culture has its own values that are unique to its members. Cultural relativism tends to focus on collective concepts and units of references, such as families, tribes, communities, and the overall society. Cultural relativists assume harmony, equal access, and respect for human rights within the cultural tenets of their societies. Since they believe men and women are inherently different and possess separate rights, cultural relativists see the division of roles as beneficial to all members in societies (Mayer 2000; Nayak 2013).

In general, cultural relativists (including the ruling elites in these societies) rank cultural values and sacred norms over the supremacy of international law (Singer 1999: 50). They embrace the status given to them by previous generations. This continuation of cultural practices adds values to their society.

Feminism, Norms, and Gender Discrimination

Feminists aim to expand the definition of human rights to include equal rights for women. While acknowledging cultural differences, feminists believe that similarities amongst the individuals should trump cultural differences and should give women the rights to ask for international changes (Nayak 2013).

Feminists critique human rights conventions, such as CEDAW, for not going far enough. They believe these conventions should use language that mirrors the strong language of the Apartheid Convention, where the terms "oppression," "domination," and "inhumane" treat racial apartheid as criminal. Feminists argue that gender discrimination should be treated as "gender apartheid." Without this language, gender-discriminating practices become a "product of culture rather than politics" (Mayer 2000: 245). Downgrading gender apartheid makes it less reprehensible than racial apartheid. Thus, feminists criticize universal and international laws and conventions for devaluing women's concerns. Feminists also highlight the subtle forms of gender discrimination that are woven into the fabric of society, in which women's status as subordinate and domestically oriented is rooted in the theory of complementary roles for men and women, which are not treated as gender-discriminating practices (Brems 1997, Mayer 2000).

Feminism calls for the eradication and revision of specific aspects and writing that have distorted the positions, aspirations, and voices of women, as they have deformed and restricted women's rights, capabilities, and functionings.

They reject the imposed norms and rules that are rooted in inherited gender-discriminating mindsets. Feminists seek to change the use of "man" and the collective units controlled or dominated by men, such as "family," as the default units of reference. Susan Okin (1989) highlights the notion of "false gender neutrality," which obscures gender-discriminating practices within the family.

Feminists see women's situation in gender-discriminating societies as unjust, contingent, and imposed. Thus, they seek to empower women through their own access to status and power (Mackinnon 1987). Women should have unconditional access to orchestration power (the power to make major decisions for themselves, their families, and their community), equal to men's status and power. Feminists define equality as the eradication of gender hierarchy, not gender differentiation. Catherine Mackinnon argues inequality is a manmade construct: "Across time and space, there is too much variance in women's status, role, and treatments for it to be biological, and too little variance for it to be individual. In this view, women and men appear biologically more alike and socially more different than is generally supposed" (1987: 25). They argue that substantial differences between men and women are socially constructed, and not natural or individual.

Liberal feminists highlight men's prejudice against women, embodied in laws or expressed in the exclusion of women from particular areas of life. They stay within the human rights framework, seeking protection of women's and structural improvement for the enforcement of human rights of women, a combination 'add and stir' approach. Cultural feminists (women's rights groups using cultural lenses) stress the differences between men and women such as the biological differences (women's comparative physical weakness that makes them more vulnerable to acts of violence), women's childbearing and lactating capacities (place them in unique childrearing situation), concentration of activities and responsibilities at home, and behavioral differences. They emphasize the positive aspects of their cultures and ignore the negative aspects, for example, Islamic feminists tend to use selected *qur'anic* versus and *hadith* that favor the status of women, while ignoring other references that violate women's rights, and their interpretations (An-Na'im 1990). Cultural feminists stress the need to revise the catalog of human rights to include reproductive rights and sexual autonomy rights. They also seek to include gender specific-violations, for example, domestic discrimination and violence. Radical feminists underscore women's oppression under a patriarchal system. They reject male dominance and female subordination. They seek to dismantle the built-in differences leading to male dominance (Brems 1997, Storey 2009).

Feminists (and Universalists) are not against religious and traditional societies. They are against the violation of human rights in the name of cultures, religions, or traditions. Differences in cultures and religions that are inclusive and uphold human rights should be respected, welcomed, and even celebrated. Exclusive and discriminating norms and practices under any slogan should be exposed, confronted, and eradicated.

The Cultural Relativist's Critique of Universal Human Rights

The cultural relativists' main critique of universal human rights is that they are the product of the Western culture. They believe these rights reflect the West's own specific needs and aspirations, most of which is foreign to non-Western cultures. They also cite lack of Eastern input. Thus, they advocate the inclusion of non-Western cultures in the catalog of human rights. Dominance theorists underscore the notion of Western conspiracy against non-Western cultures (Western imperialism and neocolonialism) as imposing Western values on the rest of the world through the catalog of universal human rights (Brems 1997).

The "difference" approach of cultural relativism underscores the difference between Western and non-Western cultures, values, and principles. It rejects specific rights on the basis of religious or cultural difference. For example, they reject the freedom of religion, since such freedom signifies a grand violation of Islamic and other non-Western norms, principles, and values. The difference approach may also accept a right, but reject the classification of particular practices as violation of it (e.g., labeling female circumcision and forced marital sex as different practices than FGM/C and marital rape, respectively) (see chapters 10 and 11). They also underscore the importance of defining rights culturally according to societal principles and values.

Radical relativists seek to exclude non-Western cultures from the universal human rights system or to transform it to accommodate cultural differences. For example, rather than the Western's individualist abstract rights, non-Westerners tend to identify themselves according to ascribed status as members of larger groups or communities (such as families, tribes, or nations). They also stress the concept of obligations and reciprocal responsibilities, above the Western concept of rights. Communitarian relativists suggest placing limitations on individual rights in favor of communal interests (Brems 1997). Cultural Absolutists call for all systems of social justice to be human rights systems (Howard-Hassmann 1993).

Critiquing Cultural Relativism

Most critiques to cultural relativism come from feminists and human rights universalists. Cultural relativism tends to overlook the importance of the global community. Members of any specific culture (or society) are also members of the global community who share common values, principles, and rights with members in other cultures (Brems 1997, Nayak 2013).

Under cultural relativism, certain gender-discriminating customs and practices, such as FGM/C, domestic violence, underage marriage, and polygyny, will not be challenged since they are unique to certain cultures (Nayak 2013). Cultural relativists may not recognize (or recognize but deny) certain gender-discriminating practices as gender discrimination, therefore failing to recognize or enforce women's rights (Nayak 2013).

Many cultures view male dominance and female subordination as integral to their principles and values (Brems 1997; Mayer 2000). Thus, cultural relativists are likely to write off calls for women's rights by calling them "Western." They accuse national human rights' activists and NGOs of being westernized and alienated elites (Mayer 2000). National feminists from the Arab world and other Muslim countries have complained about, "Westerners dismissing calls for women's international human rights coming from within Muslim countries as somehow unnatural and unrepresentative" (Mayer 2000: 269). Intimidation and prosecution of human rights activists, such as the case of ASWA (Arab Women's Solidarity Association) in Egypt, which was dissolved in 1991, is an example of how cultural relativism responds to claims of gender-discriminating practices in these societies. The court declared that ASWA had "threatened the peace and political and social order of the state by spreading ideas and beliefs offensive to the rule of Islamic *sharia* [sic] and the religion of Islam" (Mayer 2000: 264). Some of ASWA's violations were related to its critiques of the conventions of marriage, divorce, and polygyny in Egypt, which are norms based in sacred teaching and belief. The Egyptian government used "state policy," "the rule of law," and specific elements of Islamic law as instruments to suppress feminist (and universalism) activists, in Egypt. The Association for the Support of Women Voters, another Egyptian women's rights advocacy group, was shut down in 2000. Tactics and practices such as boycotting, prosecuting, dissolving, and even assassinating feminists and human rights activists are prevalent in the Arab world (Mayer 1995, 2000). Azar Nafisi stated, "In the strange world of Middle Eastern studies, any attempt to condemn gender apartheid is branded an imposition of Western values, the voices of prominent clerics who oppose the politicization of religion are ignored, and the secular dissidents are dismissed as Westernized and therefore inauthentic" (2003: par 12).

Critics of cultural relativism in the Muslim world object to CDHRI (The Cairo Declaration of Human Rights in Islam) and UIDHR (The Universal Islamic Declaration of Human Rights) for their potential violations of human rights. Both CDHRI and UIDHR are projects used by cultural relativists in the Islamic world as alternatives to universal human rights. They are customized for Muslim countries dominated by conservative patriarchal hierarchy. CDHRI and UIDHR legitimize corporal punishments (under the tenant of Islamic *shari'ah*) that violate the integrity and dignity of human beings. They also restrict many fundamental rights and freedom below existing standards in many Muslim countries. CDHRI and UIDHR both introduce an Islamic tone into the political, legal, social, and cultural spheres.

Those who are deprived from status and orchestration powers are excluded from or underrepresented in decision-making processes in many gender discriminating societies. Anne Phillips (2010) describes the "communities talking to communities" syndrome that empowers established leaders and sanctions norms and rules in which women's rights are violated and women are relegated to second-class members. Catherine Mackinnon (1987) discusses women's exclusion from inner circle status as a restriction to their ability to voice their own opinions or fight for certain rights. Female dependency becomes a cycle of brutality and need for protection if women do not have the right to report abuse on their own. In these societies, women become dependent on the same people (men) who brutalize them, so women continue to need more protection from their abusers.

Cultural relativists tend to undermine cultural diversity, dualism, and social fractionalization in almost all cultures, societies, and countries. In a given culture, there are many divisions in beliefs and values. Among the same religion, there are different denominations and affiliations. At national levels, there are different beliefs and non-beliefs (formally and informally). No one set of meanings can reflect or represent the opinions of all members in the same society. Thus, cultural relativism most likely represents the beliefs invoked by the ruling elites or the majority population in the country. This may contradict or overlook other groups' meanings and values, thus limiting or deforming these groups' identities. To sustain their status and distributional gain, the ruling elites or majority in gender-discriminating collectivist societies tend to discredit and object to any attempt to highlight the built-in bias in their society. They respond to claims of exclusion or marginalization of women in their society as attacks on the whole culture, cultural harmony, and social order. Christine Chinkin (1999) expresses this notion elegantly, "Under the relativist perspective, claims of universality, can accordingly be rejected as imperialistic and a form of conspiracy that uses human rights to uphold Western economic interests to the detriments of developing countries" (55). The marginalization and silencing of women and other population groups is an implicit admission that the imposed values and meanings are not shared by all members of the society (Singer 1999). The recent rise of religious fundamentalism in the Arab world is likely to oppress women, non-fundamentalist Muslims, and other non-Muslim population groups and subcultures further. In fundamentalists thought, calls for women's rights are seen as betrayal (Hélie-Lucas 1999). If these women or other marginalized or silenced groups were given full and free opportunity to form their views and declare them, they would reject the elite group's version of their culture or religion (Singer 1999).

Feminism, universalism, and cultural relativism are not exclusive to certain cultures. They are represented in Western and non-Western societies from around the world. Mayer (n.d., 1999) cites American opposition to the UDHR as a threat to the US Constitution, and the presence of alien concepts in UDHR that would erode American rights. The opposition to universal human rights by nationalists and cultural relativists in the USA and other European countries undermines the claim that these conventions and protocols are tools exploited by the West for political leverage against the rest of the world. The dispute is not between cultures or sovereignties, but between staticism and dynamism in every culture. It is between the winners of the status quo (who seek to sustain their distributional gains, status, and power), and the victims of such discriminating practices (and the supporters of the victims of such status quo). The debate should be reframed to make cultures inclusive and nondiscriminating.

Cultural relativism tends to assume a single culture and neutrality of norms, roles, and rules. They speak on behalf of other groups (such as women and other subcultures) in the culture, disregarding their voices and aspirations

(Singer 1999). The 'chosen' culture usually dominates other subcultures living near or within it. It assumes a culture consisting of all persons who share 'precisely' the same sense of meaning and values. Such a culture does not exist, since it is a culture of one (Singer 1999).

Discriminating norms that do violence to women in the name of culture, harmony, or unity must be opposed and eradicated if women's rights matter as well as men's rights (Butler 2004). Women's rights should triumph any claims, cultural or otherwise, that are indoctrinated in gender-discriminating societies where women are excluded or marginalized. Imposing collective identity, roles, and expectations on women in the name of culture or religion must be rejected by women and by human rights advocates elsewhere. "Social categories, imposed, from elsewhere, are always violations in the sense that they are, at first and by necessity, unchosen" (Butler 2004: 214–215). Cultural relativists imagine homogeneity where there is really diversity. They also imagine agreement or submission, where there is really silent opposition (Nussbaum 2000). Thus, they have no basis to make moral judgments and impose them on the victims of such judgment.

Gender-discriminating cultural relativism tends to draw cultural boundaries in by reference to the men and assigns the women (and other minority groups) living within the same physical environment to the same culture. Often, these boundaries are assigned without scrutiny or their sense of identity, and values (Singer 1999). Feminists believe in the equality of sexes and reject the notion of complementarity of sexes. Embraced by conservative religionists, the complementarity of sexes underscores biologically determined gender roles. In contrast, feminists view gender roles as a social construct, unsettled, and subject to change. While cultural relativists use the term 'sex', feminists use the code 'gender' in their reference to women's human rights. 'Sex' refers to the biologically fixed differences between men and women. In contrast, 'gender' is used to reevaluate women's roles, critique traditions, and advance women's rights (Mayer n.d., 1999, 2000).

Religion is a cultural marker in many countries. In the Arab world, religion is the most important marker of culture, norms, and values. Cultural relativists, including religionists, bolster and legitimize their claims by appropriating rights guarantees for religious freedom and nondiscrimination on the basis of religion. The right to religious freedom lies at the interface between civil and political rights (e.g., freedom of association and expression), and economic, social and cultural rights (e.g., access to education, health, and employment) and that between individual rights and group rights. The inclusion of group rights within a catalogue of human rights can be complex, exclusive, and discriminating. Group rights create conceptual confusion, particularly in situations where assertions of individual liberty do not conform to those of the group or the collective identity, including the religious identity. In collectivist societies, claims based on religion often have a trumping effect on other claims, such as individual freedom (Chinkin 1999). The problem becomes more serious when such religious and collective beliefs and norms, come with a clear dichotomy between the potential winners (or perpetrators) and losers (or victims).

In such cases, the winners can dictate certain identities, roles, and rules, and impose them on the losers (the victims of such cultural practices), depriving the victims of status, their ability to lead life independently, and make decisions free from the external imposition of the elite or ruling majority.

Cultural relativists tend to overlook, condone, or sanction certain human rights' violations, since such practices are meaningful to certain participants in those cultures, for example FGM/C, child marriage, polygyny, women's seclusion and veiling, and honor killing in some Arab and other similar countries, *devadasis* (temple prostitutes in India), and *sati* (burning of widows at the pyre of their dead husbands, also in India) (Abadeer 2008).

Most cultural rights tend to be positional or status rights (see chapter 9). The gains or rights of one cultural group take place at the expense of another cultural group or subgroup in the same country. The dominance theory explains the human rights' violations of groups and subcultures through the process of enforcing enculturation and acculturation.

Cultural relativists tend to romanticize about cultural harmony, social unity, complementarity of rights and responsibilities, interdependence, and homogenous members with similar values, principles, and aspirations. However, reality shows otherwise in terms of conflict, social fractionalization, dominance, and different and sometimes opposing values, principles, and aspirations; as Eva Brems puts it, "Each individual should have the right to practice his or her culture and traditions, but likewise, each individual should have the right to reject them" (164).

Cultural Relativism and Religious Values

Certain sacred religious norms that reflect Muslim patriarchy in the Arab world, are imposed and reinforced through formalization into laws. In most Arab countries (with the exception of Lebanon), the Islamic *shari'ah* is sanctioned as a main or the only source of legislation and law. Accordingly, many practices (or variations of them) that were prevalent many centuries ago, are still applicable by ruling patriarchal hierarchy, according to various interpretations of such sacred norms. Figure 3.1 shows the percentage of Arabs who believe that religion is very important in life, which is much higher (with the exception of Lebanon) than the world's average (more specifically the average of 55 countries in the survey), highlighting the important role of religion and religious teachings and norms in the Arab world.

Figure 3.2 also underscores the importance of traditions handed down by religion or family in the Arab world that is much higher (except in Lebanon, one of the least collectivist Arab countries) than the world's average, highlighting the significant role of collective and inherited culture in people's beliefs and behaviors.

The World Values Survey (2014) shows that a very high percentages of respondents from the Arab world believe that their religion (the most majority of Arabs are Muslims) is the only acceptable religion in the Arab world (see figure 5.6 in chapter 5), almost doubling the world's average. Moreover,

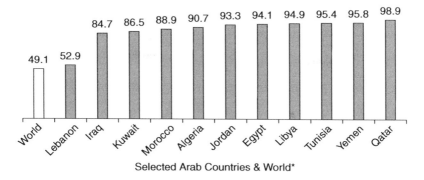

Figure 3.1   Percentage of people who agree that religion is very important in life.
*The world percentage represents the average of 55 counties included in the survey.
Source: World Value Survey (2014). V. 9, p. 6.

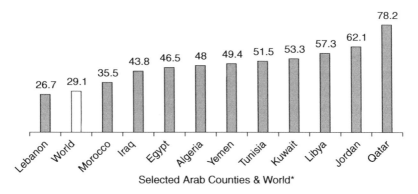

Figure 3.2   Percentage of people who agree with the statement, "it is important to follow the customs handed down by one's religion or family."
*The world percentage represents the average of 55 counties included in the survey.
Source: World Value Survey (2014). V. 79, p. 101.

according to the survey, when science and religion are in conflict, most Arab respondents believe that religion is always right, at a significantly higher rate than the world's average.

Due to the high level of religiosity in the Arab world, most of the informal norms are rooted (closely or loosely) in interpretations of sacred norms and Islamic teaching, especially in the *Qur'an* and *hadith* (the most revered sources of Islamic *shari'ah*). A good example of cultural relativism is the culture of patriarchy. Mahanz Afkhami (1999) underscores the role of cultural relativism in gender apartheid in Muslim societies. Gender discrimination (or apartheid) is defined in laws and regulations pertaining to women's role in the private and public spheres (inheritance, guardianships, space, movement, divorce, employment laws, and participation and representation in social, cultural, and political arenas) generally worked out such that, "women's dependent and separate sphere is justified, protected and perpetuated" (Afkhami 1999: 69). Women in the Arab world do not have rights according to international laws, covenants, and declarations; rather, they have privileges from sacred sources such as the *Qur'an* and the *hadith*. All rights are derived from Islam as interpreted by a select group of men (Afkhami 1999). The Islamists (cultural relativists) always posit the question of women's rights within an Islamist (a cultural) frame of reference. Afkhami made the case of women's individual rights that should not be subject to the authority of other individuals, especially the cultural relativists. Islamists and other cultural relativists suggest that the West has invented the idea of universality of rights to impose its way on other cultures and societies (Afkhami 1999).

Cultural Relativism and Gender Discrimination

The relationship between cultural relativism and individuals rights with respect to religious identity is complex. In societies where people are not free to violate certain social norms (including sacred or religious norms), the deviant members of societies expose themselves to collective punishments, which are integral in the cultural structure of the society. Without effective punishments against the deviants, certain norms may fade away. If such norms are sacred and revered by the majority population or ruling elites, these norms are accompanied by a well-defined scheme of punishments and rewards. In collectivist societies with high degrees of monitoring, potential deviants must reevaluate their options.

The dominated groups' lack of status (exclusion from or under-representation in the decision-making processes and orchestration power) is likely to leave them with the 'inferior power' to implement the major decisions (made by dominant group), according to the specification of the dominant groups. Decisions made by the elite or dominant groups usually impose certain constraints on dominated groups, in terms of restricted access to freedom, capabilities, and functionings (explained in chapter 4).

According to many cultural relativists, especially conservatives, in the Islamic world, liberal democracy or democracy in general is *kofr* (blasphemy), since it is a man-made system, not from *Allah*, the source of all human rights and laws (Hélie-Lucas 1999).

The problem resides in the sex dichotomy and the assigned identities and roles to men and women in gender-discriminating societies. Women in the Arab world are mostly praised for their socially assigned roles as wives and mothers, especially mothers of boys (Riphenbrug 1998). Women are instructed (or commanded) to be obedient to their husbands and other male relatives. Women are believed to be created with a deficiency in the mind and deficiency in faith since they cannot pray or fast during their menstruation. They are taught that they should be dependent on male relatives and husbands. A woman's body, except her face and hands, is considered *'awra* (a part of the body that must be covered), according to norms rooted in patriarchal interpretations of sacred teachings. Women should be confined to their home, not leaving the home unless it is necessary and with a permission from their husbands or other male guardians (Al-Qaradawi 1997).

According to prevailing norms in the Arab world and similar Muslim societies, women are considered minors who ought to be protected, guided, supported, and even disciplined by male guardians. As minors, women lose most status power and ability to make decision within her family, tribe, and the society in general. Based on their minor status, women's access to positive freedoms is controlled (restricted or prohibited), such as the freedom to move, travel, work, and participate in athletic, artistic, social, cultural, and political activities, and their freedom and capabilities to be leaders and rulers in many Arab countries. They are banned from certain freedoms, and need permissions to limited access in others. For example, in Saudi Arabia, women are banned from driving, are required to wear a full-length loose black gown (known as *abaya*), are not permitted to vote or run for office (until King Abdulla granted women's suffrage in municipal elections starting 2015). Women are also banned from traveling without permissions from male guardians, banned from watching sport events in stadiums and from entering or using public pools and athletic facilities, and are subject to chastisement from the religious police for behaving improperly, for example, not properly covered by the *abayas* and veils (Jensen: 2005). Women's traveling was also closely monitored through text alerts to their male guardians when they leave or enter the country. Safa Ahamad, a female Saudi freelance journalist, underscores such excessive gender-discriminating practices, "Saudi women are viewed and treated as minors by the Saudi government. A text message doesn't change that. It's just adding insult to injury" (Harding 2012).

In the Arab world (and other similar societies), a woman holds in her body, behavior, and reputation the honor of the collective community. Such a burden is imposed on women only. To uphold the honor, certain measures must be applied, generation after generation, in what is considered a sacred norm that should be upheld at any cost. Since women hold the honor in their body (specifically, their intact hymen before marriage) and their reputation and sexual fidelity after marriage, certain preemptive, on-going, and ex-post measures become integral to the culture in these societies. Preemptive measures may include gender selective feticide and infanticide, FGM/C, and underage marriage. Ongoing measures include monitoring girls' and women's behavior very closely, restricting their movement and choices, creating all-female environments for girls and women (e.g., all female school, stores, working places, health clinics), and imposing the status of legal minors on girls and women. Loss of virginity before marriage (sometimes beyond the girl's control) or tarnishing girls' and women's reputations and therefore disgracing the family' honor must be met with severe punishment, such as strict confinement, forced marriage (in the case of rape), and honor killing.

The treatment of women as legal minors in the Arab world (and other similar societies), makes these discriminating norms and practices prevalent and seemingly accepted by large percentage of women. Women—who do not have the power to make certain decisions that flourish their capabilities and functionings—depend on their male legal guardians who make decisions for the female dependents, guided in part by the prevailing collective gender-discriminating norms (see chapter 8 for more details).

Cultural Relativism, Enculturation, and Acculturation

Enculturation is the process of certain members' acclimation (voluntarily or involuntarily) to the surrounding culture and the assigned identities, roles, and rules (e.g., Muslim members in a Muslim society). Acculturation is the process of acclimation (voluntarily or involuntarily) to the prevailing norms of the dominant or majority culture by the members of minority or dominated subcultural groups (e.g., other ethnic, religious, or racial groups). In gender-discriminating societies, enculturation and acculturation impart in women the socially assigned proper behaviors and expectations according to the prevailing gender-discriminating norms, behaviors, and expectations. Gradually, women acclimate to these norms and accept them as normal nondiscriminating behaviors.

The enculturation and acculturation processes can be voluntary or imposed. If norms are not imposed and membership is voluntary, members are likely to move to the subculture that fits their aspirations and desires. In contrast, imposed enculturation and acculturation processes take place if the norms are imposed and accompanied with well-defined schemes of punishment against the norms' deviants (dissenters), in addition to the mandatory membership requirements, such that potential deviants cannot denounce their membership and leave the culture. In this case, certain members of the cultures and those of other cultures who live within the ruling culture, will be forced to act according to the imposed norms and rules sanctioned by the dominant ruling culture. Imposing the dominant culture's norms and rules on women and members of other minority cultural groups violates their rights and limits or deforms their capabilities and functionings. Examples of such processes include the acclimation of foreign women to the socially sanctioned wardrobe in Saudi Arabia, and the prevalence of FGM/C among the minority non-Muslim girls in Sudan and Egypt at a lower rate than Muslim girls there (Singer 1999; Yount 2004). In many Arab countries, non-Muslims can be punished by the virtue police (or collectivist vigilantes) if they eat, drink, or smoke cigarettes publically during the fasting time of the month of Ramadan, in which Muslims are commanded to fast sunrise to sunset, since they violate the dominant culture's norms.

Generally, minority groups tend to acclimate to imposed dominant or majority groups' norms, traditions, habits, dress, and other social markers, to avoid collective ostracism, harassment, and other punishments. In these societies, the dominated groups usually abide by many norms (including gender discriminating norms) that are specific and prevalent among the majority or the ruling elite groups.

One of the big dilemmas associated with imposed enculturation and acculturation is the seeming acceptance of the majority group's norms, traditions, and practices by the minority and dominated population groups. The seeming acceptance of gender-discriminating norms by women and other minority groups can divert attention away from the root sources and causes of these norms. Such seeming acceptance may divert or undermine the effectiveness of interventions. To tackle the problem of imposed acculturation, it is necessary to explore the root sources and causes of these norms, diagnose them, and prescribe solutions that prevent them from resurfacing. If the root causes are so embedded, or sacred, in the dominant culture, acknowledging such as such should help researchers and policy makers address them, eradicate them if feasible, or recognize them as constraints that violate human rights.

First Best Rights Versus Second and Third Best Rights

Feminism represents the first-best scenario of women's rights in terms of total and unequivocal equality between men and women free from all impediments that are rooted in various cultural, religious, historical, social institutions.

Cultural feminism represents a second-best scenario of women's rights. It calls for women's rights and equality subject to existing collectivist norms and rules, as a status quo. However, cultural feminists may challenge the interpretation of certain sacred teaching and norms that can be exploited by existing patriarchal hierarchy and the dominant power and status of fundamentalists in their society. They reject gender-discriminating norms and practices that are false, unauthentic, or exploited by gender-discriminating patriarchal dominance (Ahmed 1992; Charrad 2007; Mernissi 1987).

Cultural relativism offers the least amount of rights to women. It endorses existing cultural norms as a reflection of cultural heritage, harmony, and social order. Cultural relativists not only oppose and refute the view of the feminists, but also that of the cultural feminists who seek to stretch their rights by pushing the cultural values envelope. Martha Nussbaum underlines such discriminating notion of "social justice": "Many traditional conceptions of social justice and fundamental entitlements have made women second-class citizens, if citizens at all. Women's liberties, opportunities, property rights, and political rights have been construed as unequal to men, and this has been taken to be a just state of affairs" (2003: 48).

Women's Options under Cultural Relativism

Women's response to imposed norms in gender-discriminating collectivist societies reflects their perception of the norms. In short, women's response reflects their capability to opt-out.

The following scenarios highlight women's various views and options in a typical gender-discriminating collectivist society:

1. Women believe in the collectively assigned norms, roles, and rules and will feel content with their status because they intrinsically believe in the norms and their collective imposition. These women are likely to act according to such norms even if they live in other societies that do not

impose them. Cultural relativists are likely to sample from this group of women and use them as the representatives of women and women's aspirations in their society.

2. Women become enculturated or acculturated to the assigned norms and to their identity, roles, and rules, and will gradually internalize their cognitive dissonance, hoping for better outcomes to occur, or even for a reward in the afterlife (see chapter 7).

3. Women reject the imposed gender-discriminating norms because they disagree with the interpretation and application of the sacred norms and the absence of women's inputs (diverting from the true meaning of sacred teaching and belief), will try to reshape the interpretation or challenge the misinterpretation and the imposition of such disputed norms from within. Cultural feminism is likely to sample from this group.

4. Women reject the imposed gender-discriminating norms because they do not believe in the sacred teaching, per se. This group includes women who believe in the norms but do not want to elevate them to a sacred status (not subject to debate). It also includes women who do not share the same belief, because they are affiliated with different denomination of the same religion, different religion, or they do not believe in religion per se.

5. Women reject the imposed gender-discriminating norms because they reject the collective imposition of the norms. This group represents the secularists and individualists who do not believe in the collective imposition of certain norms, for example, religious norms.

If the norms are not imposed, only the first group is likely to follow the norms because they accept the intrinsic merits of the norms. The other groups are less likely to follow them (except the second group, depending on their degree of enculturation and acculturation).

If opting out is a viable option, such that women (and other population groups) have the capability to exit the society, the first group will stay. The second group is likely to stay, or may have a weak desire to exit. The fourth and fifth groups will exit and join other societies that do not impose such norms. The third group may stay or exit depending on their perception of the likelihood of correcting the misinterpretation leading to existing imposed norms, and the likelihood of not imposing such disputable norms.

If the norms are not imposed and exiting the society (or the country) is a viable option, such as the case in individualist societies (see chapter 5), the first group will stay. The fourth and fifth groups will exit. The second and third group may stay or exit according to their level of preferences.

In gender-discriminating collectivist societies, such as the Arab world, many norms (especially the religious ones) are imposed, and there is no access to exit (or opt-out). For example, a female member cannot leave her collective unit (family, tribe, or community), since such an act dishonors the collective unit and is subject to a harsh collective punishment.

So, in the case of imposed norms and membership, the two available options are to violate the norms and rules and be exposed to collective punishment, or to enculturate or acculturate to the existing discriminating norms, internalizing them and acting accordingly, to minimize the internal pain and dissonance.

The above spectrum of the different perspectives reflects the lack of homogeneity among women and between and among religious, racial, ethnic, and tribal members.

Imposing society's wide norms, roles and rules, is likely to disenfranchise groups of women (and men) who believe in women's equal value, status, and human rights. Cultural relativists impose their own principles and values on the disenfranchised population groups.

Norms, Cultural Relativism, and Freedom:

The influence of gender-discriminating norms on women differs according to the degree of imposition. The following three scenarios highlight the different influences of gender related norms on women, in different cultures or societies:

1. Norms are not imposed and membership is voluntary; in this case, women (and other members) can choose among the society that suit their aspirations and desires. Members can stay or leave the societies to join another one, depending on their specific aspiration, choosing the society that they feel most suited for. It is the first-best scenario.

2. Norms are imposed and membership is voluntary: in this case, members (men and women) have viable options to leave the society and join another one. This option depends on people's knowledge of the gender-discriminating norms and the availability of other viable options. An example of this would be gender neutral (or less discriminating) societies. The required knowledge and economic capability to start a new life in another society is costly and comes with significant levels of anxiety. This option is usually viable to educated and rich members who are willing to risk moving to another society, and in the process, separate from loved ones who do not have the capability or desire to leave. Under this scenario, collectivist members who agree with the imposed norms will stay. However, uninformed, poor, and risk averse members are likely to enculturate (or acculturate) to the discriminating norms, roles, and rules.

3. Norms are imposed and membership is mandatory (no exit): this is the worst scenario, in which gender-discriminating norms are imposed, converted to formal rules, or elevated to metanorms (in which not only the norm's deviants are punished, but also the shirkers—the members who fail to punish the deviants or report them) (see chapter 6 for more details). In addition, members who reject these norms have no access or capability to exit. In this case, members are forced to act according

to these discriminating norms and uphold them. Norm's deviants and shirkers will be subject to collective punishments, which range from shunning and rebuking to execution, according to the violated norms and the degree of violation. Others may gain some utility from enculturating (and acculturating) to the assigned discriminating norms.

The second and third scenarios represent the case of cultural relativism in societies with built-in discrimination, based on gender or other social markers. These societies are likely to violate the rights of certain population groups. The victims in scenario two are the uninformed and the poor who lack the capability and functioning to move out. However, in the third scenario, the victims also include women (and some men too) who are informed about the built-in gender discrimination, but cannot exercise their capability to leave. In the Arab world, female membership in the family unit is mandatory. Girls and women, according to existing norms and laws, cannot leave their families or tribe to start a new life somewhere else. They (more specifically, their virginity, fidelity, and reputation) are among the collective assets that are jointly owned or controlled by the community, such that their behaviors and acts belong not only to themselves, but also to the collective unit.

Understanding Versus Approval of Cultural Norms

Cultural relativists tend to assume that cultures are homogenous, where every member has equal access, and identities and roles are distributed fairly. They also assume that all members share in the status good, that is, the decision making process in the society. They represent a romantic picture that only exists in a utopian world. They accept what they observe as acts that are free from any threat of collective punishment or from violating certain imposed norms and rules.

Cultural relativists tend to ignore gender discrimination, especially discrimination that takes place in the private sphere. They overlook the fact that families are political institutions with built-in biases and skewed power, status and obligations, which favor male members (Okin 1989).

While advocating the respect of cultural heritage, values, and harmonies, cultural relativists overlook the negative side effects of certain cultural practices. They tend—intentionally or unintentionally—to defend collective gender discrimination by treating these practices as integral parts of the cultural heritage that serves to sustain the existing sets of values and beliefs, cultural harmony, and social order. They claim that opposing, or calling to repeal, such norms and practices or advocating other inclusive and gender-neutral norms may threaten this balance in their societies. They must therefore be rejected and refuted as blatant foreign interventions and unwelcomed cultural invasions. Ann Phillips underscores such notion, "Mistaken notions of cultural respect are said to have silenced criticism of sexually inegalitarian practices" (2010: 2). Martha Nussbaum affirms it, "We should respect people who prefer a life within an authoritarian religion (or personal relationship), so long as certain basic opportunities and exit options are firmly guaranteed" (2003: 49).

However, not all cultural opinions and practices are equally valid and respectable. Nazis, Hindu fundamentalists, the Afghan Taliban, and the support of fundamentalists in the name of freedom of thought, freedom of speech and democracy is very dangerous, "Human rights...have to identify fundamentalism as the greatest threat of our time" (Hélie-Lucas 1999: 30).

Inclusive cultures and freedoms should be promoted. Values and norms that belong to and are accessible to all population groups and members should be welcomed and shared. Examples of these include culturally specific dance, language, sports, food, music, natural endowment, and other social, artistic, and cultural features (Nayak 2013).

Cultural norms and features that exclude certain groups of population (like women and racial minorities) from voting, participating in political arenas (as voters and political candidates), accessing certain jobs (like police offices, engineers, and judges), and freely moving, socializing, and building social capital, should be expelled from the culture.

Not all cultural norms, practices, and "freedoms" should be endorsed or promoted. Men's freedom to harass women in public places, a husband's freedom to beat or rape his wife, parents' freedom to impose FGM/C on their female children, or the collective freedom to exclude women from certain rights that are accessible to men should be confronted. These forms of freedom should be penalized because they impose intended harms on victims. These freedoms must be confronted to protect gender justice (Nussbaum 2003; Rawls, 1971). Societies that allow these unjust freedoms allow fundamental injustice, involving the marginalization and subordination of vulnerable groups, such as women (Nussbaum 2003).

Relativism should not be confused with tolerance of diversity. Some people, organizations, and nations find relativism attractive because it shows respect for and acceptance of other cultures. The underlying assumption in accepting cultural relativism is that these cultures uphold the human rights of all population groups (diverse ethnicity, race, religion, gender, and so on). However, in many societies, the elite group, usually the dominant culture, dictates the cultural settings, norms, and practices, at the expense of other dominated or excluded population groups' cultures, norms, and practices. The marginalized groups are likely to acculturate to the winning cultural norms and value in the country (otherwise, they have to confront the majority groups and seek other political solutions, which are very costly, especially in discriminating collectivist societies).

Women who are members of the dominant culture are likely to enculturate to the roles, norms, and practices sanctioned by men and the men's dominant collective government. Women of other cultural backgrounds may deal with double burdens, the burden of being a minority (ethnically, racially, or religiously), and the burden of being a woman in the gender-discriminating society. Martha Nussbaum states, "By making each tradition that last word, we deprive ourselves of any more general norm of toleration or respect that could help us limit the intolerance of cultures" (Nussbaum 2003: 49). She also adds that women's apparent adaptation (enculturation) to and acceptance of hostile, exclusive, and/or discriminating surrounding social environments should not be considered as the last word on the matter (Nussbaum 2000).

Accepting a specific culture does not mean sacrificing the rights of the victims of that culture. Likewise, rejecting gender-discriminating practices of a specific culture does not invalidate the culture. It accepts all other inclusive and nondiscriminating aspects of the culture, and underscores the need to change (or eradicate) the discriminating norms and practices that victimize certain population group(s) in the society.

Summary

Cultural relativism and feminism represent unique, yet different and opposing views on the universality of human rights. Cultural relativism is the principle that people's beliefs, identities, roles, and acts should be understood and evaluated within the context of their culture. While acknowledging cultural differences, feminism holds that similarities amongst individuals should trump cultural differences. The chapter provides extensive critiques of cultural relativism and explains why cultural relativism is inadequate as an argument against changes to human rights codes. The rejection of gender-discriminating practices of a specific culture does not invalidate the culture, but simply underscores the need to change (or eradicate) the discriminating norms that victimize certain population group(s) in the society.

CHAPTER 4

The Capability Approach and Gender Discrimination

The capability approach, pioneered by Amartya Sen and Martha Nussbaum, argues that practices and policies should be evaluated based not on the means (e.g., wealth, income, social institutions) that individuals own or have access to, but on the freedom they have to utilize these means (Comim et al. 2008; Drèze and Sen 2002; Sen 1985a, b, 1992, 1999, 2002; Nussbaum 1988, 2000, 2011; Qizilbash 2009). What ultimately matters to people is their freedom. It is the freedom people have to choose from the set of valuable choices that comprises their ability to live according to what they value (Sen 1999). Functionings represent the achieved capabilities: the subset of capabilities that people actually achieve and value the most. Every person should have the freedom or capability to practice a religion, but if the person chooses to be religious, agnostic, or atheist, he/she should not fear actual or potential harm or retribution, individually or collectively. Similarly, a person should have the capability to participate in political activities, regardless of his/her preference to be politically active or not.

The core focus of the capability approach is the capability of each person to live according to what they value, that is, to have and achieve the capabilities they value (Sen 1999). The term "capabilities" is usually used with reference to specific abilities, such as the ability to have bodily integrity and safety, to affiliate with others, and to participate in the life of community.

Capabilities are equatable very closely to rights, as stated by Nussbaum "To secure a right to citizens in these areas [political participation, religious free exercise, and the free speech] is to put them in a position of capability to function in that area" (2003: 37). However, the capability approach gives more precision to the language of rights. Individuals, groups, and nations may differ in their understanding and interpretations of rights, the basis of rights, differences between rights and duties, and levels of achievement of rights. In contrast, the capability approach takes clear positions on these issues. Women may have nominal rights of political participation and access to the court system; nonetheless, they do not have the capabilities to practice these rights if they are exposed to ridicule, punishment, or threats of violence if they participate politically or access the court system, respectively (Nussbaum 2003). Furthermore, the capability approach focuses on positive liberty—the capability or the right to do, while many rights focus on negative liberty such as the absence of negative state's action. The state (or other collectivist units), for example, may not discriminate against women in employment or political participation. Such a negative action by the state is not enough to guarantee women's right to employment and political participation in the case of widespread gender-discriminating norms (Nussbaum 2003).

The capability approach encompasses capabilities belonging to both public and private spheres, while most rights regulate only the public sphere's concerns. Furthermore, the language of capabilities "is not strongly linked to one particular cultural and historical tradition, as the language of rights is believed to be" (Nussbaum 2003: 39). Capabilities thus avoid the wearisome debate about the ethnocentricity of rights, in which many states accuse the universal human rights declarations, conventions, and protocols of being Eurocentric (Nussbaum 2003). Gender inequality and discriminating practices exist in a way that restricts, deforms, and sometimes prohibits women's ability to work, travel, marry, divorce, and participate in social, cultural, and political activities. Such discriminating practices limit women's functionings subject to the imposed gender-discriminating constraints (Robeyns 2005).

The capability approach is a broad interdisciplinary and multidimensional framework for the understanding, analysis, and assessment of individual well-being and social arrangements. Generally, the capability approach serves as an evaluative approach of the well-being of individuals in different societies and cultures, especially those subject to discriminating norms and practices.

The capability approach highlights both the normative capabilities (or opportunity set or potential functionings) and the achieved functionings of the individual(s). It takes into account the influence of different social, economic, political, and cultural contexts on individuals' capabilities and functionings. The applications of the approach cover a wide range of social, economic, and political issues such as poverty, inequality, exclusive policies and practices, cultural constraints, and discrimination. The capability approach underscores the principles and practices of freedom, agency,[1] and participation, leading to a valuable life (Robeyns 2003, 2005, 2011; Sen 1992, 2000; Nussbaum 2000).

The capability approach is rooted in the philosophy of social justice philosophy. It can be traced back to the writings of Aristotle, Adam Smith, and Carl Marx (Robeyns 2005, 2011; Nussbaum 2000; Sen 1999). Much of John Rawls' emphasis on access to primary social goods (self-respect, liberty, opportunities, powers, etc.) has influenced the capabilities approach (1971, 1993; Nussbaum 2003). Paul Streeten et al. (1981) pioneered the basic needs approach to development that focuses on the possession of commodities, and furthermore, the opportunity for a full life for all people (Streeten 1984; Alkire 2002).

However, the capability approach differentiates itself from the above approaches of social justice, in that it makes explicit assumptions about the value of choice and the negative value of coercion. Both these things are implicitly assumed in the basic needs approach (Alkire 2002; Clark 2005). Choice and participation are extremely vital to human capabilities and functionings. Unfortunately, in many collectivist societies, women are both coerced to participate in certain activities and are excluded from participating in other activities, based on discriminating informal norms and formal rules. This discrimination forces women to sacrifice their own choices, agencies, and effective participation. The capability approach also responds to the limitation of the utility approach that concentrates on happiness and pleasure. Utility does not differentiate between sources of pleasure and pain, specifically, the pleasure gained from other people's pain. The capability approach focuses more on the capabilities to achieve functionings, rather than on external means to attain various functions. Having means does not guarantee their utilization. For example, having enough income to buy individualist goods but not having the freedom to do so (Hausman and McPherson 1993). The core of the capability approach lies in the notion that an individual's freedom is an end in itself. In many societies, legal, social, and cultural constraints limit women's freedom, agency, and effective participation.[2]

The capability approach shares a vision with social practices theory. The capability approach emphasizes equal worth regardless of equal contribution and the importance of access to material resources as part of the true freedom. However, access to the resources is meaningless if one is constrained from utilizing such resources, for example, driving a car, opening a business, traveling, and buying individualist goods and services that are not permitted to women in certain collectivist societies (Figart 2009; Robeyns 2003). Therefore, cultural barriers play an important role in controlling and denying women freedom. Disadvantaged groups, such as subjects of gender discrimination, are more inclined to internalize discriminating social norms and constraints by adapting their preferences in response to the cognitive dissonance that accompanies such norms. They do so in order to limit their net loss of such discriminating norms and practices (Nussbaum 2001, 2003; Figart 2009; Sen 1995). In the process, they adjust to their second-class status. Women exhibit adaptive preferences as a way to avoid harsh and excessive punishments. In this way, both cultural indoctrination and adaptive preference restrict and deform women's preference set (Nussbaum 1988, 2003). Moreover, adaptive preferences tend to favor the gender-discriminating status quo against potential changes that are more inclusive and just (Nussbaum 2003).

Amartya Sen emphasizes the importance of "responsible choice." Under certain circumstances, it is better to concentrate on the achieved functionings if an intelligent choice is complicated by uncertainty, such as fear of retribution or exclusion, or by social conditioning. Discriminating social norms and credible threats of punishing dissenters can rob a person of the courage to live or even dissent in a particular way (Clark 2005). Because of this, public actions and social policies are crucial to sustain or restore certain capabilities beyond women's own choices, such as freedom from sexual violence or gender exclusive practices.

Ingrid Robeyns (2005, 2011) highlights three groups of conversion factors that explain the relation (or gap) between a certain good and its expected functions:

- Personal: Physical condition, metabolism, sex, and intelligence.
- Social: Social norms, discriminating practices, gender roles, societal hierarchies, and power relations.
- Environmental: geographic locations, natural endowments, and resources.

This book emphasizes social conversion factors that encompass the influence of cultural norms on gender discrimination. For example, governments should direct more resources to increasing female labor force participation, reducing female unemployment rates, and increasing female political participation and representation, given the inherited/existing norms that discourage female participation in such activities in gender-discriminating societies (Nussbaum 2003).

The capability approach is well suited to decipher the issues of discrimination and exclusion based on ethnicity, religion, race, gender, and so on. The capability approach, while emphasizing the important role of economic growth in the development of societal well-being, goes further to account for the uses of such wealth—how wealth expands people's achievement of functionings. Higher levels of income or wealth may serve as a necessary but not as a sufficient condition to achieve a desired level of capabilities and functionings.

Another benefit of applying the capability approach is its application to both market and nonmarket economies (Robeyns 2003, 2005, 2011). Market based comparisons focus on the gender discrimination of traditionally measured variables (income, wage rate, unemployment). This ignores nonmarket inequality/discrimination, such as domestic violence, lack of social capital, and skewed distribution of status goods. The capability approach encompasses both market and nonmarket well-being. Standard welfare economics overlooks intra-family (or intra-household) inequality and discriminating practices, using males as the unit of interest in market setting (Robeyns 2003).

The Need for Shared/Common Universal Human Capabilities

The list of capabilities and functionings is still subject to debate and ongoing research. It is important to highlight certain capabilities that are vital not only to women's survival (negative freedom), but also to women's flourishing (positive freedom). Martha Nussbaum (2000, 2011) argues that certain capabilities and functionings should transcend cultural, social, and political structures in varying societies. Such universal capabilities and functionings should uphold the essence of human rights, corresponding with the United Nations' Universal Declaration of Human Rights, UDHR (UN 1948) and other universal conventions on human rights, such as the Convention on the Elimination of All Forms of Discrimination against Women, CEDAW (UN 1979), and the Declaration on the Elimination of Violence against Women (UN 1993).[3]

The universal list(s) of human capabilities should expose and respond to gender-discriminating norms and practices embedded in the cultural norms and traditions in different communities, societies, and countries. Inter-national and intra-national diversity (differences in historical backgrounds, government political structures, forms of art, cuisines, wardrobes, and so on) should be celebrated and welcomed without discrimination. Such diversity in norms and practices enriches individuals, communities, countries, and the world. However, discriminating norms and practices that exclude, limit, and/or distort women's capabilities and functionings should be acknowledged as practices that degrade women and relegate them to lower standards.

Examples of such practices include gender feticide and infanticide, FGM/C, domestic violence and other forms of violence against women, limitations on women's choice of individualist goods such as wardrobe, movement, travel, work, and various social, cultural, and political activities, in addition to other gender-discriminating cultural, social, and legal norms, rules, and function-ings. These norms and practices must not be accepted as part of cultural diver-sity or benign forms of cultural diversity. Rather, these discriminating norms, rules, and practices should be exposed and challenged as malignant forms of gender discrimination until women are genuinely free to choose, participate, and be able to be active agents of change in every society, without fear of humiliation, rebuke, or punishment, at all levels of social membership, from being family members as the smallest collectivist unit to being citizens in their countries, at the largest level.

Classifications of Capabilities

Capabilities can be classified into different categories. Basic capabilities, according to Amartya Sen, refer to the "freedom to do some basic things con-sidered necessary for survival and to avoid and escape poverty or other serious deprivation" (Sen 1987: 109). Basic capabilities resonate with the concept of negative freedom, which is the "freedom from" or the "freedom to avoid." This includes the freedom from abuse, punishments, discrimination, exclusive and marginalizing practices, and poverty (Sen 1985a, 1985b, 1987, 1992). Hausman and McPherson define negative freedom as the freedom to act without negative social sanctions. Negative freedom is intrinsically upstanding; in addition to promoting welfare, it promotes integrity and dignity (1993).

The transition from negative freedom and positive freedom, which is the "freedom to," is sequential, for example, abused (or marginalized or excluded) women must be first be free from many aspects that limit their freedom, such as fear, violence, and discrimination in the private and public spheres (Sen 1992: 87). Negative freedom helps reduce women's vulnerability, and restore their capabilities that are required to transform women freedom from the nega-tive freedom to positive freedom, in which women are capable/free to enjoy autonomy. It also refers to the capability to choose from a wide range and quality alternatives and to be agents of of social change too. Therefore, in addition to constructing an environment of noninterference (negative freedom), accommodating institutions must provide the required support for positive freedom and capabilities (Nussbaum 2003; Hausman and McPherson 1993). Amartya Sen summarizes, "The issue of gender inequality is ultimately one of disparate freedom" (1992: 125).

Martha Nussbaum defines basic capabilities differently as "the innate equipment of individuals that is the necessary basis for developing the more advanced capabilities" (2000: 84). Basic capabilities in this book align closer to Sen's definition. Basic capabilities play vital roles, especially in the study of poverty in less developed countries where people strive to expand their capabilities.[4] Basic capabilities are relevant to study and evaluate gender-discriminating norms and practices in certain collectivist societies, in which the basic capabilities of women (and other dominated groups, such as ethnic, racial, religious minority groups) are constrained or deformed, which in turn threaten and curtail their basic capabilities to be free from violence, marginalization, and ostracism. Examples of such practices include gender selective feticide, FGM/C, and violence against women.

Another type of capability is internal capabilities, which, according to Martha Nussbaum, refers to sufficient conditions for the exercise of requisite functions, such as the capability of social or sexual functioning as people grow, without much external interventions, "Internal capabilities develops only with support from the surrounding environments" (2000: 84). Examples of internal capabilities include the ability to love, play, practice religion, and enjoy sex. FGM/C is an example of norms that violate women's internal capabilities due to its interference with women's capabilities to enjoy sex, in addition to sending out clear signals regarding women's identity and role. Nussbaum also draws attention to combined capabilities that refer to the combined internal capabilities and proper external conditions for the exercise of the functioning (2000). External conditions, in many collectivist societies make it very difficult and costly for women to exercise their combined capabilities, such as women's capability to fall in love, since such an act may bring disgrace and shame to her, her family, and the community, especially if such an act is severely punished, with credible record of severe punishments, such as killing women, who violate certain collective norms, to cleanse the shame inflicted on the family or tribe, in what is known as an "honor killing," which is prevalent in the Arab world and other countries. In such a case, women who have the internal capability to love may not be able or free to satisfy their combined capabilities in their societies, compared to women in other societies that protect such freedom. Other examples include women's inability to exercise freedom of expression, ability to choose her wardrobe, marry, divorce, have custody of her children, ability to move or work without the permission or approval from the surrounding environment, family, tribe, and community.

Two other types of capabilities that are relevant to the analysis of gender discrimination are external and group capabilities. External capabilities are the ability of a person to function in a direct relationship with another person; the ability to function that depends on direct human relations (Foster and Handy 2008). Basu and Foster (1998) give a clear example of external capabilities, or positive externality, where members of a mostly illiterate family benefit from the only literate person in the family. Thus, external capabilities in this example refer to having access to the more informed person, in what Basu and Foster refer to as "proximate literacy." External capabilities depend on both the relationship between people and the willingness/intention of the more informed person(s) to share such information with others (members of the family, neighborhood, others) or a subgroup of them. People who are able/free to have contacts with others are more likely to enjoy this type of capability. The repeated sharing of information can lead to create individual capabilities over time (Foster and Handy 2008).

The dichotomy and separation between private and public spheres reduce women's access to external capabilities due the constraint imposed on women's movement or contacts with people other than their immediate family and their relative confinement in the private sphere. This is the case in many collectivist societies where such behaviors or patterns are the norm. The lack of women's access to external capabilities will further their isolation from the public sphere and deepen their marginalization. Other channels of external capabilities include access to media outlet such as TV news, internet, social media, books, and so on. Lack or constrained access to such external sources due to collectivist norms or rules in some collectivist societies, and the selective lack of access of certain groups of populations, such as women, to certain media or communication outlets deepen women's lack of access to external capabilities. Martha Nussbaum underscores women's lack of external capabilities in suppressive collectivist cultures in which women are generally confined in the private sphere and are not allowed to have contact with other people, other than their immediate family members, since such access to external contact is considered disgraceful and shameful that is punishable (2000). A study by Freedom House in Egypt shows that "men and women, see women as having the primary responsibility for taking care of the home and raising children, while men serve as the primary breadwinners" (Katulis 2004: 8). The study also shows that men should receive preferential employment treatments since they are considered the breadwinners by society.[5]

Group capabilities, according to Forster and Handy, are the "capabilities that belong to groups even though the groups are made up of individuals and the behavior of the group affects individuals" (2008: 12). Groups give their members the feeling of inclusion and self-respect. Group capabilities offer synergies in terms of the group collective actions, which cannot be achieved individually in the absence of the group. They also influence the members' preference formation and behavior. Generally, group capabilities represent a special class of social capital. Peter Evan's use of "collective capabilities" is very similar to group capabilities and associative freedom, "the freedom of individuals to enter into relations with others, pursue common purposes, and form intrinsically and instrumentally valuable associations" (Parekh 2004: 18). The collective capabilities highlight capabilities and functionings that are rarely being accomplished individually (Evans 2002). Labor unions, political parties, professional associations, community councils, women's groups, NGOs, and others are examples of "organized collectivities...are fundamental to people's capabilities to choose the lives they have reasons to value" (Evans 2002: 56). The ability and freedom to join others who share similar interests and values, such as families, friends, and other groups, in collective action brings about great intrinsic and instrumental fulfillment in life. Collective capabilities also bring about instrumental effectiveness in terms of securing or supplementing other kinds of freedoms or capabilities (Evans 2002; Sen 1999; Nussbaum 2003).

Individual's versus Average/Aggregate's Capabilities

Critics of specific lists of capabilities and functionings refer to the paternalistic judgment of certain people or cultures (mostly Western cultures) and their imposition of such lists on other cultures and societies.[6] However, advancing a list of capabilities and functionings "does not make it paternalistic" (Qizilbash 2009: 33). In addition, a list of capabilities and functionings that reflects the essence and aspirations of universal human rights conventions and declarations, which are accepted by all subscribing countries, should be upheld in all countries since they belong to every human, the ultimate target and receiver of human rights and capabilities. Aggregate- and average-based indicators of rights or capabilities can be misleading, since most discriminating practices are based on incomplete or deformed lists of capabilities and functionings that take place at the different levels of communities, starting from the smallest social unit, the family, due to the skewed distribution of power and liabilities among its members, especially male and female members. Families, as well as larger social units, are political institutions with built-in biases and skewed powers, status, and obligations (Okin 1989: 9). Many built-in forms of discrimination against women exist in the family, where the structure and distribution of power and obligations favors male members (fathers, husbands, brothers, and sons) against female members (mothers, wives, sisters, and daughters). In the largest societal unit, the nation, or the state, women are deprived of many political, social, and legal rights, and from effective voice and representations. Thus, higher income or economic status, based on aggregate or average international statistics, indicators, fail to highlight women's capabilities, and functionings, or lack thereof, as individuals, since these indicators are mostly based on aggregate or average data per family. In addition, most economic indicators overlook the intra-household injustices, for example the capabilities' and functionings' gaps between male and female members in the household that favor the male members. Nussbaum underscores this point even with regard to interventions and programs, which may fail because they address the average or the collective unit, not the person in need of such intervention, "Programs aimed at raising general or average well-being do not improve the situation of the least well-off, unless they go to work directly to improve the quality of those people's lives" (Nussbaum 2000: 56). Discounting or excluding women's preferences and judgments in social choices is both a cause and an outcome of socially assigned identities, roles, and norms in collectivist gender-discriminating societies. This skewed process of aggregating preferences and judgments while discounting or excluding women's preferences leaves little space for women to act as equal participants in social choices. Women can be treated as objects of decisions and judgments made without them; however, these decisions and judgment will be imposed on them (Sen 1985b; Hausman and McPherson 1993).

Internal or innate factors play a significant role in determining the capabilities and functionings of individuals who are incapable of certain things, due to their physical, mental, or emotional disabilities that prevent them from certain functionings (Sen 1990; Clark 2005). However, external social constraints, such as norms, taboos, mores, codes of conduct, and rules of law can exclude, distort, and/or reduce women's capabilities and functionings, and therefore diminish/curtail their well-being. This, in turn, discriminates against women at two levels, inter-nationally and intra-nationally: inter-nationally, since women in other societies/countries are capable of such functionings and perform them too, especially in individualist societies, and intra-nationally since women have access to a sub set or a deformed set of capabilities, compared to those accessible to men. Women in certain collectivist societies/counties are victims of social and legal injustices that restrict their capabilities just because they are women. In certain societies, various societal norms and rules exclude women from certain functionings and coerce them to behave in certain ways based on external sets of rules and norms imposed on them by the ruling government or the dominant collectivist group, mostly controlled/ruled by men (and sometimes include women who conform to such sets of constraint or prohibition).

Social norms supported by formal rules and practices in certain societies impose specific exclusions and constraints on women, for example women's working, traveling, or even appearance in public places (Clark 2005; Sen 1985b, 1992, 1999). Therefore, to understand gender discrimination, one should go beyond the commodities women command. Studies and research should focus on how women utilize these commodities to fulfill their capabilities and functioning (Clark 2005). The analysis of gender discrimination should pay close attention to what women are able to be and do, which is women's capabilities, and what they actually are and do, which is women's functionings. Functionings serve as the "positive" actualization of "normative" capabilities (Robeyns 2003, 2005).

Due to the complexity of gender discrimination, which varies among different countries, groups of countries, and between different communities within the same country, different sets of quantitative data and qualitative information should be applied to fit each context. International statistics that report higher standard of living may conceal gender-discriminating practices in terms of ignoring the internal struggle inside the family, the smallest social/collectivist unit with skewed power and decision-making process toward men's favor. Some data/statistics become less meaningful when used for international comparison. Statistics associated with higher standards of living, or even the UNDP's Human Development Index (HDI) can be misleading since gender discrimination can take place at different levels of income and socioeconomic indicators, such as HDI, since these measures provide aggregate or average data that conceal many forms of gender inequalities from the smallest social unit, family, to the largest unit, the state. These international indicators refer to the commodities accessible to people such as income, education and health; however, they fail to explain women's capabilities or functioning associated with these commodities.

The capability approach is still an ongoing process, with ongoing debates on the weights and rankings of functionings. As a human based framework, it is subject to criticisms about how to measure and/or rank the actual sets of functionings or the normative sets of capabilities, the relations or gaps between capabilities and functionings, and whether they reflect a free choice or because of formal and informal constraints or even because the prohibition on certain functionings in certain communities, societies, or countries. It is not exhaustive, such that focusing only on capability may fail to capture other aspects of freedom such as the process aspect of freedom (Qizilbash 2009; Sen 1999).

Cross-section and time-series analysis should shed some light on the presence of any constraints or barriers that prevent women from certain functionings, causing them to lag behind women's capabilities and functionings in other countries or cultures, or over time, respectively.

The gap between actual or "positive" functionings and "normative" capabilities, and whether the gap is due to women's free choice or because of imposed constraints and high transaction costs or severe punishment, are worthy of further research to understand the well-being of women living in different societies, and dealing with different sets of opportunities and/or constraints. Due to the difficulty of attaining such information, international comparisons with regard to women actual functionings should serve as proxy indicators or inference of gender discrimination.

Normative evaluations based on commodities, income, or material resources only serve as mean to people's well-being. They do not acknowledge how individuals (males and females) differ in their abilities to convert these resources into capabilities and functionings, due to discriminating norms, rules, and plays of the game (or the governance structure of transactions), such as asymmetric information, skewed distribution of social capital, and so forth.

The capability approach offers an ethically individualistic theory; yet, ontologically non-individualistic,[7] which focuses on the individual as the unit of normative judgment, not the collective unit. Ingrid Robeyns highlights the importance of the well-being of every individual: "[E]thical individualism rejects the idea that women's well-being can be subsumed under wider entities such as the household or the community, while not denying the impact of care, social relations, and interdependence between family or community members" (2003: 65). Susan Okin highlights the notions of "false gender neutrality" and "gender-neutral language" in reference to intra-household gender discrimination within the family, the smallest collective unit, where the built-in bias in intra-family roles, capabilities, and constraints differ between male and female members, "Thus gender-neutral terms frequently obscure the fact that so much of the real experiences of 'persons,' so long as they live in gender-structured societies, does in fact depend on what sex they are" (1989: 11). Okin rejects the implicit assumption of a "nonpolitical" family by cultural relativists, certain political philosophers and other theorists, and their use of the male's head of the family traditional household as the "individual," the basic subject of their theories. Thus, they rule out the principles of justice to relations between the different sexes or within the household (1989). Men are able to make the transition from the domestic to public spheres with ease because of the functions performed by (or imposed on or expected from) women in the family. Earlier theorists and political philosophers failed to recognize the family as a political institution with skewed distribution of power. Aristotle's writing assumed women's subordination. Immanuel Kant did not consider women as rational beings. John Rawls did not just assume family life, but also assumed it to be just, ignoring or overlooking the disparity in intra-family roles, capabilities, and functioning between men and women (Okin 1989). Nussbaum highlights the deficiency/inadequacy of these concepts of social justice, "[M]any traditional conceptions of social justice and fundamental entitlements have made women second-class citizens, if citizens at all. Women's liberties, opportunities, property rights, and political rights have been construed as unequal to men, and this has been taken to be a just state of affairs" (2003: 48). Nussbaum is a strong advocate of specific capabilities, "If capabilities are to be used in advancing a conception of social justice, they will obviously have to be specified" (2003: 46). She underscores ten valuable universal pluralistic capabilities that represent culmination outcomes: life; bodily health, bodily integrity, senses, imagination, and thought; emotions; practical reason; affiliation; other species; play; and, control over one's environment (2000, 2003). Ingrid Robeyns (2003) highlights an extended/definite list for gender inequality assessment that includes life and physical health; mental well-being; bodily integrity and safety; social relations; political empowerment; education and knowledge; social reproduction and nonmarket care; paid work and other projects; shelter and environment; mobility; leisure activities; time-autonomy; respect; and religion and spirituality.

All capabilities must be equally fundamental; for example, economic needs should not be met by denying liberty (Nussbaum 2000). Nussbaum emphasizes that certain rights are essential and cannot be surrendered, even with the promise of other substitutes or rewards, "Some human matters are too important to be left to whim and caprice or even to the dictates of a cultural tradition" (2003: 47). She also highlights that what people are actually able to do and to be in a given society helps explain/understand the barriers this given society erects against full justice for women (Nussbaum 2003).

Due to the difficulty in measuring individuals' capabilities, most statistics refer to achieved or actual functionings. Robeyns (2003) makes a valid argument that inequality in achieved functionings implies inequality in capabilities, unless there is a plausible reason of such systematic differences in functionings. The burden of proof should fall on whosoever claims that women are essentially different.

Gender discrimination rooted in unjust social norms, rules and governance structures of transactions should not part of cultural diversity. Opposing and rejecting gender discrimination should not be understood as an attack on the culture of that society. Instead, it should be understood as the process of celebrating inclusive cultural norms that everyone enjoy, not the discriminating cultural norms that favor one party or group against others. Zerosum and negative-sum games of social norms and rules, where the winners (or perpetrators) win at the expense of the losers (or victims), are practices that discriminate against the victimized groups, such as women in gender-discriminating societies. In such games, women are destined to lose every time the game is played since the playing field is uneven. The game is skewed against women, the victims of such games/practices. These discriminating norms and practices should not be accepted or celebrated universally; in contrast, they should be opposed universally until they are repealed, and the capabilities and functionings of women, the victims of such practices, are restored.

In sum, gender-discriminating norms, in certain collectivist societies should not be celebrated are part of cultural diversity. Such norms represent fallen aspects of cultures that should be repealed. Supporters and winners of gender-discriminating cultural norms oppose the universality of the capability approach, since it causes them to give up their distributional gain or rent extracted from discriminating against women. Advocates of gender equality and the capability approach should focus on the universality of such capabilities and functionings, which transcend cultures, and on the rights of the individuals that should be integral to the rights of the community. They should not focus on the rights of community, or collective rights, dictated by the winners of cultural norms and practices at the expense of victims of such norms and practices.

Winners of gender-discriminating norms and practices are more likely to defend and justify their norms and practices as essential parts of their heritage and culture that should be sustained, and respected by the world. They will protect their gains first by denying, the presence the gender-discriminating practices in their societies. Second, they will exploit the presence and voice of "collectivist cultural feminists" in their societies who defend the existing norms and practices as norms and practices that reflect women's aspirations, and protect their rights, dignity, and freedom (Nussbaum 2000). Third, they will attack certain universal human rights and capabilities and functionings on the ground that they are reflections of Western or foreign values that may contradict the social and cultural values and the heritage of their societies (Weiner 2004). Fourth, universal human rights and international/foreign calls to restore women's rights will be attacked as new form of cultural colonialism, an instrument of Western political agenda (Nussbaum 2000). Azar Nafisi (a prominent Iranian-American scholar) highlights this claim clearly, "In the strange world of Middle Eastern studies, any attempt to condemn gender apartheid is branded an imposition of Western values, the voices of prominent clerics who oppose the politicization of religion are ignored, and the secular dissidents are dismissed as Westernized and therefore inauthentic" (2003: par 12). Fifth, they will prosecute, silence, or slander national feminists and human rights advocates of being alienated who cease to belong their own cultures, and become puppets of the Western elite. Sixth, they will exploit forms of propaganda, such as the defense of nationalism, social unity, and harmony of their cultures. According to Martha Nussbaum raises, "We should ask whose interests are served by this nostalgic image of happy harmonious culture, and whose resistance and misery are being effaced" (2000: 38).

It is important to separate the rejection of discriminating norms in certain societies from rejecting the entire cultures. The good aspects of each culture that are mutually beneficial to all members of societies should be endorsed and celebrated as part of the cultural heritage and global diversity. However, discriminating norms and practices that benefit one group at the expense of another, should not be considered part of the culture to be celebrated and indorsed. Instead, they should be treated as ill-fated inherited practices that should be eliminated. Examples of imposed norms or assigned identity on women in many societies in the Arab world include modesty, deference, obedience, and self-sacrifice (Nussbaum 2000). However, these imposed norms and attributes on women limit and distort women's choices and flourishing. Women's choices to lead traditional life of modesty and self-sacrifice should be accepted and protected based on women's free will and capability to stay in or exit her society. However, imposing traditional life, modesty, submissiveness, and self-sacrificing norms on women violate women's human rights and curtail their functionings and flourishing (Nussbaum 2000).

CHAPTER 5

Norms in Collectivist versus Individualist Societies

Norms are likely to have more influence on people's behaviors in collectivist societies than in individualist societies.

In general, people in collectivist societies are taught, and sometimes pressured through schemes of collective punishment, to be obedient, nurturing, interdependent, and cooperative. They are more likely put the collective goals of their community (or their in-group) ahead of their personal needs. They think and communicate as groups, rather than as individuals, and their culture's language does not require the use of "I" and "you." They are also expected to conform to in-group norms and boundaries (Dayan et al. 2001; Sedikides and Brewer 2001).

In contrast, people in individualist societies think of themselves as creative, self-expressive, and independent of the in-groups. They give priority to their personal goals and are likely to use "I" and "you" (Sedikides and Brewer 2001). They are likely to follow norms that suit their own individual interest and aspirations. They are encouraged to make decisions on their own with little or no attention to the views of others. The lack of collective punishment or enforcement of norms in individualist societies tends to reduce the value and prevalence of certain norms, including gender-discriminating norms, such as FGM/C, spousal rape, domestic violence, collectively sanctioned or enforced dress-code, and other codes of conduct.

Types of Collective Groups and Membership

For the purpose of this book, collective groups can be classified into three major groups: First, in a typical individualist society, membership of any collective group is voluntary. Members join collective groups because of the potential for mutual gain to both the member and the collectivist group. Examples of such collective groups include religious institutions (churches, mosques, temples and other religious based institutions), community or neighborhood groups, boy and girl's scouts, civil society organizations, charitable organizations, political parties/associations, and other associations/group with open and voluntary membership. The benefit of joining the group is the direct individual benefit that accrues to each member and the accumulation of social capital and external capability, in terms of stronger and more efficient networks and wider scope multiplex relationships.[1] This type of collective group and membership acts as a perfect competitive industry, with characteristics like transparency, free entry and exit, and large numbers of rival groups. A second type of collective groups and membership is exclusive to certain population groups who are qualified and invited to such membership. Examples of these include exclusive groups such as labor unions, students associations, country clubs, art and cultural associations, and professional organizations and associations. However, every person in the society has the potential capability to join these groups/associations upon satisfying the required conditions. The membership depends on specific qualifications (and/or achievements) of the person. It, however, should not discriminate on the base of gender, ethnicity, race, and so on.[2] The third type are collectivist groups that are rooted in dualistic features of group members, such as superior and inferior, the center and periphery, the haves and have-nots, and the winners and losers of cultural and social norms. In these collective groups, the roles are different and well defined for the opposite members; for example, the Hindu upper caste members and lower caste (or outcaste) members in India, Whites and Blacks before the emancipation of slaves and eradication of slavery in the United States, and men and women in the Arab world and other similar cultures. A crucial feature in this collectivist group, which separates it from the other types of collective groups, is the involuntary membership imposed on some members (the inferior, peripheries and have-nots) in these societies. Severe punishments are imposed on the "involuntary" members who violate the imposed norms, reject their membership role as defined according to the collective group norms/practices, or try to exit the group (Toh and Leonardelli 2012). The term "collectivist" culture or society in this book refers to the third group, in which membership is involuntary.

Individualists in collectivist cultures are more likely to feel oppressed. They usually seek to leave their communities; however, since the membership of these collectivist societies is mandatory (i.e., forced/imposed on them), they are not free to leave. In such a case, their capabilities and functioning are severely curtailed and limited (Sedikides and Brewer 2001).

In general, the individualist-collectivist balance leans toward the individualist cultures in the US and Western Europe, and toward the collectivist cultures in South/South East Asia, the Middle East (including the Arab world), and some countries in sub-Saharan Africa and Central/ South America. At the personal level, there are individualists and collectivists in all cultures; however, more people lean toward being individualists in individualist cultures; in contrast, more people lean toward being collectivists in collectivist cultures.

Factors Influencing Collectivism versus Individualism

Collectivism is influenced by two main types of factors: individual factors and broad factors. Examples of broad factors include historical trends, political system, education system, aesthetic preference, and so on. Individual factors are divided into three sub-factors: personality, situation, and other individual factors—such as affluence, economic independence, and so on (Dayan et al. 2001). The following section explains each of these factors and their roles in explaining how norms influence people's behaviors especially in collectivist societies.

Individual Factors

First: Personality Factors
Personality factors highlight the differences between individualist (idiocentric) and collectivist (allocentric) persons with respect to their behavioral responses to collective norms and codes of conduct. If the match between personality and culture is poor, individualists may try to move out to other cultures that fit their personality better. Problems arise when individualists cannot exercise their freedom to move out of their collectivist societies because of strict norms and rules accompanied with excessive informal and formal punishments for such violations. Therefore, an individualist must choose either to conform to the existing collectivist culture (and its rules, boundaries, and limitations), or to confront the existing collectivist culture and face existing collectivist penalties and punishments. Collectivists are more likely to be under normative control, in which their actions align with cultural assumptions. In contrast, individualists are more likely to remain under attitudinal control, in which their actions mirror their own preferences. Individualists are likely to exert their control to change the situation to fit their need (primary control). Collectivists, on the other hand, tend to change their needs to fit the situation (secondary control). This may explain the widespread gender discrimination and violence against women in many societies, where individualist women are punished for violating existing norms and rules. For example, the victims of gender based violence and discrimination are punished mostly for behaving individualistically. Examples include being "too Western," too independent, not subservient enough, or for refusing socially/religiously sanctioned dress codes, wanting to advance their education and career, having relations with someone of another religion, refusing to marry an assigned person, or for leaving an abusive husband. Victims have been murdered for alleged sexual impropriety (such as allegedly having extramarital affairs), being viewed as promiscuous, or even for being victims of rape (Chesler 2010).[3]

Second: Situation Factors
The degree of collectivism in a society can be influenced by situation factors. Examples of situation factors include the "in-group" size, level of homogeneity,

in-group norms, the group situation, the status within the in-group, types of tasks, and type of instructions.

- The in-group size: smaller in-groups such as the family unit increase collectivism (compared to larger in-groups such as tribes, adherents of the same religion, and political units) due to dependable surveillance and sanctions for violating the norms of the in-group. The emotional involvement is also greater in smaller in-groups. For example, honor killings serve to reverse shame associated with a female's involvement in premarital sex, adultery, or rumors of such acts or behaviors, disobedience, or even for being a victim of rape.[4]
- The level of homogeneity: a higher level of in-group homogeneity is likely to pressure individuals to follow the in-group norms (Prietula and Conway 2009). This may explain the higher tendency of collectivism in rural areas and in-groups with same religious or ethnic backgrounds, both of which have law degrees of mobility.
- In-group norms are more likely to be imposed in strict situations like dogmatic places of worship and their extensions (religious schools and institutions) than in loose situations like nonreligious social events and activities (parties, sporting events, or bars). This explains the significance of strict religious norms or codes of conduct in tight collectivist communities. These rules are supported by a collective boycott or even prohibition of certain loose situations in which individualist behaviors may be encouraged. This is true from situations that may violate collectivist norms or strict religious rules and codes of conduct.
- People are more likely to be collectivist in in-group circles than in non-in-group circles. To ensure obedience to collectivist norms, members of such communities are instructed to trust the in-group, and to doubt the intention of the non-in-groups. This perpetuates the collectivist cultural norms and institutions.
- Compliance with in-group norms increases with the person's status of the in-group. This reflects the practices and conducts that are endorsed, and sometimes imposed, by the in-group's leaders and high-status members.
- Cooperative tasks increase collectivism compared to competitive tasks. Cooperative tasks respond to community needs and objectives that are already well established and communicated throughout the community. At this level, gains are more likely to be shared. In contrast, competitive tasks mostly reward individualist members who partake in the tasks—sometimes at the expense of other individuals (e.g., in zero-sum games).
- People who are instructed to view personal identity in terms of the collective unit are more likely to sample from the collective self (collective self-prime. In contrast, people who are taught to view identity in terms of differences are more likely to sample more from the individual self (individual self-prime) (Triandis and Trafimow 2001). In many countries, religion, ethnicity, and social caste play important roles in accentuating collective image and shared norms and customs.

The following examples from Morocco support the findings above: The percentage of uneducated women who agree that a husband is justified in beating his wife is almost four times that of educated women: 68 percent and 18 percent respectively. The percentage of women who do not work is more than twice the percentage of women who do work: 59 percent and 28 percent respectively. A similar large gap exists between women who reside in rural areas to those in urban areas: 75 percent and 40 percent respectively (Kishor and Subaiya 2008: 148). A similar study in Egypt supports the above data (El-Zanaty and Way 2009). In summary, uneducated, unemployed, rural women tend to be more collectivist—in terms of obeying and justifying genders discriminating norms and practices—than educated, employed, urban women.

Third: Other Individual Factors

There are eight other individual factors that affect the balance between individualism and collectivism in a given society: affluence, economic independence, leadership roles, migration and social mobility, exposure to out-group media, traditional and religious people, family structure, and the degree of acculturation.

- Affluence: individualism increases with affluence, since the affluent tend to be economically more independent than other members of society. This explains the prevalence of collectivism in poor communities (poor quarters, slums, and rural areas in less developed countries). Referring to the above numbers from Morocco, women from the poorest quintile are 3.5 times more likely to agree that a husband beating his wife is justified than affluent women from the richest quintile) Kishor and Subaiya 2008).
- Economic independence: people who are economically independent regardless of affluence (mostly men) are more individualist than women who depend financially on their in-group members. Economically independent members can afford to leave the in-group, whereas dependent members are less likely to leave their in-group due to their substantial financial and social dependency on their husbands, fathers, and/or brothers in many gender-discriminating societies (Triandis and Trafimow 2001).
- Leadership roles: members who have leadership roles such as fathers, husbands, and brothers are likely to be more individualist than those who have subordinate roles, such as wives, sisters, and daughters. Men in such cultures can choose to impose collectivist cultural norms and codes of conduct that match their needs and desires. Some of these needs and desires end up in zero and negative sum games, where men gain status and power at the expense of women's status and freedom.
- Migration and social mobility: research shows that those who leave or have the ability to leave to join other groups are more individualist than those who stay or are forced to stay.

- Exposure to out-group media: collectivism decreases with the exposure to out-groups' media, such as television, films, and other individualist mass media. In Western individualist novels, for example, love conquers traditions and taboos, and no one is locked into traditional prescribed roles (Howard-Hassmann 1993). In collectivist cultures, the heroes do their duty at great personal sacrifice (Tirandis and Trafimow 2001). In collectivist media, art, literature, and educational institutions, those who sacrifice for collectivist causes are more accepted than those who cross collectivist boundaries and violate the collectivist codes of conduct in the process.
- Traditional and religious people: religions can be seen as systems of social control. Religious people (and people who are forced to behave religiously), are more collectivist than nonreligious people. Traditional and religious individuals tend to sample the collective self, such as the tribe's adherents of the same religion. Some religious beliefs and norms have doctrines that expect their followers to comply with built-in schemes of rewards, or face exposure to built-in punishments. Compliance with existing religious or tribal principles and behavioral boundaries reflects the interests and wishes of the dominant members in the in-group. These dominant members, usually male leaders and scholars, can influence or dictate the reward and punishment schemes in their in-groups at the expense of members of a lower status, such as women (Toh and Leonardelli 2012). Furthermore, the disproportional status of different groups in collectivist communities may lead to informal and formal punishment on the minority out-groups (different religions, ethnicities, or tribes of "inferior" status). Such a practice sends a strong signal and credible threat to in-group members to abide by the informal norms and codes of conduct that are now imposed on other minority out-groups. Consequently, norms and rules that discriminate against women in certain in-groups are likely to be imposed on women in other groups. This effect tends to be stronger if the collectivist behavior is large-scale, such as at the national level. Extending the applications and impositions of certain norms to out-groups deprive the in-group women of a viable second source to measure themselves against.
- Family structure: individualism is likely to increase when maternal and paternal kinship is equally important. On the other hand, in the case of patrilineal or a matrilineal family structures, there is likely to be only one normative system, leading to more collectivism. In many collectivist societies, new brides are transferred from their parents' houses when they get married, to their husbands' lineage. Lineage is largely considered unilateral with patrilineal emphasis.
- The degree of acculturation: studies show that when two cultures A and B come in contact, members of the least dominant culture B have four options:
  - Adopt the new culture (assimilation into A).
  - Reject the new culture (segregation).

○ Choose elements of both cultures (A plus B, biculturalism), which depends on the balance of the collectivism-individualism in the least dominant culture, and on the level of common cultural norms and codes of conduct between the two cultures.

○ Reject both cultures (marginalization, anomie).

Studies show that the level of bicultural individuals in societies where collectivist and individualist cultures intersect is high (Tirandis and Trafimow 2001).

Broad Factors

In addition to the individual factors explained above, there are broad factors that influence the balance between collectivism and individualism in any society:

- Historical trends have played important roles in tilting the balance toward individualism. The ongoing universal declarations and conventions on human rights, and the corresponding changes in the legal systems in many societies, especially since the second half of the twentieth century, have given individuals more protections and have signaled a move toward protecting individual rights. Still, some cultures experience slow and interrupted rates of transition toward protecting individual rights. Furthermore, this trend can reverse its direction, and moves toward more collectivism (Afghanistan, Iran, Pakistan, and recent trends in Egypt after the so-called "Arab Spring," since 2011 have heightened anxiety over female rights). One important issue in the development of individualism is the property rights that are attached to groups rather than to individuals. In many cultures, especially collectivist LDCs, a women's body, virginity, and sexual behavior are treated as collective property rather than individual property.

- Religions: cultures that have highly centralized religions are generally more collectivist than religiously decentralized societies. In many collectivist cultures, religious collective traditions, codes of conduct and rules are imposed with significant informal and sometimes formal punishments to any violations of such norms/metanorms.

- Education systems: centralized educational systems increase collectivism. For example, in many societies, educational curricula are greatly controlled by the winners of existing collectivist norm and rules who seek to enforce acceptance and internalization of such norms. Peter Evans highlights the subtlety of this centralization, "Centralization of power over the cultural flow that shape preferences is more subtle from of 'unfreedom'... but no less powerful for being subtle" (2002: 99). Decentralized systems favor individualism.

- Political system: Theocracy leads to higher degrees of collectivism. This political system includes highly concentrated dictatorial and central planning systems.

- Aesthetic preferences: highly homogeneous standards of aesthetic favor collectivist cultural patterns. Collectivist visual patterns such as wardrobes, for example, *hijab* (a traditional women's dress that cover women's body, except for the face and hands), or *niqab* (a more strict wardrobe, which covers the woman's body completely, except for the eyes) in some Arab and Muslim societies/countries, are more likely to advance collectivist cultural patterns and their constraints on women's choices. Certain arts, movies, and music, associated with religious and tribal value tend to perpetuate collectivist standards. In contrast, heterogeneous standards advance individualism (Triandis and Trafimow 2001; Coleman 1990; Prietula and Conway 2009).
- Within a nation's demographics, such as poverty, population density, the presence of minority groups influences collectivism. Poverty increases the levels of dependency on community units, from the familial level to the local and even national level. In contrast, self-sufficient and affluent individuals have access to wider viable choices, without the need of collective support, participation, or approval. Higher population density increases collectivism, due to frequent encounters, transactions, engagements, monitoring, and exposure to the rest of the community. Also, states with collectivist heritage tend to perpetuate such cultural heritage, and, in the process, sustain the benefits of the dominant members of the in-groups, and the distributional effects of such norms and codes of conduct that work in their favor. In addition, collectivism tends to be higher in nations that are relatively isolated or closed to international and foreign cultures and norms. Intercultural conflicts (wars or other political and cultural clashes) typically heighten the level collectivism. Similarly, intranational conflicts tend to heighten collectivism (Tirandis and Trafimow 2001).

The tension between collectivism and individualism reflects the tension between reservation and dynamism: reservation is supported and protected by collectivists and dynamism is supported by individualists. This tension is rooted in the aspiration to achieve individual capabilities and functionings, even if such capabilities and functionings defy the prevailing collectivist norms and rules.

Mounira Charrad underscores the influence of collectivism rooted in "kin-based society" and "kin-based solidarity" in her study on Morocco, Algeria, and Tunisia: neighboring Arab countries in North-West Africa (2007). Charrad highlights the social progress that accompanied the emergence of modern states in these countries in the aftermath of colonial rules (since the second half of the twentieth century, circa). There is a contrast between Tunisia and Morocco with regard to the level of the state autonomy and the level of kin-based formation in polity. In Morocco, the state permits allegiances to patrilineal family and its extension (tribes and kin-based formations). In contrast, the Tunisian state developed an autonomy from such allegiances, "transferring loyalties from particularistic communities to the entity of the sovereign nation-state" (Charrad 2007: 238). Her findings highlight the violation of women's rights in societies, such as Morocco, where lineages and kin-based social formations remain central elements of the social structure and anchors for political power. In these societies, women's rights were curtailed in favor of the male-dominated patrilineages. Women in Tunisia gained significant individual rights due to Tunisian autonomy (Charrad 2007). Charrad highlights the role of "sacred" norms and formal rules sustaining gender discrimination in collectivist societies such as in Morocco, "Islamic family law places women in a subordinate status by giving power over women to men as husbands and as male kin. Islamic law sanctions the control of women by their own kin group." (Charrad 2007: 242). Such laws minimize the important of individual rights by giving more weight to collective rights and controls accompanied with skewed distribution of power favoring men over women.

Monitoring as an Instrument to Enforce Norms

Collectivist societies are more likely to invest in monitoring individuals' behaviors to ensure they adhere to their assigned identities, roles, and to other social norms and rules, in order to sustain the social order and cultural harmony of the society. In the process, schemes of punishment (and reward) are set up to deter any violations of socially assigned identities, roles, and social norms. This sustains the status quo, which contains built-in distributional bias and benefits favoring the ruling elites. According to Elinor Ostrom, "In all known self-organized resource governance regimes that have survived for multiple generations, participants invest resources in monitoring and sanctioning of each other so as to reduce the probability of free riding" (2000: 138). Without proper monitoring and sanctioning, certain norms will fail to survive. This may explain individual's lack of anonymity and personal freedom in collectivist societies, since behaviors are monitored, reported and punished (or rewarded) according to the violation (or conformity) of socially assigned identities and roles. In addition to informal monitoring schemes, some collectivist societies appoint monitoring units and collectivist vigilantes. An example of this is the *Hisbah* observers[5] and virtue police in Saudi Arabia. Certain individualist behaviors can be punished by these monitoring agents. Examples include, women's violating a dress code (in the public sphere), socializing with non-sibling males, or driving a car (U.S. DOSa: Saudi Arabia 2014). Effective monitoring accompanied with proper punishments is likely to deter most violations of socially assigned identities and roles. For example, the arrest of a married American business women by religious police in Riyadh, Saudi Arabia in 2008, for *khalwa* (illegal mixing of unrelated men and women) with a male colleague in public, taking her to prison, strip searching her, presenting her before a judge who reprimanded her for wearing filthy clothes, and forcing her to sign a confession before releasing her to the custody of her husband (Kelly and Breslin 2010). Another example of monitoring individual behaviors and punishing norms dissenters is arresting Saudi women who defy the ban on female driving (the informal ban on female driving became a state policy in 1990), forcing them and their male guardians to sign pledges not to drive, before releasing them to the custody of their male guardians. The root of the official ban on female driving is a *fatwa* from the Grand *Mufti* of Saudi Arabia that female driving will expose women to (sexual) temptation and can lead to social chaos (Human Rights Watch 2014c).

Monitoring people's behaviors enhances and clarifies the signals of conformity or deviance from social norms. In a typical individualist society, only a subset of social norms will prevail. Norms will be accepted and sanctioned for their internal values. These sets of norms are typically inclusive and are not associated with distributional bias.

Signals resulting from personal interactions and monitoring others' behaviors can have a strong influence on people's behaviors especially, causing some deviants to change their behaviors, seeking to gain collectivist trust, and to avoid social ostracism and collective punishment. In such cases, collectivist behaviors will dominate social behaviors and interactions in collectivist societies, "If there is a noisy signal about a player's type [collectivist, willing punisher, individualist] that is at least more accurate than random, trustworthy types will survive as a substantial proportion of the population" (Ostrom 2000: 145).

Moreover, collectivist societies tend to impart and evoke social norms through controlling sermons in worshipping places, national media, publishing institutions, and access to foreign sources, especially sources that are claimed to oppose the social fabric and moral values of the collectivist society, such as certain internet and social media outlets, and educational curricula to deepen the adherence and conformity to selected social norms.

A primary purpose of imparting and invoking certain social norms, roles, and identities in collectivist societies is to affirm social expectations of conformity in the society. Denzau and North (1993) highlight the role of individuals' learning on their behaviors, such that individuals who share the same background, learning, and experiences will behave similarly, "Under conditions of uncertainty, individuals' interpretation of their environment will reflect the learning that they have undergone. Individuals with common cultural backgrounds and experiences will share reasonably convergent mental models, ideologies and institutions, and individuals with different learning experiences (both cultural and environmental) will have different theories (models, ideologies) to interpret that environment" (Denzau and North 1993: para 2). The above analysis highlights how collectivist societies deter any potential deviance through their control of education, media and dissemination of information, and endorsing, and condoning certain social norms. They do this through emphasizing the importance of common heritage and cultural background, which in turn leads to a "collective" convergence of mental models.

Larger cognitive resources such as common information and shared ideologies, in terms of time, attention, and even indoctrination in collectivist societies are likely to be allocated to evaluating the choice and its effect. Good information is essential to improve mental models (Denzau and North 1993). This is why certain information that offers differing or opposing views or interpretations is banned and confiscated. In this mindset, such information is considered foreign propaganda that can corrupt the cultural and moral fabric of the collectivist society.

Individually accepted social norms do not require external enforcement, mainly due to the net personal benefit an individual receive from following such norms. However, external enforcement of certain social norms is necessary when individualistic members do not personally accept the norms or their implications. External forms of enforcement are used to force the opponents of such norms to adhere even though they harm, marginalize, or exclude certain members of the society (Ostrom 2000).

In collectivist societies, there is a higher percentage of willing punishers than in individualist societies. Willing punishers typically believe in the collective value of certain norms, such that certain norms act as public goods, in which the willing punishers punish the deviants (first-order violators) and even the shirker (second-order violators) of such social norms. Willing punishers are likely to invest in and expend personal resources to punish deviants and shirkers (Ostrom 2012). Formalized norms become public goods that must be held at the desired level according to the mandate of the ruling elite. Lack of effective enforcement of the law against deviants or lack of effective willing punishers is likely to reduce the level of adherence to such norms significantly.

Religious norms and traditions are perpetuated in collectivist societies. The natures of sacred (divine or supernatural) norms that are simply accepted through faith tend to be more prevalent in collectivist societies, especially religious societies such as the Arab world. These norms transcend human logic based on the belief that they are revealed by a transcending superpower. Such norms will be imposed on the believers and nonbelievers of such superpower, regardless of their authenticity, interpretations, or the exploitation of such norms. In individualist societies, such faith is not externally imposed, but is left to individuals' acceptance, given the internal value of such faith to each individual. Any built-in discriminating norms in religious texts and teachings are likely to be rejected as social norms since they may violate the tenets of liberal democracy and universal human rights in individualist societies. The collective segmentation of society into elite and subordinate groups plays an important role in gender discrimination. In the Arab world, certain religious norms have a distributional effect favoring Muslims against non-Muslims. Arab citizens are required to be monotheists: Muslims, Christian, or Jews. Muslims make up more than 92 percent of the population in the Arab world. The Arab world rejects external norms and influences that are portrayed as anti-Islamic, to give rise to Islamic identity and values in national institutions (political, social, cultural, educational, and media institutions). This also affirms a cultural identity that promotes national Islamic values. The formalization of many norms in collectivist societies, such as attire, movement, employment, social and political representation, prayers, fasting, and separation of sexes in public spheres, perpetuate such norms. Generally, Islam stresses collective obligation and solidarity within the *ummah* (Muslim nation or entire Muslim community), while the emphasis in individualist societies is on individual rights in the absence of collective conscience (Wilson 2009).

The inclusion of collective rights within a catalogue of human rights creates conceptual confusion, particularly in situations where assertions of individual liberty do not conform to those of the group or collective identity, including a religious identity. In collectivist societies with strong presence of cultural relativism, ideas and claims based on religion often have a trumping effect on other ideas and claims (Chinkin 1999: 56–57).

The Collective Image and Identity

Kenneth Boulding underscores the image of a society or a subgroup in the society, highlighting the value of "public image" that is shared by the people in a given group in a given society: "The basic bond of any society, culture, sub-culture, or organization, is a 'public image', that is, an image the essential characteristics of which are shared by the individuals participating in the group" (1956: 64). The influence of the public image on behavior is more robust in collectivist societies, where people are taught and expected to behave in certain ways to preserve such an image. A scheme of effective deontic logic of what is permitted, obliged, and forbidden is formed and disseminated to uphold the public image. In authoritarian systems with strict hierarchy of identity and roles, each role-image contains the expectation of subordination to higher roles and authority over lower roles. In these systems, "Decisions originate with the higher roles [ruling group or elites] and are transmitted to the lower roles as orders. The lower roles are expected to execute the orders without any back–talk" (Boulding 1956: 99). In the ideal democratic system, the higher roles are supposed to act on behalf of the lower roles and be responsible to them. Authoritarian societies have a stronger tendency to use violence or threat of violence in order to gain acceptance from persons occupying the lower role (Boulding 1956).

Emile Durkheim discusses the collective conscience in enforcing and sustaining certain social norms in collectivist societies. The main components of collective conscience are the shared norms and values in the society, the high level of conformity, and the low levels of tolerance for deviance accompanied with harsh and even violent punishments (1984). False consciousness (distorted view of reality) leads to internalization of discrimination and complacency with discriminating norms (Smith 2001; Brems 1997).

Durkheim (1984) underscored the role of "mechanical solidarity," where people feel connected through similar lifestyles and educational and religious training. It places a high value on societal interests. Mechanical solidarity supports collective conscience through specific roles and rules, and harsh sanctions against deviants. In contrast, "organic solidarity" is more likely to exist in individualist/secular societies. Organic solidarity is humanly oriented and attaches high value to individual's dignity, equality, and social justice, with low levels of collective conscience.

The low tolerance for deviance in collectivist societies, accompanied by harsh punishment schemes against dissenters, makes up the social norm of retribution. According to Jon Elster (1989), in these societies, the level of violence should drop since people predict a swift response to their acts. He argues against swift retribution due to the prohibitive cost of terror-based societies. Rational people would not harm others just to get even. However, in collectivist societies, the norm of retribution is more prevalent, in response to certain individualist acts that violate social norms. Even though certain behaviors are considered acceptable in individualist societies, they are considered acts of "collective violence" in collectivist societies. This is because they violate collective norms and rules, which elevates the level of collective anxiety about the cultural harmony and social order. In response, the society must retaliate against the individualists who violate the collective norms. The virtue police (or other collectivist vigilante) in many Arab communities serves as a collective agents of retribution against all behaviors that violate social norms and rules. The practice of throwing acid on the faces of women who wear makeup and violate the dress code in many societies in the Middle East and South Asia serves as a reminder of the severity of collective punishment against deviance from social norms (de Castella 2013).

The process of internalizing norms can reflect either the voluntary acceptance of the norms, if a given norm is endorsed by the person, such that violating the norm will cause an internal feeling of guilt and shame, or a forced acceptance. If the norm is externally imposed, women may internalize their cognitive dissonance, since the cost of opposing such norms exceeds the benefit. Certain collective punishments, especially those associated with violating metanorms, such as "honor killing," can sway female behavior significantly, compared to minor punishments. In such a case, the norm of collective obedience (FGM/C, restrictions on women's movement or clothing, honor killing, and so on) conflicts with individuals' moral norms such as not inflicting harm (physically or otherwise), or endorsing individual freedom of choice. The larger weight attached to the norm of collective obedience, accompanied with collective punishment against dissenters in gender-discriminating collectivist societies tilt the balance in favor of the norm of obedience, perpetuating many discriminating norms in these societies.

Antonio Gramsci (1971) highlights the role of hegemony in perpetuating certain discriminating norms in collectivist societies. Hegemony refers to how the dominant group exploits its intellectual and moral leadership to subjugate subordinate groups through consent or force. Force is usually used to assert the supremacy of the dominant group after it appears to be based on the majority's consent. Collectivist societies tend to highlight cultural harmony and social coherence, while overlooking the violation of individualist human rights, "The anti-individualist trend of the traditionalist nostalgia for community harbors a romantic tendency to ignore or disguise the many repressive and harmful effects (from a human rights perspective) of communitarian societies...It ignores the liberating aspects of individualism and forgets that collectivities can be highly oppressive social entities" (Howard-Hassmann 1993: 329–330), in contrast to individualist societies, where "no one is locked into traditional, prescribed social roles: sex roles can be ignored and deviance from traditional ways of life is permitted" (1993: 331).

Mahanz Afkhami summarizes the collectivism–individualism dichotomy with regard to imposing norms in collectivist societies: "Why is that a Muslim cleric, arrogate to himself the right to place me forcibly in preordained framework?... Does he derive his authority from God? Does he derive it from the text? Does he derive it from tradition? I reject all of these claims for his authority... I only demand that he does not force me to do what he wants me to do against my wish, in the same way that I do not force him to do what I wish; this is my frame of reference" (1999: 72). In individualist societies, people accept certain norms, roles, and identities. They are not, however, forced to accept or follow them. They have the option to overlook or even reject them, without any fear of collective retribution. In collectivist societies, people can be forced to accept imposed norms and adapt to them.

Collectivism and Perceptions of Tolerance and Foreign Cultural Invasion: A Case Study in Selected Arab Countries

More people in the Arab world believe that cultural invasion by the West is very prevalent. This ranges from 54 percent in Tunisia to 85 percent in Egypt (Moaddel 2013). This belief is both a cause and an outcome of collectivism in many Arab societies. It is a byproduct of collectivist cultural relativism and cause for further collectivity and suspicion of universal human rights, values, international concerns, interventions, or calls for reform. These international instruments are believed to be tainted by Western cultural invasion. Consequently, the Arab world is less likely to trust universal human rights protocols, conventions, and declarations. Figure 5.1 shows that high percentages of the respondents in the Arab countries agree with the notion of conspiracies against Muslims, ranging from 70 percent in Lebanon to 85 percent in Egypt.

The strength of collectivism in the Arab world is reflected in people's value of religion, and their views of other religions and their followers. The percentages of Arabs (mostly Muslims) who support prohibiting non-Muslims from practicing their religions in Arab countries range from 17 percent in Lebanon to

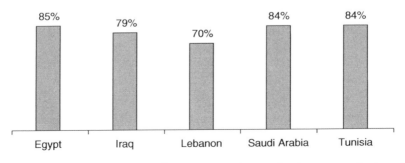

Figure 5.1   Percentage of respondents who agree or strongly agree that there are conspiracies against Muslims, selected Arab countries, 2013.

Source: Data collected from Moaddel (2013: 78).

70 percent in Saudi Arabia, as illustrated in figure 5.2. The study also highlights the higher level of intolerance in the Arab world toward foreigners.[6]

Figure 5.3 illustrates that the percentage of Arabs who believe that their children should not learn about other religions range from 18 percent in Lebanon to 67 percent in Saudi Arabia.

Moreover, figure 5.4 illustrates the Arabs' negative attitude toward the followers of other religions. The percentage of Arabs believing that the followers

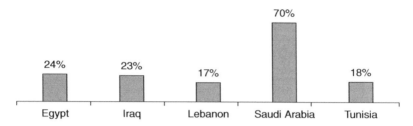

Figure 5.2 Percentage of respondents who agree or strongly agree that non-Muslims (non-Christian [for Christian respondents]) should be prohibited to practice their religion in their counties, selected Arab countries, 2013.

Source: Data Collected from Moaddel (2013: 81).

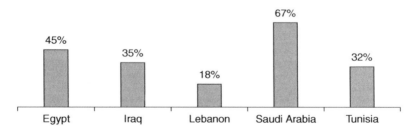

Figure 5.3 Percentage of respondents who agree or strongly agree that their children should not be allowed to learn about other religions, selected Arab countries, 2013.

Source: Data Collected from Moaddel (2013: 81).

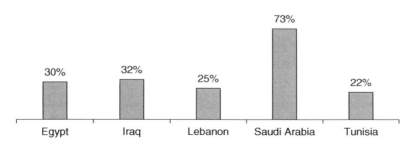

Figure 5.4 Percentage of respondents who agree or strongly agree that "the followers of other religions should not have the same rights as mine," selected Arab countries, 2013.

Source: Data collected from Moaddel (2013: 82).

of other religions should not have the same rights as Muslims, range from 22 percent in Tunisia (the least collectivist Arab country) to 73 percent in Saudi Arabia (the most collectivist Arab country).

Figure 5.5 shows the high rate of intolerance toward criticizing Islam or religious leaders, with the level of intolerance being highest in the most collectivist country, Saudi Arabia, and lowest in the least collectivist countries, Lebanon and Tunisia. Islam/religion is considered the most prized collective identity in most states in the Arab world.[7]

Figure 5.6 shows the perception of people in the Arab world who agree with the statement, "The only acceptable religion is my religion." It shows the strikingly high percentage of Arabs compared to the rest of the world, highlighting the strong influence of religion, and religious norms, Islam and Islamic norms, in the Arab world. It also signals to a high degree of collectivism in the Arab world compared to the rest of the world.

The above data highlights the prevalence of collectivism in the Arab world, which explains the high level of intolerance toward deviant and dissenting

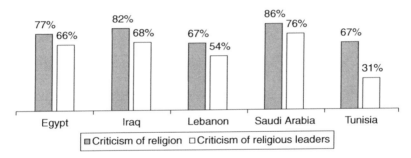

Figure 5.5 Percentage of respondents who agree or strongly agree that "Criticism of religion and religious leaders should not be tolerated," selected Arab countries, 2013.
Source: Data Collected from Moaddel (2013: 83–84).

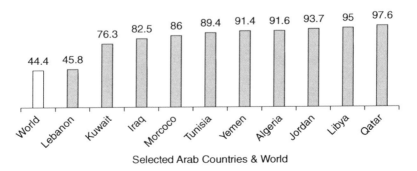

Figure 5.6 Percentage of people who agree and strongly agree with the statement, "The only acceptable religion is my religion."
*The world percentage represents the average of 55 counties included in the survey.
Source: World Value Survey (2014). V 152, P. 208.

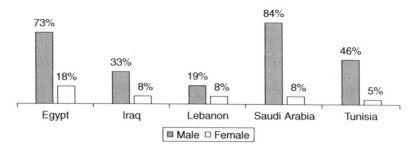

Figure 5.7   Percentage of male and female respondents who attend Mosque more than once a week, selected Arab countries, 2013.
Source: Data collected from Moaddel (2013: 87).

behavior in these societies. As the data shows, Lebanon and Tunisia are among the least collectivist Arab societies, while the prevalence of collectivism is very high in Saudi Arabia. The above trends signal a dilemma to human rights activists, especially women's rights activists (nationals and foreigners), due to the high level of intolerance to any criticism to certain gender-discriminating practices or to the teachings in sacred/religious texts and references in these countries (Toh and Leonardelli 2012).

The dichotomy between the private and public spheres and the assigned identities and roles of men and women are highlighted in the gender ratio of those who attend mosques (more than once a week). Men are more than 10 times more regular to attend a mosque than women in Saudi Arabia, compared to 2.4 times in Lebanon, as figure 5.7 shows. This may be explained by significant constraints on female movement outside the private sphere, even when leaving home to attend the mosque. This also signals the dichotomy of spheres, in which women are advised and sometimes commanded to confine to the private spheres, in contrast to men who have more access and dominance over the public spheres in the Arab world. According to valid *hadith*, it is better for a woman to pray inside her home and even better if she prays inside her bedroom. Even though not praying in the mosque denies women the reward of congregational prayer, women's obedience in their prayer at home, or even in their bedroom, has a special reward.

Summary

Collectivist women are more likely to conform to gender-discriminating norms, since these norms satisfy the collectivist goals/aspirations. In contrast, individualist women in collectivist societies have to choose from less appealing options. First, they may leave the collectivist society; however, this option is extremely costly, since women's membership is compulsory. Second, they may confront the collectivist discriminating norms and subject themselves to the collective punishment. Third, they may internalize the collectivist discriminating norms, if the net cost of dissenting or even leaving the collectivist group is too high.

CHAPTER 6

Metanorms and Gender Discrimination

Social norms exist in all societies. They are specific expectations and rules that different cultures utilize to control the behaviors of theirs members. These expectations and rules are accompanied by social sanctions. They encourage or discourage certain behaviors, and are enforced through social sanctions to approve of or reward those who conform to the norms and punish those who dissent or violate them (Coleman 1990; Horne 2007). Punishments range from snubbing and verbal reprimands to incarceration, expulsion, and killing (e.g., honor crimes). Metanorms are a special class of norms. They are the norms of enforcing norm enforcement, where norms are usually accompanied with high and multiple levels rewards or punishments (Axelrod 1986; Elster 1989; Horne 2007; Prietula and Conway 2009). Not only are first-order violators (deviants) punished, but so too are the second-order violators (shirkers) who fail to punish the deviants. Metanorms typically have very high social value, such that the collective community cannot tolerate deviation from sanctioned norms. In some societies, certain norms that are elevated to metanorms can also be elevated to a rule, either informally (routinely executed without the presence of, or the need for, a written formal law or rule), or formally (sanctioned by the formal legislative and judicial institutions). Prietula and Conway (2011) emphasize the essential importance of metanorms to the survival of collectivist societies: "Without metanorms, a norm against defection cannot survive" (Section 6).

The presence of metanorms heightens the solemnity of gender discrimination in certain collectivist societies. Metanorms make it more costly and sometimes prohibitively costly to violate or oppose the imposed collectivist norms and rules that discriminate against women. The collectivist members punish the metanorms' violators, since punishment will perpetuate metanorms that have significant value to the well-being of the collectivist members by defending the cultural harmony and social order in their collectivist community. The perpetuation of these norms is integral to the fabric of the community (Prietula and Conway 2009). Higher degrees of homogeneity and higher levels of inter-action and interdependency among community members are likely to heighten the enforcement of metanorms, since they heighten the level of collectivity and policing among the community members. Thus, metanorms reduce and punish individualism and elevate and reward collectivism and cooperation (Coleman 1990).

The degree of enforcing metanorms depends on the level of collectivist benefit that results from their enforcement (Coleman 1990). For example, honor killing will continue in some gender-discriminating societies, as long as it is elevated to a "metanorm," such that not only the female member whose behavior (or rumors about her behavior) taints the collective honor will be punished (executed) but also her family (especially her male relatives) if they fail to punish (kill) her, according to existing collective expectations or requirements.

To sustain metanorms in collectivist societies, the collective unit stands ready to punish both the metanorm's deviant and shirkers. The presence of col-lectivist "willing punishers," who are willing to punish deviants and shirkers or at least report them to the collective community for proper punishment, helps perpetuate metanorms in collectivist societies. Examples of willing punishers include the public presence of the virtue police in Saudi Arabia (and other similar countries) and other collectivist vigilantes in many communities in the Arab world, who are motivated to sustain metanorms by punishing deviants and shirkers, or report them to the authorities in cases where the metanorm is formalized into law. For example, in April 2014, the Saudi police arrested a women and her husband for violation of the ban on women's driving. Both were arrested for a while, the husband (the shirker) was fined, and their car was con-fiscated for a week. They were released after the husband (the shirker) signed a pledge not to repeat such a violation (France 24 2014a).

Metanorms and Gender Discrimination in Collectivist Societies: A Simple Model

The following tree diagram illustrates how metanorms influence the behaviors of women and other members of gender-discriminating collectivist societies for the purpose of sustaining certain norms and increasing the collective adher-ence to them.

Figure 6.1 illustrates the process of solving a sequential game in the case of metanorms, using backward induction. Backward induction is used to solve finite extensive forms of a sequential game through the iteration process. It starts with identifying the optimal strategy of the last player, then the opti-mal strategy for the player next to last, given the action of the last player. The game continues moving backward, until the first player chooses her/his opti-mal strategy.

There are three players in this model: individual A, a female who is a poten-tial deviant from the metanorm, individual B, a potential shirker, and the community.

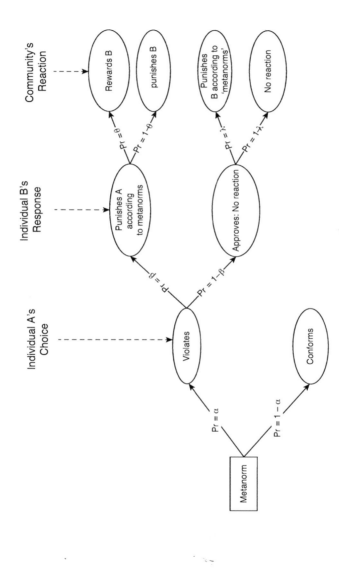

Figure 6.1 Response to a Metanorm's violations.

Let $\alpha \in [0, 1]$ be the probability that individual A, a female, violates a metanorm.

Let $\beta \in [0, 1]$ be the probability that individual B will punish A or report A's violation to the community to be punished.

Let $\theta \in [0, 1]$ be the probability that the collective community will reward (or will not punish) B who punishes A for her violation of metanorms, and $(1 - \theta)$ be the probability that the community will punish on B for punishing A.

Finally, let $\lambda \in [0, 1]$ be the probability that the community will punish B if B fails to punish A when A violates the metanorm, and $(1- \lambda)$ be the probability that the community will not punish B for failing to punish A.

The value of α reflects the net marginal benefit of violating metanorms. Higher α reflects A's increased marginal net benefit of violating the collectivist norms, and vice versa. α is a positive function of A's degree of individualism. For example α is higher for an active individualist than for a passive individualist. α is zero for a strict collectivist.

Similarly, higher β refers to B's increased marginal net benefit from punishing A if A violates metanorms. β's value increases with the level of collectiveness. It is one for a strict collectivist, and zero for a strict individualist. The values of θ and λ are high, close to one, in a strictly collectivist community, compared to lower θ and λ in a less restrictive collective community. θ and λ are zero in a strict individualist community.

In a collectivist community, high θ and λ represent the optimal strategy. They conform to the tenets of the collectivist metanorms that reward B (or not punish B) if B behaves collectively, punishing or reporting A when A violates metanorms. Similarly, the collectivist community punishes B if B behaves individualistically, that is when B does not react to, or approves of A's violation of metanorms.

Given the collectivist community's optimal strategy, B's optimal strategy is to punish A whenever A violates metanorms, otherwise B will be subject to collectivist community's punishment for failing to punish or report A.

Given B's optimal strategy of punishing A if A violates metanorms, A has two options: conform to metanorms and avoid punishment, or violate metanorms and face punishment from B. A's action is a function of the marginal net benefit from violating metanorms, which is the difference between marginal benefit of acting individualistically (e.g., benefit from acting in self-interest) and marginal cost of collective punishment.

In a typical individualist society, β, θ, and γ are equal to zero. Metanorms are downgraded to norms, where individual A may conform to or violate the norms according to her own net individual benefit, without any intervention from the collective community.

In a typical collectivist society, higher values of θ and γ increase the shirkers' cost of acting indifferently regarding the deviants' violation of metanorms, causing β to increase. This, in turn, increases the deviants' cost of violating metanorms, lowering the value of α, increasing the likelihood that women, to conform to metanorms, act collectively, and perpetuate collectivism and gender-discriminating norms.

The higher the likelihood that the collective community will reward (or not punish) collectivist members who punish the deviants of gender-discriminating metanorms, and the higher the likelihood that the collective society will punish the shirkers who fail to punish or report the metanorm's deviants, the higher is the likelihood that the deviants will be punished, and therefore the less likely is it that they will be to violate these metanorms.

Metanorms and Collectivist Societies

The enforcement of norms tends to increase with the level of societal cohesion. Collectivist members are more likely to enforce norms in more collectivist societies. This is due to the higher level of collectivity, interdependence, collective accountability, the prevalence of sacred social norms that are highly valued, and, most importantly, the collective punishment schemes against norms' deviants and shirkers.

In contrast to individualist societies, where high levels of cohesion and stronger social ties among the members of society are more likely to tilt people's interest to engage in more mutually beneficial activities and less likely to punish the violators of social norms, collectivist members in gender-discriminating collectivist societies derive high value from conforming to and enforcing collectivist norms. They punish not only the first-order violators of such norms, but also the second-order violators for their failure to punish the first-order violators for their failure to act collectively (Axelrod 1984; Horne 2007).

The enforcement of metanorms shares similar attributes with public goods in a collectivist society. If the collective society endorses and sanctions certain norms because of the collective benefit of enforcing them, the society aims to safeguard the norm's enforcement in order to maintain their cultural heritage and the social order of the society. In such cases, everyone is expected to participate in norm enforcement, even the potential victims of such metanorms, such as women in gender-discriminating societies. The metanorm's deviants are considered first-order free riders, and shirkers are considered second-order free riders. Both first and second-order free riders' behaviors should be punished accordingly to make sure that metanorms are upheld at the collective community's desired level. The failure to punish these free riders will lower the level of norm enforcement below the collective desired level, causing a decay and disintegration of the society's cultural heritage and social order (Horne and Cutlip 2002; Heckathorn 1989; Prietula and Conway 2009).[1]

Individualists living in collectivist societies will encounter four options. First, they will not conform to norms that discriminate against them personally (or norms that discriminate against the individual's rights of other groups, for example, women and dominated minority groups) if there is no punishment against violating such norms. Second, in the case of discriminating metanorms (against themselves or against other groups), they will violate the metanorms if the collectivist punishment against them is smaller than their individual gain from violating the norms (i.e., acting individualistically). Third, they will conform to discriminating metanorms if the collectivist punishment exceeds their benefit from violating the metanorm. Fourth, they will conform to the metanorms and punish the metanorm's deviants if the collectivist punishment against their shirking behaviors exceeds their benefit of letting deviants violate the metanorms.

There is also another class of individualists who are committed to not conform to discriminating metanorms. They are the committed individualists who reject the imposition of discriminating metanorms and the heavy multiple-layered punishment scheme against the deviants and shirkers. They live up to a code of conduct they acknowledge as binding to them, even if their narrow personal interest is reduced in the process (Hausman and McPherson 1993). These committed individualists act rationally, even though they may act against their narrow personal interest, since their acts seems to be morally good. This may also apply to shirkers who may act against their narrow personal interest, out of sympathy for the welfare of the deviants, to honor individualists' behaviors by not punishing or reporting them. This may explain the presence of harsh collective punishments against committed individualists in gender-discriminating collectivist societies, a reflection of the collectivist society's strong drive to rid itself of deviants and shirkers and to minimize any threat that may decay or disintegrate the cultural heritage and social fabric of the collectivist society. It also reflects the presence of committed individualists in these societies who are willing to pay a heavy price for their committed personal belief and rejection of discriminating metanorms, for example, some victims of honor killing, imprisonment, forced confinement, and of being shamed and ostracized, who choose to violate the discriminating metanorms regardless of the heavy collectivist punishment.

In contrast to individualist members, collectivist members gain intrinsic value from conforming to metanorms-punishing the deviants and the shirkers who fail to punish the deviants. They derive positive utility not only from their conforming to metanorms, but also from the whole community's collective conformity to metanorms. Therefore, they are prone to punish the metanorm's deviants and shirkers or report them. Equivalent to committed individualists, committed collectivists are motivated by a desire to do their duty even if their narrow self-interest is reduced in the process. They live up to their own collectivist code of conduct they acknowledge as binding to them. This may explain collectivist members' willingness to participate in severe collectivist punishments, such as honor killing if honor killing is a metanorm sanctioned and praised collectively. These committed members act rationally, since their acts seem to be collectively good.

Metanorms induce collectivist members to punish members who fail to punish the violators of collectivist norms. They distort the behaviors of individualist members by increasing the cost of behaving individualistically. Metanorms heighten the probability of punishing women who violate collectivist norms. Therefore, individualist women should adjust their calculations before violating these norms, by taking into account the added cost (punishments) associated with metanorms.

Metanorm and Discrimination

The weights corresponding to different groups should be taken into consideration when analyzing the effect of metanorms in collectivist societies. It is reasonable to assume that the weight of the collectivists is larger in a collectivist society than in an individualist society. In addition, it is reasonable to assume different weights (or power) are given to different groups in the collectivist societies, with more weight given to the strong or dominant group (ethnic and religious majority groups) and men, and less (or a zero, in extreme cases) weight to the weak or dominated group (ethnic and religious minority groups) and women. In collectivist societies, metanorms sanctioned or imposed by the strong dominant group will be enforced and applied to all groups: the dominant and dominated group, depending on the societal degree of collectivism. Metanorms sanctioned by a dominated group (or a subset of them) are usually applied to the dominated group members only. For example, FGM/C in Egypt and Sudan, the ban on women driving in Saudi Arabia, strict female dress codes, strict constraints on women's movements, social relations, employment, and entertainment in many communities in the Arab world, are samples of the metanorms that not only influence the behaviors of the effective majority (men-especially Muslim men), but also women and non-Muslim minority groups in these collectivist societies.

The enforcement of metanorms is likely to increase with lower cost of sanctioning, the level of support given to the collectivist willing punishers, and with high levels of homogeneity, interdependency, and cohesion among the community members (Horne 2007).

Metanorms are sustained by the informal reward and/or the high status bestowed on the willing punishers who enforce metanorms, especially when the cost of executing such norms increases (e.g., severe formal punishments against the willing punishers). In many collectivist societies, collectivist leaders (especially religious leaders) are likely to accentuate the value associated with sanctioning metanorms to offset the potential higher formal cost of enforcing such metanorms (Horne and Cultip 2002; Horne 2007). In many cases, the promise of incalculable afterlife rewards to individuals who enforce sacred metanorms and the severe afterlife punishment against the deviants and shirkers of such norms are utilized to sustain metanorms and elevate their values (Al-Qaradawi 1997).

Under normal conditions, norms are enforced because of the positive net social outcome that results from their enforcement. However, under specific circumstances, metanorms may prevail in collectivist societies such that these metanorms have negative consequences on the excluded and marginalized groups. Examples of these circumstances include skewed distribution of status and power, the exclusion or discounting of certain population groups from the decision making processes, and metanorms that are based on the strong preference of one group (mostly elites/leaders). These metanorms will be enforced as long as the effective weights of the winners of metanorms' enforcement exceed the effective weights of the victims of such norms.

Metanorms and the Minor Status of Women

Treating women as legal minors or dependents, informally or formally, in the Arab world (and other similar countries) adds power and prevalence to metanorms, since certain decisions are not made by women or are not made by them alone. As minors, women need consent or permission from their male legal guardian (husbands if married and a close male relative such as fathers, brothers, uncles, or grandfathers if unmarried) before engaging in certain activities such as leaving the house, visiting relatives or friends or inviting them, buying certain goods, working, traveling, starting a business, and so on.

Legal guardians can make certain decisions on behalf of their female dependents. In such a case, the female legal minors' behaviors reflect the choices made by their legal guardians. Accordingly, not only are deviant girls and women penalized for their violations of collectivist norms, rules, and codes of conduct, but so too are their legal guardians. The most common punishments against the male guardians are shaming and ostracizing, thus damaging their social status and tainting their honor. For example, forcing the legal guardians to sign a pledge to restrict his female dependents from driving cars on their own (in Saudi Arabia), in addition to rebuking and admonishing them for letting their female dependents violate social norms and rules and belittling them for their inability to discipline their female dependents—a reflection on their honor. Belittling and humiliating men for not disciplining their female relatives or for not treating them according to existing gender-discriminating norms and rules is very common in the Arab world. Examples include letting his wife or another female minor violate the collectively sanctioned dress code, going out without the company of a *mahram*[2], staying out late, engaging in unsanctioned social activities, playing sports, watching sporting events or movies in the public sphere, or participating in artistic, cultural, social, and political activities. These examples of unacceptable practices warrant the humiliation and even boycotting of their male guardians for not acting as a decent and a virile man. Shaming the male guardians is very costly in gender-discriminating collectivist societies where collective honor is highly valued, in terms of diminishing the male guardian's status and honor in the community. They may also be subject to shame, ridicule, and resentment from others, especially the collectivist members in the society.

The built-in double punishments (banishing the deviant and shirkers) in the dependent-guardian situation, is likely to cause the guardians to impose strict controls on their female member's freedom and behaviors that may cause collective punishment against the male guardian. To deter such collective punishment, the male guardian is more likely to prevent dissentions and violation of collectively assigned metanorms by punishing his dependent female members whenever they violate the socially assigned norms and codes of conduct.

The influence of metanorms on the male guardians' behaviors depends on the guardians' collectivism-individualism balance or preference. Collectivist guardians, who are willing punishers of metanorms' deviants, are likely to impose strict control on their female dependents and to punish them if they violate the social norms and codes of conduct, acting according to metanorms. In contrast, metanorms will have a different effect on individualist male guardians. These guardians face conflicting options. They may not impose the collectively assigned norms and restrictions on their female dependents, giving their female dependents more freedom to act according to their own individualistic set of preferences. However, this option is costly, since it exposes both the dependent female (the deviant) and the male guardian (the shirker) to collective punishment for violating metanorms. The welfare function of the individualist male guardian is positively related to acting individualistically and to the utility derived from letting his dependent females act individualistically. An increase in collective metanorm punishment is likely to increase the cost imposed on him for acting individualistically, as a shirker. Thus, the collective punishment serves to influence the guardian's behavior: first, by imposing a punishment against the female dependent (the deviant) for violating the metanorm; and second, by imposing collective punishment against him (the shirker) for not preventing the deviant female dependent from violation the collective norms. The higher the level of a metanorm's punishment, the less likely will be the individualist male guardian and the female dependents to violate the metanorms, especially when their membership in the collectivist community is compulsory; that is, there is no freedom to exit the collectivist group, as is the case in many collectivist societies. This may explain the severe and humiliating punishments that serve to deter metanorms' deviants' and shirkers' behaviors in collectivist societies.

Violating Metanorms as Negative Externalities in Collectivist Societies

Negative externalities refer to practices that affect bystanders negatively. Examples of negative externalities include the negative second-hand smoke effect associated with people who smoke in public places, which harms the health of nearby people, driving cars while intoxicated, which risks the safety of others, and firms dumping waste in ways that harm public health. These negative externalities exist in all individualist and collectivist societies and are usually penalized to discourage them and reduce their presence.

However, certain individualist behaviors that are externality-free in individualist societies can be treated as behaviors that generate negative externality in collectivist societies since such behaviors violate sacred norms revered in these societies. For example, women's choices of dress, social association and relationships, sexual preference, movement, travel, and so on, which do not conform to assigned collectivist norms, can generate negative externalities to the rest of the collectivist society, especially the collectivist members. Therefore, such individualist behaviors generate social external costs that must be deterred through proper penalties in collectivist societies. Without proper intervention, these behaviors (mostly women's behaviors) will be more prevalent, since these women do not pay for the external costs that result from their unsanctioned behaviors. In such a case, certain illicit behaviors according to collectivist norms may exceed the socially optimal level. Unsanctioned behaviors according to existing sacred norms, roles, and rules, can destroy families and corrode the social order and cultural harmony in these societies.

To reduce the level of the negative externality's behaviors, the collectivist society must increase the cost on the participants that result from such behaviors. The virtue police in Saudi Arabia are an example of intervention against negative externality behaviors. This group punishes women (and men) whose behaviors may generate negative collective externalities, such as not dressing according to the collectively assigned dress code, or mixing with unrelated people of the opposite sex in the public sphere. In certain cases, the optimal level of these behaviors is zero, such that the punishment must be severe or prohibitive enough to eradicate such behaviors, for example, honor killing. Punishing or executing Muslim women who marry non-Muslim men (in most of the Arab world) and punishing their collaborators (shirkers), flogging women for not adhering to the collectively assigned dress code and punishing or shaming their guardians publicly, send a strong signal that these negative externality behaviors will not be tolerated.

In general, the prevalence of metanorms in collectivist societies is much larger than that of individualist societies, since certain behaviors that do not generate negative externalities in individualist societies are counted as negative externalities in collectivist societies (Horne and Cutlip 2002; Horne 2007; HecKathorn 1989).

In contrast, the punishments imposed on individuals for behaving individualistically in a collectivist society can be considered activities that generate negative externalities, from the perspective of an individualist person or an individualist society. Examples of such acts include gender-based violence, spousal rape, underage marriage, and other similar punishments imposed by collectivist members against metanorms' deviants and shirkers.

Metanorms, Trust, and Trustworthiness

Trust occurs when individual A trusts that individual B views the welfare of individual A as important to the welfare of individual B. Trustworthiness occurs when A can count on B to behave according to A's expectations. In gender-discriminating collectivist societies, trustworthiness refers to the expectations that women and other individualists will behave and act in a way that satisfies the collectivist group's expectations. Two main issues of extreme value to trustworthiness in collectivist societies are effective information and effective sanctions (Guinnane 2005). In collectivist communities, women are observed, monitored, and watched closely. In addition, treating women as legal minors tend to increase their conformity to metanorms due to their constrained freedom, capabilities, and functionings. In additions, the presence of metanorms enhances the conformity to collective norms further by punishing both the deviants and shirkers. This adds another layer of monitoring and punishment against potential deviant females. The collective threat to punish the female's guardian if he shirks increases the cost of violating collective norms, thus increasing the likelihood of adhering to such collective norms, regardless of how unfair or discriminating.

Sources of Metanorms in the Arab World (and other Islamic Societies)

The enforcement of norms is widely accepted in the Arab world to uphold the cultural harmony and social Order in Islamic *'ummah* (Islamic nation or community). There are multiple references in the *Qur'an* that urge Muslim believers to do what is right and to forbid shameful deeds. Examples include, "Let there arise out of you a band of people inviting to all that is good, enjoining what is right, and forbidding what is wrong: They are the ones to attain felicity" (the *Qur'an* 3:104), "Ye are the best of peoples, evolved for mankind, enjoining what is right, forbidding what is wrong, and believing in Allah..." (the *Qur'an* 3:110), "The Believers, men and women, are protectors one of another: they enjoin what is just, and forbid what is evil..." (the *Qur'an* 9:71), and "[Believers] who repent, serve and glorify God...command the proper and forbid the improper" (the *Qur'an* 9:112). In addition, many *hadiths* by Prophet Muhammad, which are widely used in Muslim societies to enforce norms, are those urging Muslim to change what is evil or wrong, and condemn Muslims who do not intervene to stop such wrong doing or evil deeds. Examples of such *hadiths* are, "When people see a wrong-doer and do nothing to stop him, they may well be visited by God with a punishment," and "Whoever amongst you sees an evil, he must change it with his hand; if he is unable to do so, then with his tongue; and if he is yet unable to do so, then with his heart; and that is the weakest form of Faith." The verses and *hadiths* command members of the Muslim community or nation (not only governments) to forbid evil according to the resources available to them, by hand or force, reprimand, or by wishful thinking and prayer, according to their abilities, respectively (Shafaat 1989).

Summary

The enforcement of gender-discriminating norms and the elevation of some of them to formal rules deepen women's marginalization and exclusion, and deform their capabilities and functionings. Various female behaviors that are considered externality-free in individualist societies are treated as negative externalities in gender-discriminating collectivist societies that should be punished and eradicated. Accordingly, certain mere freedoms of choice and innate capabilities of women can be constrained and/or even prohibited in these societies, based on the collective perspective of these behaviors as wrong.

CHAPTER 7

Cognitive Dissonance and Gender Discrimination

C ognitive dissonance is a positive model of what will happen if individuals are able to adjust their beliefs to reduce their pain or anxiety (Akerlof and Dickens 1982). Women in many gender-discriminating societies are torn between standing up for their rights and conforming to discriminating practices. Cognitive dissonance represents conflicting desires that create the unpleasant tension that women in these societies face. The cognitive dissonance theory proposes that people are motivated to reduce this tension and may do so either by reducing their self-interest behavior, by engaging in self-deception, or by some combination of the two (Konow 2000). For example, people do not choose to work in an unsafe place. However, if they do continue to work in dangerous jobs, they try to reject the cognition that the job is dangerous. Similarly, women who do not have other viable alternatives typically believe that their situation is normal or less dire, and acclimate to it. They may believe they are being treated fairly according to the prevailing discriminating norms and codes of conduct (Akerlof and Dickens 1982). This behavior is crucial to understanding gender discrimination and violence since women's measurement of victimization has been corrupted.[1]

Individuals with a strong belief in sacred and other social norms are more likely to believe the undertaking of unpleasant tasks is good.[2] Women may believe they fare better in such collectivist societies, especially with belief of afterlife rewards. Women's acceptance of and resignation to the status quo plays right into the hands of the winners in collectivist societies. Women become oblivious to gender-discriminating norms, and therefore fail to oppose or seek to repeal them. Akerlof and Dickens explain what irrational behavior, "Analysis that takes account of cognitive dissonance gives different results from the standard analysis, and in particular, provides better explanations for some phenomena that are a puzzle according to the standard approach" (1982: 318).

Cognitive dissonance plays a vital role in perpetuating certain practices that may seem irrational to outside observers. Women are likely to become oblivious to discrimination, especially in collectivist societies. They may minimize and justify the cost and pain of discrimination against them, such that they make themselves feel less discriminated against. This is especially true if there is no other viable alternative, or if the cost of rebelling is very high or prohibitive. In gender-discriminating collectivist societies, women in general and abused women in particular are likely to censor their behaviors to conform to societal norms and practices. This minimizes the likelihood of violence and discrimination against them. Consequently, women become their own jailers (CHANGE 1999; Mathur 2004).

Women's apparent adaptation to and acceptance of hostile, exclusive, and/or discriminating social environments should not be considered the last word on the matter (Nussbaum 2000). They understand that if they resist or complain, they may expose themselves to harsh collective punishments. The severity of collective punishment serves to deter violation of social norms. The victims may even resist intervention unless there are viable alternatives and they are free of fear or retribution. Thus, external intervention is necessary to identify those who may fail to recognize themselves as victims since these victims may not initiate any intervention on their own. The victims, additionally, may object to external interventions if there is a low level of trust or because they were previously let down. Akerlof and Dickens state, "Persons tend to avoid or resist new information that contradicts already established beliefs" (1982: 316). In such a case, analyzing women's achieved capabilities (functionings) highlights their failure to reach their full potentials. Their happiness is distorted by their inability to make free choices. This is well stated by Hausman and McPherson: "Women who are systemically denied roles in public life or equal shares of consumption goods may learn . . . not to want what they have not got" (1993: 691).

Furthermore, cultural relativists who conform to existing norms and practices endorse this discrimination as benign matters related to their own culture. They allow these norms to be integral features of their cultures instead of gender discrimination.

Abused women are likely to be reluctant to report incidents of gender-discriminating practices because of their fear of police abuse, such as refusal to register their complaints. Most, if not all, police officers, court officials, and judges, in the Arab world are men, many of whom sympathize with or approve of existing gender-discriminating norms and practices. They typically refuse to enforce laws that aim to protect women at the expense of violating collectivist norms, especially sacred norms. Women may be subject to harassment, ridicule, collective resentment/rejection, or even prosecution for reporting domestic or spousal violence, sexual assault, or rape, and expose their families to shame and dishonor (U.S. DOSa 2014; Human Rights Watch 2014a). Therefore, they are likely to minimize their fear or stress. People, including women, with strong belief in informal norms, especially sacred norms, are more likely to have persistent belief that these norms are good, regardless of how discriminating

against women. Nussbaum (2000) highlights the notion of preference deformation, where unjust norms, traditions, fear, and discriminating cultural and
social backgrounds can deform people's preferences, choices, and even wishes
for their own lives. Because of distorted preferences, collectivist members and
institutions will continue their discrimination against women, with the expectation that they will not be caught, especially when norms have been formalized into laws. They believe they will treated less harshly if prosecuted, for
example in the case of violence against women and "honor" killings in the Arab
world, and other similar countries (Hoyek et al. 2005; CEWLA 2005). Jan
Morris accentuates the influence of cognitive dissonance on women's behaviors and perceptions, "The more I was treated as a woman, the more woman
I became...If I was assumed to be incompetent at reversing cars, or opening
bottles, oddly incompetent I felt myself becoming" (in Bourdieu 1998: 61).

Gender-Discriminating Norms and Cognitive Dissonance: A Simple Model

Figure 7.1 illustrates how gender-discriminating norms influence women's
behavior in collectivist societies. Starting with a gender-discriminating incident (e.g., domestic violence), let α be the probability the victim will report
the case formally to the police or court, or informally to her collectivist unit
(e.g., family or tribe). α is likely to be low in gender-discriminating collectivist
societies. Familial and societal pressure and fear from retaliation are likely to
pressure the victims to not complain.

Let β be the probability that the community (informal or formal) will prosecute and punish the perpetrator, and $(1 - \beta)$ be the probability that the accused
perpetrator will be acquitted. The value of β is likely to be low in the case of
ineffective or uncooperative informal or formal responses. The victim's fear of
being patronized and harassed (by her in-group, male police offices, lawyers,
judges, and so on), the lack of specific laws against domestic violence (in most
Arab countries), the difficulty of satisfying the witness requirement since most
of violence acts take place in the private sphere, and the difficulty of getting a
medical proof of injury and its degree of severity all contribute to a low β.

Let θ be the probability that the victim will pursue further action, such as
leaving her group (or collective unit or community) to join a supportive one,
or appeal the community's ruling. In many collectivist societies, this option is
too costly or does not exist, since a woman's membership in her collective unit
(family, tribe, and country) is compulsory. The lack of viable options available
to women can pressure them to take extreme measures such as running away,
killing their husbands, or committing suicide (Cowell 1989). However, due
to the prohibitively high costs and risks associated with these options, most
victims are likely to resign and accept gender discrimination as a "normal"
part of their cultural heritage. In doing so, they maintain social order and family unity. They may blame themselves for instigating gender discrimination
against them as a result to their disobedience or negligence. They may also
convince themselves that their acceptance of and acclimation to such violence

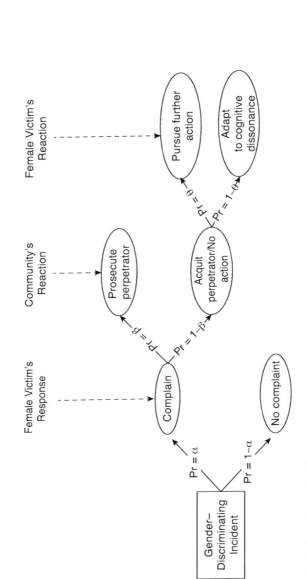

Figure 7.1 Gender discrimination and cognitive dissonance.

will make them better individuals and gain them favor with *Allah* (God) for their obedience and patience, especially in the life thereafter. Women are commanded to not let their husband be angry at them, for example, by not complaining against their husband's violent or discriminating acts against them. According to *hadith*, *Allah* will not accept the prayer of a woman who let her husband be angry about her (Al-Qaradawi 1997). This convinces victims that maintaining the status quo is highly rewarded.

In general, victims of gender violence or discrimination in collectivist societies are likely to internalize their dissonance, due the lack of viable alternatives (lower θ), the higher likelihood that society will acquit the perpetrator (lower β), and the informal pressure on the victims to not proceed with their complaints and to be patient and submissive with their perpetrators, usually their husbands or other male guardians (lower α). Looking backward, the victims of gender violence or discrimination in collectivist societies are less inclined to complain formally.

In contrast, victims of gender discrimination in individualist societies are more likely to complain formally since each of α, β, and θ are likely to be close to one due to family and social support of the victims to report the case formally (higher α), the presence specific laws and the effective enforcement of gender-neutral laws (higher β), and the availability of viable alternatives, such as leaving the abusive relationship, leaving the discriminating community, or pursuing further legal action (higher θ).

Lack of Viable Options and Cognitive Dissonance

In discriminating collectivist societies, women's lack of access to status, power, and primary goods, in addition to the excessive barriers and high cost of converting primary goods into actual functionings to achieve valued ends, are likely to lead women to find satisfaction in small mercies by adapting to such discriminating environment, and lowering their preferences and aspirations, so as to be more easily satisfied or less-dissatisfied (Qizilbash 2009: 5–6). The lengthy, costly, and complex process of recovering from abusive relations or environments makes it more difficult and daunting for abused women to start such recovering process, since the abused and victimized women lack the viable resources required for their recovery from abusive relations or environments, inter alia (CHANGE 1999: 7).

Viable alternative options for women include the followings: inclusive and non-discriminating informal norms and formal rules, freedom to move and travel, freedom to work, equal access to marriage, divorce and child custody, freedom to join the labor force and find employment and the ability to earn income, access to the public sphere, harassment-free environment, lending facilities, non-discriminating employment opportunities, education, equal access to cultural, social and political capital and participation and representation, equal access to leadership, and so on. These measures reduce women's vulnerability and empower them, depending on the availability and effectiveness of such ancillary sources. These sources also provide viable ex-post alternatives for women against gender-discriminating norms and practices.

The lack of viable options deprives women's of options regarding better trans-actions and terms, and makes them more vulnerable to gender-discriminating schemes. Even though women may have access to the legal system, familial and societal pressure can sway them to not seek legal redress, since it violates exist-ing norms and rules. Another example is female access to employment. Even though women can legally enter the labor market in most countries, they must have a permission from their legal guardian in some countries, and are likely to face multiple layers of built-in discrimination against women. This makes women's access to formal employment less viable and less rewarding. With the absence of other viable options, women may accept a bad offer if the other options yield worse outcomes. Any offer that matches women's threshold level is likely to be accepted by women (Basu 1986: 268).

Women's lack of legal knowledge, excessive delays, insensitivity of the judicial systems towards them, and the inability of women to afford the cost of obtaining justice, contribute to women's vulnerability. The lack of viable options takes away women's capabilities to choose and degrades them to mere adjuncts of the communities in which they live, whose mission is to execute the plans of someone else, men and the collective unit (Nussbaum 2000; UNICEF 2014; Kelly and Breslin 2010).

The following two case studies illustrate how women respond to domestic violence and FGM/C in gender-discriminating collectivist societies.

Women's Response to Domestic Violence

Lack of viable alternatives to victims of gender discrimination is likely to cause women to accept the least costly option available to them. For example, women's lack of access to equitable divorce and to a good life after divorce in the Arab world causes many victims of domestic violence, or spousal abuse in general, to stay in such abusive marriages and conform to the collectively assigned identity and role as submissive. Some abused wives may resign to blame themselves for the abuse inflicted on them or because of their husbands' jealousy and virility. A husband can discipline his wife according to condoned and sanctioned sacred norms. Wives are commanded to be obedient to their husbands.

In addition to husbands' access to admonish their wives verbally, abandon them in bed, and beat them (the *Qur'an* 4:34), they can divorce their wives unilaterally and unconditionally (the *Qur'an* 2:227) or take multiple wives (marry up to four wives, the *Qur'an* 4:3). In contrast to men's viable alterna-tives, women have limited options that curtail their freedom, capabilities, and functionings. Women do not have the same access to divorce as their husbands (An-Na'im 1990). They have two costly and lengthy options. First, a wife can seek a fault-based divorce through filing a legal divorce case. The court system in may Arab countries, requires the wife seeking divorce to provide proof of valid reasons to request a divorce such as the husband's sick-ness, his failure to provide maintenance or financial support, his absence or imprisonment for long period of time, and harmful behavior such as mental or physical abuse. However, the judge may reject the wife's divorce request, especially for harmful behaviors, since some levels of domestic violence are sanctioned according to Islamic *shari'ah* as viable instruments for husbands to discipline their wives (Kelly and Breslin 2010). In addition, sacred norms dictate that women should only seek divorce for strong reasons, "If any woman asks her husband for a divorce without some strong reason, the fragrance of Paradise will be forbidden to her" (*hadith* sited in Al-Qaradawi 1997: 213). Second, a wife can seek a no-fault *khul'* (separation), in which the wife, or her family, must return the *mahr* (dowry) and all gifts from her husband, according to common interpretations of *shari'ah* (Al-Qaradawi 1997). If the wife and her husband do not agree on *khul'*, the wife can petition the court for a *khul'*. However *khul'* is costly for most women, especially the poor. Given the informal norms that husbands are supposed to maintain their family financially (the *Qur'an* 4:34), wives are mostly confined to the private sphere, in their home, with no external source of income from employment. Only rich (mostly educated with employment experience) wives can afford *khul'*. Studies show that husbands can exploit the *khul'* divorce to extract more money from their wives, or abuse their wives to pressure them to seek *khul'*, instead of divorcing them, such that the husbands do not have to pay alimony or maintenance to their wives upon divorcing them. In addition to the difficulty for women to seek and get *khul'*, the process of seeking court's decision for *khul'* can take 3 months to 12 years (Fawzy 2004). Social stigma against *khul'* seeking divorcees makes it difficult for them to remarry, and adds more financial and social pressures on these women's families (since women should not support themselves but depend on male guardians) making *khul'* less practical for most women, especially the poor and uneducated from religiously conservative families or communities. Nonetheless, *khul'* is criticized by many Islamists and conservative Islamic scholars as an outcome of increasing women's independence and the influence of westernization on Islamic societies (Hamada 2010). The rate of approval of *khul'* divorce is Egypt is about 3 percent (Hamada 2010).

However, the *khul'* provision acts like a double-edged sword: on the positive side, it gives women more power to seek legal divorce from their husbands; however, on the negative side it deprives women from their right/access to financial alimony, and women must repay the dowry received from their husbands, and may give up even their rights to child custody, In addition, the provision of *khul'* can be exploited by opportunistic husbands, as stated by an Egyptian male, "If I am really fed up with my wife, I can turn her life into a living hell, and then she asks for a khul' divorce. So this way, I divorce her without paying her any money" (Katulis 2004: 23).

Consequently, most wives who can't afford divorce or *khul'* must accept the only available viable option—staying with their abusive husbands. Other than seeking extreme options such as committing suicide or murdering their husbands (Cowell 1989; Butler 2004), women are likely to convince themselves that living with an abusive husband is not so bad, and that they are responsible in part for domestic violence. The following statements are examples of how women acclimate to domestic violence, "Yes, in some circumstances the man is forced to beat his wife. Sometimes she's done something wrong and in spite of that she leaves her house to her parents' house" (Egyptian woman in Katulis 2004: 20), and "I want to say something, and please don't be upset at me for saying this: there's a crooked rib in every woman that needs fixing. Therefore, sometimes if the husband lets her do whatever she wants, she will exceed her limits. So the true husband should let the woman realize her limits and stop her if she crosses them" (Egyptian woman in Katulis 2004: 21). In many parts of the Arab world, the physical discipline of women and other minors by their male guardians is accepted as an instrument to sustain power and in-group order (Zuckerhut 2011). This norm is illustrated by a female Bahraini Islamic lecturer Fatima Bosandel, "Women should remember that obeying and tolerating the bad habits of their husbands will bring them closer to God. One day their husbands could change for the better" (Hamada 2010). Obedient and forgiving wives are rewarded, or at least not condemned. These norms limit women's access to certain capabilities that are available to men, which in turn, causes them to internalize such discriminating norms by either blaming themselves, hoping for change to happen with their husbands, or hoping for afterlife rewards.

The process of leaving an abusive relationship often includes periods of denial, self-blame, and endurance before abused women recognize the abuse as a pattern, which is the beginning of disengagement and recovery. However, not all women can afford to disengage themselves from abusive relations due to women's fear of social stigma or revenge, fear of being murdered by their spouse, being subject to socially costly rumors, loss of child custody, loss of financial support, and so on (CHANGE 1999: 7).

In instances when domestic violence occurs, the first recommendation many women have is for the woman to wait for her husband to calm down. To avoid violence, one woman in Cairo says that if the husband comes back from work upset and stressed, the wife "should not provoke him or upset him. She should try to calm him down and make him feel better" (Katulis 2004: 21). If domestic violence becomes intolerable and beatings frequent, most agree that the next best step for the woman is to take the matter to her father or an elderly person in the family. Egyptians see legal recourse, including taking such matters to the police and courts, as a last resort, if it is mentioned at all (Katulis 2004).

Mothers' Response to FGM/C

FGM/C represents another example of cognitive dissonance to the mothers of a female child undergoing FGM/C. Mothers, at least the individualist ones, are torn between gender-discriminating norms of obedience to collective norms such as FGM/C on their daughters on one side and their own desire to not violate their daughters' physical integrity and participate in a deformation of their potential capabilities and functioning. Allan Gibbard highlights such a contradiction as a "conflict between our 'better judgment' and powerful social motivations" (1985: 15). Mothers as members in collective communities (family, tribe, nation) are influenced by the norms of obedience, cooperation, and one-ness, which are likely to control the mothers' behaviors in the midst of social encounters with other members in their collective community. These mothers are "in the grip" of the norms of obedience, according to Gibbard (1985). FGM/C is a valued norm that has collective reward for the mothers (who are viewed as cooperative and obedient), and for their daughters (as they are now similar to other girls in the collective community and are described as clean and beautiful, enjoying a "normal" life among all girls who had undergone FGM/C, preserving their virginity, reputation, and increasing their likelihood of marriage later on).

FGM/C is sanctioned based on the belief that it has some roots in sacred/religious norms in many Muslim societies (see chapter 10). It is sanctioned and recommended to girls to make them clean and beautiful, to sustain their virginity, chastity, and to deter any uncontrollable sexual urges, thus reducing the likelihood of shaming the family's honor due to illicit sexual behavior, or rumors, that may stain the daughter's reputation. In addition, FGM/C spares the parents' collective punishments such as humiliation, boycotting, and attacking the parents' lack of concerns for their daughter's reputation, virginity, and fidelity through FGM/C. The severity of collective punishment against the non-circumcised girl and her family serves to deter violation of the social norm. Such punishments increase the cost of dissenting and thus the adherence level to existing rules and laws (Karayiannis and Haztis 2010). Accordingly, many parents resign to make their daughters undergo FGM/C.

An Iraqi woman shared her pain and conflicting feelings of submitting her daughter to FGM/C, "You must think we are monsters" (Human Rights Watch 2010: 54). Another Iraqi mother who was too afraid to hold her daughter or watch the procedure said, "I told my daughter that we are going to a relative's home, but then I took her to the midwife. She asked me what we are doing here. When we entered, I was too scared...I handed her to someone at the door and remained outside. Someone else held her [down]" (Human Rights Watch 2010: 4).

In these cases, societal pressures outweigh women's desires to protect their daughters. On one side, the mother's love and care for her daughter's well-being in terms of protecting her bodily and psychological integrity and her natural physical organs, desires, and sexual satisfaction and happiness when her daughter gets married will reduce the likelihood of FGM/C. On the other side, the mother (or parents) faces the fear of rejection if being uncooperative with collective expectations, norms, and practices. She fears the discomfort and harms associated with her refusal to seek FGM/C for her daughter. She also fears disobeying collective norms that are embedded in her religion/faith.

Mothers in collectivist societies are likely to resign to the thought that FGM/C is good for their daughters. They accept or trick themselves into accepting that the immediate and long-term collective benefits of the collectively enforced FGM/C exceed its immediate and long-term individualist costs. They may also resign to the idea that undergoing FGM/C on their daughters makes them more responsible parents, since they acted according to the demand of collective sacred norms.

False Conscience and Cognitive Dissonance

False consciousness refers to a distorted view of reality, where people feel happy with an otherwise miserable fate (Smith 2001).[3] Women in the Arab world are informed that they are treated with respect, not forced to enter the labor market, and not exploited like women in individualist societies, such as the Western world. They are respected in their homes and well respected as wives and mothers. They will be generously rewarded in Paradise (in the afterlife) for their submissiveness and obedience to collectively assigned norms and roles rooted in sacred teachings, upholding their reputation and the honor of their family and collective community.

Emile Durkheim (1984) underscores the importance of "collective conscience," which refers to the shared norms and values in collective societies, the high level of conformity, and the low levels of tolerance for deviance that is accompanied with harsh and even violent punishments. In his analysis of religion, he separates the sacred from the profane. The sacred involves the feelings of awe, fear, and reverence. This is separated from the profane by special taboos and rites such as ritual, prayer, and sacrifice. The collective effervescence provides a strong sense of group belonging (Durkheim 1984; Smith 2001).

Durkhim's analysis fits the state of women in many gender-discriminating collectivist societies, such as the Arab world, in which certain gender-discriminating practices such as domestic violence, FGM/C, "honor killing," inter alia, are exploited to make women feel as though they are the holder of the society's honor in their bodies and in their reputation. They may accept the collective impositions on their behaviors, through gender-discriminating norms and rules, as necessary steps and precautions to uphold the collective honor, the cultural heritage, and social order in their societies. The level of their acceptance of, and adherence to, such norms and roles is likely to be high if they are rewarded, positively through collective praises and afterlife rewards, or negatively through preventing harsh collective punishments and afterlife's condemnation.

Summary

Acclimation to cognitive dissonance usually occurs in the absence of viable alternative options when these are too costly. Victims of gender-discriminating norms, roles, and rules are more likely to adapt and acclimate to the dissonance associated with them, due to the enforcement of such norms and the high cost of deviance.

Acclimation to cognitive dissonance makes a strong case for external intervention, since the victims may not recognize that they are victims, and may not initiate any change or seek intervention. Accordingly, external interventions from NGOs, local and national governments, and international organizations, especially human rights organizations, are very crucial to decipher various gender-discriminating practices in which the victims are uniformed, ignorant, or oblivious about the violation of their rights.

CHAPTER 8

Norms, Status, and Individualist Goods

S tatus or positional goods are goods that confer utility to someone (a certain group) only at the expense of someone else (or another group) who consumes less of the status good. Hirsch (1976) distinguishes between normal goods, which confer direct utility (yielding a positive sum game in free market transactions, where everyone can gain), and positional goods, which confer utility to winners only at the expense of losers, a zero- or a negative-sum game. The distribution of status goods is a zero-sum-game in the case of no transaction costs or a negative-sum-game in the case of transaction costs. Normal goods are reproducible, but positional or status goods are not (Cooper et al. 2001: 644).

Status goods in the Arab world often take the form of authority in terms of decisions. These decisions may relate to marriage, divorce, child custody, inheritance, court testimony, travel and movement, employment, appearance (wardrobes and cosmetics), social contacts or relationships, and so on. Women's discounted share of, or exclusion from status goods in gender-discriminating societies limits their freedom and deforms their functioning. These limitations affect women's capability to choose individualist goods and activities such as buying individualist apparels, driving or traveling alone, having social relations with non-related people (especially of the opposite sex), continuing education and choosing fields of study, joining the labor force, working, working in certain fields, participating in sports and other entertainment activities, participating in cultural, social, or political activities, and so on.

The skewed distribution of status goods between male and female members highlights the perpetuation of gender discrimination. The improvement of the well-being (or utility or welfare) of men according to such norms takes place at the expense of women, the victims of such imposed norms.

Women's lack of status goods also reduces their resistance to gender-discriminating practices, and diminishes the effectiveness of many interventions to transitory or temporary effects. This is because these interventions do not take into consideration the root causes of women's lack of status goods, their deformed choices of sanctioned collectivist goods that are imposed on them, and their constrained access to certain individualist goods and activities that are prohibited or discouraged based on prevailing sacred norms.

Effective interventions should not stop at simply increasing women's access to certain goods and positions (e.g., granting women seats in parliament and other government offices or allowing women to participate in Olympic games), since all these decisions are made by men, the holders of status goods. These interventions treat the symptoms or the outcome of gender discrimination, not the root causes of the gender discrimination. Increasing women's share of the status goods should be the ultimate aim of intervention. With access to status goods, women can achieve high levels of capabilities and functionings that are authentic and sustainable.

Women's "rights" given or bestowed by benevolent collectivist rulers or governments still deprive women from earning such status. In these environments, women are still dependent on the patriarchal ruling of governments that control the status goods. Such signs of benevolence toward women are likely to have temporary effects, since women do not earn them in their own right. Without an equal or significant share of status goods, women will continue to depend on and follow the preference of the dominantly patriarchal collectivist communities and government. In such cases, women can either confront such discriminating distribution of status and power (exposing themselves to existing schemes of collective punishment), or acclimate to such imposed preference and choices (internalizing their dissonance, muting their own choices, freedom, capabilities and functionings, and resigning to a second-class position).

Allocation of Status Goods: A Simple Model

Appendix 8.1 illustrates the distribution of status goods in a society of two members—a female and a male—using a simple model. The allocation of the status good between the male and female members depends on the social preference.

In the case of a gender neutral society, in which male and female members are valued and treated equally, the status good will be shared equally between the female and male members, as is shown in figure A8.1.1.

However, in a gender-discriminating society that values the male share of the status good higher than the female share, more of the status good will be allocated to the male member at the expense of the female member, as is shown in figure A8.1.1.

In the extreme case of gender discrimination, the society discounts the female share of the status good to zero, which means males have full control over status goods, as is shown in figure A8.1.2. In such a case, the social welfare function becomes a function of the male preferences and choices due to their full control of status goods. Women's welfare, in such a case, depends on the choices and decisions made by men and the patriarchal community.

Norms and the Allocation of Status Goods in the Arab World

The main sacred norm that influences women's access to status in the Arab world (and similar Islamic countries) is the sacred norm or the principle of *qawama* of men over women, which is mentioned in sacred texts, "Men are the maintainers of women because Allah has made some of them to excel others and because they spend out of their property; the good women are therefore obedient, guarding the unseen as Allah has guarded" (the *Qur'an* 4:34). *Qawama*, according to widely accepted interpretations, means men are the maintainers of and protectors of women, the managers of affairs of women, and maintain authority and guardianship over women. In addition, *Allah* also made men to excel over women (the *Qur'an* 2:228). According to An-Na'im (1990), men's *qawama* stems from men's physical strength and their financial support of women. However, other sacred norms bestow on men superior status of "perfection," wisdom, intelligence, and reverence to women. For example, many men, according to *hadith*, reached the state of perfection that not many women can reach, "Many amongst men reached (the level of) perfection but none amongst the women reached this level except Asia, Pharaoh's wife, and Mary, the daughter of 'Imran [mother of Jesus]..."[1] Also, men's *qawama* is commanded not only for the family but also for communities and nations, according to a *hadith*, the Prophet said, "Never will succeed such a nation as makes a woman their ruler."[2] This *hadith* is one example of other supporting sacred teaching and norms that are used or exploited in patriarchal societies to reduce women's access to status goods, including leadership positions. Thus, women should be ruled, maintained, protected, managed, and live obediently and righteously under the guidance of such sacred norms, especially in gender-discriminating patriarchal societies.

Some norms, based in sacred teachings, support the notion that men should rule and have authority over women, not just because of men's superiority, but also because of women's inferiority or deficiency. For example,

> *Once Allah's Apostle went out to the Musalla (to offer the prayer) o 'Id-al-Adha or Al-Fitr prayer. Then he passed by the women and said, "O women! Give alms, as I have seen that the majority of the dwellers of Hell-fire were you (women)." They asked, "Why is it so, O Allah's Apostle?" He replied, "You curse frequently and are ungrateful to your husbands. I have not seen anyone more deficient in intelligence and religion than you. A cautious sensible man could be led astray by some of you." The women asked, "O Allah's Apostle! What is deficient in our intelligence and religion?" He said, "Is not the evidence of two women equal to the witness of one man?" They replied in the affirmative. He said, "This is the deficiency in her intelligence. Isn't it true that a woman can neither pray nor fast during her menses?" The women replied in the affirmative. He said, "This is the deficiency in her religion." Sahih Bukhari (Volume 1, Book 6, Number 301)*

A modified version of the above *hadith* is widely used in many parts of the Arab and Muslim world, "women are deficient in mind and religion," which is widely exploited to marginalize women, lower their status, and exclude them from decision-making processes and from leadership positions. These interpretations of *qur'anic* verses and *hadith* are being used as the foundation of women's identity and role in religious collectivist communities in the Arab world. Even though the Qur'an and *hadith* have various references and instructions to treat women properly and with dignity, the above (and other) references are used or exploited in the mostly patriarchal hierarchy in the Arab world to perpetuate women's lower status and to exclude them from many decision-making processes and leadership positions, or at least minimize the effectiveness of their presence.

According to prevalent and accepted interpretations and opinions of Islamic scholars, women can have the same qualities of self-reliance and leadership; however, they cannot lead since they do not have the right to be a judge or a witness. Some women can be wiser than some men are, however, this is not the usual rule and such women are not in the majority. Most Islamic scholars also argue that women's leadership will conflict with their proper place and role as a wives, mothers, and housekeepers. Others mention that women, more often than men, are more taken by their emotions when making decisions. In addition, leadership requires traveling and staying out of home, meeting in public place, and mixing with strangers of the opposite sex. Some of these functions are prohibited (meeting and negotiating with foreigners, especially of the opposite sex), some require permission from, or the company of their husbands or male guardians (leaving the house and traveling), and most, if not all, women cannot perform all these tasks efficiently while performing their job as a mothers and wives as well.

Orchestration Versus Implementation Powers

Women will sustain some decision-making power, even in gender-discriminating societies. However, one should distinguish between types of powers. Safilios-Rothschild (1976) distinguished between a superior/independent power, "orchestration power," and an inferior/dependent power, "implementation power." Orchestration power is an example of a status good that gives the winners the right to make major and critical, important, and less frequent decisions. The balance of power between orchestration and implementation power tilts towards the winners of the surrounding social norms and practices. In gender-discriminating collectivist societies, most orchestration power is held by men who hold more of the status goods, while women are stuck with most of the implementation power.

In gender-discriminating societies, men who hold the orchestration power usually make important and infrequent decisions to be implemented by their wives and other female dependents. Men must allocate enough time and energy to their activities in the public sphere, such as working, socializing, entertaining, and so on. Wives and other female dependents, mostly confined to home (their private sphere), are generally relegated to implementing the orchestration's decisions. Most implementation powers are treated as less valuable (or inferior) and time consuming, such as shopping for food, cooking, cleaning, and so on. This notion is well stated by Safilios-Rotheschild,

> Spouses who have "orchestration" power have, in fact, the power to make only the important and infrequent decisions that do not infringe upon their time but that determine the family life style and the major characteristics and features of their family. They also have the power to relegate unimportant and time-consuming decisions to their spouse. ... (1976: 359)

Implementation power is driven from the orchestration power. It is the inferior power implemented by relegated members in the family and in the community in general. Wives and other female dependents can derive a feeling of power from implementing certain orders made by the holders of orchestration power. Wives and other female dependents must abide by the constraints imposed by holders of the orchestration power.

In a gender-discriminating collectivist society, the relation between men (holders of orchestration power) and women (holders of implementation power) is similar to the principal-agent problem. Men who are in charge of "big decisions" have a well-defined set of orchestration power that is usually accompanied with very well defined set of instructions and a set of reward-punishment scheme. This is well known by the agents (women) who are in charge of "small decisions" such that the agent is constrained in her choices of implementing the instructions to satisfy the preference/desires of the principal. The agent knows what might happen if she does not act according to the principal's instructions or preferences (Pahl 1983).

Allocation of Orchestration and Implementation Powers: Cases from the Arab World

Figure 8.1 gives an example of the distribution of orchestration power (large household purchasing decisions) and implementation power (daily household purchasing decisions) in Egypt. It shows that men's share of orchestration power is more than ten times women's share, while more implementation power is left to women.

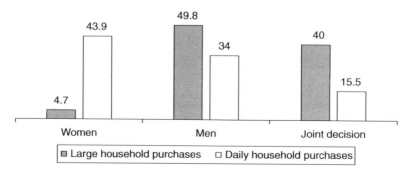

Figure 8.1 Participation in decision-making, Egypt, 2008 (%).
Source: Date collected from table 3.12, P. 41 in El-Zanaty and Way (2009).

Almosaed (2008) highlights the family as a patriarchal hierarchal institution in Saudi Arabia, with rights and responsibilities assigned according to sex and age. Female and young members are subordinate to male and older members respectively. Gender roles are assigned in a way that grants the male members privileged positions (orchestration power) in the family and in the society in general. Women are assigned to the private sphere to take care of the house, children, and the elderly (implementation power). Mostly, men have access to both the private and public spheres, while women are mostly confined to the private sphere, except in cases of necessity, in which they may access the public sphere with permissions from their male guardians.

Collective opposition to women serving in judicial or political leadership positions (judges or ministers) is another example of skewed distribution of status goods in gender-discriminating societies. A 2004 study in Egypt shows that most men and women oppose women serving in leadership positions. The following statement from an Egyptian man illustrates such opposition, "There is a week every month when the woman is unstable; this is because she is physically different from the man. During this week, she cannot make the right decisions, and so she is not qualified to be a judge" (Katulis 2004: 20). Others underscore sacred norms, for example, a woman is not allowed to testify in court without another woman to corroborate her testimony, which implicitly contradicts the notion of women being trusted as prosecutors or judges in many Arab countries (Katulis 2004).[3] These positions are associated with making decisions or judgments and providing distributional power in the decision-making processes—something which should be allocated only to men in many gender-discriminating societies, such as the Arab world.

Norms and the Allocation of Individualist Versus Collectivist Goods

In societies where gender discrimination is widespread and accepted, women's access to certain individualist goods and activities is constrained or even prohibited, if accessing such goods violates existing norms and rules.

Women, and everyone in general, are pressured to substitute collectivist (collectively sanctioned) goods and activities for certain individualist good and activities that are collectively discouraged or prohibited. Collectivist goods and activities are those sanctioned by the collectivist society. Examples of collectivist good and services include female wardrobe sanctioned by the collectivist community, such as sanctioned dress-code, for example, *hijab, niqab,* or *burka* (according to the societal degrees of conservatism and collectivism), staying at home, socializing only with other females, going to all-girl schools, all-female-stores, and so on. They also include purchasing sanctioned goods, books, media and entertainment materials (sometimes in collectively sanctioned and subsidized stores and outlets), participating in sanctioned activities (religions and all female activities) approved and recommended by the collectivist community.

In General, women, in gender-discriminating collectivist societies such as the Arab world, lack status and access to certain individualists goods and behaviors, for example, their choice of wardrobe, leaving the house without permission or in the company of the spouse or a male *mahram*, socializing with non-related individuals, traveling without consent or the company of the spouse or a male *mahram*, participating in social activities (such as sport, arts, cultural, political, and entertainment events that take place in the public sphere), working without a consent from their male guardians, applying for certain jobs or working in certain shifts, being admitted to hospitals or having certain medical procedures, falling in unsanctioned love, marrying without permission or consent, divorcing, and so on. In contrast, men have access to wider varieties of goods, and all activities and events in the public sphere, due to the effective dichotomy of spheres in the Arab world and other similar countries, in which men have unrestricted access to the public sphere, supported by informal norms and formal rules that restrict women's presence in the public sphere, and the collectively assigned private sphere for women, their residences. In addition, men have unconditional and unlimited access to the private sphere.

Women's access to the public sphere, and thus to goods and activities that belong to the public sphere, depends on the degree of gender discrimination and collectivism each society or country. Saudi Arabia and Yemen are usually ranked the most collectivist societies in the Arab world, accompanied with the strictest norms and rules against women's presence in the public sphere and access to status and certain unsanctioned individualist goods. In contrast, Lebanon and Tunisia are usually ranked the least collectivist societies in the Arab world (Kelly and Breslin 2010).

Norms and Allocation of Individualist Goods: A Simple Model

Appendix 8.2 provides a simple model of women's choices between collectively sanctioned goods (referred to as collectivist goods) and collectively unsanctioned goods (referred to as individualist goods). In the absence of gender-discriminating norms, women will choose the optimal amounts of collectivist and individualist goods and activities according to the market price (or cost) of these goods and according to women's preferences (point E_0 in figure A8.2.1 in the appendix).

To control or limit women's access to unsanctioned goods and activities, the gender-discriminating society can impose a price barrier to increase the cost of acquiring or accessing the good or quantitative barriers, such a ceiling (a maximum level) on the targeted good or behavior. The collectivist society can increase the price though specific taxes on goods, and through imposing higher thresholds or requirements on activities. Examples of this would be requiring females to be accompanied by a male *mahram* to leave the house or to travel (if they are prohibited from driving, or going out by themselves), increasing the cost of female employment by forcing them to rent a cab to go to work, requiring permission from male guardians to be admitted to the hospital or before certain medical procedures, requiring permission to get married, or to choose a field of study, or to apply for a job.

Kuwait University's requirement is that female students must maintain a higher grade-point average than male students to be admitted into certain fields, for example the engineering department. This is an example of increasing the cost (by imposing a higher threshold) on women seeking certain unsanctioned individualist goods or acts (Kelly and Breslin 2010).

The virtue police in Saudi Arabia (and similar collectivist vigilantes in other Arab countries) punish women who defy the collectively assigned wardrobe (*abaya*), for laughing or speaking loudly (to draw attention) or for walking in a way to attract attention to their adornments, according to their level of defiance (more lashing is imposed for defiance that is more aggressive). A 2004 study by Freedom House in Egypt highlights a collective backlash to women's relative freedom to choose their attire. Women, not adhering to the collective norm of covering their head and wearing long dresses, were harassed, and some were attacked by men because they did not adhere to the collectively assigned dress code. The rise in sexual harassment was blamed in part on claims that women are not dressing as modestly as they did in the past (Katulis 2004: 9). Since the veil became the collectively assigned attire, anything less than that can be considered more revealing, indecent, and imitating foreign immoral cultures. Increasing the cost of unsanctioned individualist goods reduces their demand of such goods (point E_1 in figure A8.2.1).

The collectivist society can impose quantitative constraints on women's access to certain individualist good and activities, as is shown in point E_2 in figure A8.2.1. Examples of such constraints include limited working hours, being forbidden from working night shifts, limited access to certain jobs that seem dangerous or immoral, access to only one husband in countries that permit polygyny (men's access to marry more than one wife), and so on (Kelly and Breslin 2010; Human Rights Watch 2014a; U.S. DOSa 2014).

In extreme cases, the collective community can impose extreme prohibitive access to certain goods and activities. In such a case, women only access the sanctioned good. The ban (zero access) on unsanctioned goods and activities is shown in point E_3 in figure A8.2.1. To enforce a ban on certain goods or behaviors, strict collective punishment (by virtue police, the *hisbah*, or collectivist vigilantes, and formal laws) must accompany the ban. For example, women who drive cars in Saudi Arabia even when accompanied with their male guardians have been arrested, and their guardians have been punished as well (France 24 2014a). In many Arab countries, women have zero access to watch public sport events, since it may violate the norms of sex segregation in the public sphere. In December 2014, the Saudi police arrested a woman who disguised herself as a man to be able to watch a soccer match (Arab News 2014). In Algeria, the government, for the first time in 2014, allocated certain sections in stadiums for women. Algerian women used to be banned from watching soccer games in stadiums due to prohibiting social norms. Men used to have a monopoly on watching soccer games in Algeria, rejecting women's presence there since it hurts their virility and ego (France 24 2014b).

Norms and Women's Clothing

The social norms regarding women's clothing and appearance, in the Arab world (and other similar Muslim countries) are abundant. They mostly come from religious sources, such as the *Qur'an*, for example (the *Qur'an* 24:30–31; 33:59) and *hadiths* that warn against certain choices regarding women's clothing, appearance, and behaviors. For example, the Prophet said, "I will not be a witness for two types of people who are destined for the Fire: . . . and women who although clothed, are yet naked, seducing and being seduced, their hair styled like the tilted humps of camels. These will not enter the Garden nor will its fragrance even reach them, although its fragrance reaches a very great distance" (in Al-Qaradawi 1997: 83). Also, "The woman who perfumes herself and passes through a gathering is a *zaniyah* (adulteress or fornicatress)" (Al-Qaradwai 1997:162). In contrast, men are permitted to wear perfume, since the Prophet used to wear perfume. In addition, the Prophet cursed women who used artificial hair (wigs or hairpieces) and women who make them. Also cursed are women who shorten their teeth or widen the gap between them for beauty, women who pluck their eyebrows (too thin or shape them), women with tattoos, and women who tattoo. Moreover, women who imitate men in clothing or behaviors are cursed too (Al-Qaradawi 1997: 88). According to sacred norms, a Muslim woman's clothes should cover her entire body, be non-transparent, not too tight, and should not imitate men's or foreigner's clothes. Women should also not be too pleasant when speaking in public and should not draw men's attention by using perfume or jingling or toying with their ornaments. Women, when dressed properly, are allowed to serve their husbands' guests only during the presence of their husbands (Al-Qaradawi 1997). These examples underscore the detailed degree of specificities of sacred teachings that still influence norms and rules associated with women's appearance and behaviors, which in turn, constrain women's choices and prohibit certain behaviors and acts, especially in collectivist societies that adhere to these norms.

Furthermore, the Prophet commands Muslim believers not to imitate the non-Muslims, in their appearance. This command highlights, in part, why conservative Muslims and collectivist Islamic communities distinguish themselves from other population groups, using Islamic clothing and appearances as an identifier or a social marker. For example, the Prophet instructed Muslim men to dye their hair, trim their mustaches, and grow their beard to differentiate themselves from Christians and Jews who do not dye their hair and grow their mustaches, in order to develop Islamic distinctive and independent characteristics in appearance and behavior (Al-Qaradawi 1997). Therefore, such norms regarding appearance and behaviors serve as differentiating physical and social markers that separate women from men and Muslims from non-Muslims.

Norms and Women's Clothing: Case Studies
As explained above, according to sacred norms in the *Qur'an* and *hadith*, women are commanded to cover themselves. Women's bodies should be covered except

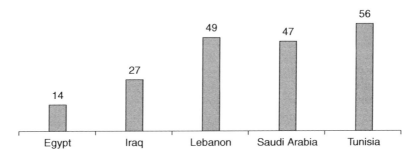

Figure 8.2　Percentage of respondents who agree with the statement, "Women Should Be Able to Choose their Own Clothing."
Source:　Data collected from Moaddel (2013).

their face and hands. Thus, women's choice of dress reflects their degree of freedom to choose among varieties of individualist goods. A recent study on selected Arab countries (Egypt, Iraq, Lebanon, Saudi Arabia, and Tunisia) shows the influence of norms and women's access to individualist goods, such as women's clothing. Figure 8.2 shows that more than 50 percent of respondents (except Tunisia) agree that women should not be able to choose their own clothing; rather, they should adhere to the collectively assigned clothing, influenced by sacred norms that are accepted and sometimes imposed.

When asked which dress style is the most appropriate for women in public places, the most common response was the *hijab* (with hair, neck, and ear fully covered). In Tunisia, agreement for this was 57 percent, with Egypt at 52 percent, and Iraq at 44 percent. Sixty-three percent of Saudis (the most collectivist country in the Arab world) chose the *niqab*, which exposes only women's eyes and hands. In contrast, 49 percent of Lebanese (the least collectivist society in the Arab world) chose no head cover as the most appropriate dress (the sample in Lebanon included 27% Christians) (Moaddel 2013; Poushter 2014). The survey highlights the influence of sacred norms on what is considered proper for women to wear in public places. It also highlights the large gap of choices between strict collectivist societies, such as Saudi Arabia, and relatively individualist (or less collectivist) societies, such as Lebanon.

The Head of Al-Azhar Institutes (Al-Azhar is the largest and leading Islamic institution in Egypt) issued a statement in 2014, requiring female employees to wear loose clothing and prohibiting the use of cosmetics. The new guideline specifies that all female employees must commit to the proper attire for Muslim women. Clothing should be loose, such that they do not specify the details of women's bodies and to give the impression of commitment and dignity. Female employees must abandon finery. Some female teachers, who asked to be anonymous, shared that the freedom to choose clothing is for all, and that they are keen to wear clothes worthy of the teachings of Islam without the need of such publications (El-Fagr 2014).

In Sudan, the police arrested women for wearing trousers, violating the country's Islamic law. The court ordered some of them to be flogged in public (NBC News 2009). One of the arrested women, Lubna Hussein, a Sudanese lawyer and Journalist, challenged the charges. She gained international fame and publicity when she announced that she would not pay the financial fine imposed on her by a Sudanese court for wearing pants in public. She said "When I think of my trial, I pray that my daughters will never live in fear of these police... We will only be secure once the police protect us and these laws are repealed." She was also ready "to receive (even) 40,000 lashes" if that what it takes to abolish the law (CBS News 2009).

In November 2014, the Sudanese State Television ordered all its female employees to change their appearance, prohibiting dresses with bright colors or heavy makeup (Amin 2014). In 2013, Amira Osman, a Sudanese female activist was sentenced to 40 lashes for acting in a manner contrary to public morals when she refused to cover her hair (Amin 2014).

Women' Access to the Public Sphere

In addition, according to sacred norms, women also should not leave their home without permission from their husbands or male guardians, preferably only when necessary. Women must wash all traces of perfume before leaving home to attend mosque for prayer. In contrast, men are free to go out of the house, work, travel about, mix with other people, and are permitted to wear perfume in public. Men, according to widely accepted interpretation of *shari'ah*, are thought to be weaker than women, are to give in to sexual thoughts and desires, thus there is more burden laid on women's appearance and behavior in the public sphere. Azar Nafisi (2003b) underscores how women's appearance can cause *fitna* (disorderly behavior), that is, men's disorderly behaviors when sexually tempted by women, driving men to destruction and distraction. The Prophet warned in a *hadith*, "there is no *fitna* more harmful to men than women" (Sherif-Trask 2004: 397). To avoid such a *fitna*, certain separation of the sexes must take place in the public sphere, accompanied with constraints on women's appearance and behaviors that serve to avoid such *fitna*, such as covering the body, limited access to certain public spheres, and preferred confinement of women in the private sphere, except for necessities (Nafisi 2003b; Sherif-Trask 2004; Al-Qaradawi 1997). The following *fatwa* from the Permanent Council for Scientific Research and Legal Opinions (the official institution entrusted with issuing *fatwas*), underscores how societies must prevent *fitna* by imposing strict constraints on women's appearance and access to public sphere, "God Almighty... commended women to remain in their homes. Their presence in the public is the main contributing factor to the spread of *fitna* [strife]. Yes, the *Shari'ah* permits women to leave their home only when necessary, provided that they wear *hijab* and avoid all suspicious situations. However, the general rule is that they should remain at home" (Human Rights Watch 2008: 6).

Norms and Women's Right to Drive

The capability to drive and the actual functioning of driving are examples of women's access to status and individualist goods. Driving gives women more access to the public sphere, which is not sanctioned for women in some conservative societies in the Arab world, such as Saudi Arabia. The following *fatwa* by the Grand *Mufti* of Saudi Arabia underscores the social and moral harms of giving women the access and freedom in the public sphere, "There is no doubt that such [women driving cars] is not allowed. Women driving leads to many evils and negative consequences. Included among these is her mixing with men without her being on her guard. It also leads to the evil sins due to which such an action is forbidden." (Al-Musnad 1996: 310). He supported his fatwa with a *qur'anic* verse, "And [women] stay quietly in your houses, and make not a dazzling display, like that of the former Times of Ignorance..." (the *Qur'an* 33:33).

Driving can be considered a status good that gives women access to orchestration power in terms of their capability to leave their home, access the public sphere, and access to certain unsanctioned activities. This leads to the norm of prohibiting *khalwa* in many parts of the Arab world and similar Islamic countries. *khalwa* (the meeting of a women and a non-*mahram* man, or the meeting of a woman and unrelated man) is prohibited according to the prophetic *hadiths*, "Whoever believes in Allah and the Last Day must never be in privacy with woman without there being a *mahram* (of hers) with her, for otherwise Satan will be the third person (with them)" (in Al-Qaradawi 1997: 147). Also, "A man is never alone with a woman except that Satan is the third" (in Al-Musnad 1996: 311). Some Saudi clerics made extreme excuses to support the ban on women driving, for example, driving may excite women sexually and lead them to behave erratically, and driving may affect their ovaries (Begum 2013).

Saudi women who drove their cars in protest of the 1990's ban on women driving were met with harsh punishment. They were arrested, their passports were confiscated, they were fired from their jobs (the employed ones), prohibited from speaking to the press, and were released after their male guardians signed pledges to not allow them to drive again (Human Rights Watch 2008). The purpose of such severe punishments is to send a clear signal that such violations will not be tolerated, such that the punishments must outweigh any feasible benefit for women exercising their capability to drive.

The above may explain the reluctance of the Saudi society to give women access to privacy or the public sphere for the fear of illicit social contacts with men, which can tarnish their reputation, and damage their families' and communities' honor and pride. Sacred norms and their enforcement may also explain the lack of collective support to the victims of sexual harassment and sexual violence (including rape), since female members should not be in contact with unrelated men in public sphere.

In 2008, the Saudi Consultative Council recommended that women above 30-years of age be allowed to drive under the conditions that they have permission from their legal guardians, drive during daylight, carry a cell phone, and wear modest clothes (Doumato 2010). The same recommendation was repeated in late 2014 (BBC 2014b); no decision has been made so far. Even, if these recommendations pass, women will still be treated as minors.

Norms and Women's Participation In Sports and Sporting Events

In response to a question regarding women practicing sports or exercising in public athletic clubs, a *fatwa* states that women should practice sport activities that do not require leaving their homes. The fatwa also mentioned the benefits of women's housework, Islamic prayer (involving standing, bending and kneeling), and diet on women's health (Islamweb.net 2001).

In addition, according to a prophetic *hadith*, "A woman who removes her clothes (i.e., goes naked) outside her husband's house tears down the veil (*sitr*) between herself and her Lord" (Al-Qaradawi 1997: 158). The significance of this *hadith* stems from its instruction that women should never change their clothes outside their homes, for example in athletic clubs, especially with the presence of advanced spying technologies (taking pictures) that can be exploited to tarnish their reputation and disgrace the honor of their families.

Professor Amna Nosseir (female professor of Islamic doctrine and philosophy at Al-Azhar University, Egypt) sees no contradiction between the Islamic faith and female participation in sporting events as long as the woman is dressed properly (wearing *hijab*). Nosseir recommends that women can practice light sports and refrain from "violent" sports. She warns women from going to athletic clubs in which women mix with men to protect women's reputation, adding that women must be trained by a female coach, such that no male can touch them or to get to know specific details about their bodies. Other professors of Islamic doctrine and jurisprudence agreed with Dr. Nossier. They added that men, spectators or otherwise, must not be allowed in women's sporting events and such events must not be broadcasted. Moreover, women must not participate in sporting events that make them imitate men, such as wrestling, boxing, auto racing, and so on. This is based on the prophetic *hadith* that women who imitate men are cursed (Islamweb.net 2001; Al-Bayan 2009). Women also should not swim or participate in swimming sports that require wearing swimsuits (or otherwise) that show parts of their bodies (Al-Bayan 2009). According to *hadith*, a man's *'awra* (body parts that must be covered) only includes the area between the naval and the knees, such that wearing long shorts satisfies the *shari'ah* requirements. However, a woman *'awra* covers all her body, except her face and her hands (Al-Qaradawi 1997), which add more constraints on women practicing sports.

Women and girls are banned from practicing sports in Saudi Arabia. However, Saudi Arabia sent two Saudi female players (who have been raised and trained outside Saudi Arabia for several years) to the 2012 London Olympics for the first time in the country's history after immense pressure from the International Olympics Committee which threatened to exclude the entire Saudi team if the country does not comply with the Olympic Charter of racial and gender equality. The senior sport official in Saudi Arabia, Prince Nawaf bin Faisal, said that women could participate if they "wear suitable clothing that complies with *Sharia*[sic] law, are accompanied by their guardian...and they do not mix with men during the games..." (Shihab-Eldin 2012). Abeer, a 26-year old Saudi female, underscores the collective pressure on Saudi females to play sport, in her reaction to the first two Saudi female athletes participating in the 2012 Olympics, "I wish the girls in the Olympics well, but it's not something I would do. And even if I did, my father would not even consider it. There is too much at stake. Even if my family supported my right to compete in sports, our relatives, our neighbors would condemn it. There is too much at stake. It just does not affect me but my entire family" (Willis 2012). Another Saudi academic female expresses the immense pressure on families letting their daughter participate in sporting events, "It's almost incomprehensible to the average Saudi to see a beloved daughter on television parading on the field for all to see...It is too much for family members to see their daughters exerting themselves in some outfit even remotely form-fitting. It is a big shame for the family. As hard as it is to understand, it boils down to 'what will the neighbors think'" (Willis 2012). In 2014, Saudi Arabia did not send any females with its 199 male athletes to the seventeenth Asian Games, South Korea (Linden 2014).

In March 2014, The UN Relief and Work Agency (UNRWA) sponsored a marathon in Gaza, Palestine, which was canceled after the governing Islamist Hamas movement refused to allow female runners to participate in the marathon. Hamas said the marathon could go ahead if local traditions were respected, "We regret this decision to cancel the marathon, but we don't want men and women running together...We did not tell UNRWA to cancel the marathon and we haven't prevented it, but we laid down some conditions: We don't want women and men mixing in the same place," said Abdelssalam Siyyam, cabinet secretary of the Hamas government (BBC 2013b). Previous summer camps for children in Gaza were attacked after complaints that boys were allowed to mix with girls.

Another commonly held belief is that physical exercise and sports can tear girls' hymeneal tissue, leading to the loss of virginity which would tarnish the girl's reputation and disgrace her family and community. Girls' virginity, preserved in an intact hymen, is one of the most treasured collective assets in many gender-discriminating collective societies in the Arab world. The collective fear and anxiety of losing girls' virginity (if the hymen is torn) is high enough to exclude girls from such activities.

Norms and Women's Access to Health and Medical Treatment

In some gender-discriminating societies, women must get permission from their male guardians with regard to medical treatment, admission to, or release from a hospital. Women's dependency on male guardians reflects their lack of status goods. Such decisions are examples of orchestration powers, as stated by a Saudi woman, "Even if you go to a hospital for an operation, you need a guardian. It's your life. Why do you need his signature?" (Human Rights Watch 2008: 12). In certain cases, women and girls are not allowed to get medical attention or treatment if a female doctor is not available (Weiner 2004). Dealing with women in labor is critical in Saudi Arabia, if a pregnant woman arrives to a hospital without a male guardian, due to the fear that the pregnancy is related to an extramarital affair. According to a Saudi doctor, "If a [pregnant] woman comes in to the hospital with a guardian, then she can leave with anyone, even the driver. If she comes in without a guardian, it becomes a "police case," and she'll need a guardian to come to the hospital in order for her to get discharged. She stays here if no one picks her up" (Human Rights Watch 2008: 13). In 2013, a Saudi hospital postponed the amputation of an injured woman's hand because she did not have a male guardian; her husband, who died in the auto accident that hurt her, was not there to authorize the procedure (Human Rights Watch 2013). The need of a male guardian's authorization for medical treatments is very costly to foreign women who have been divorced by their Saudi husbands, since they do not have male guardians in Saudi Arabia (Human Rights Watch 2013).

These are just examples of treating women as second-class citizens, legal minors, who lack status goods and need someone else to make decisions on their behalf.

International Comparisons

The WHO's 2014 World Health Statistics highlights two statistics that can be used to measure women's access to certain individualist goods: The female-to-male ratio of smokers, and the female-to-male ratio of obesity.

Women are discouraged from smoking in the Arab world. Most societies in the Arab world believe smoking is a bad habit that taints the reputation of women. They view such activity as an illicit imitation of both men who smoke, and foreign women. These imitations are criticized and condemned in Islamic societies according to prevailing norms and sacred teaching. Women are also discouraged from smoking since it is considered a behavior that aims to equate women to men and is a sign of women's independence (The Islamic Awareness 2010; Al-Bayan 2013). Figure 8.3 shows the ratio of female-to-male smokers. Most Arab countries, 12 of 14, are significantly below the world average of 22 percent. The low ratios in the Arab world highlight the influence of gender-discriminating norms on women's access to smoking as an individualist.

The second comparison is the female-to-male obesity ratio. Figure 8.4 shows that female-male ratios of obese in most Arab countries—15 out of 19—are much higher than the world's ratio. As explained earlier, women's confinement to the private sphere, lack of access to physical education in some Arab countries, and lack of access to athletic clubs or health spas compared to men's access to both the public sphere and athletic clubs, and to exercise and play sports can explain, in part, the higher ratios.

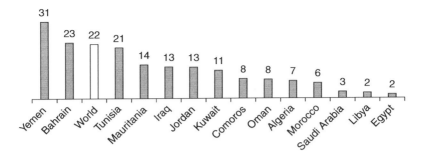

Figure 8.3 Adult female-male smoker ratio (%) Arab countries and the world, 2011.
Source: Date collected from World Health Organization (WHO) (2014). World Health Statistics 2014. Table 5: 118–127.

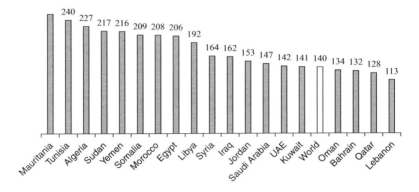

Figure 8.4 Female-male ratio of adult≥20 who are obese, 2008 (%).
The ratio for Mauritania is 542.
Source: Date collected from World Health Organization (WHO) (2014). World Health Statistics 2014. Table 5: 118–127.

Other Examples of Norms and Women's Access to Individualist Goods and Behaviors

Gender-discriminating norms in the Arab world impose higher costs and thresholds on women to access certain goods and behaviors, compared to men, in addition to prohibiting women's access (zero access) to certain goods and behaviors. The following list gives examples of such goods and behaviors in the Arab world:

- A wife cannot fast without the permission of her husband. A husband can fast without any need for permission from his wife.
- A wife is required to satisfy her husband's sexual needs upon his request (unless sick or menstruating); otherwise she is condemned. This norm applies to wives only, not husbands.

- A husband has access to satisfy his sexual need with his other wives (if he has more than one wife). A woman can be married to one man only. In such a case, she must share him with the other wives.
- A husband who fears disloyalty or disobedience from his wife can discipline her physically (beat her). A wife who fears disloyalty or ill treatment from her husband is advised to settle with her husband and be obedient.
- A husband can divorce his wife with ease by verbally stating that he repudiates her. A wife must file a legal request to the court and must provide proof to support her request for divorce. Legal requests are costly, difficult to prove, take a long time, and can be rejected.
- Men have unrestricted access to the public sphere. Women's access is restricted.
- Women may need to get permission from their male guardians (husband or a close male relative) to leave the house and to have access to the public sphere.
- Women may need to have permission from their male guardians to apply for passports. Men do not need any permission to get passports.
- Men can travel freely without any restrictions. Women may be required to be accompanied by male guardians, especially for international traveling.
- Women may need permission from their male guardians to work.
- Women may be banned from certain fields of education that are deemed inappropriate for women.
- Women may be banned from certain jobs, especially what is collectively deemed dangerous or immoral.
- Women may be banned from working in late shifts.
- Women may be excluded from certain leadership positions.
- Women may be banned from driving.
- Women do not have access to file complaints against certain domestic violence crimes.
- Muslim women cannot marry non-Muslim men; however, Muslim men can marry non-Muslim women (e.g., Christians and Jews).
- Foreign wives and children of national men can have automatic citizenship rights. In contrast, foreign husbands and children of national women do not have such rights in most Arab countries.
- A Muslim female's share of inheritance is a fraction (usually half) of an equivalent male's share.
- The legal value of a female witness is a fraction of the value of a male witness in civil cases. In serious criminal cases, women are considered incompetent witnesses.
- Women may not have access to vote or to run for certain political or judicial offices.
- The money compensation paid to the family of a female victim is only a fraction (usually half) of that of male victim.

The above examples illustrate women's lack of status and their restricted access to certain individualist goods and behaviors, which are not restricted to men in many gender-discriminating societies in the Arab world. In certain cases, women are excluded from certain goods and activities accessible to men. The prevalence of the above examples depend on the degrees of collectivism in different countries, where the above list (or most items mentioned) are prevalent in most collectivist countries, for example, Saudi Arabia and Yemen, and less prevalent (or absent) in other less collectivist countries, for example, Lebanon and Tunisia.

Summary

This chapter explains, using a simple model, how gender-discriminating norms and rules deprive or exclude women from status goods, that is, their ability to make decisions on their own and their share in the collective units' (e.g., families') decision-making process. The chapter draws attention to how male and male-dominated collectivist units gain status and orchestration power, and impose certain collectivist goods on women—depriving them from their own choices of individualist goods. Case studies are used to illustrate how gender-discriminating norms distort women's choices and limit their access to certain individualist goods and behaviors in the Arab world such as women's wardrobe and access to public sphere.

Appendix 8.1: A Model of Allocating Status Goods between Females and Males

Assume a fixed stock of status goods equals one, and an implicit price of the status good of one. The status good is to be allocated the community members: a female, F, and a male, M. The budget constraint is $F + M = 1$. Also, assume a simple Cobb-Douglass welfare function, $W = F^{.5}M^{.5}$. In equilibrium, F and M will share the status good equally, 0.5 each.

Allocating status goods in an individualist society: in the case of no gender bias, the female-male ratio, $F/M = 1$ in equilibrium, at E_{ind}, where the female's share of the status good equals the male's share, each has one-half of the status good, since the marginal values (or utility) of the status goods attached to female and male are equal, as is illustrated in figure A8.1.1.

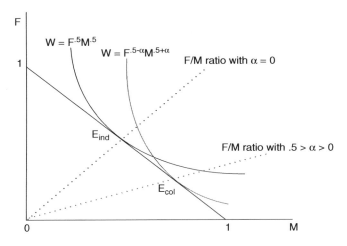

Figure A8.1.1 Allocation of status goods: Preference$_{individualist}$: $W = F^{.5}M^{.5}$; Preference$_{collectivist}$: $W = F^{.5-\alpha}M^{.5+\alpha}$, where α refers to the male bias factor; Constraint: $F + M = 1$.

Allocating status goods in a gender-discriminating collectivist society: let α refer the bias against women in the welfare function, where $0 \leq \alpha \leq 0.5$. Higher α refers to a stronger gender bias against women. The welfare function becomes: $W_{col} = F^{.5-\alpha}M^{.5+\alpha}$, where W_{col} is the welfare function in a collectivist society. In equilibrium, $(F/M) = [.5 - \alpha]/[.5 + \alpha]$, with $0 \leq (F/M) \leq 0.5$. In the case of gender discrimination, women's share of status goods decreases with the rise of α, the male bias factor.

In an extreme case, where $\alpha = 0.5$, the female's share in the status good drops to zero, and male's share increase to one, The male members will control 100 percent of status goods, as is shown in figure A8.1.2. In such a case, male members of the collective unit will have absolute control over the decision-making process. Women should acclimate to men's choices and internalize cognitive dissonance resulting from their lack of the status good. When women violate the collectivist society's distribution of status goods, they expose themselves to the collective punishment, since rejecting their discounted share of status goods is similar to rejecting social norms. In the extreme case of gender discrimination, where $\alpha = 0.5$, females' share in status goods drops to zero, and males' share increase to one. In this case, the collective society drives all gain from allocation the status good to the male members, as is shown in figure A8.1.2.

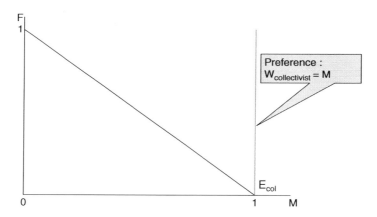

Figure A8.1.2   Case of extreme gender discrimination: Women's zero position of status goods: $\alpha = 0.5$.

Appendix 8.2: A Model of Allocating Collectivist–Individualist Goods

In societies where gender discrimination is widespread and accepted, collectivist women and pressured individualist women are likely to substitute collectivist goods and activities for individualist goods activities.

Let X be an index (or vector) of collectivist goods: goods that confer utility to the collectivist unit. Collectivist goods confer utility to the collectivist unit; however, they may generate negative utility (disutility) to the female members of the collectivist unit who are pressured or forced to use these collectivist goods.

Let Y be an index (or vector) of individualist goods. They confer utility to the ultimate individual users, participating women in this case. Certain individualist goods may violate certain sanctioned collectivist norms and rules as shown in the chapter. The collectivist societies are likely to restrict, or ban, women's access to these unsanctioned good and behaviors.

Let P_x the price index (or cost) of X; P_y the price index (or cost) of Y; and the following Cobb-Douglass utility function: $U = X^\alpha Y^\beta$.

Equilibrium in an individualist society: the objective function, $U = X^{.5} Y^{.5}$ subject to $I \geq P_x X + P_y Y$.

The equilibrium (X_0 and Y_0) at point E_0 as is shown in figure A8.2.1.

Now, assume that the collectivist society raises the price (or opportunity cost) of individualist goods to $P_y(1+a)$, where "a" is the higher cost of individualist goods. The higher prices/costs of individualist goods are likely to cause women to substitute the less costly collectivist goods for the more costly individualist goods.[4]

Figure A8.2.1 shows women's choice (more specifically, the choices available to women) of individualist goods decreases from Y_0 (in the case of no distortion) to Y_1 (in the case higher cost of Y), and to Y_2 when a ceiling is imposed on women's access to individualist goods. In the case of prohibited goods or activities (i.e., a zero ceiling), Y will drop to zero. In such a case women have access only to collectivist goods, X.

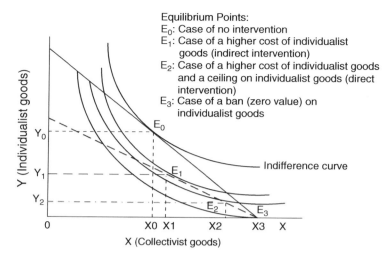

Figure A8.2.1 Gender discrimination and women's choice between individualist and collectivist goods.

This simple model shows that women in collectivist societies are more likely to replace individualist goods with collectivist goods due to the higher costs of attaining individualist goods. Imposing a quantity ceiling will limit their choices and reduce their utility levels. In summary, women are induced or even forced, indirectly (through increasing cost of individualist goods) or directly (through a ceiling or a quota on the amount of individualist goods), to alter their choices.

The model can be extended to show the case of prohibited individualist goods that violate collectivist norms, such as living alone, traveling alone, having a relation that is prohibited, or choosing individualist goods that violate the collectivist norms drastically. In such a case, the quantity ceiling can be set at zero for such individualist goods.

The model can also be extended to show the effect of gender-discriminating norms in terms of the effect of these norms on the preference (utility) function. This reflects the bias toward the collectivist goods and against the individualist goods, which in turn causes the indifference curve to be steeper, leading to more collectivist goods and less individualist goods. In extreme cases, this lead to a corner solution with zero individualist goods.

Discriminating informal norms can enter this simple model in the utility function, "a," the budget constraint, "b," and the ceiling on the amount of individualist goods women can get, $\overline{Y}$.

$U = X^{.5+a} Y^{.5-a}$, where $0 \leq a \leq 0.5$ where "a" represents the collectivist preference toward X and away from Y, subject to the constraints: $I = P_x X + P_y (1 + b)Y$, and $Y \leq \overline{Y}$.

In equilibrium, $X = (.5 Ĺ a)I/P_x$ and $Y = (.5 - a)I/[(1 Ĺ b)P_y]$ where $Y \leq \overline{Y}$.

As is shown, the equilibrium value of Y is reduced by three factors: a, b, and $\overline{Y}$ Higher a and b and lower $\overline{Y}$ will lower the equilibrium value of Y.

CHAPTER 9

Measuring Gender Discrimination

The Problem: "There Is No Problem"

Certain practices of gender discrimination in many societies do not exist on official records; there are no official records of domestic violence and spousal rape in the Arab world. At best, they are reduced to secondary problems rather than primary problems. The collectivist unit of reference or measurement (family, tribe, larger community) usually discounts or disregards the negative effects of collective decisions on women in such societies. The lack of women's effective participation in the collective decision-making process is likely to discount women's interests or preferences. In certain cases, women are excluded from the decision-making process altogether. Certain acts of violence are not treated as acts of violence in these societies, partly due to the absence or lack of victims' voice and status.

In addition, the cumulative effects of inherited gender-discriminating norms and rules make these norms and practices integral part of the daily life for both the perpetrators and victims. They are therefore not to be counted as gender violence or other forms of gender discrimination, especially when such norms are classified as sacred. Furthermore, domestic violence incidents are less likely to be addressed or reported in the public sphere.

In certain societies, domestic violence and other forms of gender discrimination may not be considered problems when the loss of women's well-being is more than offset by a gain in men's, or the collective unit's status.[1] "Laws ostensibly intended to address violence against women often define violence very narrowly or entail evidentiary requirement for proving violence that are extremely burdensome" (The World Bank 2001: 119). Therefore, official records will fail to record many incidences of gender discrimination and violence against women. The true problem becomes the mindset that "there is no problem." The absence of "official" records of gender violence, such as domestic violence and spousal rape, conceals and perpetuates such appalling practices in many societies. Consequently, the silence of the victims of domestic violence should not be considered as the last word (Nussbaum 2000), rather it should be approached as a starting step in deciphering these appalling human rights violations, and consequently confronting and eradicating them.

Official records of violence may not be documented due to many factors, such as preserving national pride, avoiding international sanctions or boycott, protecting the collectivist units, upholding cultural heritage and identity, denying the prevalence of shameful and inhumane practices, and, sustaining certain beliefs that condone or even endorse gender discrimination and violence against women.

No Unit of Measurement: Domestic Violence and Spousal Rape

Domestic violence and spousal rape are examples of social norms that are not considered violations of women's human rights according to social norms rooted in sacred texts and teachings in many societies, including the Arab world. According to prevalent interpretations of sacred norms rooted in the *Qur'an, hadith*, and other sacred texts, certain forms of physical discipline against women are condoned and even sanctioned as a last resort against disobedient women.

According to sacred norms and teachings in Muslim societies, men have access to their wives to satisfy their sexual needs at their will. Wives should respond obediently to the needs of their husbands according to this socially assigned identity and role of women. No reasons, other than sickness of menstruation, should prevent a wife from not satisfying her husbands' sexual needs. In these societies, spousal rape or forced sex do not exist on records, since women are taught to act according to their husbands' wills.

Spousal Rape: When Gender Violence Is Not Violence

Norms rooted in sacred teachings show that obedient woman are blessed, and women who act defiantly toward their husbands are cursed. For example, Prophet Muhammad said, "If a man invites his wife to sleep with him and she refuses to come to him, then the angels send their curses on her till morning."[2] In a similar *hadith*, the angels will curse the woman until she responds to her husband's desire.

Further *hadiths* demand wives to be subordinate to their husbands in other areas of daily living. One *hadith* states that a wife should seek their husband's permission before starting voluntary fasting. The Prophet said, "A woman should not fast (optional fasts) except with her husband's permission if he is at home (staying with her)."[3] Since sacred teaching commands the fasting person to abstain from sexual acts, a wife who plans to fast must obtain permission from her husband. Husbands do not need permission from their wives to fast. Wives, according to this norm, are expected to accommodate their husbands' sexual needs even at the expense of skipping a sacred act of voluntary fasting, giving their husbands' sexual satisfaction more credence than their religious desires. This reflects the skewed distribution of status (or status goods), favoring men in gender-discriminating societies. Thus, as a concept, spousal rape does not exist in certain gender-discriminating societies. As a result, many countries reject the claim that spousal rape is a form of gender violence or a violation of women's human rights, and therefore voice reservations to many articles in universal human rights' treaties and conventions.

Since spousal rape is not a crime or a violation of women's rights in the Arab world, there is no unit of reference or measurement, and no official statistics. The case of spousal rape is an extreme example of discounting women's weight in the well-being of the collective unit to zero, such that the harm inflicted on women does not affect the collective unit's welfare.

Abusive husbands are able to force their wives to have sex involuntarily just to affirm their manhood, humiliate their wives, or retaliate against previous acts of disobedience by their wives. However, Islamic teaching, in general, advise against such an abuse, for example, the Prophet said, "None of you should flog his wife as he flogs a slave and then have sexual intercourse with her in the last part of the day."[4]

Domestic Violence Is Not a Crime Unless It Crosses Sanctioned Levels

In debating whether to report domestic violence to an authority or not, the victims of gender violence must weigh the costs and benefits associated with potential outcomes, pursuing the least costly option.

Women in collectivist societies often think twice before filing legal complaints against their abusers—mostly their husbands, fathers, or brothers. Victims may not have the capability to leave their homes without permission from their male legal guardians (husband, father, or brother) according to existing sacred norms and rules. Leaving home to report violence can expose the victim to informal retribution from her collectivist unit, since this act violates her socially assigned identity. Moreover, the victim may not have access to health services to obtain treatment or to record the physical proof of injury required by law. She may not be able to afford the costs of hospital care or the cost of initiating a court case due to her financial dependence on males. Furthermore, her complaint may be rejected or ridiculed. In some countries, such as Yemen, a deputized male relative usually submit the female's complaint and speak on her behalf in the court (U.S. DOSa: Yemen 2014). In addition, she may fear being scorned or ridiculed by male health workers, police officers, or judges, "Laws are often enforced by male judges, prosecutors, and police officers who may share the abusers' value" (The World Bank 2001: 119). In many gender-discriminating societies, the victims are generally uninformed or misinformed about the process of filing a formal complaint due to their confinement in the private sphere (U.S. DOSa 2014).

The availability of other informal channels such as extended families or customary councils to report victims' grievances puts more pressure on the victims to forgo filing formal reports. Consequently, victims of domestic violence are likely to resign to informal mediation within the family or the collective unit, which are more likely to invoke the socially sanctioned gender-discriminating norms. Violating the assigned social norms exposes the victims to possible retribution from their abusive husbands or male siblings, especially when they lack other viable options. The court typically orders the victim to return to her abusive husbands or male guardians. This is prevalent outcome in many Arab countries, for example, Morocco and Saudi Arabia (U.S. DOSa 2014).

Laws such as a requirement for a minimum amount of days in the hospital for something to be considered abuse further prevent victims from filing formal complaints. Similarly, the legal requirement of minimum number of qualified witnesses (mostly males) to testify on behalf of the abused women is difficult to provide since most acts of domestic violence take place in the private sphere (U.S. DOSa 2014). Abused women typically face collectivist pressures from family and other collectivist members not to file formal complaints, since such filing may harm and stain the honor of the family or collectivist unit. Accordingly, women are less likely to file formal complaints in gender-discriminating collectivist societies.

Reports from various Arab countries underscore the high threshold of verifying gender violence (U. S. DOSa 2014; Human Rights Watch 2014a). For example, in Morocco, slow police response to reports of domestic violence, where husbands commit 80 percent of gender violence, is the norm. In addition, the police occasionally document complaints of domestic violence. Domestic violence is generally treated as a social rather than a criminal matter in most Arab states (Human Rights Watch 2014a; U.S. DOSa 2014). Due to the absence of specific laws against domestic violence, courts usually use existing criminal laws, for example, in Morocco, "By law high-level misdemeanors occur when a victim suffers injuries that result in 20 days of disability leave from work. Low-level misdemeanors occur when victims suffer disability for less than 20 days" (U. S. DOSa: Morocco 2014- section 6). Courts in Morocco rarely prosecute perpetrators of low-level misdemeanors.

Repeated failed cases of formal complaints serve to perpetuate domestic violence and other forms of gender discrimination. The typical victims of domestic violence learn that filing a complaint is likely to backfire. Their reputations will be tainted for acting defiantly against social norms in the eyes of other collectivist members. They will be perceived as uncooperative, disobedient, and selfish. They also know that certain forms of domestic violence are sanctioned or condoned as social norms and rules. Accordingly, the court may order them to return to their abusive husbands, fathers, or brothers, as the case in many Arab countries. Moreover, in Morocco, the penal code criminalizes individuals and NGOs, such as domestic violence shelters, if they hide or subvert the search of a married woman (U.S. DOSa: Morocco 2014).

In general, what matters in some gender-discriminating societies is not the violence and violation of women's bodily and emotional integrity per se, but rather, the degree of severity of domestic violence. Incidents of condoned or sanctioned domestic violence are not treated as crimes; They are treated as norms integral to cultural heritage and social order and harmony in these societies. For example, a 2011 survey in Egypt shows that 81 percent of men believe they have the right to beat their wives and daughters (U.S. DOSa 2014). Beating and disciplining disobedient women, within the socially sanctioned range, is usually internalized in the minds of perpetrators as well as the victims of the beating. Only excessive beatings that go beyond the socially sanctioned level can be considered acts of violence or assault.

Victims of domestic violence are usually advised to behave properly and obediently according to their socially assigned identities and roles to deter any physical disciplining from their husbands, fathers, or brothers. In case of excessive injuries, the victims are usually advised to refrain for instigating such violence when they act disobediently, to share their grievances internally within the collectivist community (family or tribe), and to accept its informal traditional judgment.

Victims may also resign themselves to the belief that they should blame themselves as the instigators of domestic violence, especially when they violate their assigned social roles, such as not cooking for their husband or burning the food, neglecting their children, leaving home without their husband's permission, not cleaning the home, raising their voices against their husbands, or rejecting/not satisfying their husband's sexual needs. Studies show that majority of women in the Arab world (see chapter 11 for more details), and other similar countries, believe that their husbands have the right to beat them if they violate their socially assigned roles and expectations (CHANGE 1999; Roumani 2006; Ghanim 2009; U.S. DOSa 2014; Human Rights Watch 2014a; UNICEF 2012, 2014). The victims may also accept domestic violence and adapt to it as an integral part of the cultural identity. In this mindset, violence is treated as a normal fact of life that should not diminish their self-worth or well-being, but simply be coped with. Furthermore, victims of domestic violence may acclimate to cognitive dissonance associated with domestic violence, either by blaming themselves as stated above, or through believing that somehow, especially through their faith, they will be rewarded for their obedience and tolerance of domestic violence.

Using the family, instead of each individual, as the unit of reference conceals the intra-family distributional bias, gender discrimination, and gender violence in the family. It means that the well-being of each individual is evaluated according to the weight attached to each individual in the collective unit, the family. Domestic violence against women may prevail since the weight attached to the perpetrators, mostly men, exceeds the weight attached to victims, mostly women. In contrast, in a typical individualist society, each individual has an equal weight of status good and the unit of reference belongs to each individual. This explains, in part, why women in individualist societies are more likely to report domestic violence and the police and court officials are likely to give the victims due justice by prosecuting the perpetrators. Consequently, victims of domestic violence in an individualist society are likely to report their grievances since their well-being is not discounted or summed up with other weights in collective units.

In summary, the threshold of injury is higher by design in gender-discriminating collectivist societies than in individualist societies. As stated above, the threshold of injury is associated with women's share in status goods: the lower women's share in the status good, the higher the threshold level of injury, in case of domestic violence or sexual assault.

The Likelihood of Reporting Domestic Violence in Individualist and Collectivist Societies

The following analysis and tree diagram (figure 9.1) explain why victims of domestic violence in gender-discriminating collectivist societies are less likely to report such incidents formally. This is based on three high thresholds: the threshold of reporting incidents of domestic violence (with probability α), the threshold of passing the medical requirement of injury (with probability β), and the legal threshold of proving the violent crime (with probability 0).

First, let α be the probability that abused women will file a formal complaint, seeking legal assistance. α is likely to be high in individualist societies with the prevalence of gender equality's norms and rules. In gender-discriminating collectivist societies, α is likely to be lower for many reasons. Fist, the victim may be hesitant to violate social norms by seeking external legal assistance outside her collectivist unit (family or tribe). She may feel internal shame of betraying her collectivist unit when she circumvents existing informal interventions or reconciliations. Second, the victim may fear violating other social norms such as leaving her residence without permission to file legal report of domestic violence. Third, she may fear harassment or ridicule by collectivist male police officers, lawyers, and judges. Fourth, she may fear a forced return to her abuser, according to existing norms and rules. Fifth, she may fear backlash from the abuser or other collectivist members. The compound informal fear is likely to lower the victim's likelihood of pursuing formal action outside her collective unit.

Second, let β be the probability that the victim's injury exceeds the legal threshold required to file a formal complaint. In individualist societies, β should be relatively high since any injury, or even a credible threat of violence or injury, is generally accepted as a form of criminal act of violence against women. However, gender-discriminating societies, with high thresholds of injury, such as formal documentations from a hospital attesting the severity of the injury and the duration of the victim's treatment in the hospital, lower β.

Third, let 0 be the probability of pursuing legal action, after passing the injury threshold requirement. 0 is a decreasing function of legal barriers such as the requirement of a minimum number of qualified witnesses, and the victim's access to the court system. 0 is likely to be high in individualist societies due to women's equality in filing legal complaints. In contrast, 0 is likely to be low in gender-discriminating societies that require excessive legal prerequisites before the case is accepted.

Figure 9.1 shows that in a perfectly individualist society with $0 = 1$, $\beta = 1$, and $0 = 1$, the victim will always report domestic violence and perpetrator will always be prosecuted. Accordingly, in individualist societies, women are more likely to report domestic violence incidences and the perpetrators will be

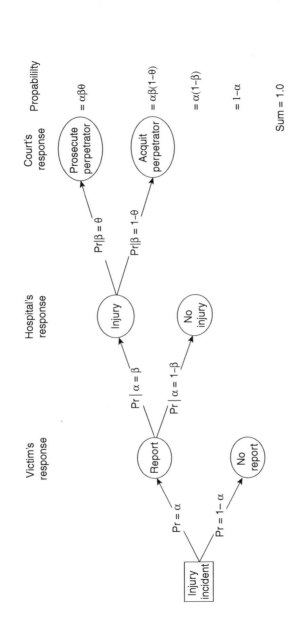

Figure 9.1 The likelihood of reporting incidents in case of a high threshold of injury.

prosecuted with a probability $\alpha\beta\theta$. In contrast, in gender-discriminating collectivist societies with low values of α, β, and θ, the likelihood that the victim of gender violence files a formal complaint drops significantly as explained above.

The likelihood that a victim of gender violence choose not to report incidences of domestic violence = $(1 - \alpha) + \alpha(1 - \beta) + \alpha\beta(1 - \theta) = 1 - \alpha\beta\theta$.

In summary, victims of domestic violence in individualist societies, with high α, β, and θ, are likely to report incidences of gender violence and receive proper justice and protection. In gender-discriminating collectivist societies, the combined effect of the higher costs associated with three phases: filing a formal report (with probability α), passing the medical threshold (with probability β), and passing the legal barriers (with probability θ), are likely reduce $\alpha\beta\theta$ significantly, convincing the victims of domestic violence to forgo formal reporting, accept the informal judgment, or acclimate to the cognitive dissilience associated with domestic violence.

Furthermore, women who file formal reports of domestic violence, in some Arab countries, may be subjected to accusation of lying or spreading false information, harassment, and even detention, as in Sudan (U.S. DOSa 2014).

Treating Women as Legal Minors

In many states in the Arab world, women are treated as legal minors under the guardianship of close male relatives such as husbands, fathers, or brothers. Treating women as minors or dependents limits their capabilities and freedoms. The designation of legal minor undermines both women's capabilities and their freedoms. It violates their "negative freedom," such as their freedom from violence, and their capabilities to seek legal assistance and prosecute their abusers, and the freedom from fear and feeling of subjugation. The designation also violates their "positive freedom," such as the freedom or capabilities to study, work, move and travel, buy and entertain individualist goods and services (such as wardrobe and cosmetics), watch and participate in sport, artistic, cultural, and political events, fall in love and marry the person of their choice, and to exit their societies and join other ones. These are just examples of what women may not be free or capable to do when they are treated as legal minors or dependents.

Designating women as minors deepens their dependency on their male legal guardians. For example, in Saudi Arabia, women are forbidden from traveling, concluding official businesses, or undergoing certain medical procedures without the permission of their legal guardians (U.S. DOSa 2014). They are also forbidden from playing sports or watching public sport events. Until recently, in Saudi Arabia, information regarding women's traveling abroad, such as their departure and arrival was automatically sent to their legal guardians (BBC 2012b). In most Arab countries, women cannot travel abroad without the company of or formal permission from their legal guardians (Human Rights Watch 2014a; U.S. DOSa 2014). In Yemen, women are restricted from exercising property rights, owning land, and accessing formal credit, especially in rural areas (U.S. DOSa 2014). In most Arab countries, women cannot get married without the presence of two male witnesses to the marriage contract, which is conducted by a male matrimonial guardian. Women cannot marry men of their choice, except with a permission from their male legal guardian, in most Arab countries. Forced marriages and underage marriages are related to treating women as legal minors where their male legal guardians make the decisions on their behalf (U.S. DOSa 2014).

Consequently, women are limited to collectively sanctioned goods, activities, and places. Examples include sanctioned wardrobes (*hijab*, *niqab*, or *burqa*), schooling (all female schools), and activities. Their capabilities to attain individualist goods such as clothing, cosmetics, and entertainment in public spheres are restricted if not forbidden in many Arab countries.

Treating women as minors or dependents removes their basic rights of defending themselves against certain human rights violations, such as physical discipline. It also has negative effect on women's share of status or positional goods. The share of legal guardians in status goods (their share in the decision-making process), outweighs the minors' share. Women, deprived from their capability to make decisions on their behalf, are constrained to accept choices made by their male guardians, even though these choices violate their human rights, and deform and restrict their capabilities and functionings.

In such a case, the minor victims face challenging barriers since they cannot exercise their capabilities and functionings to leave home without permission and to file legal reports against their legal guardians' physical discipline. Furthermore, police officers and judges can order or force them to return to their abusive legal guardians, such as the cases seen in Morocco, Saudi Arabia, and Yemen (U.S. DOSa 2014). Explicit formal laws that give male guardians exclusive rights to discipline their wives and children, including the use of physical violence, exist is some Arab states, for example, in the United Arab Emirates, "The penal code gives men the legal right to discipline their wives and children, including through the use of physical violence. The Federal Supreme Court has upheld a husband's right to 'chastise' his wife and children with physical abuse" (Human Rights Watch 2014b: 625).

Reporting Rape: A Double-Edged Sword

Social stigma associated with sharing or reporting certain crimes such as rape deters the victims from reporting. Women fear multiple aspects of social stigma and immense fear of collective punishment if they report honor related crimes, such as rape. Studies and reports show that women are less likely to report rape crimes in gender-discriminating societies. Rape victims fear reprisal, damaged reputation, diminished marriage opportunities, criminal sanctions, accusations of adultery or even death (as the case of "honor killing") in many Arab countries (U.S. DOSa 2014; Human Rights Watch 2014a).

The extremely high burden of proof for a rape case in *shari'ah* courts, for example in the United Arab Emirates, contributes to the relatively low conviction rate for rapists. In addition, female victims of rape or other sexual crimes may face prosecution for consensual sex instead of receiving assistance from government authorities. This may also explain why the rape incidences of foreign female workers (working as maids or housekeepers) in some Arab countries (especially in the Gulf states), is severely underreported (Human Rights Watch 2014b: U.S. DOSa, b 2014). Unfortunately, unreported rape crimes and acquitted rape incidents that result in pregnancy will most likely lead to severe collective punishment on the rape victim, including death, to cleanse the honor of the family or tribe.

In many Arab countries, the victims of rape are pressured by their family—or the collective unit—to commit suicide as a last act to spare her family the cost of cleansing the shame and disgrace resulting from her rape, disgraceful rumors, or socially illicit sexual misconduct. The victim's suicide will spare the family the legal cost of reclaiming the honor by killing her (U.S. DOSa 2014; Human Rights Watch 2014a).

Moreover, rape victims in many Arab states may be advised or even forced to marry their rapists to save the honor of the collectivist unit, even at the expense of extending the violation of the victim's human rights (U.S. DOSa 2014; Human Rights Watch 2014a).

The Likelihood of Reporting Rape Crimes

Figure 9.2 illustrates the likelihood of reporting rape crimes in the case of a high threshold of prosecution, and the possibility of prosecuting the victim in the case of perpetrator's acquittal.

In individualist societies, with the prevalence of gender equality's norm and the proper use of modern technology, the rape victim is more likely to succeed in proving her case. Therefore, the likelihood of reporting the rape crime and receiving just treatment is high. In addition, the typical victim of rape in individualist societies does not fear any collective retribution or externally induced shame associated with being a victim of rape. Furthermore, the victim may be encouraged to report the rape crime and seek justice.

In collectivist societies, the scenario and outcome can be very different. First, the internally and externally induced shame and guilt may cause the rape victim to reevaluate her choices. Collective pressure on the victim and sometimes the implicit accusation of the victim's role in the rape (such as the way she dresses or socializes with unrelated men, or leaving the private sphere without permission or the company of a legal guardian) will impose further burden on the victim. That may prevent her from reporting the rape or even sharing the rape incident with her in-group. The victim may also fear negative rumors that may shame her and her family, which in turn deter her from reporting or sharing the rape with her siblings.

Second, the high threshold of proving rape, such as the presence of minimum number of qualified witnesses to testify against the perpetrator adds more barriers against the victim in her pursuit to seek justice and uphold her reputation. The witness requirement is embedded in religious norms and rooted in interpretations of sacred texts, such as the *Qur'an* (4:15, 24: 4, and 24:13) and *hadiths*. Objecting to the use of modern technology to prove rape crimes, or

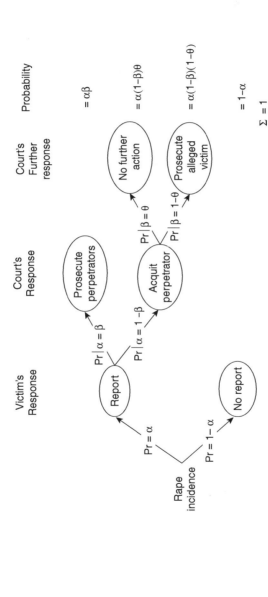

Figure 9.2 The likelihood of reporting rape.

paternity tests, in some court systems, since it may stir unwarranted conflict between sacred texts/belief and modern technology to solve certain legal issues, gives more weight to outdated norms and prevents women from proving their complaint of rape and other similar crimes. The absence of qualified witnesses and the barriers against using modern technology to prove the rape are likely to allow the acquittal of the alleged rapist (U.S. DOSa: United Arab Emirates 2014).

Third, in some Arab countries, the police and court systems may investigate the victim's role in the alleged rape crime. Possible conviction includes alleged sexual misconduct, such as consensual fornication or adultery. The resulting possibility of prosecuting the rape victims is likely to reduce the reporting of rape significantly, perpetuating "un-reporting" rape and women's human rights violations in gender-discriminating collectivist societies, for example, Saudi Arabia, United Arab Emirates, and Yemen (U.S. DOSa 2014).

The acquittal of the alleged rapist brings about immense ramifications on the alleged victim and her family (or in-group) exposing her and her family to informal collective shame and disgrace that must be punished according to collective norms and rules.

Based on the above analysis, the victim must go through four insurmountable barriers: the decision of whether or not to report; whether or not the court exonerates her and prosecutes the rapist; whether or not the court charges her if the rapist is acquitted; and whether or not the collectivist community punishes her based upon the acquittal of the rapist. Looking backward at these responses and outcomes, with low α, β, and θ in collectivist societies, the rape victim is less likely to report rape crimes against her, due to the high costs associated with each step of seeking justice and protecting her human rights.

Women's Involuntary Participation

The involuntary participation of women in many collectivist norms and practices is an important characteristic of gender discrimination supported with well-defined schemes of reward for conformists and punishment for deviants. Examples of involuntary participation include women's adherence to collectively imposed strict dress codes, required permission from male guardians to work outside home, travel only with the company of, or permission from, a male guardian, and obedience to husbands or male guardians. Women's deviance is deterred by credible threats of punishments, such as confinement (imposed by the collectivist unit or legal guardians), beating (mostly by close male relatives), and, in extreme cases, killing (e.g., case of "honor" killing).

Coercion refers to the choice between different alternatives that reduce the victims' well-being. Certain alternatives, such as rebelling or exiting the society are too costly to choose. Consequently, women are likely to obey the socially imposed dress code in order to be allowed to leave the private sphere, to attend all female schools if they want to continue their education, to forgo certain essential rights (e.g., alimony, child custody) if they want to leave abusive husbands and cannot get a divorce, such as the case of *khul'*(separation of wife from her husband in return of a payment based on the *Qur'an* 2:229), and to serve their husband's sexual need, including coerced sex to avoid possible physical violence due to the absence of laws against spousal rape or domestic violence (CHANGE 1999; Human Rights Watch 2014a; U.S. DOSa 2014).

Sociologists distinguish between the actual exercise of physical force and the threat of such force. Both engage women in involuntary acts to submit to collectivist norms and rules (Basu 1986). The threat of force supported by credible history of punishment can alter the mental model of both the perpetrators and victims, such that they both would act as if the physical punishment exists. The threats of honor killing and domestic violence, for example, are usually made to induce or pressure women to behave according to social norms. Records of honor killing and domestic violence and the informal approval of such acts and praise for the perpetrators are likely to give more credence to the threats alone.

Male-dominated collectivist units can increase their status by forcing women to adhere to the discriminating norms and rules. "Unreasonable commands" and "unwilling obedience" refer to the acts of collectivist units and women, respectively, in gender-discriminating collectivist societies. Unreasonable command and unwilling obedience separate gender-discriminating practices from normal exchanges or transactions, which are associated with "reasonable commands," and "willing obedience" (Commons 1931: 653). Furthermore, male-dominated collectivist units can also threaten or punish individualist men and women who do not participate in the punishment of women who violate or challenge the imposed norms and rules, a pressure instrument to ensure women's obedience and participation.

Women fear they will face worse scenarios if they refuse to abide by such discriminating norms and rules. They know that if they rebel, they will be harshly punished, so most of them opt to obey these norms and rules in the first place.

In summary, the violation of collectivist rules and norms in gender-discriminating societies exposes women to harsh informal and formal punishments, since such violations confront or oppose the main tenets in these societies. Such harsh punishments serve as a signal to other women not to rebel against, or confront such collectivist norms. In addition to physical punishments or threat of such punishments, other forms of punishment, such as confinement, social shame, and so on, can be imposed on women when they fail to act accordingly.

"Imposed" Trust and Gender Discrimination

Women are subject to institutional constraints that are specific to their person and their sexuality or exposure to sexual environment. Examples include the expectation that women should be obedient, stay at home, go to female exclusive schools, malls, hospitals, and so on.

Women know that if they violate the norm, regardless of how unfair, they will pay an excessive price. Family (or collectivist unit or group) members have various means to collect information about each other and therefore use such information to influence and control female behaviors.

In the context of gender relations, the collectivist unit seeks to know whether women can be counted upon to obey and conform to social norms. The main variable in such a case is not the trust between the different sides of transactions, but the trustworthiness of specific actors, women in this case, and the upholding of their part of transactions. The collectivist unit or group counts on the existing institutional structure of information gathering and the formal and informal instruments of enforcement to make all members, especially women, conform to such imposed norms (Guinnane 2005). Women know if they violate the imposed collectivist norms and rules, regardless of how unfair, they will pay for it, especially in the smallest collectivist unit, where family members have various means to collect information about each other and to influence women's behaviors.

Collectivist groups can impose preemptive and precautionary measures that reduce the likelihood of violating the informal codes of conduct and honor. For example, they can impose well-defined and well-enforced preemptive measures such as gender-selective-feticide, gender-selective-infanticide, and FGM/C.

They can also impose on-going measures, such as all-female-public spheres in school, work, hospitals, markets/malls, as well as imposing limitations on appearances, limitations on privacy, limitations on travel without the company or the approval of a male guardian, limitations on social contact especially on mixing of unrelated men and women, and so on.

Furthermore, the collectivist group can impose ex-post measures, such as physical disfigurement (which punishes the violators of codes of conduct and honor and sends a clear signal of executing credible threats), severe confinement with minimum necessities imposed on dissenting women, shaming the family (e.g., social exclusion and lower social status in the collectivist group), and killing women whose behaviors disgrace the collective unit, to uphold the collective "honor."

Furthermore, some women will be subject to collectivist punishment for reasons beyond their ability to control, such as women who are the victims of rape, sexual assault, incest, and other forms of sexual violence and harassment, and women who are subject to false rumors. The common rationale for punishing these women is the collective society fear that if these victims are not punished, other women may fake such incidents in their pursuit of violating the collectively imposed informal norms and rules.

Trust versus Control

People require trust because of their vulnerability to the behavior of others. To increase the effectiveness of trust based on intention, people can set up tighter contracts, constraints, and/or monitoring schemes. Trust differs from control. Control causes individuals to behave according to the contract or expectations because they fear punishment or retribution if they dissent or breach the contract, or because it is beneficial for them to do so. Trust occurs when individuals acts properly according to the contract or expectations even though they have both the opportunity and the incentive to cheat but choose not to. These individuals behave properly based on intrinsic motive of ethical conduct or solidarity (Nooteboom 2009).

People and groups tend to impose control and boundaries when dealing with relational risks. For example, trusted women will be allowed to go out and even work, since they gain the reputation of acting according the expectations of their family or collective community, "Trust and trustworthiness begin where control ends and may help to reduce the need for control" (Nooteboom 2009: 551). Lack of trust (or imperfect trust) is a major cause of restrictions on women's acts and behaviors in gender-discriminating societies. There is a need to control women's behaviors and acts to be aligned with the socially assigned identities, roles, and norms, which are mostly controlled by patriarchal hierarchy.

Trust can take place under certain conditions, but not in others. This may explain the strict expectations and constraints imposed on women in many collectivist societies. Studies show that those who are dependent on others are more inclined to take the interest of the others into account. Accordingly, women (sisters, daughters, and wives) are more inclined to take the interest of men (brothers, fathers and husbands) into account. This may explain imposing more control and constraints on women as an ex-ante condition to induce (of force) women to behave according to their collectively assigned identity and roles, and imposing severe punishment on women if they violate the collectively imposed trust, as an ex-post reaction. Husbands who are in control of a decisions that can harm wives—such as divorce, violence, confinement, constraint on movement, travel, and employment—can use such control to retaliate against their wives when they do not behave according to their socially assigned identity, roles, and social norms (Nooteboom 2009).

Reputation is a matter of self-interest. Women will find it in their best interest to behave according to their assigned identities and roles, to uphold the collective trust in them, internalizing their cognitive dissonance in the process, in order to be accepted in the collectivist community and to deter further collective punishment or exclusion.

Unit of Interest: The Collectivist versus Individual Unit

The unit of interest, and therefore the unit of analysis, plays a crucial role in explaining gender discrimination and violence against women. In individualistic societies, each individual is counted and measured as a separate and independent unit, subject to some constraint such as the individual age (legal minors or dependents below certain age). The unit of measurement (or interest) is the individual, and the collective unit (if there is such a thing) is the sum of the individual units. Each individual in the individualist society should have the same access and same weight with regard to sharing his/her preference for or against the issue of concern.

In contrast, in collectivist societies, the unit of analysis or measurement is larger and more complex, since it includes more than one person. It can vary from the immediate family to the whole tribe or community to the whole society or country. The complexity arises from the unequal distribution of costs (responsibilities, duties, family's reputations, and honor) and rewards within the collective unit, and the method of summing up the collective preference.

The collectivist unit of measurement conceals gender-discriminating practices that take place within the collectivist unit, by assuming the neutrality of the collectivist unit, "Standard approaches to inequality measurement presume that there is no inequality within the household" (Woodley and Marshall 1994: 420).

Studies show the prevalence of gender-discriminating norms and practices within the collectivist norms, starting from the smallest collective unit, the family, to the largest unit, the state. This may explain why the capability approach rejects the notion of collectivist units, instead, focusing on the capabilities and functionings of each individual. The well-being of the collectivist unit may increase if the gain of the winners of the gender-discriminating norms (e.g.,˙ fathers, husbands, brothers, communities, society), exceeds the loss of the victims (wives, sister, daughters, female members of the community or society). Using the collectivist unit as a unit of reference may lead to the implementation and sustenance of gender-discriminating practices that exclude and marginalize women, lower their status and well-being, and violate their human rights.

Reports show that the primary goals of government interventions against domestic violence in many collectivist societies is family reconciliation rather than protecting the abused victims. The sway of government intervention contributes to very low rates of prosecuting the perpetrators of domestic violence. In Iraq, only 6 percent of domestic violence complaints came to the court (U.S. DOSa: Iraq 2014). Such government bias helps perpetuate domestic violence and gender discrimination, since it sends clear signals to victims not to file complaints or pursue legal interventions. Similarly, in Morocco, and other Arab countries, laws designed to protect women and to prosecute perpetrators of domestic violence were mostly unenforced in response to societal pressures not to break up the collectivist unit, the family, in addition to the collectivist mentality of people, and of authority, such as police and court's officials (U.S. DOSa: Morocco 2014).

Norms and the Discounting of Women's Relative Value

Some of the social norms and rules that discriminate against women can be traced to the interpretations and applications of early sacred teachings, which have significant and sometimes undisputed values in certain societies. Features of gender-discriminating norms can be traced to sacred teaching in most religions and beliefs. However, in collectivist societies, some of these discriminating beliefs and norms are informally accepted and formally enforced. This is highlighted in many countries in the Arab world, where formal laws correspond to various interpretations of Islamic *shari'ah*. For example, the penal code in United Arab Emirates permits husbands to discipline their wives and daughters physically (U.S. DOSa 2014). In most countries in the Arab world, formal laws do not criminalize domestic violence or spousal rape, based on interpretations of sacred teaching in the *Qur'an* and *sunna*. For example, domestic violence that does not cause bleeding, broken bones, or damage to the face, or permanent disability is condoned as a last resort (the *Qur'an* 4:34). Excessive domestic violence however, is not permitted, and can be prosecuted as acts of physical assaults according to the penal code in most Arab countries.

According to certain norms and rules based on interpretations of scared teaching, a woman's value equals about half of a man's value. Most of these norms are rooted in sacred texts in the *Qur'an* and *sunna*. There are a number of implications of this.

First, the female share in inheritance is one-half of the male share, according to the sacred text, "Allah (thus) directs you as regards your Children's (Inheritance): to the male, a portion equal to that of two females" (the *Qur'an* 4:11). According to Badawi (1995), this is because men assume the responsibility for providing for their families. The notion of men's responsibility to provide for their families is cited frequently in the *Qur'an* and *hadith*.

Second, the *Qur'an* and *hadith* support or explain the notion that a women's testimony is only a fraction of a man's, "and get two witnesses, out of your own men, and if there are not two men, then a man and two women, such as ye choose, for witnesses, so that if one of them errs, the other can remind her," (The *Qur'an* 2:282), and in *hadith*, "The women asked, 'O Allah's Apostle! What is deficient in our intelligence and religion?' [Prophet Muhammad] said, 'Is not the evidence of two women equal to the witness of one man?' They replied in the affirmative. He said, 'This is the deficiency in her intelligence. Isn't it true that a woman can neither pray nor fast during her menses?' The women replied in the affirmative. He said, 'This is the deficiency in her religion.'"[5] According to various *hadiths*, women's discounted testimony is related to women's deficiency in intelligence that, according to many interpretations, is related to women's menses, causing them to act unpredictably or erratically. Bleeding also makes women impure, such that they cannot pray, fast, or read the *Qur'an* during menses.

Third, women's blood money is worth one-half of men's according the current *shari'ah* law in some Arab countries, for example, Egypt, Saudi Arabia, and Somalia. Blood money refers to the *diyya* (fine or compensation) paid by the accidental killer or by the killer's collective unit to the victim's family or tribe, according the Islamic *qisas* (the principle of equal punishment). There is no explicit reference in the *Qur'an* with regard to the value of a woman's life compared to a man's, however, the *Qur'an* highlights the foundation for *qisas*, separating men from women, from slaves, such that the *qisas* for a free man is a free man and for a women is a women (the *Qur'an* 2:178).[6] Prophetic narrations and the consensus of Muslim scholars support valuing women's life as one-half of men's. The widely common rationale of the discounted value of a woman's life is that men's economic status exceeds women's and the primary responsibility of men to provide for the economic needs of the family, supported by sacred teaching and norm, for example, "Men are the protectors and maintainers of women, because Allah has given the one more (strength) than the other, and because they support them from their means" (the *Qur'an* 4:34).

These examples reflect the state of women's dependency and sometimes as legal minors relative to the status of men with full witnessing power, full share in inheritance, and full value of blood money. Based on these valuations, the social identities and roles are set up such that women will continue to be valued less than men are. This discriminating measurement and the rationale behind them violate female human rights as equal to men, and violate their capabilities in terms of their access to the labor market, since it is one of the primary duties of men to work, earn income, and support their family, as the sacred text says. Female choices are also discounted due to the implicit assumption of their mental deficiency.

Discounting women's value to men leads to chain effects that support and sustain the discounted valuation of women or the superiority of men. For example, men have the option to marry more than one wife. They also have easy access to divorce (by saying clearly that his wife is divorced), compared to women's arduous process of seeking divorce. Women must file a formal legal request to get divorces, with reasons accepted by the judge or court, a process that can sometimes takes years and also be rejected. This may explain the practice of polygyny in the Arab world, and other similar countries, since a man can marry up to four wives according to sacred teaching, "Marry women of your choice, two or three or four" (the *Qur'an* 4:3). Polygyny is an outcome of valuing women less than men. The decisions to marry, practice polygyny, and to divorce, are made easy for men in the Arab world. Men do not need any permission to get married, in contrast to women who must get a consent from a male legal guardian (usually a male relative). Men's access to marry multiple wives put great pressure on wives to please their husbands, obey them, and to accept or internalize their pain and suffering that result from verbal and physical domestic violence. The availability and easy access of men to both divorce and marry multiple wives tilts the balance of power favoring husbands at the expense of the well-being of their wives. Divorce and polygyny are available options to men that can be exploited to violate their wives' human rights and degrade them to second-class citizens.

To offset the skewed balance of power that favors husbands, wives (and women in general) are advised to be obedient and submissive, and to act collectively, putting the preference of their husbands ahead of their own, to minimize the likelihood of divorce and polygyny. Dissenting women who reject gender-discriminating norms and roles expose themselves to divorce and sharing their husbands with another wife (or wives). In summary, women are taught to accept their socially imposed discounted value. Thus, they face a catch 22 dilemma, to be obedient and patient, internalizing their cognitive dissonance, or to dissent, exposing themselves to more violence, divorce, and sharing their husbands with other wives.

Summary

This chapter shows that in gender-discriminating collectivist societies women are less likely to report incidences of gender violence, such as domestic violence, spousal rape, and other rape incidences due to the high medical and legal thresholds of injury and due to social and legal barriers imposed on victims of such gender-discriminating crimes, including violence. Informal and formal barriers impose immense pressure on victims to forgo their legal rights, or even their right to share their blight with family or other members in their collectivist community. Failure to prove a rape crime can expose the victims to legal prosecution of adultery or fornication, in addition to the immense informal retribution.

PART III

Gender Discrimination in the Arab World

CHAPTER 10

Norms and Female Genital Mutilation/Cutting (FGM/C)

According to the World Health Organization (WHO), "Female genital mutilation (FGM) comprises all procedures that involve partial or total removal of the external female genitalia, or other injury to the female genital organs for non-medical reasons" (WHO, UNICEF, UNFPA, 2007: 3). The four types of FGM/C known to be practiced today are:

Type I Clitoridectomy: partial or total removal of the clitoris (a small, sensitive and erectile part of the female genitals) and, in very rare cases, only the prepuce (the fold of skin surrounding the clitoris);

Type II Excision: partial or total removal of the clitoris and the labia minora, with or without excision of the labia majora (the labia are "the lips" that surround the vagina);

Type III Infibulation: narrowing of the vaginal opening through the creation of a covering seal. The seal is formed by cutting and repositioning the inner, or outer, labia, with or without removal of the clitoris; and,

Type IV Other: all other harmful procedures to the female genitalia for non-medical purposes, for example, pricking, piercing, incising, scraping, and cauterizing the genital area (WHO 2013).

The most common type of female genital mutilation is excision of the clitoris and the labia minora, accounting for up to 80 percent of all cases. The extreme form is infibulation, which constitutes about 15 percent of all procedures (WHO 2013). WHO recognizes FGM/C as a violation of the human rights of girls and women (WHO 2013).WHO and other groups adopted the term female genital mutilation (FGM) to emphasize the permanent damage done by the cutting of female genitalia. Some researchers and organizations such as USAID use the term female genital cutting (FGC) for its neutrality. Throughout this book, the term female genital mutilation/cutting (FGM/C) will be used to highlight both the neutrality of the research and the severity and harms of FGM and its violation of women's and girls' rights. The term FGM/C is used by the US Department of State's recent reports on Human Rights Practices (U.S. DOSa 2014). The term 'female circumcision' is mostly used in societies where this FGM/C practice is prevalent (Yoder et al. 2004).

More than 140 million women and girls have undergone FGM/C. More than six thousands girls are genitally mutilated/cut daily, two million annually in the name of this discriminating tradition, most notably in the North East and West parts of Africa and parts of the Middle East (WHO 2013).

Historical Background

While the exact origins of the practice of female genital mutilation are unknown, scholars have concluded the practice predates the monotheistic religions. Historical records show "signs of excision were detected among female Egyptian mummies of the sixteenth century B.C." (Yount 2004: 1064). Theories surrounding the expansion of FGM/C into social practices frequently cite that the ancient trade of female slaves who had undergone the procedure for "fidelity-promoting purposes" of FGM/C (Yount 2004). To what extent can a woman's position be likened to that of a slave? To the extent that FGM/C is conducted as a means to promote her presumed fidelity, to increase her value to her owner, to decrease her autonomy, to take control over her circumstances, and to transform her into an object (Yount 2004).

Even though FGM/C predates monotheistic religions, religion has been used or exploited to promote and perpetuate the practice, where contemporary interpretations of religious tenets have been cited as rationale to sustain it. FGM/C is still prevalent in many places of the world due to collectivist group identities and pro-FGM/C religious interpretations. For example, FGM/C is very prevalent among Muslims women in Sudan, but less so among Christian women in the region. In addition, different types of FGM/C were used as markers of ethnic identity: for example, FGM/C is practiced only among Muslim ethnic groups in Guinea Bissau as a cleansing rite to enable women to pray in the proper fashions.

Most of FGM/C is practiced in Muslim communities, according to UNICEF, "While the majority of cut girls and women are Muslim, other religious groups also practise FGM/C" (2013a: 73). The types of FGM/C differ among different ethnic groups and even different countries. While clitoridectomy is believed to be the religiously correct type of FGM/C in West Africa, infibulation is considered the religiously superior choice in Sudan (Guernbaum 2001; Yount 2004). Kathryn Yount, a public health scholar, found that the effect of maternal education on reducing FGM/C among Christian Women is stronger than the effect in Muslim families in Egypt (Yount 2004).

The above trends highlight the influence of traditions and customs, some rooted in interpretations of religious texts and practices, and the important role of group identification, especially in collectivist societies, and those with multiple ethnic or religious groups/affiliations. Yount (1994, 2004) highlights both the roles of traditions and group identity in her research on FGM/C in Egypt. Christian and secular non-government organizations call for the eradication of FGM/C as a goal, among other integrated visions and initiatives to empower women, and to expand women's participation in the process of development. Such initiatives are made easier since they don't conflict ideologically with the leadership of the church(es). They succeeded in forming state-approved voluntary institutions that are accepted as nonsectarian society development even though their vision of women's empowerment differs from revivalist/fundamentalist Islamic view on gender (Yount 2004).

On the other hand, the 'authentic' national Muslim identity pursued by revivalists and fundamentalist Muslims hampers the effort of other Muslims and national NGOs, for example, the FGM-Free Village Model and Egypt Task Force against FGM, to reduce the prevalence of FGM/C and change the support for FGM/C (Barsoum et al. 2011). This may explain Yount's finding that FGM/C among Muslim girls is significantly higher than Christian girls in Minia (a governorate in Upper Egypt), especially among the younger-age cohort, the form of FGM/C was more severe among Muslims girls, and Christian mothers are less willing to circumcise their daughters (2004). Christian mothers, as opposed to Muslim mothers, are less likely to perceive positive effect of FGM/C and face fewer negative consequences of non-circumcision (Yount 2004). The study also shows that Christians' voluntary opposition to 'traditional practices' may have encouraged dramatic decline of the prevalence of FGM/C among Christians.

Yount's finding highlights the role of the "copying effect," by minority groups, of certain practices that are more prevalent among the majority population group. A minority group (or groups) is likely to copy certain collectivist practices that are deeply rooted or widely prevalent in the majority population. Reasons for this include deterring potential exclusion or harassment, submitting to certain collectivist traditions of the majority group, and avoiding being marked as the other, inferior, or marginalized. The dynamic of relationship between strong and weak groups, especially in collectivist societies, makes practices like FGM/C more prevalent and elevate them to cultural norms that perpetuate themselves, because they have been practiced generation after generation.

Media outlets, education curricula, religious sermons, and even national propaganda, make practices such as FGM/C an integral part of national, ethnic, or religious identity that should be protected and perpetuated. The image and role of women as keepers of 'cultural authenticity' and "traditional identity" in certain interpretations of Islamic ideology, therefore, may hinder the decline of FGM/C and other practices that discriminate against women (Yount 2004).

Prevalence of FGM/C

According to WHO, FGM/C is mostly concentrated in some parts in Africa. Figure 10.1 shows the prevalence of FGM/C among women 15–49 years in countries 50 percent or more of girls and women have undergone FGM/C.

In addition, there are 13 other African countries with prevalence rates between 1 to 44 percent. The only non-African countries cited in the report are Yemen with prevalence rate of 14 percent in 2013, and Iraq 8 percent (UNICEF 2013a, 2014).

Twenty-four African countries and Yemen and Iraq have enacted laws to prohibit FGM/C, in addition to 33 countries in other continents that mainly serve to protect children with origins in foreign practicing countries (UNCEF 2013a: 8–9). Some governments have started high profile national publicity campaigns and outreach to religious leaders against FGM/C (U.S. DOSa 2014). A recent UNICEF survey of 29 countries shows 80 percent of girls and women in 10 countries think FGM should end. However, in 13 other countries, less than 55 percent of girls and women think FGM/C should end, including six Arab countries: Mauritania, Sudan, Djibouti, Yemen (the only non-African country in the survey), Egypt, and Somalia (2013a).

Studies show that FGM/C is practiced in other countries in the Arab world such as Yemen[1], Oman, Kuwait, Saudi Arabia, United Arab Emirates, Jordan, Syria, the Occupied Palestinian Territories in Gaza, and Libya. Studies show that FGM/C practice is accepted and common in Oman, even though the government prohibits FGM/C in public hospital and clinics, due to the fact that there is no law prohibiting undergoing FGM/C procedure somewhere else (Cuthbert 2012; U. S. DOSa: Oman 2014). FGM/C is still considered a sensitive issue that belongs in the private sphere (Cuthbert 2012). A 2011 study in Kuwait and Saudi Arabia reveals that the prevalence rate of FGM/C was 38 percent (Chipper et al. 2011). Also, a 2011 study on FGM/C practice in

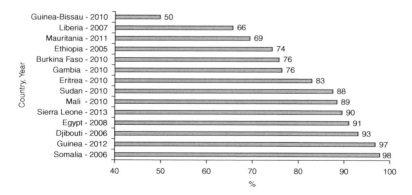

Figure 10.1 Countries with FGM/C prevalence of 50 percent or more among girls and women aged 15–49 years.

Source: UNICEF (2014). Female genital mutilation and cutting. http://data.unicef.org/child-protection/fgmc. Accessed October 28, 2014.

the United Arab Emirates shows that 34 percent of women said that they have undergone FGM/C. Forty percent of the circumcised women favor the practice and would have their daughters circumcised (Al Marzouqi 2011). "I was feeling every needle prick as I was circumcised without any painkillers," Marian Humaid, a university student says; however, FGM/C is a must in her tribe. "Those who are circumcised will be respected and appreciated while those who are not will be looked down on." Marian tells the story of her female friend who was forced to undergo FGM/C at age 22 in order to get married. Miriam affirms her own loyalty to her tribe and to her faith, "Of course, I will circumcise my daughters and if my husband doesn't like the idea, I will do whatever it takes to persuade him" (Al Marzouqi 2011).

FGM/C is also practiced throughout the Arabian Peninsula, particularly in Northern Saudi Arabia as well as in Southern Jordan, occupied Palestinian Territories (Gaza), and among Iraqi's Kurds. For example, a 2003 survey by WADI, a European NGO in Iraq, showed that 60 percent of women who took the survey were circumcised. Most women declared that female circumcision is a "normal" practice, a tradition, and a religious obligation sanctioned by many Islamic clerics in northern Iraq (Von der osten-Sacken and Uwer 2007; U.S. DOSa: Iraq 2014).

Human Rights Watch estimates 63 percent of Kurdistani women in Iraq have undergone FGM/C (Al-Sharq Al-Awsat, 2010). In 2011, the Kurdistan Islamic Scholars Union (in Kurdistan, Iraq) issued a formal *fatwa* (an Islamic decree) that FGM/C is not a legitimate obligation (Al-Sharq Al-Awsat 2010). Furthermore, The Kurdistan Regional Government (in Iraq) approved the Family Violence Law in 2011 that bans FGM/C (Basem 2012; Shelton 2010). However, a recent Human Rights Watch report shows that the ban of FGM/C in Iraqi Kurdistan is currently not enforced. Rather, the law drove FGM/C underground. Women have expressed concerns about the conflict between government's law to ban FGM/C and anti-FGM/C NGOs and the Pro-FGM/C religious leaders, as stated by a Kurdistani woman, "The NGOs come and tell us this [FGM] is bad for our girls, but the religious leaders have always told us it is good for them, ... who should we believe? ... The NGOs tell us that it [FGM] is against the law, but we do not hear this from anyone but them" (Human Rights Watch 2012). Other women cited reluctance to discontinue the practice because of the overpowering influence of FGM/C norms in their society. One woman, Sirwa, shares her pain on submitting her daughter to FGM/C, "You must think we are Monsters" (Human Rights Watch 2010: 54). Recent UNICEF reports included Iraq as a country practicing FGM/C with prevalence rate of 8 percent, with 1.3 million women between the age of 15 and 49 being submitted to some forms of FGM/C (UNICEF 2013a, 2013b; U.S. DOSa: Iraq 2014).

A study by two Saudi researchers in Saudi Arabia, shows that about 50 percent of the surveyed women had been subject to FGM/C, some of them were born in Saudi Arabia (Randerson 2008). According to a senior UN official well acquainted with the Middle East, the problems lies in the attitude of the Arab governments (IRIN 2005).

The Taboo of FGM/C: Case Study, Indonesia and Malaysia

Until recently, Indonesia, the world most populous Muslim country, was overlooked when it comes to the issue of FGM/C. This is partly due to the Indonesian government and officials' dismissal of reports about FGM/C practices as rumors. The taboo was broken when reports of annual mass circumcisions, sponsored by a local Muslim charity '*Yayasan Alssalaam*' (The Peace Foundation) surfaced. The reports claimed the circumcisions were performed free of charge or even with gifts. According to a 2003 study by the Population Council, an international research group, 96 percent of parents had their daughters circumcised before age 14 (Corbett, 2008). FGM/C is prevalent despite the Ministry of Health's decree forbidding medical personnel to perform FGM/C in 2006; however, this decree is yet to be supported with legislation. Surveys show that many Indonesians view female circumcision as a religious duty, supported by the country's religious leaders as a sacred duty. About 83 percent of FGM/C in Indonesia involves cutting (type I according to WHO's classification). In a few animist communities in Indonesia, FGM/C is more ritualistic, simply drawing a symbolic drop of blood; in other parts it is more invasive (Corbett 2008; Haworth 2012). "Nationwide studies found that between 86 and 100 percent of households surveyed subjected their daughters to genital cutting" (Haworth, 2012). *Nahdlatul Ulama*, the largest Muslim organization in Indonesia, issued an edict of its approval of FGM/C, without cutting too severely, also known as the *sunna Circumcision* (Haworth 2012). In 2012, the Indonesian Parliament reversed the ban on FGM and approved guidelines for trained doctors on how to perform FGM/C, since the earlier ban had failed. The stricter moral climate, after the fall of the Suharto regime in 1998, and the resurgence of some forms of radical Islam, had devastating effect on efforts to eradicate FGM/C in Indonesia (Haworth 2012). According to Hdjella, a teacher and midwife supervising the cutting at *Assalaam* Foundation "It [FGM/C] balances their [the girls] emotions so they don't get sexually over-stimulated ... It also helps them urinate more easily and reduce the bad smell" (Haworth 2012). In 2012, The Chairman of the *Majelis Ulama Indonesia,* the most powerful council of Islamic leaders in Indonesia, issued the following statements, "Circumcision is a requirement for every Muslim woman ... It not only cleans the filth from her genitals, it also contributes to a girl's growth" (Haworth 2012). A study published in 2010 by Yarsi University in Jakarta, Indonesia, shows signs of trauma among girls subjected to FGM/C. They experienced "depression, self-loathing, loss of interest in sex and a compulsive need to urinate." When chosen at random, six of seven visited hospitals performed female circumcision. A female gynecologist in one hospital, representing the anti-FGM/C side in Indonesia, stated, "You can have it done here if you wish ... But I don't recommend it. It's not mandatory in Islam. It's painful and it's a great pity for girls" (Haworth 2012).

In Malaysia, the National Council of Islamic Religious Affairs issued a fatwa ruling that FGM/C is obligatory for Muslims. A 2012 study shows that 90 percent of Muslim women in Malaysia (Muslim population makes about

61 percent of the total population in Malaysia) have undergone FGM/C, mostly in rural areas. The main rationales for undergoing FGM/C were satisfying religious obligation, cultural traditions, and for hygienic purposes. In response to the above fatwa, the Ministry of Health developed a guideline for FGM/C practice allowing health-care facilities to perform it (U.S. DOSa 2014)

Norms and FGM/C

Informal norms play a significant role in the prevalence and perpetuation of FGM/C. Figure 10:2 shows that more than one-third of surveyed men and women believe that FGM/C prevents adultery. About 50 percent of men and women believe FGM/C is required by religious precepts. Moreover, the majority of men and women believe that FGM/C should continue. Surveys show that a gradual reduction in the percentage of ever married women who believe that FGM/C should continue dropped from 82 percent in 1995 to 63 percent in 2008 (El-Zanaty and Way 2009: chapter 15). FGM/C is another manifestation of gender discriminating norms and societal control over women in many societies.

The acceptance of FGM/C, especially in collectivist societies, brings collective and individual rewards to not questioning practices such as FGM/C. In these collectivist communities, FGM/C is considered necessary to raise a girl properly, and to prepare her for adulthood and marriage. FGM/C also frees girls from social rejection and stigmatization, and it imparts sense of pride, a coming of age, cultural identity, and society membership to girls and women (WHO 2008). FGM/C helps women restrain sexual desire and resist forbidden sexual acts thus preserving virginity and fidelity. In addition, FGM/C is believed to make girls and women clean, pure, and beautiful since it removes the genital parts that are thought of as masculine, such as the clitoris. Violating norms such as FGM/C subjects the dissenters to condemnation, punishment, and ostracism, such as the non-circumcised girls would not get married, be

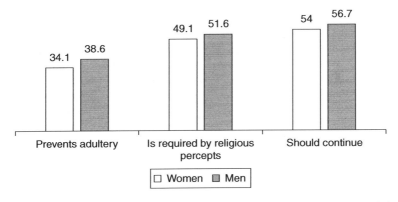

Figure 10.2 Beliefs about female circumcision among women and men in Egypt, 2008 (%).
Source: Data collected from El-Zanaty and Way (2009, chapter 15).

guilty of misbehaviors, and would be possessed by the devil (Aldeeb 1995: WHO 2008). According to an Egyptian circumciser midwife, "one should lynch the fathers who were opposed to circumcision of their daughters, because these fathers were in fact willing to see their girls become whores" (Aldeeb 1995: 85). Studies show that most Egyptians, including women, strongly prefer the continuation of FGM/C, in response to religious mandate and societal expectations (Katulis 2004).

There is strong tendency of religionists and collectivist leaders to justify religious norms *a posteriori* (Aldeeb 1995). Collective support and endorsement deepens the roots of the discriminating norms and attract more followers to practice and perpetuate them by rewarding assenters and punishing dissenters. The sacred roots of norms make it easier to convince the public to agree with the norms' benefits, and minimize their harms. Meanwhile the opponents of the sacred norms will try first to vacate these norms from any sacred value, and then prove the factual harmful effects of following and practicing them.

Harms and Costs of FGM/C

The practice of FGM/C varies in terms of its severity. While some individuals and communities subscribe to a method in which the woman is not "cut severely" (meaning only part of the clitoris is removed), other groups and communities, such an in Ethiopia, Somalia and Sudan, adhere to a much more severe method of circumcision, the infibulation, also known as the *Pharonic* circumcision (Human Rights Watch 2010; WHO 2013). Infibulation, according to the prominent Egyptian feminist and author, Dr. Nawal El Saadawi, "removes all of the clitoris, the labia minora, and the labia majora. The sides are then sutured together, often with thorns, and only a small matchstick-diameter opening is left for urine and menstrual flow. The girl's legs are tied together and liquids are heavily rationed until the incision is healed" (Goodwin 1995: 335). While the prevalence of FGM/C is indeed shocking and varied, it is the individual stories of women who were submitted to FGM/C that reveals its deeper effects. El Saadawi relates her personal story from the perspective of a six-year old girl, taken from bed in the middle of the night:

> *They carried me to the bathroom. I do not know how many of them there were, nor do I remember their faces, or whether they were men or women ... All I remember is that I was frightened and that there were many of them, and that something like an iron grasp caught hold of my hand and my arms and my thighs, so that I become unable to resist or even move ... At that very moment I realized that my thighs had been pulled wide apart, and that each of my lower limbs was being held as far away from the other as possible, gripped by steel fingers that never relinquished their pressure. I felt that the rasping knife or blade was heading straight down towards my throat. Then suddenly the sharp metallic edge seemed to drop between my thighs and there cut off a piece of flesh from my body. I screamed with pain despite the tight hand held over my mouth, for the pain was not just a pain, it was like a searing flame that went through my whole body ... I did not know what they had cut off from my body, and I did not try to find out. I just wept, and called out to my mother for help. But the worst shock*

of all was when I looked around and found her standing by my side. Yes, it was her, I could not be mistaken, in flesh and blood, right in the midst of these strangers, talking to them and smiling at them, as though they had not participated in slaughtering her daughter just a few moments ago. (Nawal El Saadawi 1980: 7–8)

The immediate physical effects of female circumcision include, but are not limited to, shock, severe pain, hemorrhage, bacterial infection, damage to the vagina, urethra, bladder, or bladder area, keloid scarring, resulting in obstructed walking, and even death (Goodwin 1995; WHO 2013).

According to WHO, women who were subjected to FGM/C suffer from incidences of caesarean section, post-partum hemorrhage, and higher death rate in their newborn babies and immediately after birth compared to those who had not: 15 percent higher for babies whose mothers had type I, 32 percent with type II, and 55 percent for those with type III FGM/C. In addition, one to two percent of delivered babies die because of FGM/C (WHO 2008). Furthermore, girls frequently suffer from lagged effects of FGM/C such as mental and sexual distortions because of this traumatic experience (El Saadawi 1980). The sexual effects of FGM/C include decreased sexual stimulation and extreme pain and danger if it is necessary for the woman to be "cut open" after infibulation (WHO, UNICEF, UNFPA 1997; WHO 2013). Other harmful effects, according to study by medical researchers at Kuwaiti and Saudi universities shows that among women who were submitted to FGM/C in the Arabian Gulf, 80 percent suffer from flashbacks, 58 percent from psychiatric disorder, 38 percent from anxiety disorder, and 30 percent suffer from post-traumatic stress disorder (Chibber et al. 2011).

According to El Saadawi, FGM/C is often a girl's first "signal" of her status. While El Saadawi's story demonstrates a girl's confusion and fear prior to the experience, she concludes her story with a reflection, "Now we know where lies our tragedy. We were born of a special sex, the female sex. We are destined in advance to taste…misery" (1980: 8). Therefore, not only does FGM/C have a profound physical and mental effect on a girl, but a social effect as well. This experience is her induction into the social hierarchy—to the bottom of the social hierarchy. In the FGM/C transaction, the girl becomes the object of transaction rather than an agent or a participant of transaction. This experience signals to her not only that she does not have sexual autonomy but also that there is something inherently and naturally deficient with her that must be humanely corrected—an often repetitive theme in the lives of women in many collectivist societies.

Religious and Cultural Norms and FGM/C: Egypt

The religious and cultural embedded norms are likely to continue even after the government's ban. According to a midwife in Egypt, "Some women say they won't have their daughters purified [circumcised] when the social worker is around. They humor her until she leaves and once she is gone they come and ask me to circumcise their girls" (BBC 2012). This sentiment is supported by an Egyptian mother, Olla, from a village in South Egypt, "It is important that she [my daughter] loses that part of her body that awakes sexual desire. If not, she may play with herself or ask a boy to touch this part for her, not specifically a stranger, but one of her cousins for instance, and she might enjoy it…When she feels the pain of it she will be more careful about this part. I know the doctor might be punished for this, but still there are doctors who are practising it…And if the doctors won't do it then we will get the daya [a local midwife]" (BBC 2012).

Tensions and disputes among religious and societal leaders highlight the intricacy and uncertainty regarding the legitimacy of FGM/C. An *Imam* (Sheikh) in a village in upper Egypt, stated his support for the eradication of FGM/C, "In the past, the imams in mosques didn't have enough information on this issue, but now cultural and educational expansion have allowed people to know more and understand the wrong acts that were done before. We are here working hard with the NGOs on spreading the word of not having FGM. We are ordered by the Prophet [Muhammad] not to do it" (BBC 2012).[2] However, in a direct contradiction to the Imam's view, when asked about the anti-FGM campaign in upper Egypt, his superior thundered, "No, I am not. The Prophet has ruled that [female circumcision] must be done" (BBC 2012). These two views clearly contradict each other and highlight the ongoing tension between pro-FGM/C and anti-FGM/C advocates. The BBC report (2012) highlights the anxiety among anti-FGM/C NGOs in Egypt after the 'Arab Spring', and the rise of Islamists, including the Muslim Brotherhood, and the more hardline Islamists, *salafis,* to power (until the toppling of the Islamist regime in July 2013 by the Egyptian army in what is known as another populace revolution or an outright military coup). Nivine Rasmi, an anti-FGM/C campaigner shared her fear about the Islamist government and its campaign, "Of course we fear this new parliament won't tackle issues like FGM because already there are extremists who want FGM unlike the previous regime…We know that there will be a decline in women and children rights with this new government and parliament" (BBC 2012*)*.

FGM/C is likely to prevail due to the high collective pressures imposed on the girls and their families, as stated by Anti-FGM/C campaigner in Egypt, "If a girl is discovered not to have been genitally mutilated on her wedding night, a husband or mother-in-law might demand that she is sent back to her family and her chances of marriage can be destroyed forever" (BBC 2012).

Because of the government's formal ban on FGM/C in Egypt in 2008,[3] parents face a catch 22. If they do not subject their daughters to FGM/C, they subject themselves and their daughters to many informal forms of collective punishment. If they seek FGM/C and their daughters end up bleeding, suffering, or dying from the procedure, they cannot take them to hospital, because of their fear of prosecution, as stated by Dr. Randa Fakhr El Din of the Cairo Coalition against FGM, "Their parents won't take them to the hospitals in case they get reported and imprisoned" (BBC 2012). In November 2014, an Egyptian court acquitted the first prosecuted doctor on charges of FGM/C, disappointing many activists and NGOs in their call and pursuit against FGM/C (BBC 2014c).

Costs and Benefit analysis of FGM/C in Collectivist Societies

FGM/C can be thought of as an ex-ante or a preemptive practice, a norm, to sacrifice human rights and to marginalize women for the sake of potential collective 'benefits'.

A simple cost–benefit analysis can explain the prevalence of FGM/C and its trend into the future, in collectivist societies.

In societies where the male is the dominant gender, informal norms and traditions reflect male dominance and their collective effect on aligning formal rules into the governance structure of female-male transactions. The distributional effect explains the gains males make at the expense of females.

FGM/C places the burden-of-proof on women with regard to their chastity and fidelity, while giving men the benefit-of-doubt. This places immense burden on women who become subject to strict scrutiny and severe punishment if these informal customs are violated.

The parents and daughter benefit from the practice when they are under the belief that, 'no girl or woman will be marriageable unless she has submitted to the process' (Crossette 2000: 184). As girls are conceptualized in part as liabilities to the parents, both socially—in terms of the potential shame they can bring—and economically—in terms of their lack of financial contribution to the family—increasing the sexual value of the daughter (i.e. protecting her chastity) becomes paramount to increasing her chances of marriage, thereby limiting familial liability and minimizing their fear and anxiety and shame. To the future husband, FGM/C in an extreme sense renders "the women they marry uninterested in sex or unappealing and inaccessible to any other man—a safe, albeit damaged, piece of property" (Crossette 2000: 184). Again, FGM/C is a means to decrease the sexual utility of the women in order to increase her sexual value to her husband. As conceptualized as a liability in the collectivist framework, girls are forced to bear a tremendous cost (both immediate and lagged) with minimal, if any real, intrinsic benefit. Men (the father and future husband) on the other hand, are able to control women's sexuality, ensure their fidelity, and decrease their likelihood of bringing shame, through the practice of FGM/C.

Although the preemptive and irreversible nature of FGM/C makes the practice appear to force the entire cost of the transaction on young girls, this is not necessarily the case. Mothers are often forced to bear a portion of the cost of FGM/C in that they are often the ones forced to perpetuate the tradition. Many mothers, especially individualist ones, are torn between the violation of their daughters' human rights on one side, and the collective benefit of seeking FGM/C for their daughters on the other side. Collective gains and pressures usually outweigh the cost of submitting to FGM/C, especially in collectivist societies with low respect and status for women. Thus, the fate of FGM/C is a function of the costs and benefits associated with it; most of the cost accrues to the girl, and most of the benefits accrue to the collectivist unit. Given the higher weight attached to the collective unit's preference and the lower weight attached to the young girl (usually zero), or her mother, FGM/C is likely to prevail in many collectivist communities until this weight and status distortions are corrected. *See the appendix at the end of this chapter for a detailed analysis of the net social benefit of norms, such as FGM/C, in collective societies.*

As shame is frequently conceptualized as a larger communal embarrassment, society, or at least the collectivist members of society, benefits from the practice of FGM/C. According to a prominent Islamist leader, Sheik Mohammad Al-Berri,[4] "A woman can be aroused at any moment. Even if a woman is riding in a car, if she hits a few bumps, she can become sexually aroused. Once this happens, a man loses control. So you see, this practice [clitoridectomy] is not meant to punish women. But it is necessary" (Weiner 2004: 54). Therefore, the girl is forced to sacrifice for the good of her family, but she is also forced to sacrifice for the greater good of the collective society and social stability—for those men who she does not even know.

When justifications for practices like FGM/C are based on ignorance due to poverty or limited second sources, as opposed to collective sacred norms like religion, it becomes much easier to combat the problem of FGM/C.

In addition to FGM/C being a preemptive procedure that is supposed to repress women's sexual desire, enhance the likelihood of their chastity before marriage, and reduce the likelihood of adultery once they are married, it is also a signal of obedience to collective norms and traditions. It brings collective rewards to the circumcised girl, her family, and the collectivist unit in general. FGM/C serves as an initiation into womanhood and enhances the husband's sexual pleasure (with the circumcised wife). It improves fertility and prevents infant and maternal immorality. It is a religious obligation since it prevents sexual immorality. At the same time, FGM/C saves the circumcised girl and her family the wrath of collective punishment in the forms of shame, exclusion, expulsion, harassment, and being tagged/shamed for her uncleanliness, bad reputation, high exposure, and tendency for adultery and promiscuity, having part of her sexual organ looks like male sexual organ, and so on.

FGM/C: The Complexity of Debating Religiously Based Discriminating Norms in Collectivist Societies

FGM/C is one of the most sensitive practices that violate the human rights of girls and women. It is an extremely offensive practice, especially since the victims of FGM/C are defenseless female infants and children. In light of the violent and inhumane FGM/C practices, many scholars and leaders make the claim that FGM/C practices in their countries and communities are not based on sacred/religious norms or teaching. In addition, many governments in the Arab World and the Middle East (e.g., Iraq, Syria, Bahrain, Oman, Saudi Arabia, and the Palestinian Occupied Territories) deny the presence of FGM/C and/or dispute its prevalence in their countries. While globally known, discussing or researching FGM/C in many societies is still considered a taboo, such that no one talks about it, except when referring to it as an "African phenomenon."

It is essential to recognize and admit the presence of a problem and to start thinking of how to solve it. It is, therefore, important to explore the roots of FGM/C and why certain governments deny/conceal FGM/C practices. Thomas Von der Osten-Sacken highlights one main reason, "There is a clear link between freedom of expression and knowledge of FGM ... If we know the phenomenon exists in Egypt, Jordan and Iraq, it is because these countries had an embryonic civil society" (IRIN 2005). According to a senior UN official, referring to certain practices in Saudi Arabia, "Issues of FGM and violence against women in general are not open for discussion within the country, let alone to UN agencies" (IRIN 2005). Issues belonging to the private sphere in collectivist societies are likely to be kept in the private sphere and should not be discussed or researched, especially by outsiders, which is stated well by Von der Osten-Sacken and Uwer, "It would be a mistake to interpret lack of public discussion of many sexual issues in the Middle East as indicative of a lack of problems. Rather, the silence only reflects the strength of taboo" (2007: 30). David Ghanim in his book 'Gender and Violence in the Middle East' adds, "In the Middle East they overlook violence rather than acknowledging it and acting against it" (2009: 5).

Many organizations and writers in the West support the notion that FGM/C is not rooted in religions but rather in cultures. Other scholars and experts, NGOs, and civil society organizations, seek to broaden the research of relevant religious and cultural precepts and practices that may shed more light on the root causes that perpetuate practices like FGM/C in certain societies. For example, the practice of FGM/C in North Africa, the Middle East, and some sub-Saharan African communities, especially in Islamic communities, shares religious roots that are accepted by dominant religious leaders and religious organizations and institutions in these communities and countries. The cautious recognition by international organizations, such as WHO, of the presence of various religious positions with regard to FGM/C is a welcomed step toward finding the root causes of FGM/C in different societies/countries. A more careful examination shows a strong, yet disputable connection between religious norms and FGM/C norms and practices in many Muslim communities and countries, for example, in the Arab World. These different religious teachings, traditions, and norms should be explored and scrutinized further with regard to the validity of the claims about FGM/C in religious teaching/scripts (WHO 2013).

The following references, which are generally overlooked or ignored (in part because they are written in Arabic) in many researches and studies of the norms and causes of FGM/C practices in societies in the Arab World, highlight the crucial role of religious norms with regard to FGM/C.

The dynamic of relationships between strong and weak groups, especially in collectivist societies, makes practices like FGM/C more prevalent and elevate them to cultural norms that perpetuate themselves, because they have been practiced generation after generation.

The Authenticity of "Sacred" Teaching Regarding FGM/C

The most cited sacred references used by the proponents of FGM/C in Muslim societies are two *hadiths* (recorded sayings of Prophet Muhammad), mentioned by various Islamic references in similar phraseology. The first *hadith* regarding the religious legitimacy of FGM/C is a conversation between the Prophet and Um Habibah (or Um 'Atiyyah), a genital exciser of female slaves, the Prophet replied to her question about the legitimacy of female genital excision, "Yes, it is allowed. Come closer so I can teach you: if you cut, do not overdo it *[la tanhaki]*), because it brings more radiance to the face *[ashraq]* of the girl and it is more pleasant [ahza] for the husband". According to similar phraseology, the Prophet said, "Cut slightly and do not overdo it *[ashimmi wa-la tanhaki]*, because it is more pleasant *[ahza]* for the woman and better *[ahab,* in other sources *abha]* for the husband"[5] (Aldeeb 1995; Ahmad n.d.; Badawi 1995). In this *hadith*, the Prophet agreed that female genital excising is allowed (not forbidden), but the cut should not be too severe. Thus, the dispute is not to excise or not, but it is how deep to excise. The second *hadith* Narrated by Aisha, the Prophet said, "If both circumcised parts *(khitanan)* meet or if they touch each other, it is necessary to wash before prayer" (Aldeeb 1995)[6]. In similar phraseology, "If the two circumcision organs meet, grand ablution, i.e., ghousl, becomes obligatory" (Al-Sabbagh 1996: 38), which implicitly implies the circumcision for both men and women.

However, other Islamic scholars reject the above *hadiths* as "none aspire to a degree of authenticity which would indicate that female circumcision is obligatory" (Al-Sabbagh 1996: 17). They reject the *hadiths* about female circumcision, based on the following rationales: first, the *hadith* narrated by Um Habibah does not exist and its argument in not valid. Second, some *hadiths* lack authenticity. Third, these *hadiths* are weak especially in terms of the chain of transmission of each of these *hadiths*. Fourth, even if these *hadiths* are authentic, these scholars consider female circumcision not as a *sunna*, but below it in degree, such as a habit or honor. Fifth, because female circumcision involves tampering with God's creation and the Prophet forbade any meddling with God's creation (Al-Sabbagh 1996; Aldeeb 1995). Lastly, the Prophet did not require Muslim women to undergo circumcision as stated by a prominent Islamic thinker, Dr. Mohammad Salim Al-Awwa, "had the Prophet intended an equal ruling for men and women, he would have said, 'circumcision is a *sunna* for men and women'" (Al-Sabbagh 1996: 38; Badawi 1995). Al-Awwa, highlights the role of traditions and interpretations of sacred texts by Islamic scholars. His comments underscore the role of informal norms in perpetuating certain practices even though they are still disputable, "The conclusion of the jurisprudence scholars are a human endeavour carried out by specialists in Islamic law to point out for Muslims, and even non-Muslims, the ruling of Islam in everything they are interested in. Any conclusion reached by these scholars, however, should not be regarded as law, nor can be cited as a creed to be followed. It can only be cited as an interpretation of the original texts and an application of what they say to actual cases." He also adds there is a possibility of unintended errors made by the interpreters of Islamic jurisprudence, "A qualified interpreter of Islamic jurisprudence is doubly rewarded when he makes a correct interpretations and receives a single reward when he errs" (Al-Sabbagh 1996: 34).

Dr. Youssef Al-Qaradawy, a well-known Islamic scholar, supports the "*light circumcision*," which represents the most impartial and practical opinion among Islamic Scholars, since it protects girls' morality. He leaves the choice to parents according to their beliefs (Al-Qaradawi 1987: 443; Aldeeb 1995: chapter 2). And, according to Dr. Mohammad Hasan Al-Hifnawi (professor of medicine at Al-Azhar University, Cairo, Egypt), female circumcision must be upheld for the public desire to conserve women's pride, dignity, and femininity, according to the Islamic instructions of cutting part of the clitoris to restrict female sexual desires (October Magazine 1994).

The Politicization of Religious Perspectives: Views and Reversals

In 1994, The Grand *Mufti* of Egypt, Dr. Mohammed Sayyed Tantawy, acknowledged that female circumcision is permissible in Islam, and it is not permissible to outlaw it. Tantawy explained that the Prophet's guidance serves to balance the girl's sexual feeling and control her sexual desires. The Prophet prohibits cutting or removing the source of this sexual feeling, such that this balancing act (of no deep cut) does not prevent a woman from the source of enjoyment and at the same time protects her from behaving irreverently and from losing self-control when sexually aroused. Therefore, female circumcision is one of the unspoiled natural dispositions that Islam agrees with and urges its followers to abide by, according to the teaching of the Prophet (Dar Al-'Ifta' Al-Massreyya, in Arabic, 1994). However, years later, Tantawy reversed his position, and opposed FGM/C as un-Islamic practice (The National Council for Children and Motherhood 2003).

Sheihk Ali Jom'a, days before being appointed as the Grand *Mufti* of Egypt in 2003, said that male circumcision is required and female circumcision is a recommended habit or honor (*makramah* in Arabic), such that a woman may have it or not, and it may be elevated to a *sunna* (a custom). According the *Sahfe'i* school of Islamic thought, female circumcision is an obligation. According to the *Hanifi* and *Hanbali* Schools, female circumcision is a *sunna*. According to *Imam* Ahmad, it is a *sunna* and obligation. Furthermore, according to the *Hanifi* School, a group or a tribe should be fought if they choose to abandon female circumcision. Jom'a calls for proper female circumcision in hospital under the supervision of medical doctors, and rejects the improper practice of circumcision using non-sterile instruments, without the presence of medical doctors. According to Jom'a, there is no harm in female circumcision, especially the Islamic (or *sunna*) circumcision associated with no deep cut of the clitoris (The Egyptian Society of Medical Ethics, 1994). Like Tantawy, however, he later reversed his position in 2007 and issued a *fatwa* criminalizing FGM/C and declaring FGM/C an un-Islamic practice, as will be explained later (Reuters 2007).

Sheikh Al-Azhar,[7] the highest Islamic official position in Egypt, The Grand *Imam* Jad El-Haq Ali Jad El-Haq,[8] issued a *fatwa* that considers male and female circumcisions to be features of unspoiled natural disposition. He also highlighted certain benefits of female circumcision, such as it achieves moderation, does not prevent women from enjoying and responding to sexual act, and it protects women against irreverence and against her inability to control herself when aroused (Jad Al-Haq 1994: 14–15). It is worthwhile to mention that Al-Azhar (the most respected Islamic institution in Egypt, and many countries around the world) had issued several *fatwas* endorsing FGM/C in 1949, 1951, and 1981. In 1950s, the Egyptian government tried to regulate FGM/C by stopping FGM/C performed by midwives, allowing doctors only to perform it.

Sheikh Nasr Fareed, a former Grand *Mufti* of Egypt, also affirmed that female circumcision is a *sunna* (a custom) and it is not permitted to illegalize it, except if it done by nonspecialists, which may cause harm (Al-Lewa' Al-Islmali 1996b). The Saudi's General Presidency of Scholarly Research and Ifta' agrees with the view of the Egyptian *Muftis*, and Sheikh Al-Azhar mentioned above.[9]

The proponents of FGM/C also exploit the notion that 'what is not prohibited is allowed' according to the norms of Islamic law, since there is no single verse in the *Qur'an* or in *hadiths* that prohibits FGM/C (Ahmad 2000; Al-Liwa' Al-Islami 1996a, b; Aldeeb 1995). In addition, when asked if female circumcision is illegitimate, the Prophet's response was, "no." He just advised the circumciser to not cut severely.

Due to the increasing pressures from international organizations, NGOs, and foreign states to eradicate FGM/C, some Islamic leaders and scholars appear to agree with the calls to eradicate FGM/C; however, they (or at least many of them) do not consider *sunna circumcision* a form of mutilation, believing mutilation only applies to Type III FGM/C.

In a TV interview in 2003, Sheikh Ali Jom'a (former Sheikh Al-Azhar) shared his view on Islam, culture in Islamic societies, and the fear and rejection of cultural imperialism especially Western cultures. He rejected foreign interventions in Egyptian religions and *shari'ah* and shared some of his perspectives on the foreign propaganda against Egypt and Islam. He stated that the Western model of knowledge, which is saturated with secularism, considers virtue and chastity as forms of limiting human freedom. He continued that the United Nations documents discussed during the 1995 Population Conference in Beijing discussing female circumcision, rights to inheritance, the right to divorce, sexual freedom, abortion, and prohibition of polygamy are all matters that clearly violate the provision of religion (Islam). The Islamic Research Board in Egypt studied all these claims and objected them.[10]

Other Islamic scholars and leaders think that the calls to end FGM/C is politically and ideologically motivated by fanatic secularists driven by antipathy to religion (Ahmad n.d.), Dr. Mohammad Al-Mosseir, professor of religion and philosophy at Al-Azhar University, Egypt, underscores that prohibiting female circumcision is an attack on Islam, and female circumcision is a legitimate matter (Al-Liwa' Al-Islami 1996a). Dr. Safwat Lotfy and others (Egyptian professors of medicine) state that the *sunna* (Islamic) female circumcision usually corresponds to the removal of prepuce covering clitoris and part of labia minora, and to a lesser degree involves the removal of part of the clitoris and parts of labia minora, if the clitoris is abnormally enlarged, as recommend by Prophet Mohammad. Lotfy, however warned that more excessive cuts such as infibulation, or the *Pharonic* circumcision, are against *Sunna* regulation (1996: 711). These scholars and scientists discount the alleged harms and highlight many benefits of the *sunna* circumcision including lower incidents of vulva's cancer among circumcised women.

Another study by a professor of medicine in Egypt supports the above findings, adding that *sunna* circumcision if performed properly, by medical specialists, would not generate any harm or side effect (Fawzi n.d.). According to Fawzi, without *sunna* circumcision, girls may suffer from the followings medical problems: chronic inflammation, poor hygiene, uninhibited sexual effects and sexual self-consciousness, interference and pain with sexual intercourse, pain and discomfort from underwear and physical exercises and sometimes from walking or sitting, and it may lead to some wrong 'sexual' practices because of the external part of the girl/woman's sexual organ, which in turn may have negative effect on the sexual relation between the non-circumcised woman and her husband (Fawzi n.d.). Fawzi backs his finding by referring to the presence of similar procedures to female circumcision in other countries, such as the USA and other European countries. In addition to the above list of the medical benefits of *Sunna* female circumcision, Fawzi affirms the Islamic religious legitimacy of female circumcision according to the opinion of the four main Islamic schools of thought. Fawzi warns against the criminalization of female circumcision as a serious violation of a legitimate matter ordered by Prophet Muhammad, and rejects the politicization of FGM/C and the "international propaganda" against it (Fawzi n.d.).

The politicization of FGM/C and the conflict it creates with other/foreign cultures or religions serves to elevate female circumcision into the state of a national 'sacred norm' that should be upheld as a symbol of Muslim resistance to international propaganda and attacks against Islamic culture and traditions.

After the death of an eleven-year-old girl while undergoing the procedure in 2007, the then state-appointed Grand *Mufti* of Egypt, Sheikh Jom'a declared (issued a *fatwa*) that FGM/C is forbidden by Islam, reversing his earlier support for FGM/C.[11] However, other Islamic scholars have declared their support for FGM/C (Reuters 2007). In response to Jom'a's declaration, the Muslim Brotherhood (then, *Jama'a Islameyya*) in Egypt demanded the *mufti* (Sheikh Jom'a) to renege on the prohibition of circumcision, saying the decision was based on the ill-fated death of a girl during the circumcision procedure, where such an unfortunate death may occur with other medical procedures. The Muslim Brotherhood rejected the 2007 *Fatwa* since it violates the main tenets of Islamic teaching and *sunna,* and arguing that criminalization of female circumcision will move its practice underground, leading to more serious harm (Al-Arabiya 2007). In 2008, members of the Muslim

Brotherhood of the Egyptian Parliament called for organizing female circumcision rather than criminalizing it (Tadros 2012). Members also attacked the then new Child Law because it would cause moral collapse and loss of moral identity. They attacked the new laws as examples of the episodes of foreign intervention. In early 2012, a Salafist (fundamentalist) member of the parliament in Egypt and a member of El-Noor (Light) Party, second largest party in the new elected Parliament called for the restoration of female circumcision, as it is a part of the *Sunna* (of Prophet Muhammad). In May 2012, the Muslim Brotherhood's Freedom and Justice Party, the largest party in the Egyptian Parliament (before the toppling of the government and disbanding the Egyptian Parliament and the Muslim Brotherhood in 2013), launched a charity medical campaign for female circumcision for a nominal fee at the Islamic Institute in Abu Aziz village, Minia, South Egypt, which raised serious concern about the intent of government (before its toppling) in Egypt and its perspective on many issues related to gender discrimination, including FGM/C that was formally banned by the previous government in 2008 (Malik 2012; Tadros 2012).

Regional and international arenas have witnessed many conferences, conventions, declarations, and protocols to highlight the harm of FGM/C and its violation of women's human rights, and to call for ending FGM/C.[12] These declarations, conventions, and protocols underscored the importance of a multidisciplinary approach to stop FGM/C.[13]

Sheikh Jom'a's and Sheikh Tantawys's changes of position reflect the political pressure that is sometimes imposed on religious leaders, especially state-appointed leaders, in response to international condemnation of FGM/C. It also reflects the ongoing theological tensions between the pro-FGM/C and the anti-FGM/C groups in Egypt (and other similar countries), and the rising tension between 'secularists' and the well-established 'religionists' in many collectivist societies in the Arab World and other regions.

Globalization, faster and wider dissemination of information, and wider access to information regarding what used to be taboos, have exposed many unknown facts and practices about FGM/C and other discriminating norms almost everywhere in the world, exposing many practices to inquiry and investigation that may tilt the balance in favor of the opponents of FGM/C. Aiding this is higher levels of awareness in many LDC societies that used to suffer from high rates of illiteracy just a few decades ago and wider and faster access to information. On the other hand, many collectivist members in these societies have become more adamant about sustaining norms and practices, such as FGM/C, supported by instructions, teaching, and traditions mentioned in 'sacred' texts, sermons, lectures, and videos, to counterbalance the views of the opponents of FGM/C, and to sustain FGM/C in their societies.

It remains to be seen whether collectivist and religionists will hold onto this practice, discrediting governmental decisions as anti-Islamic, or if human rights organizations will help to stop the perpetuation on FGM/C.

Recent studies and surveys show that the practice of FGM/C has become less prevalent in Egypt, after 1996's ban of FGM/C in hospitals (FGM/C still could be performed elsewhere) and the 2008 criminalization law of FGM.[14] Recent research in Upper Egypt shows FGM/C procedures performed by general practitioners doubled to almost 100 percent in 2009. Most of previous FGM/C used to be performed by a *daya* (a local midwife). FGM/C prevalence rate is still high at 89.2 percent. The study shows 88.2 percent of nurses, 34.3 percent of young physicians, and 14.9 percent of senior physicians preferred to uphold FGM/C (Rasheed et al. 2011).

Is *Sunna* Circumcision a Form of FGM/C?

While some leaders in many Muslim dominant societies have expressed their opposition to FGM/C, they are not against the *sunna* female circumcision. FGM/C refers the more severe forms of excision, such as type III, infibulation, or the more severe form of type II as explained above. This may explain how many Arab and Muslim countries accept and subscribe to international calls to end FGM/C, since such a definition is not used in these countries. What is practiced in these countries is *sunna* circumcision that does not belong to FGM/C, according to their interpretation. As highlighted with the example of Indonesia, FGM/C is practiced and widespread in more countries than those reported in international agencies such as WHO and UNICEF. The recent references to the presence of FGM/C in other countries may shed more light on FGM/C practices in more countries, where officials do not distinguish *Sunna* circumcision from FGM/C.

The Medicalization of FGM/C: Taking the Cultural Norm Away From FGM/C

The new trend to transform FGM/C practices from a norms to a cosmetic medical procedure further complicates the discussion surrounding FGM/C. Under the new trend, FGM/C will be will be performed in operating rooms in hospital/clinics under anesthesia, and in accordance with proper medical procedures. Given this new concept, some societies can claim that they oppose FGM/C, since what takes place in their societies is a cosmetic medical procedure based on proper medical diagnosis, not just a continuation of a gender discriminating norm.

Summary

FGM/C is a norm that is rooted in religious and social norms in some countries in the Arab world. Collectivist leadership and members in many societies aim to perpetuate FGM/C and other gender discriminating practices as long as such norms and practices suit their aspiration and align with their beliefs. These beliefs can be combatted with appropriate government intervention and education. Counselling parents and religious leaders is integral to eradicate FGM/C. In collectivist societies, disputes regarding norms with religious roots tend to favor religious leaders, as political leaders face international pressure to speak against the beliefs that most of the society holds. In the end, "what protects a boy or a girl from making mistakes is not the removal of a small piece of flesh from the body, but consciousness and understanding of the problems we face, and a worthwhile aim in life, an aim which gives it meaning and for whose attainment we exert our mind and energies" (El Saadawi 1980: 42).

Appendix 10.1: The Economics of FGM/C: A Simple Cost Benefit Analysis of FGM/C

The fate of FGM/C depends on the costs and benefits associated with all involved parties: female children, their parents, and the collective unit. FGM/C belongs not only to the private domain, but also to collectivist domain. Female children are subjected to FGM/C due to insufficient understanding of FGM/C and proper evaluation of the costs and benefits associated with such practice. FGM/C is likely to continue in many collectivist societies as long as the cost–benefit analysis warrants such a practice. Adherence levels to practices such as FGM/C depends on the following factors:

1. The social net benefit, NB_s, from adhering to the norm: the sum of the individual's net benefit, NB_i, and the collective net benefit, NB_c: $NB_s = NB_i + NB_c$. If the collective benefit, B_c, exceeds the collective cost, C_c, associated with a certain norm, NB_c will be positive and the norm will be more prevalent, and vice versa. The same can be said for NB_i. The parents act as proxy for their daughter since FGM/C is usually performed during the daughter's infancy/childhood.

2. The degree of collectivism in the society: Let α refer to the degree of collectivism in a given society. A larger α refers to a higher degree of collectivism, making such norms as FGM/C more prevalent in high-degree collectivist society than lower degree collectivism (or a high degree of individualism). $1 \geq \alpha \geq 0$, with $\alpha = 1$ in a perfectly collectivist society, and zero in a perfectly individualist society.

3. The degree of norm's sacredness, β: $1 \geq \beta \geq 0$, with $\beta = 1$ for authentic/sacred norms (or informal institutions), and zero for unauthentic norms. For disputed norms such as FGM/C, β's value will be less than one and higher than zero, depending on the degree of authenticity of the norm.

4. The level of collective punishment, θ, to violators of sacred norm: higher level of punishment against norm's violators will sustain the norm and

widen its prevalence compared to lower levels of punishment against the norm's violators. $\theta \geq 0$, with $\theta = 0$ in a perfectly individualist society.

5. Degree of forced membership and immobility, γ: $1 \geq \gamma \geq 0$, with $\gamma = 1$ in a perfect collectivist society with compulsory membership and lack of mobility, and zero in a perfect individualist societies with voluntary membership and free mobility.

6. Type of norms, $\Phi\{0, 1\}$: norms are classified into norms and metanorms. In the case of metanorms, where $\Phi = 1$, not only the norm's violators (deviants) are punished but also the collaborators (shirkers), which in turn increases the level of adherence to these metanorms compared to the norms, where $\Phi = 0$.

In a perfectly individualist society with an absence of metanorms and collective punishment and presence of effective formal institutions, norms are likely to endure and to be prevalent only if the individual's net benefit is positive. Otherwise, such norms are likely to fade away.

In contrast, norms like FGM/C are more likely to endure and be prevalent in a perfect collectivist society in which norms are supported by sacred traditions, elevated to metanorms, and supported by excessive collective punishment.

It is reasonable to assume the individual's net benefit is negative in regards to FGM/C, and these practices will not exist in individualist societies. Likewise, most of benefits associated with FGM/C are the collective benefits of deep-rooted 'sacred' norms in certain collectivist societies. It is reasonable to assume that the collectivist net benefit is positive.

The possible scenarios (excluding zero's net benefit, for simplicity) are:

1. Both $NB_i > 0$ and $NB_c > 0$: the norm will be practiced in both individualist and collectivist societies.

2. Both $NB_i < 0$ and $NB_c < 0$: the norm will not exist in either the individualist or collectivist societies. An example of such norm is incest.

3. $NB_i > 0$ and $NB_c < 0$: the norm will be practiced in individualist societies, for example, participating in secular or 'foreign' activities/festivities such as Valentine's Day[15]. These activities will be opposed and even punished in collectivist societies if they violate any of the core beliefs.

4. $NB_i < 0$ and $NB_c > 0$: the norm will be opposed and will not exist in individualist societies, for example, FGM/C, under-age marriage, 'honor' killing, and so on. However, it will be practiced/followed in some collectivist societies.

The following analysis corresponds to scenario 4.

The Degree of Collectivism, α

The weighted social net benefit function will be,

$$NB_s = (1 - \alpha)\, NB_i + \alpha\, NB_c$$

The critical value of α that makes $NB_s = 0$ is

$$\alpha = \frac{-NB_i}{NB_c - NB_i} \, , \, 1 \geq \alpha \geq 0; \text{ note that } NB_i < 0.$$

In a perfect individualist society, with $\alpha = 0$, $NB_s = NB_i < 0$, the practice does not exist.

In a perfect collectivist society, with $\alpha = 1$, $NB_s = NB_c > 0$, the practice exists

In the case of imperfect individualist or collectivist society, with $1 > \alpha > 0$, NB_s will be positive if $\alpha > \left(\dfrac{-NB_i}{NB_c - NB_i} \right)$

Given NB_i and NB_c, NB_s depends on the value of α. Higher α increases the weight of the collectivist net benefit, causing NB_s to increase. Thus, certain norms will be prevalent in collectivist societies, when $NB_s > 0$, even though $NB_i < 0$, depending on the values of α and NB_c. For example, in perfect collectivist societies, NB_c captures all the weight, with zero weight allocated to NB_i, making $NB_s > 0$.

In order to sustain any norm in a collective society, leaders and policy makers have three options: increase α, increase NB_c, or decrease NB_i. Any of the above three options, separate or combined, serves to increase NB_s, and therefore sustain certain gender discriminating norms and traditions.

The Degree of Norm's Sacredness, β, $1 \geq \beta \geq 0$

β ranges between 0 for non-sacred norms and one for strictly sacred norms. The modified net social benefit function will be,

$$NB_s = (1 - \alpha)^* \, NB_i(\beta) + \alpha^* NB_c \, (\beta)$$

Higher sensitivity or responsiveness of net benefit to norms' sacredness on the norms will increase NB_s: $\dfrac{\partial NB_s}{\partial \beta} = \left[(1 - \alpha) \dfrac{\partial NB_i}{\partial \beta} + \alpha \dfrac{\partial NB_c}{\partial \beta} \right] > 0$

$\partial NB_c / \partial \beta > 0$: it is reasonable to assume that NB_c is very sensitive to the degree of norms' sacredness. For simplicity, assume $\partial NB_i / \partial \beta = 0$. Therefore, $\partial NB_s / \partial \beta > 0$.

Depending on the degree of sensitivity of the NB_s to β, norms that are more sacred prevail and endure in certain collectivist societies regardless of how such norms marginalize certain population groups, and violate their human rights, e.g., FGM/C and 'honor' killing.

The Level of Collective Punishment of Norms' Violators/Dissenters, θ: $\theta \geq 0$

Higher levels of punishment against norm's violators, $\theta > 0$, will sustain the norm and widen its prevalence compared to low or no levels of punishment against the norm's violators. In an individualist society, θ is zero. The further modified net social benefit function will be,

$$NB_s = (1 - \alpha)^* \, NB_i(\beta, \theta) + \alpha^*NB_c(\beta, \theta)$$

θ affects both NB_i and NB_c similar to the effect of the norm's sacredness. Punishing the norm's violators will reduce their opposition to, or rejection of, the norm, since the punishment increases the individual's cost of violating the norm. The formal/informal virtue police in some Arab countries is a good example of the collective punishment on norm's violators, for example, punishing women who do not adhere the proper attire that is collectively sanctioned. The collectivist's punishment reduces the individual incentive to violate the norm, thus increasing his/her incentive to follow the norm, even though NB_i is negative. Higher θ increases NB_c since it allows the collectivist unit to assert a higher degree of control over individuals' behavior, therefore increasing collective utility.

Degree of Social Norms, Φ: Φ{0, 1}

Social norms can be classified into regular (or normal) norms and metanorms. Metanorms help sustain collectivist norms for three main reasons: first, punishing the shirker will further reduce the deviant's net benefit. Second, shirkers are likely to report or even punish the metanorm's deviants just to deter any collectivist punishment against themselves. Third, collectivist members gain from reporting the deviants and shirkers to the collectivist unit or directly from punishing them for their unsanctioned acts/behaviors. Thus, adherence to metanorms is higher than the adherence to regular norms, where $\Phi = 0$.

Let P_j represent the collective punishment against the second-order norm's violators (the shirker). The effect of collective punishment of deviants (first-order violators) and shirkers (second-order violator of norms) in collectivist society on the net social benefit of the norms will be, $NB_s = (1 - \alpha)^* \, NB_i(\beta, \Phi, P_j(\Phi)) + NB_j \, (P_j(\Phi)) + \alpha^*NB_c \, (\beta, \theta, P_j(\Phi))$ where $P_j \geq 0$.

In the case of metanorms, $\Phi = 1$, the potential shirker faces a catch 22: to report or punish the deviant and suffer from internal inflicting harm or to not report or punish the deviant and be exposed to the collectivist punishment. Either way, the shirkers net benefits are decreased. Punishing the shirkers should also increase NB_c, since it increases the collective conformity to sanctioned norms and metanorms. The net effect on the social net benefit is still indeterminate: even though the net individual benefits of both the deviant and shirkers decreases, metanorms increase the collectivist net benefit due to the higher rate of adherence. The net effect on the social net benefit depends on the weights attached to the individualist and collectivist units as explained above.

Levels of Freedom of Membership and Mobility, γ: 1 ≥ γ ≥ 0

The effect of the level of individual's freedom of membership and mobility on the net social benefit of certain norms reflects their degree of mobility into and out of society. In collectivist societies with fully forced membership, collectivist norms will be imposed on all members regardless of their effects. In contrast, members of individualist societies are free to relinquish their membership or move out of such a society if the social norms and practices cause them to suffer, feel excluded, or marginalized. The effect of γ on the social net benefit function is, $NB_s = \gamma \{(1 - \alpha)^* NB_i (\beta, 0, \Phi, P_j) + \alpha^* NB_c (\beta, 0, \Phi, P_j)$.

The effect of perfect mobility and voluntary membership, $\gamma = 0$, in collective societies is the gradual drop in membership in these societies, with all individualists leaving the collective society, $NB_s = NB_c$. The collectivist society will only include collectivist members who voluntarily accept such collectivist norms. This also happens in certain clusters of collectivist groups living in individualist societies, for example, some immigrant groups living in the West, who impose their practices only on the collectivist members, since the individualists member are capable of relinquishing their membership. However, in many collectivist societies, individualists are incapable of moving out.

In the case of $\gamma = 0$, the social net benefit of adhering to the norm will be reduced only to the collectivist net benefit, $NB_s = NB_c > 0$; however, it is applied only to a sub-section of the population, the collectivist group[16]. With $\gamma = 0$, the collectivist society acts similar to an individualist society when deviants and shirkers have the capabilities and means to move out of the society. The only exceptions are those who lack sufficient means to leave.

In summary, gender discriminating norms are more prevalent in societies with higher levels of collectivism, norm's sacredness, collective punishments, immobility, and where membership is forced.

Appendix 10.2.1: Backward-Induction Analysis FGM/C as a Regular Norm

L et α be the probability that parents will choose to not have their daughter(s) undergo FGM/C, and β be the probability that the collective unit will punish parents who make this choice.

Assuming that net individual benefit of FGM/C is negative, $NB_i < 0$, parents in a perfect individualist society will choose to not have their daughter(s) undergo FGM/C. In contrast, in a perfect collectivist society, with a high value attached to the sacred norm of FGM/C, that is, with $NB_c > 0$, parents will choose FGM/C for their daughter(s). The case becomes more complex for individualist parents in collectivist societies. Individualist parents who reject the norm have two options, they may conform to the norm if the expected collective punishment exceeds NB_i, or they may not conform if the effect of the collective punishment is lower than their net benefit from opposing the norm.

Figure A10.2.1 shows, in a perfect individualist society with $\alpha = 1$ and $\beta = 0$, Pr (FGM/C) = 0. In a perfect collectivist societies: $\alpha = 0$, and Pr (FGM/C) =

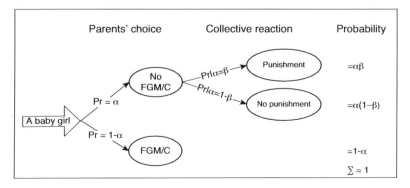

Figure A10.2.1 FGM/C, the case of a regular social norm.

1. In an imperfect collectivist society with $1 > \alpha > 0$, $1 > \beta > 0$, $\Pr(FGM/C) < 1$. Therefore the prevalence of FGM/C depends on the parents' choice and on the probability of collective punishment against deviant parents. Higher levels of collective punishment against deviants can sway some individualist parents to have their daughter(s) undergo FGM/C.

Appendix 10.2.2: Backward-Induction Analysis of FGM/C as a Metanorm

Elevating FGM/C to a metanorm will influence the decision made by individualist parents by increasing the effect of the collective punishment on the individualist parents' choice. A successful application of metanorms will impose collective punishments on deviant parents and on the shirkers (usually family members and other close friends and neighbors) who observe the deviant parents' behavior and do not punish them or report them to authorities.

Given α and β as illustrated in Figure A10.2.2, let θ be the probability that the collectivist unit will punish the shirker who reports the deviants to the collectivist unit of punishes them directly corroding to their un-sanctioned act. Also, let λ be the probability that the collectivist unit will punish the shirker for failing to punish the deviants or report them to the collectivist unit.

In a perfect individualist society where $\alpha = 1$, $\beta = 0$, $\lambda = 0$; Pr (FGM/C) = 0.

Figure A10.2.2 shows that in a perfect collectivist societies with perfect collectivist members, $\alpha = 0$, and Pr (FGM/C) = 1.

In an imperfect collectivist society with $1 > \alpha > 0$, $1 > \beta > 0$, $1 > \theta > 0$, and $0 > \lambda > 1$: $0 < $ Pr (FGM/C) $ < 1$.

- Higher β will increase the cost to deviant parents; therefore increasing Pr (FGM/C).
- Lower θ will induce other collectivist members to punish or report the deviant parents, increasing the collective cost on the deviant parents. This may cause the parents to reevaluate their choice, especially with higher β and lower θ.
- Higher λ will increase the costs on potential shirkers, inducing them to punish or report the deviants parents, thus heightening the punishment imposed on the deviant parents and causing some of them to change their choice and accept the FGM/C norm.

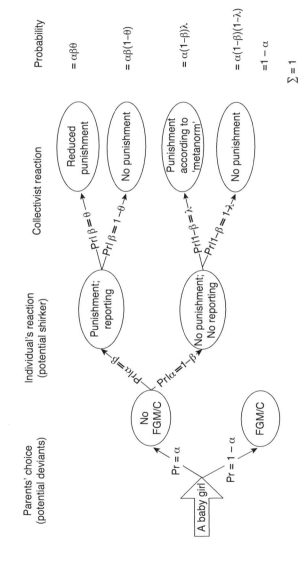

Figure A10.2.2 FGM/C, the case of a Metanorm.

The above analysis highlights the variables that influence the choices of different agents regarding gender discriminating norms, such as FGM/C: individualist parents, collectivist parents, other members in the collective society such as potential shirkers, and the collective unit. Potential intervention to eradicate or diminish certain gender discriminating norms such as FGM/C should take into consideration the dynamics of such variables, the different participants, and the collective schemes of reward and punishment.

CHAPTER 11

Norms and Gender Violence

Norms play a very important role in sustaining and perpetuating gender violence in the Arab world (and other similar countries). CEDAW's definition of gender violence encompasses varying levels and forms of violence, "For the purposes of this Declaration, the term 'violence against women' means any act of gender-based violence that results in, or is likely to result in, physical, sexual or psychological harm or suffering to women, including threats of such acts, coercion or arbitrary deprivation of liberty, whether occurring in public or in private life" (UN 1993). However, various cultural, social, and legal definitions of gender violence do not recognize certain forms and levels of violence. This allows socially and culturally sanctioned acts of violence against women to exist without them being considered as violent acts. Examples of practices that are not considered violent acts in many Arab countries (and other similar societies) include FGM/C, domestic violence, marital rape, and underage marriage. These practices are condoned or accepted as features of normalcy that are integral to the cultural heritage and social fabric of their societies. Cultural relativists underscore the importance of analyzing violence according to its cultural specific meanings (Zuckerhut 2011).

Gender violence, especially within the socially assigned norms and rules, serves as a constructive instrument in some gender-discriminating societies. It strengthens and maintains the social order and societal hierarchy. Likewise, gender violence creates and promotes solidarity within groups by punishing dissenters and shirkers of social norms and rules, thus sustaining order. Violators of socially assigned gender, religious and ethnic identities in discriminating societies (e.g., disobedient women in gender-discriminating societies) should be disciplined and punished to keep the social order intact (Zuckerhut 2011).

Treating women, informally, and/or formally, as legal minors in some Arab societies reduces women's status, especially with regard to making decisions on their own, or participating in decision-making in their collectivist units. As legal minors, girls and women are subject to minor-like treatment, such as their exposure to verbal admonishment, confinement, and physical disciplining when they violate their assigned social identities and roles as submissive and obedient. The high percentage of women in the Arab world who believe that their husbands are justified in beating them if they violate or neglect their assigned roles is a de facto admission of their status as minors and their acceptance of physical violence against them. A 2011 survey in Egypt shows that 81 percent of men believe they have the right to beat their wives and daughters (U.S. DOSa: Egypt 2014). Another survey shows that almost 40 percent of Egyptian women agree that husbands are justified in hitting or beating their wives under certain circumstances (El-Zanaty and Way 2008).

Using cultural concepts of gender violence makes it impossible to have a meaningful international analysis and comparison of gender violence. The differences of forms and levels of violence in various societies complicate international comparison, and distort many international statistics. Underage marriage and FGM/C are not considered acts of gender violence in many Arab countries. Spousal rape is condoned in all Arab countries. Many Arab countries condone and even sanction certain levels of physical discipline of women and girls by their husbands and male relatives/guardians (U.S. DOSa 2014; Kelly and Breslin 2010; Human Rights Watch 2014a).

Gender-discriminating norms influence collective and individual behaviors to control and sometimes constrain women's capabilities and functionings at different stages of their lives. FGM/C serves as an ex-ante measure to control and weaken female sexual desires. Underage marriage also serves as another ex-ante measure to uphold honor and minimize possible shame associated with illicit sexual behaviors or rumors that can damage the girl's reputation and family's honor. Both serve to control young girls' sexuality, enhance the likelihood of female fidelity, and thus reduce the likelihood of dishonor. Domestic violence (including spousal rape), confinement to the private sphere, and sexual harassment are examples of ongoing measures to ensure women's submission and obedience. Honor killing (and other excessive forms of violence) serves as an example of ex-post measures used as a collective punishment against women whose behaviors, rumors about their behaviors, and sometimes acts beyond their control (victimized by rape, genetic features such as girls born without hymen, and girls who do not bleed after the defloration of hymen (France 24 2014c), stain some of the most prized collective assets—female reputation, girls' virginity before marriage, and women's fidelity after marriage.

Domestic Violence

Domestic violence is an appalling violation of women's rights. It is present in all societies. Nevertheless, in certain gender-discriminating collectivist societies, some prevalent social norms and rules condone and even sanction certain forms and levels of violence against women. "In many parts of the Middle East (and other regions of the world) the beating of women and other dependents by men in the household or male relatives is (still) accepted as a form of discipline to retain inner-domestic relations of power" (Zuckerhut (2011: 16)).

Domestic violence is used as an instrument of social order and cultural harmony. According to WHO, "[O]ne of the most common forms of violence against women is that performed by a husband or male partner. This type of violence is frequently invisible since it happens behind closed doors, and effectively, when legal systems and cultural norms do not treat domestic violence as a crime, but rather as a 'private' family matter, or a normal part of life" (2002). International and national research and statistics tend to overlook or underestimate the prevalence of gender violence because they use an incorrect unit of reference or measurement—the family rather than the individual. Using the family as the unit of reference undermines the political structure and the skewed distribution of power and status within the family. In gender-discriminating collectivist societies, most acts of gender violence take place within the family, inside the domestic residence of the victims. Domestic violence is a result of norms, traditions, and formal rules that favor men over women in their distribution of power and status. Therefore, although domestic violence occurs in all societies, its prevalence and acceptance varies significantly between countries, or groups of countries, according to collectively sanctioned norms and rules.

In the absence of norms that sanctions domestic violence, women in individualist societies have, in general, more access to report violent acts and receive justice through effective law enforcement. However, in many gender-discriminating collectivist societies, victims of domestic violence are trapped in the presence of norms that condone this violence. Victims often fail to report such acts due to an internal and external feeling of shame that results from betraying the collective unit. In addition, the lack of formal rules to protect victims (or prosecute perpetrators), along with ineffective enforcement of existing rules, discourages the victims of domestic violence from sharing such acts with others, especially non in-group members, for example, through filing formal complaints to authority.

Cultural and social factors that increase the likelihood of spousal abuse/violence include family and relationship factors such as male control of wealth and decision-making process, in addition to marital conflict. Community factors include the isolation and lack of social capital of women due to their lack of access to the public sphere, as well as the presence of male groups that condone and legitimize abuse, predict higher rates of violence. Societal factors show that violence against women is most common in societies where gender roles are rigidly defined and enforced, and where the concept of masculinity is linked to toughness, male honor, and dominance (CHANGE 1999).

Norms, Normalcy, and the Concept of Violence

In many gender-discriminating societies, domestic violence and the practice of disciplining wives and children are accepted as normal. Media, soap operas, religious sermons, and educational curricula, among other things, condone and even sanction certain norms and traditions associated with gender violence as integral to the society's cultural heritage and social order. Violence against wives and other female dependents by men is accepted as a normal form of discipline to retain domestic order and/or power (Zuckerhut 2011). Identifying women as legal minors in certain societies reduces their status, especially with regard to making decisions. Consequently, it subjects them to 'normal' forms of discipline, including physical discipline. "Studies around the world have found that violence against women is most common where gender roles are rigidly defined and enforced and where the concept of masculinity is linked to toughness, male honor, or dominance. Other cultural norms associated with abuse include tolerance of physical punishment of women and children, acceptance of violence as a means to settle interpersonal disputes, and the perception that men have 'ownership' of women" (CHANGE 1999: 8).

Wife beating is accepted as a normal punishment for a woman's disobedience, arguing with her husband, or for the mere fact that her husband was upset and needed to vent, as is stated by an Egyptian female: "Yes, in some circumstances the man is forced to beat his wife. Sometimes she's done something wrong and in spite of that she leaves her house to her parents' house" (Katulis 2004:20). It is clearly stated by police to an abused wife in the United Arab Emirates, "In the UAE husbands are allowed to beat their wives" (Human Rights Watch 2014a).

In gender-discriminating societies, perpetrators typically argue for their rights to punish or discipline victims as a response to victims' failure to fulfil their duties or to behave properly according to social norms and assigned roles. For example, the husband's (or other male guardians) de facto impunity to punish his wife gives certain normalcy and legitimacy to such acts of violence (Zuckerhut 2011: 14). Legitimacy is related to norms, laws, and ethical codes in each society. It is typically related to status and power of the perpetrators and victims. High levels of status and power for male perpetrators make their acts legitimate and normal (Zuckerhut 2011). What matters in gender-discriminating societies is not violence per se; it is the legitimacy and 'just cause' of using violence as an instrument of discipline that is integrated and accepted in the social fabric of the community. Gender violence within the socially sanctioned norms is accepted as a part of the ongoing measures to remind women of their identities and roles as obedient and repository of collective honor. Violence serves also as a normal response to women's disobedience or negligence. It is socially accepted as a normal behavior to uphold social order and cultural harmony.

The prevalence and legitimacy of gender violence in different societies differs according to each society's perception of what violence is, what counts as violence, the attributes of perpetrators and victims, the socially assigned roles of men and women in the societies, the prevalence of gender-discriminating collective norms, and the collective power to enforce norms within the society.

Figures 11.1 and 11.2 illustrate the rate of women's acceptance of domestic violence under certain circumstances in selected countries in the Arab world (with the exception of Lebanon[1]), ranging from 30 percent in Tunisia to 76 percent in Somalia. This differs significantly from smaller rates in selected countries in the Caribbean and Latin America, ranging from 2 percent in Argentine to 17 percent in Haiti. Many countries in the Arab world condone or even

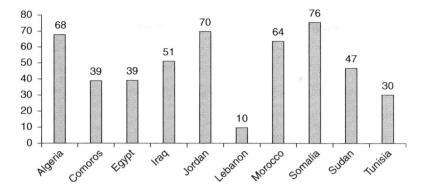

Figure 11.1 Percentage of girls and women aged 15–49, in selected Arab countries, who think that a husband/partner is justified in hitting or beating his wife/partner under certain circumstances (Data Range:2003 to 2012).

Source: Data collected from UNICEF: UNICEF Global Database. http://data.unicef.org/child-protection/attitudes. Updated: November 2014.

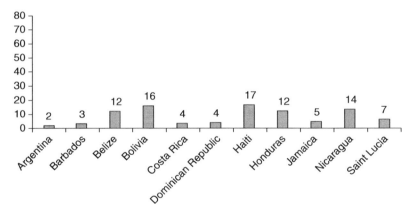

Figure 11.2 Percentage of girls and women aged 15–49, in selected Caribbean and Latin American countries, who think that a husband/partner is justified in hitting or beating his wife/partner under certain circumstances (Data Range:2006 to 2012).

Source: Data collected from UNICEF: UNICEF Global Database. http://data.unicef.org/child-protection/attitudes. Updated: November 2014.

endorse the 'just cause' of certain acts of domestic violence, within socially sanctioned limits (CHANGE 1999: 6–7).

The high percentage of women who believe that their husbands are justified in hitting or beating them if they violate or neglect their assigned roles, is a de facto admission of women's status as minors and second-class citizens, and consequently, their acceptance and justification of domestic violence against them.

Figure 11.3 illustrates the prevalence and normalcy of domestic violence in Egypt and Morocco. It shows women's acceptance of wife beating under different circumstances, such as going out without his permission, neglecting the children, arguing with him, or for refusing to have sex with him. Justifying domestic violence mirrors the norms of women's submission and obedience, and their acceptance of collectively assigned punishment. In gender-discriminating societies, the blame is usually imposed on women for perceived disobedience and/or negligence.

Women, in gender-discriminating collectivist societies, can avoid domestic violence if they act obediently. In these societies, incidences of domestic violence can be blamed in part on women who instigate such acts when they violate their social roles and attributes as obedient and submissive. The internalization of gender violence in women's minds distorts their cognitive models, such that women, in their effort to minimize such suffering and pain, may resign to accept the blame for the beating by their husbands or guardians as a response to their negligence and disobedience. Domestic violence or the threat of it becomes a normal feature in women's lives. A woman can avoid or minimize the likelihood of being chastised or beaten by being submissive and obedient to her husband, therefore fulfilling her socially assigned role. In the process, many women suffer significantly. They sacrifice their own individual capabilities and functionings so they can acclimate a lower level of domestic violence, a lower level of negative freedom. It is an unfair game between women and their husbands or male guardians, in which women "win" only by avoiding or minimizing the physical violence inflicted on them.

The surveys also show that the rate of acceptance of domestic violence depends on different socioeconomic markers such as wealth, education, and residences. Rich, educated, and urban women are less likely to agree that a husband is justified in beating his wife, while poor, uneducated, and rural women are more likely. Studies show that when women have power and authority outside the family, rates of spousal and domestic abuse appear to be lower (CHANGE

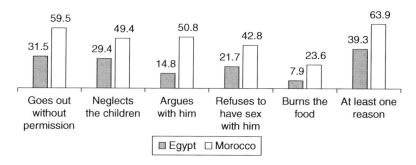

Figure 11.3 Percentage of ever-married women agreeing husband is justified in hitting or beating his wife if she... (Egypt 2008; Morocco 2003).

Note: Ever-married women include married, divorced, and widowed women.

Sources: Data collected from table 3.14 in El-Zanaty & Way (2009: 43), and tableau 3.13 in Ministère de la Santé, Maroc (2005: 39).

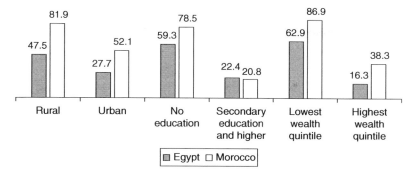

Figure 11.4 Percentage of ever-married women who agree that a husband is justified in beating his wife for at least one reason, Egypt (2008), Morocco (2003).
Source: Data collected from table 3.14 in El-Zanaty and Way (2009: 43) and Tableau 3.12 in Ministère de la Santé, Maroc (2005: 39).

1999). These findings support the notion that collectivist-prone women, such as poor, uneducated, and rural women are more likely to act according to the collective norms and roles of obedience, accepting and internalizing collective gender-discriminating practices in the process, as figure 11.4 shows.

The Norms of Domestic Violence (or Discipline)

Domestic violence is prevalent today in non-Muslim communities as well, but the apparent religious sanction in Islam makes the challenge especially difficult. Asra Nomani (2006, par 18)

Some widely accepted informal norms of discrimination imposed on women include women's dependency on and submission to men, since these norms provide men more power and higher status than women do. In many Arab and similar Islamic societies, men, supported by informal norms, formal rules, and the governance structure of transactions, can and do, to different degrees, abuse their wives and deprive them from certain basic human rights, capabilities, and functionings.

An important aspect of domestic violence is not the actual incidence of violence per se, but the collective acceptance of physical violence as a norm in the Arab world and other similar societies, that makes domestic violence normal. The mere access to violence by a husband (or a legal guardian) as an instrument to discipline his wife (or a female dependent) is enough to instill fear and violation of women's human rights and capabilities, and to diminish their well-being. This explains why domestic violence is often not considered or even recorded as an act of violence against women. Not admitting domestic violence as a form of violence against women gives precedence to informal norms rooted in sacred teaching and texts, over women's well-being, human rights, capability, and functioning.

According to widely accepted interpretations of sacred texts such as the *Qur'an, hadith,* and *sunna*, husbands can admonish their wives verbally, abandon them in bed, and beat them, respectively, to disciplines their wives if husbands fear their wives' disobedience or disloyalty. The 'fear' is based on men's fear or perception, not the actual act of disloyalty or disobedience (the *Qur'an* 4:34). In summary, beating wives serve as a preemptive and ongoing instrument to make them act to fulfill collectively assigned norms and rules.

Asra Nomani (2006) uses "the 4:34 dance" to highlight the complexity and the influence of norms on gender violence in Islamic societies, such as the Arab world, and its exploitation to endorse or condone violence against women. The 4:34 dance refers to a *qur'anic* verse that instructs husbands on how to respond if they fear their disobedience or rebelliousness from their wives:

> *Men are the maintainers of women because Allah has made some of them to excel others and because they spend out of their property; the good women are therefore obedient, guarding the unseen as Allah has guarded; and (as to) those on whose part you fear desertion, admonish them, and leave them alone in the sleeping-places and beat them; then if they obey you, do not seek a way against them; surely Allah is High, Great.* The *Qur'an* (4:34)

First, men should admonish their wives in hope that their wives will behave accordingly by obeying their husbands and abandoning any act of disobedience.

Second, if wives fail to response properly to their husbands' verbal admonishment, husbands can extend the punishment by abandoning their wives in bed, deserting them sexually. Men have the right to marry, and satisfy their sexual needs/desires with up to four wives according to widespread acceptance of interpretation of sacred scripture (the *Qur'an* 4:3). Husbands have the capability to satisfy their sexual needs, while wives are left unable to satisfy their sexual desires, since a woman cannot marry anyone besides her husband. Accordingly, the deprivation from intimate/sexual relations is effectively forced on women only. Furthermore, the husband can desert his wife sexually for up to four months, according to sacred teaching (the *Qur'an* 2:226–227). Moreover, other sacred norms condone certain forms of domestic sexual violence, such as spousal rape (or forced sex). Relegating women's sexual need and desires is echoed in other norms rooted in sacred teaching. For example, according to *hadith*, wives must put their husbands' sexual desires ahead of their own religious aspirations, such as optional fasting. Wives must get their husbands' permission first, since fasting Muslims should refrain from sexual contact during their fast. In contrast, husbands do not need a permission from their wives before fasting. According to *hadiths*, angels curse women who reject their husbands' sexual desires. In contrast, there is no divine punishment for men who reject their wives' sexual desires. In the above examples, women, behaving according to the norms, can be forced to act against their free will. They can internalize these discriminating norms/practices, or expose themselves to collectivist punishment if they violate such norms. These examples of discriminating norms signify multiple violations of women's capabilities and functioning in comparison to men's. The intimate (sexual) relation between a husband and wife, according to these norms, sets up a game in which women are destined to lose, since men have access to second sources (access to other wives).

Third, husbands have the right to beat their wives as a last resort, if admonishing and abandoning their wives fail to convince them to correct their behaviors. Beating wives or just the right of men to beat their wives continues to be a very hot topic of in many Islamic societies. In general, a high percentage of Arab men, and a significant proportion of Arab women (though lower than the men's percentage) believe that men have the right to beat their wives. The implicit approval of such discriminating norms is reflected in the absence of laws in most Arab countries against domestic violence. Domestic violence is largely considered as a private or social matter, not a legal one (U.S. DOSa 2014). This also explains the strikingly high rate of reservations made by the Arab world to specific articles in CEDAW, with regard to such gender-discriminating norms sanctioned by interpretations of Islamic *shari'ah*. In many Arab countries, domestic violence against women is tolerated, in part, through legal high thresholds of injury, such that many cases of domestic/spousal violence are practically non-punishable (U.S. DOSa 2014; Human Rights Watch 2014a). Only excessive cases of violence, which exceed the norm-based threshold of injury, can be prosecuted.

Most Islamic scholars and commentators set limits on beating wives, such as avoiding beating the face and other sensitive parts or causing an injury. Proper beating, according to some scholars and commentators, should not hurt much, break bones, leave marks on the body, or be on the face. Men are also commanded not to exploit or misuse such right, according to the Prophet, "None of you should flog his wife as he flogs a slave and then have sexual intercourse with her in the last part of the day."[2]

Nomani highlights the dilemma facing many Islamic scholars and leaders, "they reject outright violence against women but accept a level of aggression that fits contemporary definitions of domestic violence" (2006: par 4). The dilemma stems from the conflict between universally accepted human rights and prevalent interpretations of sacred teaching in the *Qur'an* and *hadith* (Nomani 2006; Badawi 1995). Nomani also reflects on the contradiction between beating wives and other Islamic tenets that stand against cruelty, such as, "The Believers, men and women, are protectors one of another: they enjoin what is just, and forbid what is evil: they observe regular prayers, practice regular charity, and obey Allah and His Messenger" (the *Qur'an* 9:71).

However, according to critics of sacred discriminating norms, 4:34 is just another reference to misogyny and violence (Nomani 2006). The presence of sacred references that condone violence should not invalidate other sacred references that call on men to treat women justly. However, the presence of verses and *hadiths* that condone violence are used and sometimes exploited by the beneficiaries of the status quo in many patriarchal Islamic societies.

To understand the influence of sacred norms on gender discrimination, one should compare the sacred instruction to wives who fear their husband's ill treatment or cruelty to the instruction to husbands who fear their wives' disobedience:

> And if a woman fears ill usage or desertion on the part of her husband, there is no blame on them, if they effect a reconciliation between them, and reconciliation is better, and avarice has been made to be present in the (people's) minds; and if you do good (to others) and guard (against evil), then surely Allah is aware of what you do. The *Qur'an* (4:128)

Wives are instructed to seek reconciliation and amicable settlement with their abusive husbands. In contrast, according to the *Qur'an* 4:34, men have more options, all of which deal with different levels of punishment.

The following example highlights the normalcy of domestic violence in the Arab world, and other similar societies: in a recent TV interview, Dr. Muhammad El Gendi (Professor of Islamic *shari'ah* and a member of the Islamic Research Center, Egypt), stated that a wife should not be permitted to file a formal complaint of her husband's physical abuse against her. Instead, she should complain informally to her or his family. His rationale is that a formal complaint may cause a family's breakup. He also states that a husband should not beat his wife unless all other possible ways to correct her behaviors have failed (Sada El-Balad 2014). El-Gendi's view represents a good example of solving problems (or coping with them) informally in a typical gender-discriminating collectivist society. In these societies, domestic violence should be condoned and treated as a family or private matter, not a legal or criminal one.

Spousal Rape: A Concept that Does Not Exist in the Arab Culture

Spousal rape is a form of domestic violence that is condoned and sanctioned in the Arab world (and other similar countries) in accordance to widely accepted interpretations of sacred religious norms. Nonetheless, spousal rape exploits women's sexual capabilities and functionings. It deforms female sexuality, since a woman's role in sexual relations is demoted to serving as an object designated for the purpose of satisfying the husband's sexual needs. Moreover, wives are expected (or forced) to live with their abusive husbands and serve them obediently. Spousal rape turns marital intimacy into a traumatic violation of women's bodily, psychological, and emotional integrity.

As explained in chapter 9, the term "spousal rape" does not exist in these gender-discriminating cultures. Spousal rape and other forms of spousal sexual violence can be used by opportunistic husbands to retaliate against their wives or to humiliate them as a form of corrective punishment.

Polygyny and Domestic Violence

A man's access to viable alternatives, such as divorcing his wife or taking more than one wife, is likely to cause him to invest less in the relationship with any one wife (Charrad 2007). First, men can divorce their wives and stay single or marry other women. Second, men can marry more wives. Third, men know that their wives do not have access to easy divorce or polygamy. Fourth, it is easier for men to accumulate more social capital in gender-discriminating societies than it is for women. Fifth, men are more likely to be able to afford living expenses on their own due to their ability to work in the public sphere. Women are expected to be financially dependent on male guardians. The subsequent discrimination against women is manifested in strikingly lower female labor force participation rates, higher female unemployment rates, and lower female wage rates relative to men in the Arab World. In this uneven-playing field, men can dictate and tilt the marital relation to their favor.

Most Muslim jurists agree that polygyny is impractical nowadays, except if the first wife is barren, or becomes sick (Katulis 2004:22).[3] It is widely acceptable, in most Islamic societies, that a man can/should marry a second wife if the first wife in barren, due to the great value and rewards of having children and the high value of a fertile wife (the *Qur'an* 18:46;[4] Al-Qaradawi 1997). However, in addition to the man's easy access and right to divorce his wife, polygyny offers men a set of viable options or alternatives to the first wife, "Since a man may either repudiate his wife or take a second, third, and fourth wife, there is little incentive for him to invest much of himself in the relationship with any one wife" (Charrad 2007: 248). Fatima Mernissi (1987) highlights a game associated with polygyny, in which the husband can make himself more valuable by creating a sense of competition among his wives. She also underscores the effect of polygyny on impoverishing the husband and wife's investment in one another as lovers, "Polygamy is . . . a direct attempt to prevent emotional growth in the conjugal unit and results in the impoverishment of the husband's and wife's investment in each other" (Mernissi 1987: 115). Bahira Sherif-Trask (2004) underscores the contractual nature of marriage in Islam, which validates the sexual relation between the husband and wife upon the consent of the bride and her legal guardian, in the presence of two witnesses and upon the payment of *mahr* (the dowry). The contract entitles the bride to a residence and maintenance from her husband. A wife is expected to submit to her husband's authority and allow him access to her sexually.

Accordingly, the husband can dictate the decision making process—holding most, if not all status/positional goods and leaving very little to his wife. In such a case, wives are at the mercy of their husbands. The potential exploitation of this distributional power has a significant effect on the female perceptions, expectations, and mental models. It is a hostage-like situation for the wives of opportunistic husbands. Wives, seeking to minimize the likelihood of their husband divorcing them or adding new wives are likely to invest tremendously in the marriage. They will obey their husbands and give up many positive freedoms (e.g., their freedom to choose individualist goods such as their choice of attire, their freedom of movement and socialization, and so on). In the process, women tend to internalize marital related anger, abuse, and anxiety. In contrast, there is no equivalent drive for husbands, except their inner moral standard, to invest properly in the marriage.

According to sacred norms, men are the primary breadwinners for their families (the *Qur'an* 4:34). Restricting women from earning potential automatically empowers men at the expense of women. Women serve as keepers of the private sphere, cooking, cleaning, managing the house, and rearing children. Men also have an opportunity to accumulate social capital in the public sphere, which, in turn, ensures and increases their income and independence. Meanwhile, gender-discriminating norms deprive women of viable alternatives such as entering the labor force, finding a job, building viable social and cultural capital, and gaining skills and seniority in order to make a living. The World Bank (2014) statistics show a strikingly low percentage of females in the total labor force in the Arab world. In 2012, 22 percent of women are part of the labor force in the Arab world whereas 39 percent of the world's female population are included in the labor force. In addition, the data show a strikingly high ratio of female-to-male unemployment rates in the Arab states, that is more than twice the World's ratio. In addition, the female labor-force-participation rate (of the qualified female population) in the Arab world was 23 percent, compared to 50.5 percent for the world in 2012 (World Bank 2014). Furthermore, women are prohibited from certain jobs (Engineers, fire fighters, police officers prosecutors, lawyers, judges, certain fields in medicine, and other jobs) that are deemed dangerous or immoral for women in many Arab countries. Laws in many Arab countries ban women from working at night (with few exceptions, such as working in hospitals). Women also need to be accompanied by a male guardian or rent a cab in order to go out in the public sphere. This is the case in countries such as Saudi Arabia, where women are banned from driving (U.S. DOSa: Saudi Arabia 2014). Women, in general, are restricted or banned from taking certain senior or leadership positions in many Arab countries (U.S. DOSa 2014). Moreover, sacred and social norms of the Arab world discourage women from remaining single, or living on their own, due to perceived collective shame and adverse rumors associated with being divorced, unmarried, or living alone (Al-Qaradawi 1997). Most single and divorced women in the Arab world typically live under the guardianship and financial support of their fathers, brothers, or other male guardians. The fear of being divorced, or having to share their husbands with other wives, influences women's behavior and mental models in such a way as to turn women into victims of fear and anxieties, reduce their expectations, give up certain freedoms and human rights, and accept a lower status as second-class citizens.

Given the above, women are still exposed to the risk of being divorced or of sharing their husband with other wives even if they invest significantly in marriage. In many cases, external factors beyond the wife's control may influence her husband's decisions, such as his desire to marry a younger wife. Wives are typically pressured to invest and employ significant resources, including submission and obedience, to minimize the likelihood of domestic violence, divorce, or polygyny (Mernissi 1998).

Women tend to lose more in divorce due to the distributional bias of resources accumulated during the marriage. Most women's contributions are in the private sphere, while men are the income earners. Women's confinement in the private sphere depreciates their skills and reduces the likelihood of success in the labor market and other public spheres, which women are excluded from during their marriage.

Another cultural and religious norm that is elevated to a formal rule in most Islamic societies is the prohibition on adoption (the *Qur'an* 33:4–5). Adoption serves as a substitute for parents who love children but are unable to have them naturally (through pregnancy), and for parents who want to raise orphaned or abandoned children as adopted children. In the absence of adoption, a husband's alternatives to having children in the case of a barren wife are either to divorce the barren wife and marry another woman, or to keep the barren wife and marry another woman (in order to have children).

Furthermore, the norms and rules of child custody have far-reaching effects on wives and mothers, since informal norms and formal rules in most Arab countries give divorced wives only transitory custody of their children. Thereafter, children typically belong to their father and his family.

The above summarizes the many factors that work against women's well-being in marriage. Most if not all, of these factors are direct and indirect outcomes of informal norms, many of which become formal rules in the Arab world, and many other similar countries.

Sexual Harassment

There is no specific law against sexual harassment in most Arab countries. In Egypt, people can be prosecuted for 'public displays of affection,' but not for sexual harassment. Ninety-nine percent of Egyptian women and girls said that they were exposed to sexual harassment (U.S. DOSa: Egypt 2014). According to Kelly and Breslin (2010), about 50 percent of all women in Egypt are subjected to sexual harassment on a daily basis (Kelly and Breslin 2010).

Women are usually blamed, in part, for sexual harassment, for the way to dress or socialize with others, or for their mere presence in the public sphere. Sexual harassment, in gender-discriminating collectivist societies, serves as an instrument against individualist women who do not abide by their collectively assigned roles, such as a strict dress code (*hijab* or veil). According to strict conservative interpretations of sacred teachings, women should only leave the home in case of necessity. They should be accompanied by their husbands, male guardians, a *mahram*,[5] or should have permission from their male guardians to leave the house or travel. Women, according to sacred norms, should cover their adornment except theirs hands and faces, according to most Islamic scholars and jurists, by wearing an *'abaya* (a loose non-transparent cloak that covers the body) over their clothes. Women must not wear perfume in the public sphere since it makes them adulterous according to *hadith*. Women are commanded to not be very pleasant in speaking to strangers (Al-Qaradawi 1997). Thus, girls and women who do not abide by these sacred and collectively assigned norms are to blame if they cause men to harass them in the public sphere. Remarkably, more fully covered girls and women are sexually harassed in the public sphere, mostly because they are not accompanied by their husbands, guardians, or *mahrams* (Katulis 2004). Widespread sexual harassment discourages female participation in many activities that take place in the public sphere such as work, school, shopping, entertaining, and so on. In addition, it put pressures on families to impose restraints on women's movements—crippling their capabilities and functionings. In Oman, as well as other Arab countries, fear of losing employment and of being blamed for instigating sexual harassment prevents women from reporting sexual harassment in the work place. Social responsibility for moral behavior places more blame on women, rather than on the male assailants (Kelly and Breslin 2010).

Women are mostly harassed when they are alone or in groups of females without the presence of a male guardian or a *mahram*. The need for a male guardian or *mahram* to accompany women in the public sphere adds more cost as an inconvenience to the collectivist unit. Thus, female members are commanded, according to sacred teaching (in the *Qur'an* and *hadith*) to stay at home and leave home only in the case of necessity.

Victims of sexual harassment are less likely to file police complains against their offenders, because of their distrust of the criminal justice system, and their fear that their complaints or sharing the incidents with relatives may backfire by limiting their access to the public sphere where sexual harassment takes place (U.S. DOSa 2014).

Rape and Other Forms of Sexual Violence

Rape is an appalling and complex crime and an extreme violation of women's rights. First, the violation of women's physical, emotional, and psychological integrity and well-being is accompanied with shame, self-defeat, fear, mistrust, and so on, which can spiral into a chain of long-term detrimental effects on the rape victim. Second, rape deprives girls of their most precious and valued asset in gender-discriminating societies—their virginity and their virtuous status. Third, rape victims can be blamed, in part, for their role (or perceived role) in rape incidences. For example, in Saudi Arabia (and other Arab countries), both the rape victim and the perpetrator(s) can be punished for illegal mixes of genders, or for illicit consensual sex, especially with the difficulty of proving rape legally in the Arab world. The required testimony of minimum number of credible witnesses, which is rooted in sacred religious norms, is required in most courts (the *Qur'an* 4:15, 24:4), is likely to reduce the rate of prosecuting rape perpetrators, and consequently raise more doubt about the victim's role in the alleged rape. Fourth, the immense shame inflicted on the rape victim's family, which adds great burden and immense fear for the rape victim, since women's reputation and their honor (girls' virginity and women's chastity and fidelity) are considered collective assets. In these societies, rape victims are usually suspected and even accused for their perceived role in exposing themselves, encouraging or even tempting the rapists to rape them, by the not dressing according to the assigned norms, wearing makeup and perfume, being in a public place without the presence of a male guardian, being active in the public spheres, instead of staying at home, or by mixing illicitly with unrelated men.

Women who do not act according to gender-discriminating norms, gender segregation, dress codes, and confinement to their private spheres, share the blame for being raped and must be punished accordingly. Women must wash all traces of perfume before leaving home, even to attend mosque for prayer. In contrast, men are free to leave the house, work, travel, mix with other people, and are also permitted to wear perfume in public (Al-Qaradawi 1997). Men are thought to be weaker than women, and easily given to sexual thoughts and desires. Therefore, there is more burden laid on women's appearance and behavior in the public sphere, so as not to tempt men. The significant constraints and burdens imposed on women, especially in the public sphere, are usually exploited to blame, punish, or even prosecute women who violate them.

Excessive harassment and insensitive treatment of rape victims by police and medical workers (partly, in response to their suspicion of women's role in such a crime) often prevent victims from sharing what has happened. The rape victims are usually subjected to a virginity test that is very humiliating and dreadful. In addition, the victims must answer questions regarding the clothes they were wearing and other questions, all of which can be used to raise more doubt on the victims' characters. In summary, the victim can be blamed/accused informally (by her collectivist unit) and/or formally (by police and court) of violating collective norms and rules, and can be subjected to formal punishment (e.g., lashing or imprisonment) and informal punishment (e.g., forced marriage to the rapist, and killing the victim in the name of honor). In Algeria, for example, the rape victims' fear of societal pressures and judicial obstacles leads to underreporting rape crimes to secure conviction against rapists. According to the Algerian Director of the Judicial Police for the Protection of Childhood, Juvenile Delinquency, and the Protection of Women Victims of Violence, "Reporting rape and other sexual violence remained 'taboo' in Algerian culture ... [Women] prefer to suffer the pain in silence rather than face the possible rejection by their families and societies" (U.S. DOSa: Algeria 2014; Mackinnon 1987).

The legal proof of rape is usually daunting and can lead to the victim's prosecution instead of exoneration. The required number of eligible witnesses (usually a forum of credible males) or the confession of the alleged rapists makes passing the legal threshold very difficult, especially when rape take place in the private sphere away from potential witnesses. According to women's rights groups in Egypt, the rate of rape crime prosecutions is less than 0.5 percent. The actual number of rapes is estimated to be several times higher than the number reported by the government (U.S.DOSa: Egypt 2014). This miniscule rate of prosecuting rape perpetrators sends a clear signal that rapists can get away with a crime and sends a discouraging message to all women that rape is, in large part, a problem for women instead of a crime against women.

The rape victims also may fear prosecution if the alleged rape perpetrator is acquitted. The court can charge the rape victims with illicit sexual conduct. The acquittal of the alleged rape perpetrators and/or prosecution of the victim usually stir up grave informal reactions, for the sake of cleansing the disgrace and shame inflicted on the victim's family or collective unit. Examples of collective informal punishments include killing the rape victim or pressuring her to commit suicide to cleanse the family or the collective unit's honor. In Jordan, authorities incarcerate the victims of rape to protect them from potential retaliation from their families until the family of the victim signs a legal form promising not to harm the victim. However, in most cases, even with the signed form, the victims end up being killed or pressured to commit suicide (U.S. DOSa: Jordan 2014).

The victim of rape may also be pressured to marry her rapist, as an informal or formal settlement. In such a case, the court drops any charge against the rape perpetrators. This is common practice in Jordan, Morocco, and other Arab countries. In Jordan, the law forces rape perpetrator to stay married to the rape victim for a minimum of three years (Kelly and Breslin 2010). In Iraq, the family of the rape victim may seek official intervention to force the rapists to marry their raped victims (U.S. DOSa: Iraq 2014). In Lebanon, rapists who marry their victims are not prosecuted (U.S. DOSa: Lebanon 2014). In Oman, judges offer lighter sentences to rape offenders if they offer to marry their rape victims (U.S. DOSa: Oman 2014). The rationale for such solution is to minimize the shame and save the honor of the victim and her family, and in many cases, it can be settled informally to avoid any undue publicity that further harms and stains that honor. It is also a solution to incidents of rape and sexual violence that take place between close relatives, such as cousins.[6]

The above examples highlight the notion of rape as an honor crime, rather than a gender violence crime, such that the offender is acquitted if he offers to marry to victim, saving the victim's and family's "honor." Since the honor is somehow upheld, there is no crime, or the crime is mitigated. If the family of the rape victim (the rapist's bride to be) drops the charge, the rape offender is usually acquitted. However, many of the rape victims would suffer since their fate is being dictated by external acts imposed on her: first, being raped, and second, being pressured or forced to marry her rapists. In the process, the victim' rights and her physical, psychological, and emotional integrity are violated for as long as she remains married to the rapist. The rape victim is less likely to reject the marriage, since such a marriage restores her family's honor and/or based on the fear that she will be murdered as another case of honor killing. The victim's collective value in this case is tarnished by the rape and then restored by the marriage. Both can be beyond the victim's control. Rape victims in such cases are treated as objects: to be destroyed (honor killing) if their reputations tarnish their families' (or the collectivist units) honor, or to be restored if their marriage to the rapists restores their families' reputation.

Sexual violence (including rape) within the family or the collective unit in gender-discriminating collectivist societies complicates the matter further. This is a result of the taboo of sexual relations outside marriage and constraints on social interaction between sexes, which, in turn, reduce women's value to sex objects or targets. The higher rates of rapes inside the family places more pressure on the victims to internalize the rape and to not share the crime publically.

Built-in gender discrimination can backfire against the victims of rape or sexual assault. This was true in the case of a Saudi girl who sought police protection after her father sexually molested her and her sisters, only to be turned away and told to bring her father (legal guardian) in to file the complaint (Human Rights Watch 2008). The requirement to get the permission of male guardian (or *wali*) to file formal reports of violence against women, in many Arab states, complicates the process of reporting gender violence and sexual violence against women. It also imposes immense pressure on the victims of such acts of violence to internalize these acts and to refrain from sharing or reporting such crimes with others. There is no other viable alternative available to these victims if the perpetrators are their legal guardians (or a *mahram*). In such a case, women must resign to internalizing gender discrimination and sexual violence against them (Human Rights Watch 2008).

The story of Amina Filali, a 16 year-old Moroccan girl who was raped at the point of a knife in 2012, is an example of the entrapment of rape victims in gender-discriminating collectivist societies. Amina was forced to marry the man accused of raping her. Two years later, Amina committed suicide, highlighting the blight of rape victims who are pressured and even forced (by social norms and rules) to marry their accused rapists. Amina married her rapist at the expense of violating her rights and distorting her capabilities and functionings. She was then expected to be obedient and submissive to her now husband. Such social settlements sacrifice the rights of the individual victims for the sake of preserving the collective units' interest and honor. "Many families prefer to marry daughters off rather than let people know that they were raped or that they had lost their virginity" (Alami 2014: para 8).[7]

Honor-based Violence or Honor Killings

While rape (and other sexual violence) is treated as a 'gender violence' crime in a typical individualist society, it is treated as an 'honor' crime against the collective unit of the rape victim in a typical collectivist society. Rape is considered an assault on the community's honor, and a failure of the ex-ante and ongoing measures to minimize the breach of the collective unit's reputation. Any infringement of such collective honor must be dealt with forcefully. The collective extreme response to honor-based violence reflects the extreme value of collective honor, which resides in women as the repository of the collective honor's sexual behavior and reputation (Sen 2005, Amnesty International 2012).

The collective honor, which resides in women's reputation and body, cannot be fully controlled by women, especially for women with active public lives, or active public presence. To sustain women's 'negative honor' (borrowed from Pierre Bourdieu 1998: 51) and minimize the violation of women's honor, women should lower their exposure to all incidents that may cause their reputation and their honor to be tarnished. Consequently, women are likely to confine themselves to their private sphere, home, and do their best to reduce any interaction that may damage their honor, such as contact with strangers and exposing their bodies to strangers, by covering their bodies and with a *hijab* or *burka*, and ceasing communication with non-related men. Men, especially collectivist ones, restore honor by guiding or forcing women, especially their wives and other female dependents, to behave according to the collective traditions and expectations.

Difference between Domestic Violence and Honor Killing

Honor killing serves as an ex-post measure used against individuals, mostly women, who violate the collective norms regarding their reputation, virginity, and fidelity. It is a unique class of gender violence. It differs from ongoing domestic violence that serves to discipline girls and women into behaving according to assigned norms and rules. Honor killing serves as the collective ex-post or terminal measure used against girls and women who, despite the ex-ante and ongoing measures, violate the collective norms and rules regarding their reputation, virginity, or fidelity. It serves to send a clear message to all members of the collective society that crossing the line of collective honor is met with a credible threat. This increases the cost of violating the collective norms and thus reduces the likelihood disobedience.

Honor killing is a collective, premeditated murder of a female relative who is accused of tarnishing the honor of her family (or the collective unit) in collectivist societies. In many gender-discriminating societies, the behavior of a female is a collective matter. Women's wardrobes, movements, hobbies, social contacts, and their feelings are collectively owned and guarded. This may explain the immense pressure and constraints imposed on female members in these societies. A girl's reputation and virginity are hers, her family's, and her collectivist community's most prized assets before her marriage.

According to sacred norms in Muslim societies, the female body, except the face and hands, is 'awra (a part of the body that is illegal to be seen by others, Al-Qaradaw 1997). Rumors about a woman's reputation, or any behavior or act that violates the collectively assigned norms and roles can inflict a collective wrath on her, since she hold the collective honor in her body and her reputation (Sen 2005, UN General Assembly 2014).

Treating women as repositories of the collective honor and also as legal minors or dependents subjects girls and women to multiple layers of constraints starting from their childhood. This may explain the multiple measures imposed on women to uphold the collectivist honor. FGM/C is an ex-ante measure that serves to prove the girl's collective identity, lower her sexual drive, and increase the likelihood of her virginity before marriage and her chastity after marriage. FGM/C also serves as a reminder of the price paid for girl's reputation and honor and her expected submission to collective norms and rules. Underage marriage is another ex-ante measure to uphold a girl's reputation and reduce her family and collective unit's anxiety about her reputation and virginity. In extreme cases, young girls are married even before they reach puberty.

The strong connection between women's behavior, reputation, and the collective honor puts most of the burden on women. In this game, women are destined either to lose or to continue their lives according to the collectively assigned norms and roles. If women uphold their reputations, they get married, raise families, and move on. If they fail to uphold their reputation, or act in a ways that stain their reputation, or become subjects of false rumors about their reputations, they expose themselves to the collective punishment. To reduce the probability of losing the honor and reputations games, women are taught, advised, and forced to behave in collectively sanctioned ways.

Behaving in a collectively sanctioned way comes at a high cost: a forced relinquishment of individualist capabilities and functionings. Other acts that may lead to honor killing include women's rejection of arranged marriage, seeking divorce, and failing to avoid suspicion of immoral behavior.

Honor killings take the lives of about 5000 girls and women annually, according to the United Nations Population Fund. However, due to the tendency of official statistics to be grossly underestimated, women advocacy groups estimate this number to be around 20,000 annually. Honor killing occurs mostly in Muslim, Hindu, and Sikh communities in the Middle East and South Asia (UN General Assembly 2014). Studies showed that 91 percent of worldwide honor crimes are carried out by Muslims, mostly in the Arab world (and the Middle East in general) and South Asia, including 84 percent of the perpetrators of honor killings in North America and 96 percent of all honor crimes in Europe (Chesler 2010).

The collective unit (family or tribe) usually chooses the assailant (usually a young male or an older relative) to kill the victim as a last resort to cleanse the disgrace and restore the family honor. Electing a young, minor, male or an elderly member to commit the honor crime is intended to lower the punishment against them, if such a punishment exists (UN General Assembly 2014). The collective unit can also pressure the 'disgraced' female to commit suicide or make the killing appear like a suicide, such as in Iraq (U.S. DOS: Iraq 2014).

In some Arab countries, honor-related crimes are rarely prosecuted and the law is rarely enforced according to the severity of the crime. Sentences are usually far less than similar crimes without the honor dimension (UN Assembly General 2014). Informal norms and formal rules in most Arab countries protect husbands who murder their wives for alleged adultery. Courts usually pardon honor crime perpetrators, if the victims' family drops the charges. This practice makes honor killing almost unpunishable, especially since the assailant (or assailants) is most likely a member of the victim's family (e.g., brother, father, uncle, cousin, husband). Collective approval and even praise of the honor-killing's perpetrator is likely to perpetuate such appalling practices in many collectivist societies. It also elevates such a practice to an admirable act in which perpetrators are hailed as restorers of the family's honor. Bourdieu (1998) also highlights the notion of women's negative virtue and honor (virginity and fidelity) versus men's positive virtue and honor, where a real man increases his honor by "pursuing glory and distinction in the public sphere" (Bourdieu 1998: 51).

In some Arab countries, law enforcement often turns a blind eye or fails to enforce proper punishments for the murder of women. They may even help the killer's family cover up the murder by refusing to register it as a crime or delay the process until the assailant escapes. In many cases, these crimes are treated as suicides (U.S. DOSa 2014).

Mothers and other older female relatives (grandmothers and aunts) are supposed to raise the younger females according to the collective norms and also to monitor the younger females' behaviors and discipline them for disobedience or illicit behavior. A tainted reputation reflects the failure of the in-group to prevent the disgrace of the family's honor. The collective complicity serves to perpetuate such acts of gender violence, and treats it as family, not a judicial matter. Reports show that mothers and other female relatives participate in the honor killing of their daughters (U.S. DOSa: Jordan 2014).

Leniency toward honor murderers is the norm in many Arab states. It is codified in penal laws. For example, in Iraq, the maximum sentence for a man murdering his wife for committing adultery is three years imprisonment (U.S. DOSa: Iraq 2014). In Kuwait, the maximum punishment for honor crimes, committed for an act of adultery, is three years imprisonment and a small fine (U.S. DOS$_a$: Kuwait 2014). In Jordan, Article 340 of the penal code gives those who commit a murder out of extreme anger (or temporary insanity) brought on by illegal acts committed by the victims, the benefits of a reduced penalty. It exempts the killer from any penalty if he discovers his wife or a female relative while committing adultery. According to a human rights' activist, Article 340 of the Jordanian penal code is a license to kill (Feldner 2000). Attempts to abolish or amend Article 340 were met with fierce rejection. According to a 2000 survey, 62 percent of Jordanians oppose amending Article 340 because of their fear of moral corruption in Jordanian society. The lower house of the Jordanian parliament rejected the amendment in 1999. In Algeria, Egypt, Kuwait, Syria, and other Arab countries, the law permits judges to reduce the penalty for murder or assault if the defendant asserts an honor defense. In Egypt, judges sentenced honor killing perpetrators to as little as six months' imprisonment (Kelly and Breslin 2010).

Lenient punishment is likely to perpetuate honor killing if the net benefit of the crime exceeds the cost (a lenient legal punishment or even an acquittal). The benefit from committing an honor crime mostly reflects the collective praise and admiration of the perpetrator(s) who cleanse the family's honor and rids the family (and collective community) from shame and disgrace. The collective praise is likely to be high in gender-discriminating collectivist societies, in such a way as to make honor killing a rational choice.

Compulsory Marriage & Divorce

Male matrimonial guardians, in the Arab world and other Muslim countries, have the power to force marriage contracts on their daughters (or other female dependents), regardless of their consent, in what is known as the compulsory marriage (Charrad 2007). Compulsory marriage is a clear example of gender-discriminating practices in collectivist societies, since the matrimonial guardian, supported by collectivist informal or formal power, makes the very individual decision on behalf of minors/dependents.

The case of Amina, explained earlier in the chapter, is a clear example of a catch 22, facing collective shame (resulting from her loss of virginity, and rumors about her behavior and her role in the rape) and subsequent collective punishment of marrying her accused rapist, who had already violated her human rights, capabilities, and functionings. Amina chose neither. Sadly, ending her life was her choice.

Girls are not always consulted as to when they want to get married. They may not know the person they are to marry. Many girls meet their husbands for the first time on their wedding night. Some male guardians exploit their authority, morally and legally, by not asking the female dependent for a clear approval regarding the marriage. Cultural pressures prevent girls from saying no to a marriage proposal offered to them by their legal guardians. Saying no can creates a doubt about an illicit relation between the female dependent and another man. In addition, saying no to a proposed marriage offered to her by her male guardian violates the collectively assigned norms of female obedience. This challenges the authority of the male guardian. Therefore, the likelihood of a female rejecting a marriage proposal is low in gender-discriminating collectivist societies. Amal, a Yemeni women who was married at age 15, illustrates this notion very clearly, "The girl is put under an imposition, and there's no benefit in making trouble" (Human Rights Watch 2011: 26). Kawkab's, another Yemein girl, statement reflects similar pressures on girls to get married, "I didn't want to get married . . . but the decision was stringent . . . My father and father-in-law went to court, and my father came back to the house and told me 'You're married.' I was surprised, I knew that I would be married one day, but I didn't know that this would be the day" (Human Rights Watch 2011: 26).

Compulsory divorce is usually initiated by the male guardian seeking to annul a wedding contract or forcing a divorce, regardless of the wife's objection. The story of Hamda Al-Thani, a female member of the royal Qatari family highlights the influence of gender-discriminating norms. Hamda violated the collective norms twice: first, when she married an Egyptian without the consent of legal guardian, her father (her Egyptian fiancé asked her father to marry her, but her father rejected). Second, when she flew to Egypt and got married there in 2002, violating another collective norm and rule of traveling without the required permission from her father. Later she was abducted by members of Qatari security forces while in the process of getting a valid passport at the Qatari Embassy in Cairo, Egypt. She was taken to Qatar where she was sent to a government jail and was forced to abort her unborn baby. After her story became popular in the Arab media, she was transferred to her parents' residence in 2003. She was held in confinement in addition to being exposed to frequent beating (Edemariam 2006). In a statement to Amnesty International, Hamda said, "I do not see anyone or go out to see the sun . . . I am mature and sane, educated and aware of my decisions . . . Where is the Qatari law?" (Fields-Meyer 2006). In October 2007, she was permitted to leave Qatar and rejoin her husband in Egypt (Amnesty International 2008).

Underage Marriage

Underage marriage is an act of violence against female children, which deprives them from many capabilities and functionings. It causes detrimental physical and psychological effects on young girls' health. The death of Ilham Al-Assi, a 13-year-old Yemeni girl of internal injuries from forced sex a few days after her marriage in 2010 to a man twice her age, is an examples of the of the dire effects of marrying underage girls. Poverty and sacred traditional norms play crucial role in this appalling practice that affects more the 15 percent of Yemeni girls who are married or forced to get married before age 15. In 2013, Rowan, an 8-year-old Yemeni child, died on the first night of her marriage to a man in his 40s due to internal injuries (AlJazeera America 2013).

According to prevailing cultural and religious norms, younger girls are more likely to be obedient, kept away from sexual temptation (an ex-ante measure), and bear more children. The negative health effects of underage marriage include complication with pregnancy at younger age. Compared to adult women (20 to 24 years old), the death rate from pregnancy complication is doubled for girls age 15–19 and five times higher for girls between the age of 10 and 14 (Human Rights Watch 2011). The rate of miscarriage for girls under age 16 is double the rate for adult women and four times the combined risk of fetal death and infant mortality (Human Rights Watch 2011).

Gender-discriminating norms play an important role in perpetuating child marriage, especially in conservative collectivist communities. Some poor families view girls as a financial burden, such that the family can alleviate that burden by marrying their daughters at a younger age. In addition, poor families benefit from the dowry payment given to the bride by the groom before marriage (Human Rights Watch 2011). As extreme as it is, underage marriage protects the family's honor as a preemptive measure (similar to FGM/C) to shield girls from male sexual attention, to protect girls' reputation, and to prevent shame and dishonor associated with premarital sex. Marrying girls at younger age is both an effective economic tool, and a prevention of potential shame. A clear example of the influence of norms on formal rules is the Yemeni government's repealing the minimum legal age of 15 for marriage in 1999, making it legal to marry a child of any age (Human Rights Watch 2011; UNICEF 2011). According to cultural norms, a man can marry an underage girl but cannot have sexual relations with her until she reaches physical puberty. The younger bride's role is to keep up the domestic chores, remains obedient to her husband, and to stay at home unless she must leave for necessity (with permission of her husband) according to the Yemeni Personal Status Law (Human Rights Watch 2011).

The story of Nujood Ali sheds more light on the blight of child bride in Yemen. When she was eight years old, she was forced to marry a 32-year-old man. At the age of ten, she went to the court and asked for divorce from her husband after he repeatedly beat and raped her. She was granted divorce only after she paid her husband back the *mahr* (marriage dowry). Her husband was not penalized, since he did not violate any informal norms or formal laws (Kelly and Breslin 2010; Human Rights Watch 2011). Consequent national and international pressures on the Yemeni government to amend the law and raise the minimum marriage age failed due the rejection of the *shari'ah* legislative committee in parliament and other subsequent *fatwas*. In 2010, the Yemeni

Shari'ah Legislative Committee issued a document citing that the proposed bill to set a minimum age for marriage contradicts the teaching of sacred texts, such as the *Qur'an* and *sunna* (Human Rights Watch 2011). In support of the committee's perspective, a group of clerics issued a fatwa stating that defining a minimum age for marriage is contrary to Islamic *shari'ah*. They supported this with evidence of prominent Muslim women who were married at a young age, such as Lady A'isha (one of the Prophet's wives) who was married at the age of nine (Human Rights Watch 2011). The above dispute underlines the power of the informal norms, especially those rooted in sacred religious belief.

Studies show that underage and uneducated women are at higher risk of physical and sexual violence from their husbands than older, more educated women are. This is due, in part, to their lack of status in their husband's home, and the expectation of their obedience not only to their husbands, but also to their husband's family who usually live in the same residence. This is illustrated by another Yemeni girl, Rhadia who was married at age 16, "He upsets me a lot, and he beats me. One day he beat me because of his mother. She tells him that I don't do anything at home. I had problems [with my husband and in-laws] when I first had my son, but I can't leave now because of my children...They [my family and in-laws] ruined me. They ruined my life" (Human Rights Watch 2011: 32). Thuraya, another Yemeni girl, married at age 16, illustrates the influence of discriminating norms and identity roles such as women's obedience and patience, "I would go back to my father's house and my family would tell me that these are normal problems. They would say that a woman has to have patience and would return me to my husband's home as if I was wrong, and I would think that maybe I was wrong after all. I would be quiet...just to avoid problems" (Human Rights Watch 2011: 33–34).

Underage marriage deprives young girls of their adolescence and transforms them prematurely to the life of adult women responsible for managing the same responsibilities that normally belong to adult women, who are mature enough (physically, emotionally, psychologically, and intellectually) to start a married life. The 1989 Convention on the Rights of the Child (CRC) regards childhood, up to age 18, as a process of development that does not end with the menstruation 'maturity' marker (UNCEF 2011). However, "In many traditional societies, the idea of an adolescent period between puberty and adulthood is alien. A girl who menstruates can bear a child, and is therefore 'a woman'" (UNICEF 2011: 6).

Sacred norms and customs of marrying young girls are prevalent in many religions and beliefs. Islamic teaching sanctions young age marriage as long as the girl reaches puberty. The story of Prophet Muhammad getting engaged to his wife Lady A'isha when she was six-years-old and her move to his home when she was nine-years-old highlights the sacred norm and tradition of underage marriage.[8] Furthermore, according to conservative interpretation of Islamic law, there is no minimum age for legal marriage. Marriage contracts can be legally formed at any age with consummation to occur after puberty (Charrad 2007).[9] The collective notion of underage marriage may reflect the collective obedience to sacred norms, and/or collective fear of shame and dishonor. The ongoing cost and fear of shame that damages the family's honor are too high for the family to wait until girls reach maturity and are able to choose spouses for themselves (Charrad 2007). In collectivist Islamic societies, the father (or another male guardian) serving as matrimonial guardian can give verbal expression of consent to the marriage contract, on behalf of the daughter or other female relative, making the marriage legally valid (Charrad 2007).

In Saudi Arabia, a judge in 2009 refused for a second time a petition by the mother of an 8-year-old girl to annul a marriage between the girl and a 47-year-old man. The girl's father, her legal guardian, arranged the marriage to settle a debt with the man who married his daughter. The judge made the girl's husband sign a pledge to not have sex with her until she reached puberty. The grand *Mufti* of Saudi Arabia, Sheikh Abdul Aziz Al-Sheikh defended parents who force their underage daughters to marry, "It is incorrect to say that it's not permitted to marry off girls who are 15 and younger ... A girl aged 10 or 12 can be married. Those who think she's too young are wrong and they are being unfair to her" (in Jamjoom 2009: para 9). He added, "We should know that *Shari'ah* law has not brought injustice to women" (in Jamjoom 2009). International NGOs and other human rights organizations in Saudi Arabia expressed their objection to the above ruling. The divorce case was settled out of court. This story underscores the influence of sacred norms and the high status of the conservative Muslim clergy in Saudi Arabia who oppose the calls to end child marriage, according to their interpretations of Islamic teaching and norms. This is heightened by the Grand *Mufti* of Saudi Arabia's *fatwa* that it is permissible for ten-year-old-girls to marry, and that people who disagree with this *fatwa* are doing the girls an injustice (USA Today 2009). Arwa, a Yemeni girl, was married when she was eight years old to a man 27 years her senior, after her father accepted an offer for the man to marry his daughter for a $150 dowry. She did not know that she was married. She did not even understand the meaning of the word 'marriage' at the time. She ran away after eight months, when her husband tried to force her to have sex with him. One of the NGO's concerned with children in Yemen offered to care for and defend her (Khalil 2008).

Case Study: Underage Girls and Tourist Marriage in Egypt

Reports from Egypt show that tourism marriage (or summer marriage) is growing in popularity. This is a marriage between Egyptian underage girls and Arab tourists, mostly from the Gulf countries. A study by the Ministry of Family Affairs and Population shows that the rate of marriage between underage girls and non-Egyptian men is about 74 percent. The study also shows that 57.5 percent of families accepting such marriage contracts are middle-income families, compared to 30 percent in poor families that accept such marriage contracts. This shows that poverty is not the only motive behind these marriages (Awadallah 2009).

Other studies show that underage girls between the ages of 11 and 18 are sold in marriage contracts by their parents to wealthy, much older Gulf Arabs.

Azza El-Ashmawy, the director of the Child-Anti-Trafficking Unit at the National Council for Childhood and Motherhood in Egypt states, "The man pays a sum of money and will stay with the girl for a few days or the summer, or will take her back to his country for domestic work or prostitution . . . It's a form of child prostitution in the guise of marriage . . . Most 'marriages' last for just a couple of days or weeks" (McGarth 2013). These temporary marriages serve as a way to circumvent Islamic restriction on premarital sex. Marriage brokers usually forge the birth certificate or substitute the identity card of the girl's older sister, since the law prohibits underage marriage. However, the laws are poorly enforced (McGarth 2013). The *mahr* (dowry) paid by the Arabian Gulf men serves to convince parents to accept the marriage contracts. A 2009 survey showed that 80 percent of the men came from Saudi Arabia and the rest were from other Gulf countries. Studies also show that in about a third of all marriages, the girls were pressured into the marriage. Another rationale for summer/temporary marriage (and also for polygyny) is to protect men from engaging in adultery or other illicit sexual activity. Studies show that 35 percent of all women in these summer or temporary marriages (that last between two weeks and two months, with the exception of shorter marriages that can last only a few hours) were 19 years old and younger. El-Ashmawy summed up this process of child abuse, "It's not simply about poverty or religion . . . It's cultural norms that support this illicit trade—people believe it is in the best interest of the girls and the families at large. And brokers succeeded in finding common ground with families in order to exploit young girls" (McGarth 2013).

There are multiple influencing factors on this phenomenon of temporary underage marriage, such as the family's fear of any illicit behavior by their daughter, rumors about her reputation, and their anxiety of waiting for proposals; It is the legal guardians, especially, who feel enormous pressure to accept proposals to marry their daughters (and other female dependents) prematurely. Once a daughter is married, the burden of protecting their daughters' virginity and preventing any rumors about their daughters' sexual behaviors is removed. In addition, the norm that the female's role in the home is to serve her husband and raise her children appeals to poor collectivist rural communities (Mansouri 2013). Another rationale for summer marriage (or temporary marriage) is to protect men from engaging in adultery or other illicit sexual activity.

Reports from Yemen support the phenomenon of temporary marriage between underage Yemeni girls as young as 10 years old, and Saudi men, with some of these girls being abandoned in Saudi Arabia and/or being subjected to sex trafficking there (U.S. DOSa,b 2014).

A report by The Ministry of State for Family and Population in Egypt on summer marriages between underage Egyptian girls and Arab tourists from the Gulf states shows that this phenomenon is widespread in certain rural areas in Egypt, especially with some religious endorsement of such marriages, as long as the young girl is capable of having intercourse, according to some religious decrees from conservative Islamic scholars and sheikhs. These religious decrees appeal to many parents. Anti-underage marriage advocates seek more govern-ment intervention to prevent the abuse of Egyptian female children. They call for more stringent restrictions against such marriages, such that the husband must hold a minimum deposit in the name of his Egyptian wife and sign legal documents to admit his fatherhood of the born babies of such marriages and to buy an apartment in the name of his wife to guarantee a decent life for the Egyptian girls after separation (Oreibee 2014).

Summary

Gender violence is condoned and sometimes sanctioned in collectivist soci-eties to uphold sacred norms. The norm of collective honor that resides in the female body (especially her virginity) and reputation (especially regarding sexual behavior), and the norm of treating females as legal minor or depen-dent may explain the prevalence and acceptance of various forms of gender violence against women. Examples of such violence start early with ex-ante or preemptive measures such as FGM/C and under-age marriage that are done to under-age girls. Ongoing domestic violence and various forms of restric-tions on women's freedom and capabilities (movement, marriage, socialization, dress code, travel, education, employment, entertainment, etc.) are supposed to restrain female's behaviors and sustain their reputation and the collective honor. The ex-post measures such as honor killing (and other forms of excessive violence or credible threat) serve as the ultimate punishment to deviant female members who dare (or are victimized) to deviate from the collective norms and to violate them, gravely tainting their reputation and disgracing the collective honor, such that they must pay the ultimate price. As noted before, the collec-tively assigned honor is retained in the female's body and reputation, thus the collective unit or community must uphold and sustain the honor by controlling women, their behavior, and their reputation. Failing to uphold honor and repu-tation is a grave collective matter that must be dealt with accordingly.

CHAPTER 12

Norms and Women's Economic Rights

In the Arab world, women's economic right are largely determined by social norms. These norms influence women's participation in the labor force, their right to an inheritance and their rights to own and manage properties and business. Prevailing norms in the Arab world impose significant barriers to women's gaining economic rights. Most gender-discriminating norms in the Arab world (and similar Islamic societies) are rooted in the principle of *qawama*—men's authority and guardianship of their female relatives (the *Qur'an* 4:34). These norms include treating women as legal minors, stressing obedience to their legal guardians, confining women to their residence (the private sphere), preventing women from imitating men by participating in certain activities and jobs, treating girls' virginity and female's sexual reputation and fidelity as collective assets (property that belongs not only to the girls and women, but to the collective unit), not mixing opposite sexes, and forming men's roles and responsibilities to support their female relatives and provide for their economics and financial needs (this norm is supported by sacred teaching that gives the male twice the female's share in inheritance[1]).

Accordingly, women must get permission from their male guardians to leave the house, apply for a job, work, and to travel, and so on. Furthermore, if permitted to leave the house, women face social barriers such as the assigned dress code (preventing them from performing certain tasks or certain jobs), inability to mix with men (preventing them from working or activities where men are present), disapproval of working certain hours and locations (preventing them from working in late or night shifts and from traveling). Women's exposure to sexual harassment in the public sphere and at work is another barrier that deters woman's participation in economic activities in the public sphere. Moreover, women's participation in the labor force is negatively impacted due to discriminating norms that deny or discount benefits such as retirement and health care to working women. The resulting glass ceiling obstructs women's advancement in the business world regardless of their qualifications. The above list of a few of the many gender-discriminating norms and rules in many Arab countries (especially the more conservative and collectivist ones) explains the strikingly low female participation rates in the labor markets.

The first and largest part of this chapter covers the influence of norms on women's rights and capabilities to participate in the labor market, including statistical comparisons of women's participation in the labor markets and cases studies from Saudi Arabia and Egypt. The second part covers the gender-discriminating norms of women's rights to inheritance in the Arab world. The last part covers women's access to properties and business activities.

Norms and Women's Access to Labor Market in the Arab World

According to the prevalent norms (based in sacred norms) in the Arab world and other similar societies, the female body is created to serve the function of motherhood, and the female psyche may have been created to be a housewife and mother. The Islamic *shari'ah* does not require women to work outside her home. Under the guardianship system, the male guardian (husband, father, etc.) is responsible for caring for his female relatives financially. Therefore, a woman may work outside the house but she is not obliged to do so. According to widespread interpretations of Islamic *shari'ah*, a woman's work should not contradict her main role as a housekeeper, wife, and mother. She must receive permission from her male guardian to work outside her residence. Women should only work in fields suitable to their nature, such as in the fields of education, medicine and nursing, sowing, sales, and in public offices. These jobs do not require physical strength, late night shifts, traveling, or staying away from home. Women's dress and appearance must be proper and respectful. They should abide by existing norms, especially religious ones, such as refrain from wearing cosmetics and perfume, and from behaving in a sexually tempting or exciting manner in the public sphere. Moreover, women should not mix with unrelated men, or have other suspicious relations. These gender-discriminating norms constrain women's choices regarding their capability to move (outside her residence), to work, and to choose the type of jobs and locations that suit their aspirations and preferences.

In the Arab world, and other similar Muslim countries, men are responsible for their families' financial and economic needs and are in charge of the public sphere's affairs. Women take care of house chores and family members, especially the children and elders. According to *shari'ah*, women's work outside their residence should ought to not have a negative effect on their families' life.

The 2014 World Value Survey statistics highlight to prevalence of women's roles as housewives in the Arab world. It shows that in most Arab countries, people agree that "being a housewife is as fulfilling as joining the labor force and working for pay," at higher rates than the world's average.

Since men are financially responsible for their families, women are discouraged from working, especially if their work may have negative effects on men's employment, such as increasing the male unemployment rate. Figure 12.1 underscores this gender discrimination. This norm highlights the role of men

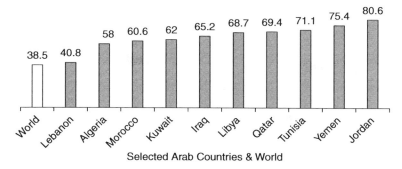

Figure 12.1 Percentage of people agree with the statement, "when jobs are scarce, men should have more right to a job than women."

Source: Data collected from World Values Survey (2014). V45, P. 63.

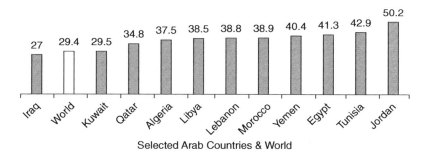

Figure 12.2 Percentage of people who agree with the statement, "if a woman earns more money than her husband, it's almost certain to cause problems."

Source: Data collected from World Values Survey (2014). V47, P. 65.

as the primary breadwinner, such that women should not compete with men in the labor market. Rather, women should behave according to their natural attributes as wives and mothers. The percentages of people in the Arab countries (ten selected countries in the survey) agreeing with "when jobs are scarce, men should have more rights to a job than women," are much higher than the world's average, reaching as high as 80.6 percent among Jordanians.

Moreover, figure 12.2 highlights a perceived problem associated with working women earning higher incomes than their husbands, since it violates men's role as the primary breadwinners and affects their masculinity and *qawama* (authority and guardianship). The percentage of Arabs who agree that a wife's income exceeding her husband's income will cause problems is much higher than the world's average.

Furthermore, according to prevailing sacred norms, female work should match women's feminine nature. The *hadith* that women should not imitate men is exploited to ban women from certain types of work that are deemed dangerous or immoral to women. Women's emotional composition makes it unfair to ask women to do men's work, or work usually done by men, since it will be more difficult and painful for women to do that. Thus, women are encouraged to perform certain jobs that serve specific women's needs, such as obstetrics and gynecology, teaching in all-female schools, administrative work, social work, and volunteering for female causes and organizations.

Another *hadith,* the Prophet said, "He who imitates a people is one of them" (Al-Qaradawi 1997: 92) commanding Muslims not to imitate non-Muslims, is also used to persuade women to stay at home and to act according the prevailing social norms in the Arab and Muslim world in order to affirm their distinctive Muslim identity. Many Muslim scholars use women's menstruation as a natural cause for women to stay at home, since her productivity will suffer during her menstruation.

In addition, female work that causes her to ignore her family's need, without any legal necessity is prohibited since it violates men's *qawama,* and can break down the foundation of the family. Figure 12.3 shows the high percentage of Arabs who agree that when women work, their children suffer.

The percentages range from 56.9 percent in Jordan to 20.4 percent in Iraq, which are significantly higher than the world's average of 15.5 percent. The higher percentages in the Arab world reflect the influence of norms of women's assigned identities and roles as wives and mothers, such that women working outside the house is perceived to generate negative externalities on their children. Thus, women should stay at home to raise their children properly. The distributional effects of women's work outside the house includes the inability to care properly for children and the added burden on women working and taking care of their home, children, and husbands.

There is also a perception that women may lose their femininity and natural features from their excessive mixing with men at work. Women's work outside their homes generates suspicion about their fidelity. In addition, their participation in the labor force and competition with men for jobs may increase

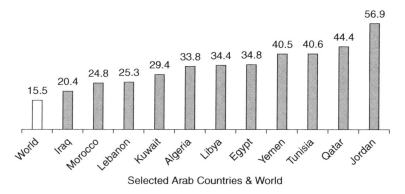

Figure 12.3 Percentage of people who agree with the statement, "when a mother works for pay, the children suffer."

Source: Date collected from World Values Survey (2014). V50, P. 68.

the unemployment rate, leading to more unemployment among men who are responsible to raise their families. Other scholars fear that women working outside home may lead to illicit relations between women and men. Women work outside home may also lead to lower the rate of marriages, since working women may be satisfied with their work, and due to the fact that some men may refuse to marry working women.

Deborah Figart (2009) underscores the institutional theory of discrimination and the segmented labor market theory in explaining gender discrimination in the labor market. Social constraints on women, such as their mobility, attire, their interactions with strangers (other than husbands and *mahrams*), and exposure to sexual harassment, tilts the decision regarding the division of labor between "labor market" and "domestic labor." Women are likely to stay at home, specializing in domestic labor, while men specialize in the public sphere's labor market, explaining in part the higher female unemployment rates and lower female-to-male wage rate. Accepting this discriminating status quo, will perpetuate such unjust distribution of labor between men and women, since women become more productive and skilled in domestic labor activities, while men are more productive and skilled in public sphere market activities. Furthermore, the higher levels of interaction with others in the public sphere give men more access to acquire higher levels of human capital (through training and learning) and higher levels of social capital through membership in effective social networks. This has positive external effects that benefit men in their participation in the labor markets.

Women in the Arab world (and other similar societies) are also victims of statistical discrimination since they are discriminated against based on characteristics associated with groups (of women in gender-discriminating societies) rather than their individual qualifications. Women in these societies are widely perceived to have cognitive and religious deficiencies. This, paired with their status as legal minors, deepens the discrimination against women in the labor market. Figart (2009) highlights the rigid structural features of the labor market and employment practices, while explaining the institutional theory of discrimination. Limiting women (and other ethnic minorities) to employment in the "secondary sector" of the labor market is highlighted in the segmented labor market theory, which underscores the employment barriers and gap in wages. Women as organizational outsiders do not enjoy traditional employment compared to the organizational insiders. In gender-discriminating collectivist societies, gender can be treated as a type of productive property, generating power and wealth for men who consequently resist any attempt to weaken their property rights (Ogilvie 2004a; Figart 2009[2]).

Figure 12.4 shows people's attitudes toward women's leadership and executive skills compared to men in the Arab world. In most Arab countries (except Lebanon, one of the least collectivist Arab countries), the percentage of people who believe that men make better business executives than women is much higher than the world's average, reflecting the prevailing norms in the Arab world that men are superior to women in intelligence.

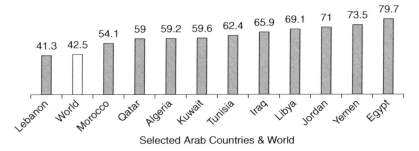

Figure 12.4   Percentage of people who agree with the statement, "on the whole, men make better business executives than women do."
Source: Data collected from World Values Survey (2014). V53, P. 71.

Structural barriers and customs prevent the flow of labor between segmented labor markets, which, in turn, prevents the equalization of wages for workers (men and women) with equal potential productivity (Figart 2009).

Pierre Bourdieu (1998) argues that women need to possess not only what is explicitly required by the job description, but also what is called natural authority, for which men have been taught and trained as men, such as a physical structure, a strong voice, or dispositions such as aggressiveness and self-assurance. However, in a society of masculine domination, women are expected to be feminine, that is to say, "smiling, attentive, submissive, demure, restrained, self-effacing" (Bourdieu 1998: 66). "Femininity is often a form of indulgence toward real or supposed male expectations. As a consequence, [women's] dependence on others (and not only on men) tends to become constitutive of their being" (Bourdieu 1998: 66).

Norms and Women's Participation in Labor Markets: International Comparisons

The interpretations of the sacred texts and teachings are complex and sometimes contradict each other. Certain cultural norms are based on sacred texts and references that call for equal and just treatment of women and men. Other sacred texts, and other parts of the same texts, give explicit instructions and commands that marginalize women and discriminate against them. Men, the winners of such discriminating texts and norms, exploit such teaching and norms to sustain their favored status.

Worldwide statistics support the significant influence of gender-discriminating norms on women's access to the labor market, female relative (to male) participation in the labor force, female relative unemployment rates, and female relative income in the Arab world compared to the world's standards. The World Bank's gender statistics show that the female labor-force rate as percentage of total labor force in 2013 in the Arab World was 22.2 percent, significantly lower than the world rate of 39.6 percent. This significant gap

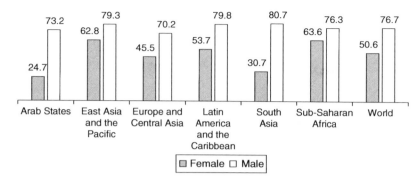

Figure 12.5 Labor force participation rate, regions, 2012, %.
Source: Data compiled from UNDP. Human Development Report 2014. Statistical Tables, Table 4.

reflects the presence and influence of real barriers against women's share in the labor force in the Arab world (the World Bank 2014). Furthermore, there is a striking gap between female labor-force participation rates (the percentage of female population ages 15 to 64 who are members of the labor force) in the Arab world and the world rates. The 2013 world female labor-force participation was 55.2 percent, more than double the Arab world's rate of 24.6 percent. Moreover, the World Bank's statistics show that the world's ratio of female-to-male labor-force participation rate in 2013 was 68.2 percent more than double the Arab world ratio of 32.4 percent (The World Bank 2014).

Figure 12.5 shows a significant gap between male and female labor force participation rate in the Arab world (and South Asia) and other world's regions. A main reason for such wide gaps is that women's capabilities to enter the labor force is curtailed and distorted due to gender-discriminating informal norms and formal rules that restrict women's free participation in the labor force..

In addition to females' low labor force participation in the Arab world, the ratio of female-to-male unemployment rate in the Arab world is remarkably higher than the world's rate, as Figure 12.6 shows. In 2013, the Arab world's ratio of female-to-male unemployment rates was 2.49, more than double the world's ratio of 1.13.

Figure 12.7 takes a closer look at each of the Arab countries and their international rankings in terms of female-to-male ratio of labor force participation, in which Arab countries are ranked at or near the bottom of the world. Fourteen Arab countries were among the bottom 20 countries. Other bottom-ranked countries (such as Afghanistain, Iran, Pakistan, and India) share some of the Arab world's gender-discriminating norms and cultrues (UNDP 2014).

Figure 12.8 reveals the compound effects of the low female-to-male labor force participation rate (in figure 12.7) and the strikingly high ratio of female-to-male unemployment (Figure 12.6) in the Arab world compared to the rest of the world in terms of the low ratio of female-to-male income per capita in the Arab countries. The Arab countries took 18 of the lowest 23 ranks at the global

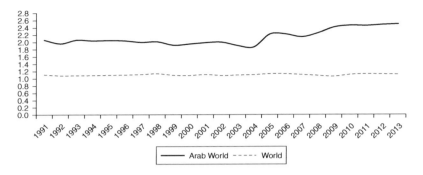

Figure 12.6 Ratio of female-to-male ratio unemployment rates, 1991–2013.

Source: Data collected from the World Bank: Gender Statistics. Last update: December 16, 2014. http://data.world-bank.org/data-catalog/gender-statistics.

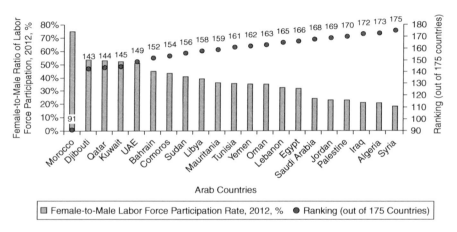

Figure 12.7 Female-to-male ratio of labor force participation in Arab countries and their ranking, 2012, %.

Source: Data compiled from UNDP, Human Development Report 2014, table 4, pp. 172–175. http://hdr.undp.org/sites/default/files/hdr14-report-en-1.pdf

level. The other five countries share similar gender-discriminating norms and rules (Afghanistan, Iran, Pakistan, India, and Turkey).

Sample Case Studies: Saudi Arabia and Egypt

Saudi Arabia
In addition to the gender-discriminating norms and rules explained earlier, women in Saudi Arabia (one of the most collectivist Arab countries) suffer from further forms of discrimination. Women's lack of status and orchestration power explain their exclusion from leadership in the Saudi religious institutions, such that women can only act according to decision and restrictions

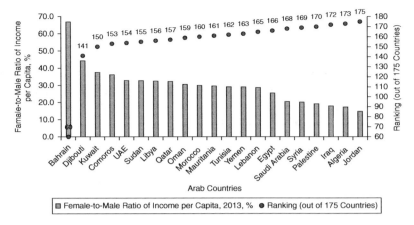

Figure 12.8   Female-to-male ratio of income per capita in Arab countries and their ranking, 2013, %.

Source: Data compiled from UNDP, Human Development Report 2014, Table 5, pp. 176–179. http://hdr.undp.org/sites/default/files/hdr14-report-en-1.pdf

made by male religious leaders. For example, women are encouraged to pray at home instead of going out to pray at mosques (Doumato 2010). Women's need for permission from their male guardian to access the public sphere or to work imposes significant constraints on their participation in the labor force.

The female-to-male ratio of labor-force participation rate was 25.8 percent in 2013, reflecting a strikingly low female labor force participation (among all qualified female) of 20.2 percent. Moreover, the female unemployment rate was 21.3 percent in 2013, more than seven times the male unemployment rate of 2.9 percent (The World Bank 2014). Saudi Arabia is ranked near the bottom (137 out of 142 countries) in terms of female economic participation and opportunity, and ranked 138 out of 142 countries in terms of female-to-male labor-force participation (World Economic Forum 2014).

Women's freedom to access the labor market and to manage assets or run a business is controlled by the authority of their male guardians, who approve certain types of business licenses. Even though women can legally work without the guardian's permission, existing social norms pressure employers to require the guardian's permission first (U.S. DOSa: Saudi Arabia 2014). The Saudi Central Bank's data shows that the percentage of working Saudi female citizens is less than one percent of the total labor force in Saudi Arabia. Most working females in Saudi Arabia are foreigners (U.S. DOSa: Saudi Arabia 2014).

Religious norms based in the provision of *shari'ah* trump government laws that aim to improve women's capabilities and functionings (e.g., permitting women to work in jobs suitable to women's nature and banning women from jobs that are deemed dangerous or risky—these are determined by the secretary (minister) of labor). According to a 2012 ministerial decision, women are prohibited from working in 18 types of jobs. According to the law, women can only work between 6 a.m. and 5 p.m. (Asharqia Chamber 2012). These norms and laws underscore women's lack of status and orchestration power to make independent decisions.

Another factor that restricts women's participation in labor force is the lack of protection for women against sexual harassment. The Saudi Consultative Council withdrew a proposed law against sexual harassment (proposed by four male and four female members) in 2014, after criticism that such law may encourage the mixing of opposite sexes in the public sphere, decaying the social fabric of the Saudi society as a result (Lahamag.com 2014).

The following statement from the Saudi Permanent Council for Scientific Research and Legal Opinions comments on women's access to labor market and working in the public sphere:

> In an Islamic society, the call for women to join men in their workplace is a grave matter, and intermingling with men is among its greatest pitfalls. Loose interaction across gender lines is one of the major causes of fornication, which disintegrates society and destroys its moral values and all sense of propriety. (Human Rights Watch 2008: 9)

Thus, the fear of violating the collective honor (girl's virginity, and female sexual reputation and fidelity) plays a crucial role in constraining women's access to labor market, and to the public sphere in general.

Furthermore, men's *qawama* over women can be used to force a woman to resign or to be fired from her job upon a request from her male guardian that she should not work outside the home (Human Rights Watch 2008). The norm against *khalwa* (banning meetings between a women and unrelated man, to prevent any illicit sexual relation) is used to prevent women from driving (since it gives women access to *khalwa*). Thus, women must rent cab, get a ride with a *mahram*, or the employers must arrange transportation for female employees, which result in added costs, barriers, and inconvenience. This restricts women's access to the public sphere and participation in the labor market. It also provides a disincentive for employers to hire female workers (Human Rights Watch 2008). Furthermore, employers are likely to hire male employees who can interact with government agencies and other businesses (without violating the norm of mixing of sexes).

Egypt

Even though formal rules in Egypt call for gender equality, social pressure against female employment is strong. Gender-discriminating norms and rules exclude women from high-level positions, especially in large sectors such as the military, since women are not allowed to serve (U.S. DOSa: Egypt 2014). Data show that the female labor-force participation rate was 25.8 percent, less than one-third of male rate of 79.1 percent in 2013. The number of female in the labor force was less than 25 percent of the male labor force in 2013. In addition, the female unemployment rate, 29.3 percent, was four times the male unemployment rate, 7.4 percent, in 2013 (The World Bank Gender Statistics 2014). According to the 2014 World Economic Forum's Global Gender Gap Report, the female earning estimate in Egypt is less than one-third the male's, ranking Egypt near the bottom of all countries (125 out of 139 countries)—highlighting women's economic and financial dependency on men. Egypt ranked near the bottom (131 out of 142 countries) in terms of women's economic participation and opportunity (World Economic Forum 2014).

A 2004 survey by Freedom House on women rights in Egypt shows that there has been some progress that is met by growing fear of increasing immorality and women's imitation of Western cultures in education and attire, as is stated by an Egyptian man, "Women now have more rights than men, because the West keeps talking about women's rights continuously" (Katulis 2004:9). Many men and some women agree that the primary role and responsibility for a woman is to raise her children and take care of the family at home (Katulis 2004). Men should receive preferential treatment in hiring since men are expected to be the main breadwinners according to social norms and traditions based in sacred teaching and commands (for example, the *Qur'an* 4:34). According to an Egyptian male, "there are priorities in life. A man is the one that spends his salary on his house; the government should realize that when there are no more unemployed men they can start hiring females" (Katulis 2004:18). Among the reasons to hire women in Egypt are their submissiveness, diligence, and willingness to accept lower salaries and fewer benefits (Katulis 2004).

Women's rights advocates report that Islamist influences, as well as traditional and cultural attitudes and practices, further prevent women from having careers. In addition, weak labor laws and lack of equal opportunity increase women's vulnerability to arbitrary dismissal (U.S. DOSa: Egypt 2014). Even though the labor law does not discriminate against women in general, it imposes certain restrictions based on gender, such as excluding women from night shifts and bars women from certain "unwholesome and morally harmful areas of work for women" (Tadros 2010: 104). Such gender-discriminating practices and rules affirm and reflect the norm of women's minor status, such that certain decisions can only be made by males.

The Egyptian labor law's protections do not cover work done mostly by poor, rural, and uneducated women, such as domestic servants and agricultural laborers. This further aggravates gender-discriminating practices against the most vulnerable women (Tadros 2010).

Permitting an earlier retirement age for women (45) than men (50) sends many deterring signal to women's economic independence and career advancement: the monetary compensation given to women is significantly lower if they choose to retire earlier, early retirement is likely to increase women's dependency on their male relatives, reduces women's chances for promotion and positions of authority, and heightens the social pressure on women to retire early (Tadros 2010).

Norms and Women's Rights to Inheritance

Inheritance norms and laws in the Arab world reflect a distributional bias that favors men. They give men access to more resources since men's share in inheritance exceed (usually double) women's share according to sacred norms, "Allah instructs you concerning your children: for the male, what is equal to the share of two females" (the *Qur'an* 4:11). The general rule is that the female's share of inheritance is half of the equivalent male's share. The norms and rules also give more inheritance privileges to male relatives on the paternal side. The most common rationale and interpretation for the inheritance norms and rules is that males should spend from their income to support female minors and dependents in their homes. According to Mounira Charrad (2007), current inheritance norms and rules are considered an improvement compared to the pre-Islam norms of excluding women from inheritance. However, these norms discriminate against women who have no male relatives/guardians, or who live by themselves, or who want to free themselves from dependency on male relatives male dominance.

In discounting women's share in inheritance, women are treated as legal minors who should not have equal access to the collective assets and wealth. Because of this, their share should be supervised and managed by their male guardians. The male should have more share in the collective (e.g., family) wealth (assets and property), due to their obligations to support their female relatives and children. Women still require a male guardian's permission to manage their property, to leave home, and to make certain business transactions in many Arab countries (U.S. DOSa 2014). Prevailing norms and traditions encourage and sometimes pressure women to give up their share of inheritance to their male relatives, especially their male guardians. In some cases, women who refuse to give up their inheritance share are exposed to collective punishment (Azzouni 2010).

The women's discounted share in inheritance deepens their dependency on their male guardians financially, and serves as an admission that male relatives have authority and guardianship over women, as is commanded in the men's *qawama* (the *Qur'an* 4:43).

Moreover, according to the sacred norms of *shari'ah*, non-Muslim widows are banned from inheriting their Muslim husband's wealth (U.S. DOSa 2014). This special case represents double discrimination based on sex and religion. Non-Muslims should not share the collective wealth of Muslims, or in the status since the inheritance is considered a collective asset to be distributed among collective members; Christian women who marry Muslim men are not considered members, since their association with the collective group (family), is severed with the death of their Muslim husbands (Muslim men can marry Christian or Jewish women, but Muslim women are banned from marrying non-Muslim men). Sharing the inheritance with the non-Muslim women violates the collective norms. A proposed amendment to change this discriminating practice against non-Muslim female widows in Egypt was rejected for its violation of Islamic sacred norms (Tadros 2010). However, in Tunisia (one of the least collectivist Arab countries), non-Muslim women gained the right to inheritance from their Muslim husbands in 2009 under the constitutional provision of freedom of worship (Ben Salem 2010). Norms, especially religious norms, dictate the distribution of inheritance in Lebanon (one the least collectivist Arab countries). The Civil Law of Inheritance is applied to non-Muslims, in which the inheritance is distributed equally between men and women (Lebanon has a significant Christian population, the highest by far in the Arab world; 40.5 percent of the population). As for Muslims, women's share in inheritance is assigned according to the way their sect (for example, *Sunni* and *Shi'a*) interprets *shari'ah* (Kelly and Breslin 2010).

In Jordan, to avoid women's discounted share in inheritance, real assets are usually transferred to male family members during the owner's life. This circumvents the transfer of female members' share to other families when the female members marry men from other families. If the transfer of the asset to male members does not take place, the female members are pressured to waive their share in the inheritance to their parental families' male members (Husseini 2010). Showing good progress, the 2004 Family Law in Morocco allowed, for the first time, the children of a man's daughters to inherit from him. Prior to that, only the children of a man's sons could inherit (Sadiqi 2010).

Norms and Women's Right to Property and Business

The laws in many Arab countries do not prohibit women from owning and managing assets and property, however, existing gender-discriminating norms pressure women to delegate the responsibilities of properties to their male guardians (or assigned male relatives) out of obedience to patriarchal norms (Tadros 2010; Kelly and Breslin 2010). In this, patriarchal control of assets can be exploited to violate women's economic rights.

In Tunisia, for example, women rarely exercise their right to own property, including land. Property is transferred from father to sons. Land is considered part of the family's 'honor' that should be kept in male hands. This prevents the transfer of land to another family through marriage, and keeps the collective assets in the hands of males who have status and orchestration power. Women are allowed to inherit only if they marry a paternal cousin, keeping the property in the male dominated collective unit through the paternal lineage (Ben Salem 2010). However, in Tunisia, parents and husbands can circumvent the gender-discriminating law by giving tax-exempt gifts at very low registration fee to daughters or non-Muslim wives (Ben Salem 2010).

In Saudi Arabia, women's ability to manage their own assets or to earn income are restricted and controlled by commercial and retail regulations, public codes of conduct, and sex segregation in the public sphere (including the workplace) and in mindsets (Doumato 2010). In Yemen, due to the gender-discriminating norms that pressure women to stay at home, only a limited number of women can exercise their right to own and run their businesses and assets, mostly in the upper-middle and upper classes (Manea 2010).

The prevailing norms in the Arab world encourage working women to give their income to their families, and for married working women to pay for their families' expenses directly, for example, in Jordan (Husseini 2010). In certain communities, women cannot even open a bank account or hold assets in their names, for example, in rural Morocco (Sadiqi 2010).

In most Arab countries, women's decision to manage property is traditionally made in consultation with male relatives such as their male guardians. Otherwise, women expose themselves to familial and social opposition and obstacles (Kelly and Breslin 2010; Al-Talei 2010).

Summary

This chapter asserts that gender-discriminating norms in the Arab world limit and deform women's capabilities and functionings with regard to their economic rights. Their assigned identities as wives and mothers and their roles as housekeepers and care providers for the young and elderly members in the family put more pressure on women to stay at home. Treating women as minors or dependents deprives them from making decisions that reflect their own preferences, such as joining the labor force or starting a business. Norms that prevent mixing with the opposite sex impose a significant barrier on women's participation in the labor force, since the public sphere is designated to the male members of society. The prevalence of restrictions on women's employment to protect the collective honor collectively puts downward pressure on women's participation in labor force, and public sphere in general. These restrictions include collectively mandated attire, certain types of work and hours deemed appropriate for women, and so on. Furthermore, women are discriminated against in terms of their right to equal inheritance, property ownership, and running businesses. Gender-discriminating norms pressure them to give up the active role in ownership and management. Instead, women are likely to delegate these activities to their male relatives—especially male guardians—accepting their assigned roles as wives and mothers who should depend on their male legal guardians.

CHAPTER 13

Norms and Women's Political and Legal Rights

Prevailing gender-discriminating norms and rules explain women's lack of legal and political rights in the Arab world. Women's access to political and legal rights varies according to the balance of collectivism and individualism in different Arab countries. Women, in general, have more rights in the more individualist countries such as in North-West Africa (Tunisia, Algeria and Morocco), than in more collectivist countries (Saudi Arabia, Yemen). Within each country, women who are prone to individualism (e.g., rich, educated, employed women living urban regions) tend to exercise more rights than women in poor, illiterate households in rural regions.

The first part of this chapter highlights the influence of norms on women's political rights using examples from various Arab countries. The second part covers how prevailing norms influence women's legal rights in the Arab world. The chapter samples the effect of norms on certain political and legal rights.

Norms and Women's Political Rights in the Arab World

In general, women in the Arab world have limited access to political rights and are excluded from political spheres. Prevailing norms that limit or deform women's political rights can be classified into two groups: general norms and specific norms. General norms include the following:

- Treating women, formally or informally, as minors who need permission from their male guardians before engaging in certain activities, such as leaving the house, working, traveling, and so on;
- Resigning women to the private sphere;
- Assigning certain attributes to women such as obedience and submissiveness;

- Assigning certain primary roles for women, such as wives and mothers;
- Assigning certain types of jobs that fit women's nature;
- Prohibiting women from imitating men and men's behaviors;
- Prohibiting women (and men) from imitating foreign (non-Muslim) communities and nations;
- Regarding women as having a deficiency in mind and religion.

As a result of these general norms, women have limited access, among other things, to work, to earn income, travel, join social networks, and participate in political activities without the consent of their male guardians.

The main specific norms regarding women's political rights are related to sacred teaching such as, "Men are in charge of women, because Allah hath made the one of them to excel the other, and because they spend of their property (for the support of women)" (the *Qur'an* 4:34), and the prophetic *hadith* that women should not rule a nation, or a community, in which the prophet said, "No people will ever prosper who appoint a woman in charge of them."[1] Together, these general and specific norms play a significant role in hindering women's capabilities and functionings in the political sphere as voters, activists, candidates, representatives, and leaders (Toh and Leonardelli 2012). Commentators of the *Qur'an* support the notion that *Allah* gives men virtue over women, that men are superior to women, and that only men should rule and govern. Accordingly, women should not be permitted to the role of a ruler or a judge because women lack the required wisdom and resolve. Others refer to women's lack of adequate management skills because women have been created with a deficiency in their intelligence, and with strong emotions that can outweigh their abilities to make proper and objective public decisions. These two combined contradict the required attributes of leaders and judges, especially in matters belonging to Islamic *shari'ah*. In addition, rulers are required to appear in public and handle matters directly, they meet with male delegates and leaders, and sometimes lead the army for *jihad*—it is, of course, forbidden for women to do so. According to Islamic scholars, banning women from positions of authority does not belittle women's capabilities in leadership, but redirect it into proper ways, mostly in the private sphere as wives and mothers. This protects women from wasting their capabilities in matters that do not fit their personal, physical, and psychological dispositions, and do not fit the Islamic *shari'ah* laws that aim to protect women from corruption and from corrupting others.[2]

According to broadly accepted interpretations of *hadith,* many men have reached the state of perfection, while very few women have reached that state.[3] This *hadith* and other supporting ones are used or exploited, especially in religious male-dominant societies, to perpetuate the notion that men in general are superior in their faith and in their intelligence to women. Therefore, women should be guided by men, and should not have leadership over them, especially in the legislative systems or national parliament as illustrated in figure 13.1 where the percentage of seats held by women in national parliaments in the Arab world is significantly lower than the world's average. In certain countries,

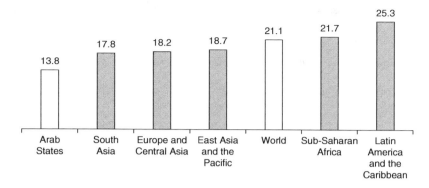

Figure 13.1 Percentage of seats held by women in parliament by regions, 2013.

Source: UNDP. Human Development Report 2014, Statistical Tables, table 4. http://hdr.undp.org/en/content/human-development-report-2014.

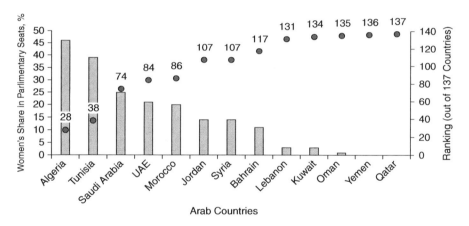

Figure 13.2 Women's share in parliamentary seats in Arab countries, and their international ranking, 2014, %.

Source: Date compiled from the World Economic Forum (2014), Table E12, P. 75.

women are completely excluded from for running for political office (especially at the national level), for example, in Saudi Arabia and Qatar.

Figure 13.2 shows the percentage of seats held by women in parliament in the selected Arab countries (Global Gender Gap Report 2014) and their international ranking. Four Arab countries took the bottom ranks out of 137 countries. Other Arab countries had higher rankings due to the ruling patriarchal hierarchy's appointment of women to the parliament, for example, in Saudi Arabia and the United Arab Emirates. The figure also shows the higher percentage of women's shares in Algeria, Tunisia, Morocco, and Jordan, benefiting from the women's quota of parliamentary seats in these countries (Kelly and Breslin 2010; U.S. DOSa 2014).

The World Economic Forum's 2014 Global Gender Gap Report also shows a significant gender gap between Arab countries and the rest of the world in terms of women's broader political empowerment—the ratio of female-to-male legislators and senior officials in each country—in Figure 13.3. The Arab countries ranked in the bottom 20 percent of the world ranking. Ten Arab countries ranked among the bottom 12 countries out of 125 countries (the other two countries were Pakistan and Bangladesh).

The low ranking of the Arab countries signifies the influence of gender-discriminating norms and rules against women holding positions of power. Figure 13.4 illustrates the informal perception among Arab citizens who agree

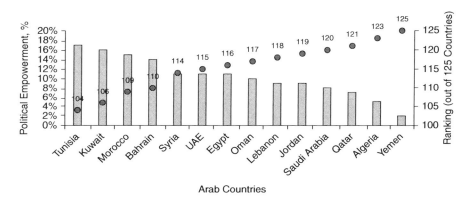

Figure 13.3 Female-to-male ratio of legislators and senior officials in the Arab world and their international ranking, 2014, %.

Source: Data compiled from the Global Gender Gap Report (2014), Table E4, P. 67.

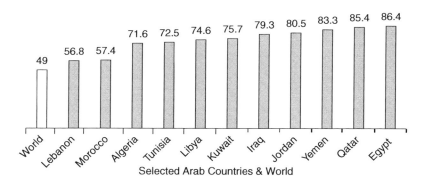

Figure 13.4 Percentage of people who agree or strongly agree with the statement, "on the whole, men make better political leaders than women do."

Source: Data collected from World Value Survey (2014), Table V 51, P. 69.

that men make better politicians than women do (Toh and Leonardelli 2012), which is much higher than the world average.

In some Arab countries (Bahrain, Oman, Saudi Arabia, and United Arab Emirates), women are appointed by the ruling patriarchal hierarchy, with limited roles and specific constraints on women's participation. Such appointments are encouraging first steps, however, they are not yet earned by women through their effective participation, capabilities, and functionings in political arenas. Rather, they reflect male superior status and control over the orchestration power, which bestows such positions on women under assigned conditions such as appointing female cultural relativists. Former King Abdullah of Saudi Arabia appointed 30 women to the Saudi *Shura* (consultative) Council (a formal advisory body) in 2013, giving women 20 percent of the Council's seats. According to the royal decree, the appointed women must commit to the principles of Islamic *shari'ah*, must adhere to wearing proper *hijab* (veil), must enter and exit the chamber from a separate gate, and sit in separate reserved seats. In addition, the King also granted women the right to vote and run for offices in municipal elections, for the first time, starting summer 2015 (Al-arabyia 2013; U.S. DOSa: Saudi Arabia 2014). However, critics of the new wave of royal decrees to give baby-step rights to women, consider these steps a window dressing at best, or "an attempt to obscure the fact the Saudi Arabia still systemically discriminate against women" (Begum and Coogle 2014) at worst.

Even though women in many Arab countries have the legal right to vote or run for office (except Qatar and Saudi Arabia), women's participation in political activities and community life depends on the balance between collectivism and individualism in their countries overall and in their families specifically. Educated, employed females such as teachers, professors, doctors, social workers, journalists, and religious scholars are more likely to participate and voice their concerns and aspirations, especially working women. However, women's participation and influence is mostly self-censored, due to the significant influence of gender-discriminating norms and the overwhelming power of the patriarchal hierarchy in Saudi Arabia (Doumato 2010). In Jordan, the government added a quota for female members in the lower house of the parliament and in municipal councils (Husseini 2010). Even though women are allowed to vote and run for office, social norms still pressure women to focus more on their household and children, their collectively assigned identities and roles (Husseini 2010).

In Yemen, as in some other Arab countries, women have the right to run for office. However, the major political party rejects female candidacy, even though it has women members in its internal party hierarchy. As a result, women's participation in politics remains very low (Manea 2010). Prevailing social and official biases have led to women's exclusion from political life in Yemen, regardless of women's formal rights. This underscores the effective gaps between what women are capable of doing (capabilities) and what they actually do (functionings). Women's formal capability to run for office and to participate in the political, social, and cultural life is not materialized in to effective functioning due to significant barriers. Yemeni women represent about half of one percent in legislative and local councils in Yemen, regardless of the claim by Yemeni politicians that they support women's participation in political life (Manea 2010). Islamic fundamentalists oppose women's participation in public and political life on religious grounds, petitioning against the female quota in Yemeni political affairs since "Opening the door for women to leave their houses and mix with men will lead to sexual chaos" (Manea 2010: 505). The dominant religious, patriarchal hierarchy controls and dictates the state of women's standing and rights in Yemen. Since women do not have orchestration power, the fluctuations in their rights are mostly outside their control. Women are just the recipients of decisions and mercies bestowed on them by the dominant patriarchal hierarchy. This is stated by Belquis Al-Salami, a Yemeni human rights activist: "The political mood towards women changes often, sometimes championing women and other times discriminating against them" (Al-Azizi 2013).

On a positive note, the percentage of women in Morocco's parliament (and similarly in Algeria and Tunisia) increased significantly after the government assigned a minimums quota for women's seats in 2002—reserving 30 out of the 325 seats in the Chamber of Representatives for women. In addition, women's representation in the local governments has improved with the quota (Sadiqi 2010).

Norms and Women's Legal Rights in the Arab World

Gender-discriminating norms also hinder women's capabilities and functionings with regard to their legal rights in the Arab world. The collectivist nature of most Arab countries, dominated by patriarchal hierarchy, places various limitations and exclusions on women's legal rights in the Arab world. Gender discrimination becomes more complex when its practices are internalized in individual and collective mindsets such that it is not considered gender discrimination. Instead, such discriminating and exclusive practices are considered just and inclusive. For example, according to a 2004 Freedom House study on women's freedom in Egypt, most Egyptians believe that women have equal legal rights, and, that in most cases, laws treat women and men equally (Katulis 2004). Also, most Egyptians do not dispute the legal argument regarding the weight of female testimony, in which the testimony of two women equals the testimony of one man, since it is clearly instructed in the sacred text, the *Qur'an* (Katulis 2004), nor do they consider it gender discrimination.

The following examples highlight prevalent gender-discriminating norms and practices regarding women's legal rights in the Arab world.

Norms and Women's Access to the Court System in the Arab World

Women's effective access to the court system and legal remedies is one of the most hotly debated issues in the Arab world, due to the prevalence of various discriminating norms and rules. Prevalent norms pressure the victims of gender violence to not complain formally at all and to settle domestic violence and other gender-discriminating cases within their collective units (families). In these cases, the victims are more likely to be blamed, according the existing gender-discriminating norms and traditions, for their dissention and disobedience to their husbands or other male guardians. Women's obedience is integral to their identities and roles and is reinforced in many aspects of the Saudi culture, such as media, laws, and in education curricula. Women fear that their formal complaints of gender violence would damage their reputation and their families' honor (Doumato 2010). If women do choose to file a formal complaint, the guardianship law in Saudi Arabia serves as a double-edged sword against them: the victims are required to bring their guardians (the accused perpetrators) to file the legal report, and the court can order the victims to return to their residences, which are ruled and controlled by their male guardians. A 2008 Human Rights' report underlines women's standing in Saudi Arabia as "perpetual minors." Saudi courts can deem women's voices to be 'awra (an intimate part that must not to be heard in public), preventing women from speaking in the court. Women's mahram can speak on their behalves. Furthermore, the court can refuse to accept a Muslim woman's testimony as a witness in criminal case. Women are only allowed to speak if they a wear a full-face veil (Human Rights Watch 2008). The court requires the presence of a Mu'arrif (a person able to identify a woman wearing niqab; usually her male guardian or a mahram) before entering the courtroom. According to a Saudi lawyer, "Unfortunately, judges consider women to be lacking in 'aql [reason] and faith, so generally do not agree with their arguments" (Human Rights Watch 2008: 15). The cost and inconvenience of bringing a mu'arrif to the court discourages women from seeking legal justice. Women cannot file complaints without the presence of their male legal guardian, creating a dilemma for women who wish to file complaints against their male guardians, for example, their abusive husbands as mentioned above. Women in Saudi Arabia are not allowed to be judges or lawyers (Doumato 2010). However, female students were allowed for the first time to study law in Saudi Arabia, starting in 2007, a step welcomed by women's rights organizations as a first step toward affording women effective access to legal rights (Doumato 2010; U.S. DOSa 2014). The absence of a written penal code in Saudi Arabia underscores the value of the prevailing norms and traditions that are mostly dominated by the patriarchal hierarchy (Doumato 2010).

The lack of laws against sexual abuse in the public sphere in many Arab countries deepens and extends gender discrimination. Police and courts are less likely to sympathize with female victims. Moreover, the victims can be accused of asking for such an encounter or for having illegal sex. This is common, for example, in Saudi Arabia. This is a result of women's restriction from entering the public sphere by themselves; they should be accompanied by a mahram. A rape victim in Saudi Arabia must provide four witnesses to the rape according the sacred teaching (the Qur'an 4:16, 24:6), or the perpetrator's confession to the rape. Otherwise, the victim will be prosecuted for having illicit sex, which is punishable with lashes if she is single, and death if she is married (Doumato 2010). Any resulting pregnancy exposes her to criminal prosecution or to the wrath of informal collective punishment (e.g., honor killing). Such legal rules impose most, if not all, of the burden of proof on the female victims. Similarly, victims of domestic violence who can't provide eyewitnesses to the violence, which usually takes place in the private sphere, can be ordered to return to their abusers' home, exposing them to further abuse. Moreover, a Saudi court sentenced a male lawyer (who defended a rape victim) to 90 lashes, for bringing the case to international media, undermining the reputation and honor of the country (Doumato 2010). Furthermore, the authorities also harass and imprison human rights activists. They force them to sign pledges to stop engaging in certain activities, such as participating in public protests, or sharing their thoughts on social media outlets (Doumato 2010). In Morocco, it is common for men to file legal cases against the behavior of female relatives. It is also common for women to not defend their cases in courts for fear that such an act could damage the honor of their families (Sadiqi 2010). In the United Arab Emirates, social norms pressure women not to seek legal protection or legal professions since they expose women to the male-dominated public sphere (police officers, lawyers, and judges), which violates the norms of gender separation. Police continue to be reluctant to get involved in domestic matters (Kirdar 2010). In Jordan, women's access to legal rights allows them to present their cases in the court as witnesses. However the testimony of a man is equivalent to the testimony of two women in *shari'ah* courts (the *Qur'an* 2:282) (Husseini 2010). In general, a woman's testimony is discounted to half of a man's testimony in various courts in the Arab world, especially in *shari'ah* courts, according to collective norms based in sacred teaching, "And bring to witness two witnesses from among your men. And if there are not two men [available], then a man and two women from those whom you accept as witnesses—so that if one of the women errs, then the other can remind her." (the *Qur'an* 2:282), and in *hadith* too. In the United Arab Emirates, the testimony of a woman equals half of a man's testimony in criminal courts; however, a woman's testimony equals a man's in certain civil cases (Kirdar 2010). In Egypt, the testimonies of two females in family courts and in matters related to personal status law are equivalent to the testimony of one male (Tadros 2010; U.S. DOSa 2014). A 2008 plea represented by Zeinab Radwan (a female expert in Islamic Jurisprudence) to the lower house of the Parliament in Egypt to contest the law that denies the testimony of women with equal weight was defeated, since the plea represented a distortion of Islam and Islamic *shari'ah* (Tadros 2010: 94–95).

The high cost of litigation, women's fear of social retribution, and inadequate training of police and court officials to deal with female cases, impose significant pressure on women not to seek legal remedies to violence and crimes against them (Husseini 2010). The Jordanian penal code, for example, drops rape charges against rapists if they marry their rape victims. The Jordanian law still treats women under the age of 40 as minors, and as dependent on their male guardians. In this case, a female minor loses her right to financial maintenance if she disobeys her guardian (e.g., husband) (Husseini 2010). Yemeni police consider women who complain against domestic violence to be indecent; respectable women should tolerate assaults committed against them by family members. Women's misbehavior is widely considered the major cause of domestic violence (Al-Azizi 2013).

The most vulnerable women to gender discriminating norms are the poor, rural, illiterate women who are isolated and dependent on their male guardians. They are the victims of higher degrees of collectivism in gender discriminating societies (Doumato 2010; Sadiqi 2010).

The absence of effective gender equality articles in the constitutions and in family and personal status laws in most Arab countries reflects the significant influence of gender-discriminating norms, which, in turn, makes women more vulnerable to gender-discriminating practices that are rooted in discriminating norms and traditions (Kelly and Breslin 2010; U.S. DOSa 2014).

Just as in the political sphere, norms and rules in most Arab countries discriminate against women's leadership in the legal sector, especially in leadership positions such as judges. Women are prohibited from serving as lawyers and judges in Kuwait and Saudi Arabia (Kelly and Breslin 2010; U.S. DOSa 2014). Women serve as judges in many Arab countries, but mostly in cases related to family matters. Women's engagement and representation in the legal sector in Tunisia, Algeria, and Morocco is significantly higher than the rest of the Arab world, and specially the Arabian-Gulf countries (e.g., Saudi Arabia, United Arab Emirates Oman, Bahrain, and Kuwait). However, recent developments show ongoing signals toward allowing women more access to and employment in the legal sectors as future lawyers and even judges in Saudi Arabia and Kuwait (U.S. DOSa 2014).

Governments in many Arab countries have effective control and influence over human rights organizations, directing them to promote traditional norms, customs, and values, including gender-discriminating norms. The members of these organizations are mostly chosen by the government to engage in collectivist activities and praise the government's role in protecting human rights. They are not allowed to engage in human rights and gender matters such as women's civic and political rights or autonomy. Such governmental control is supported by laws that punish human rights' activists for acting against the interest of the country, enticing social disorder, or insulting the government (Mayer 2000; Manea 2010; Al-Talei 2010; U.S. DOSa 2014).

Norms and Separation of Ownership in Marriage

In most Arab and other similar Muslim countries, husbands and wives do not have joint ownership of the couple's assets—each has his or her separate assets. According to Islamic law, the wife's property belongs to her, and the husband's property belongs to him. Joint ownership of the couple's assets increases the cost and inconvenience to husbands to take advantage of other options accessible only to men according to informal norms rooted in sacred religious teaching, such as divorcing their wives or adding another wife (or wives, up to four wives at a time). In the Arab world, husbands are the primary income earners and are in charge of supporting their families because of their *qawama* over women. As a result, men earn most of the family's monetary income and own most of the family's assets. Men earn and control most assets, open bank accounts in their names, inherit more shares than women (double women's share in general), have unrestricted access to the labor market, have near monopoly on land and in-kind assets.

Furthermore, the collective pressure on women (who are minors confined to the private sphere) to give up their shares of inheritance to their male relatives, especially their male guardians, is likely to compel women to delegate the management, and sometimes the ownership, of their assets to their male legal guardians. Men have the exclusive right over the assets accumulated during marriage. According to prevailing norms and rules, a wife is entitled to food, housing, clothing, and furnishing. She does not have a say in how her husband uses his income or assets beyond the mentioned specified needs (Charrad 2007).

In summary, women's lack of monetary contribution to a marriage puts her at a disadvantage, since men earn monetary income, which, in turn, deprives women from a fair share of assets accumulated during their marriage. This deepens women's dependency and vulnerability. Thus, divorced women normally move back to their parents or other male relative (e.g., brothers). In such a case, women's male guardianship is switched back to an assigned male member (father or brother).

Norms and Women's Rights to Child Custody

Existing norms and rules regarding child custody vary in the Arab world, yet contain certain similarities. The norms and rules for divorced mothers' custody of sons differ from those of daughters. A mother's custody of sons is usually shorter and generally ends once the sons reach puberty. The custody then is passed to the sons' father. However, the custody for daughters is longer and can remain until the girls get married (Charrad 2007). In general, a son belongs to his father's (paternal) side of the family once he reaches adulthood, to be groomed in the patrilineal system, and to affirm his preferred status over female members and his *qawama* over them, such that he should be removed from his mother's custody and start belonging to the paternal side of his parents. Thus, a mother's right and custody last as long as they are needed to take care of their children. Such a need ends when the son reaches adulthood.

Since daughters lose their father's lineage once they get married (especially to men outside the family) the norms allow mothers to have longer custody of their daughters, sometimes until they get married (Charrad 2007). In Saudi Arabia, child custody for a mother lasts until the boy reaches the age of seven and the girl reaches her puberty (Doumato 2010). In Jordan, mothers have custody of their children until they reach puberty. After that, children decide whom they will live with. Mothers (in Jordan and other Arab countries) lose the custody of their children if they remarry. The father is considered the legal guardian of his children even when the mother has custody of them, giving the father the status and orchestration power to make important decisions such as children's education and place of residence (Husseini 2010; Kelly and Breslin

2010; U.S. DOSa 2014). In many Arab countries, noncitizen mothers lose custody of their children if they divorce their citizen husbands "without just cause" (Kelly and Breslin 2010). In Saudi Arabia, mothers lose the custody of their children even if the children's father dies. In such a case, the custody is transferred to the deceased father's family (U.S. DOSa: Saudi Arabia 2014).

Norms and the Right to Marry Non-Muslims in the Arab World

The laws in most Arab countries allow Muslim men to marry non-Muslim women (Christians or Jews); however, they prohibit Muslim women from marrying non-Muslim men. The rationale for this norm and rule is the dual rulership rooted in sacred texts and teaching: men's *qawama* (guardianship or rulership) over women (the *Qur'an* 4:34), and Muslims' rulership over non-Muslims (the *Qur'an* 3:38; 4:59; 4:141; 5:51). The inferior status of non-Muslim men does not equip them to have guardianship over Muslim women. Such *qawama* cannot be offered to a non-Muslim man, since it contradicts the norm of no *welaya* (rulership) of non-Muslims over Muslims. This explains, in part, the sacred norms and laws that prohibit Muslim women from marrying non-Muslim men (unless these men convert to Islam) in the Arab world and other similar Islamic societies.[4] Consequently, the children of the mixed marriage between Muslim men and non-Muslim women are Muslim by default, since children are related to their paternal parents (Kelly and Breslin 2010, U.S. DOSa 2014). In addition, the non-Muslim wife (unless she converts to Islam) is excluded from any share in the inheritance of her deceased Muslim husband, since she does not belong to the family (the collective unit) after his death, due to the absence of a male Muslim's *qawama* over her (Kelly and Breslin 2010).

Norms and Marrying Noncitizens: Rights to Citizenship

The following cases of gender-discriminating practices in the Arab world deal with a family's right to citizenship. Men in the Arab world can transmit their nationality to their foreign wives and to their children in order to sustain collective identity. In contrast, women cannot transmit their nationality to foreign husbands since these foreign husbands have high status in terms of their *qawama* over the national women. By preventing foreign husbands from getting easy access to nationality or citizenship, most of the status and orchestration power will be tied to the national male—helping sustain collective norms, cultural heritage, and social unity in the society. A few Arab countries do give unrestricted citizenship to foreign husbands, and the children of the marriage, such as Tunisia, Algeria, and Morocco (Kelly and Breslin 2010; U.S. DOSa 2014).

In the United Arab Emirates, Emirati women can lose their citizenship upon marrying a non-Emirati man under certain circumstances. Emirati men can transfer the Emirati nationality to their foreign wives and children automatically, while Emirati women must get permission from the Presidential Court before marrying foreign men to be able to apply for a transfer of nationality to their husbands (Kirdar 2010; U.S. DOSa 2014). In Saudi Arabia, applications by men to marry foreign women are usually approved without delay; however, women's applications to marry foreign men are subject to delay and more requirements, without a guarantee of approval (Doumato 2010). Jordanian men can automatically transfer the citizenship to their foreign wives and their children, while Jordanian women are not allowed to transfer their nationality to their foreign husbands and children, disqualifying these children from free education, in addition to requiring the foreign spouses and children to pay recurring residency fees (Husseini 2010). Bahraini women cannot transmit nationality to their foreign spouses or the children of such marriage (U.S. DOSa: Bahrain 2014). In Kuwait, female citizens cannot pass citizenship to their foreign spouses or children, except when she divorces her foreign husband or becomes a widow (U.S. DOSa: Kuwait 2014). In Saudi Arabia, a 2004 royal decree granted gender equality regarding the Saudi nationality; however, in truth, women cannot pass their Saudi citizenship to their noncitizen husbands and children. Since 2005, noncitizen husbands who have professional qualifications can apply for citizenship after ten years of living in Saudi Arabia (Doumato 2010), and the sons of Saudi women can apply for citizenship after they reach the age of 18. The daughters can get Saudi citizenship if they marry a Saudi man (Doumato 2010). Women in Egypt cannot transfer nationality to their foreign husbands. Egyptian men automatically transfer nationality to their foreign wives and children. In 2004, Egyptian women gained the right to transfer citizenship to their children of foreign husbands. However, these children cannot join the army, police, or other government posts (Tadros 2010).

On the other hand, recent developments in other countries like Algeria, Tunisia, and Morocco, grant women the right to marry foreign spouses and transmit citizenship to their spouses and children—giving these children access to free services and amenities such as education and healthcare (Kelly and Breslin 2010; U.S. DOSa 2014).

Summary

Gender-discriminating norms in the Arab world hinder women's capabilities and functionings, especially when it comes to women's authority and leadership, such as women serving as political representatives, leaders, prosecutors, and judges. In addition, legal rules discriminate against women, such as women's discounted legal testimony, barriers against women's access to legal rights, prohibiting Muslim women from marrying non-Muslim men, discrimination against women's right to transfer citizenship to their foreign husband and children, and on mothers' rights to child custody. These are examples of many practices that permit specific rights, capabilities, and functionings to men only, especially in the most collectivist countries.

PART IV

Summary and Conclusion

CHAPTER 14

Summary and Conclusion

Community-based strategies can focus on empowering women, reaching out to men, and changing the beliefs and attitudes that permit abusive behaviors. CHANGE (1999: 2)

Gender-discriminating norms, especially those rooted in sacred texts and teachings, have been exploited for centuries and even millennia to impose assigned identities and roles on women. This is especially in the gender-discriminating collectivist societies, such as many countries in the Arab world, with varying degrees of collectivism and impositions of such norms. Gender discrimination is treated with varying degrees of normalcy in different Arab countries; most discrimination is internalized by Arab women. The formalization of sacred beliefs and social norms have detrimental effects on women's capabilities and functionings, which, in turn, violate women's rights and freedom—rights that are sanctioned in universal human rights declarations, protocols, and conventions.

This book analyzes the influence of informal norms on women's status and their freedom to achieve the capabilities they value. Gender-discriminating norms, like other discriminating norms, exist in communities and societies in an imperfect world, in which a certain group (or groups) aims to gain status and dominance over another group (or groups).

Gender discrimination is prevalent in the Arab world for two main reasons: the presence of gender discriminating norms in this region and the collectivist foundations of Arab societies (with different degrees of collectivism among Arab countries). The collectivist social and political structures in Arab world impose gender-discriminating norms that label women as submissive to men (especially their male guardians), belonging to the private sphere as wives and mothers, excluded from, or having limited access to, many activities in the public sphere, and, most importantly, as the holder of the collective honor (girl's virginity and women's sexual reputation and fidelity).

The norm of women's obedience to their male relatives, the norms of women's deficiency of intelligence and faith (or mind and religion), the norm of women's holding the collective honor in their bodies and their behaviors (especially their sexual behaviors), and the norms of treating women as minors all add to the prevalence and acceptance of gender discrimination in the Arab world at a much higher rate that the rest of the world. Jointly these norms impose significant limitations on women's capabilities and functionings to make decisions on their own, to lead an independent life, and to seek equal status that is accessible to men. The fear of women's freedom, especially the fear of women's sexual behavior, explains to a large degree the many measures to guard and sustain the collective honor. Gender-discriminating norms in the Arab world largely confine women to the private sphere, constrain their mobility, especially their access to the public sphere, and therefore limit women's mixing with unrelated men. Women's status as minors prevents them from participating in the collective decision-making processes and from status and orchestration power, delegating women to implement decisions made by males and male-dominated collective units (e.g., family, tribe, and society) according to their specifications and aspirations.

Sacred norms in the Arab world (based in widely accepted interpretation of sacred Islamic texts and teaching) impart on women economic and financial dependency on men in addition to male rulership and guardianship. These norms explain, in a large part, the Arab world's (and other similar countries) ranking near or at the bottom of the whole world in terms of female labor-force participation rates, the female-to-male unemployment rates, female-to-male per capita income, and female-to male economic participation in general. International surveys show that Arabs believe men make better business and economic leaders than women, at much higher rates than the rest of the world. In addition, world statistics show the Arab world ranks near or at the bottom of the world in terms of female political empowerment, female-to-male ratios of legislators and senior officials, and the percentage of parliament's seats held by women. These statistics reflect the deficiency in women's capabilities in the Arab world compared to women in the rest of the world. This is due, in part, to the collective punishment against deviants and shirkers of norms related to gender-discriminating metanorms. The influence of gender-discriminating norms in the Arab world is also highlighted in the Arab people's negative perceptions of women's leadership and presence in the public sphere.

Because women in the Arab world do not have access to orchestration power (the power to make major decisions), they are not free to act independently, for example, to choose from individualist goods and behaviors (fashion, cosmetics, education, work, travel, sport, driving). Instead, they are constrained to choose only from collectivist goods and behaviors endorsed and sanctioned by males guardians and the collectivist community.

The collective control of women's behaviors includes various forms of violence against women. Such violence starts early with ex-ante or preemptive measures such as FGM/C and female underage marriage. Ongoing measures of controlling women's behaviors include domestic violence and various forms of restrictions on women's freedom and capabilities (movement, marriage, divorce, child custody, socialization, dress code, travel, education, employment, entertainment, etc.). The purpose of such measures is to restrain female behaviors and sustain their reputation and the collective honor. Ex-post measures, such as honor killing (and other forms of excessive violence or credible threat of violence), serve as the ultimate punishment to deviant female members who dare (or are victimized) to deviate from the collective norms and to violate them, gravely tainting their reputation and disgracing the collective honor, such that they must pay the ultimate price—death, such as in honor killing. Women's acceptance of men's right to beat or chastise their wives under certain circumstances in the Arab world underlines the influence of gender-discriminating norms. The norms are imposed to ensure women's submission and to guard and sustain their sexual fidelity.

After laying down the foundations of gender-discriminating norms, the book highlights the difficulty of measuring gender discrimination and violence in the Arab world. Many gender-discriminating practices and crimes in the Arab world are not considered crimes or even gender discrimination, such as domestic violence, spousal, rape, and female circumcision (FGM/C). These are examples of practices that are condoned or sanctioned according to prevalent norms that are based in sacred teaching and interpretations of sacred texts, especially by males or the male-dominated patriarchal hierarchy in the Arab world (and other similar societies). Some other gender crimes are underreported due to the fear of tainting the victims' reputation and the honor of their collective unit. Also, the female victims' fear of prosecution (if they fail to prove rape or sexual harassments) for their perceived roles in initiating such acts by the way they dress, mix with men, or are in the public sphere without the company of a *mahram* leave many abuses unreported. The husband's right to discipline and beat his wives, prevents women from reporting many incidences of gender-based crimes and violence against women in the Arab world. Furthermore, informal collective pressures, supported by formal rules, impose great barriers on women to not share or formally report such gender crimes, since such acts are likely to taint the collective honor and ruin the complaining woman's reputation. Arab women are likely to internalize such gender-discriminating norms and practices due to their fear of violating collectivist norm. This includes their fear of collective retribution, gender-discriminating practices in police and court systems, and women's lack of other viable options, causing women to accept such gender discrimination as integral to their daily life in the Arab world.

Recent developments in many Arab countries show promising steps toward reducing gender discrimination in the Arab world. These developments include recent laws against sexual harassment, and increasing female participation in political and judicial institutions, such as women's gained right to vote and run for political office and judicial positions in many Arab countries.

Where to Go from Here?

Effective and long-lasting interventions must come from within the Arab societies, especially those supported by effective demystification and reinterpretation of "sacred" gender-discriminating norms and practices, in inclusive and equitable ways to women. Women's reformed thinking is vital to their empowerment and freedom from gender-discriminating norms. Authentic and long-lasting reforms are likely to emerge from progressive thinking that takes place in the Arab world. This is easier said than done! However, ongoing pressure supported by informed modernized Islamic thought in the mostly Muslim Arab world, and the emergence of secular voices, can reduce gender inequality in the Arab world significantly.

Tilting the Collectivism–Individualism Balance

Gender relations and women's rights are likely to improve with the tilting of citizens' loyalties from paternalistic hierarchy rooted in tribal and local aspiration, to the entity of the sovereign nation-state (Charrad 2007). This goes beyond statist and stagnant social identities and roles to more dynamic and inclusive membership in the nation-state. This membership applies to people from different tribes, ethnic and racial backgrounds, and gender identities. Effective interventions should give women the freedom to pursue the capabilities and functionings they value the most without any fear of collective retributions rooted in gender-discriminating norms and traditions. Making membership to collective groups and organizations voluntary with freedom to enter and exit without any fear of collective punishments is a necessary step to reducing discrimination. Likewise, repealing gender-discriminating laws rooted in gender-discriminating "sacred" norms in religious texts can help tilt the balance. Tilting the collectivism-individualism balance toward individualism should give more credence to international human rights protocols and conventions that are inclusive and universal, and are not based in any particular ideology, faith, or history. In such a case, human rights will be standardized around the world.

Choosing the Battle: The Need to Dig Deep

It is important to decipher the causes of gender-discriminating norms in different countries (or societies), and dig deeper than selective, usually superficial, aspects of gender discrimination (e.g., the veiling of women, especially in the public sphere) (Ahmed 1992; Abu-Lughod 2002; Mernissi 1991; An-N'aim 2002). Women's veiling is a symptom of gender discrimination; it is, however, an inventive way for women to access the public sphere without violating existing norms of gender separation and covering women's 'awra (Papanek 1982). A deeper understanding of gender-discriminating norms—their credence, authenticity, and ability to accommodate and modernize norms to modern world—can serve women's issues and women's rights in more effective ways than focusing on one selective issue (or issues) (Ahmed 1992; Mernissi 1991). Shirin Ebadi, an Iranian human rights activist and the 2003 Nobel Peace Prize Laureate, emphasizes this notion, "When my husband can marry three other women, when my husband can take my children, when my husband can kill me, I have more important problems. When I find a solution for these problems, then I will worry about hijab [veiling]" (in Weiner 2004).

Demystifying Gender-Discriminating Norms

There is a strong need for modern Islamic thinkers and theologians, especially female theologians and feminists to demystify the misinterpretations and the exploitations of sacred norms, expose their distortions, and offer a more accurate picture of the world, especially in religious collectivist societies, such as the Arab world (Smith 2001). Demystifying the norms is needed to provide modern reformed perspectives on century-old norms (or even those that have existed for millennia) and traditions that should correspond to needs and circumstances over time. Islamic feminists should be able to evaluate the authenticity, credibility, and the appropriateness of such norms to modern life, and the level and form of applying such norms. Reformed thinking should also offer modern substitutes for old norms to fit societal needs and aspirations in modern life. For example, some Islamic scholars believe that veiling which was used to protect women in the Prophet's (Muhammad) era should be replaced with women's education to protect their interests in modern world (Hélie-Lucas 1999). Charrad (2007) argues that Islam provides a framework that is subject to interpretation, opening the door for Islamic reformists, including Islamic feminists, to seek more rights and dignity for women, within the tenet of Islamic *shari'ah*.

First-, Second-, and Third-Best Scenarios

Chapter 3 explains that feminism (or human-rights universalism) represents the first-best scenario for women's rights in terms of total and unequivocal equality among men and freedom from all impediments that are rooted in various cultural, religious, historical, and social institutions. Cultural feminism (Islamic feminism in the Arab world) represents a second-best scenario for women's rights. It calls for rights subject to existing collectivist norms and rules, such as the status quo. In addition, cultural feminists can challenge the interpretations of certain sacred teachings and norms exploited by the existing patriarchal hierarchy and the dominant power and status of fundamentalists in their societies. They reject gender-discriminating norms and practices that are false, unauthentic, or exploited, according to the true intention and meaning of Islamic *shari'ah* (Ahmed 1992; Charrad 2007; Mernissi 1987).

Cultural relativism offers the third and worst level of rights to women in gender-discriminating collectivist societies. It endorses existing cultural norms as a reflection of cultural heritage, harmony, and social order. Cultural relativists not only oppose and refute the view of the feminists, but also the cultural feminists who seek to reform or stretch women's rights by pushing the cultural values' envelope.

Effective International Interventions: Transparent with Clear Agenda

International intervention should be transparent with a clear agenda to serve women's interests, reduce their vulnerability, and empower them, mostly through complementary activities of national women and human rights organization in each country. Competing interests or hidden agendas are likely to divert energy and resources and be exploited by certain winners of the status quo in these gender-discriminating countries in order to neutralize such international intervention or to reject it (Ostrom 2012). International intervention should avoid the use of inappropriate modes or programs that fail to take into consideration the specific needs and cultural contexts in each country (Abu-Lughod 2002; Abadeer 2008). They should utilize universal norms of human capabilities without associating them with a certain culture or faith or ideology. Moreover, international interventions should support and utilize internal initiatives that are authentic to the culture to provide more support for women and women's rights (Abadeer 2008).

The Last Word

What is taking place in the Arab world is the combined effect of century- or millennia-old gender-discriminating norms based in sacred texts and teachings, and exploited and sustained by male dominance in patriarchal hierarchies. The fate of women and women's rights in the Arab world (and similar countries) will be determined by the outcomes of multiple tensions and balances: between collectivism and individualism, secularism and theocracy, collective (or community) rights and individual rights, staticism (traditionalism) and dynamism (reformism), and between human rights universalism and cultural relativism.

In countries in which the balance tilts toward collectivism, theocracy, community rights, staticism (traditionalism), and cultural relativism, women are likely to continue to suffer from gender discriminating norms, rules, and practices.

These intricate tensions and balances underscore the complexity of tackling gender discrimination in many countries, especially in gender-discriminating collectivist societies, such as the Arab world.

Notes

1 Introduction

1. Women, especially Muslim women, in prominent Muslin counties are advised and sometimes required to wear *abaya* or similar long dress (and head cover), especially in public. The rationale is rooted in the Muslims' holy book, the *Qur'an,* revealed to Prophet Mohammad, the Prophet of Islam, regarding his wives' dress code, "O Prophet, tell your wives and daughters, and the believing women, to cover themselves with a loose garment. They will thus be recognized and no harm will come to them" (the *Qur'an*, 33:59). A similar *qur'anic* verse related to women's dress is, "And say to the faithful women to lower their gazes, and to guard their private parts, and not to display their beauty except what is apparent of it, and to extend their head coverings (*khimars*) to cover their bosoms (*jaybs*), and not to display their beauty except to their husbands, or their fathers, or their husband's fathers, or their sons, or their husband's sons, or their brothers, or their brothers' sons, or their sisters' sons, or their womenfolk, or what their right hands rule (slaves), or the followers from the men who do not feel sexual desire, or the small children to whom the nakedness of women is not apparent, and not to strike their feet (on the ground) so as to make known what they hide of their adornments. And turn in repentance to Allah together, O you the faithful, in order that you are successful" (the *Qur'an* 24:31).
2. See Elster (1989) for more details and examples of social norms.
3. Customs refer to socially accepted standards of views, behaviors, and acts that are not morally significant, or do not have significant moral inclination.
4. Taboos refer to certain moral behaviors and acts that are socially forbidden. What is considered a taboo in one society may not be a taboo in another; for example, polygyny is considered a taboo in Western societies; however, it is accepted in the Arab world, except Tunisia.
5. Mores are moral behaviors; norms based on definitions of right and wrong. Violating mores tends to offend most members in a community. Examples of mores includes attending prayer, fasting, and women's adhering to socially sanctioned dress codes in many collectivist societies in the Arab world.
6. For more definitions and deeper understanding of culture, see Kroeber and Kluckholm (1952), Durkheim (1968 and 1984), William (1976), Smith (2001), Storey (2009), and Gramsci (2009).
7. Other definitions of culture refer to the range of intellectual and artistic activities and their products, which are synonyms with "the Arts," and the intellectual,

spiritual, and aesthetic development of individuals, groups, or society (Smith 2001; Williams 1976; Storey 2009). Smith (2001) highlights six main understandings or definitions of culture: descriptive, historical, normative, psychological, structural, and genetic definitions of culture.

8. Most, if not all, taboos are legislated (e.g., incest). Not all mores are legislated. Not adhering to women's dress code and other constraints on female behaviors are formally punishable only in some Arab countries.

9. UNRWA refers to the United Nations Relief and Work Agency for Palestine Refugees. For more details on UNRWA, see http://www.unrwa.org/.

10. See Al Marzouqi (2011), Alarabiya (2008), Aldeeb (1995); Al Jazeera (2013), Basem (2012), BBC (2002, 2012a,b, 2013a,b, 2014a,b,c), Charrad, (2007), El Saadawi (1980), El-Zanaty and Way (2009), Ennaji and Sadiqi (2011), France 24 (2014a,b,c), Ghanim (2009), IRIN (2005, 2010), Jamjoom (2009), Kassem et al. (2012), MacFarquhar (2011), Malik (2012), NBC News (2009), Rassam (1980), Reuters (2007), U.S. DOSa (2006–2014), Washington Times (2013), Weiner (2004), WHO (2014), Yoder et al. (1999, 2004), and Yount (2001, 2003, 2004).

11. The Gender Inequality Index (GII measures the loss in human development index due to inequality between women and men in three dimensions: gender discrimination in reproductive health, empowerment, and the labor market. It ranges from zero where women and men fare equally to one where women fare as poorly as possible in all measured dimensions. For more detailed information see UNDP. http://hdr.undp.org/en/statistics/gii/.

12. The Gender Empowerment Measure (GEM) is "A composite index measuring gender inequality in three basic dimensions of empowerment—economic participation and decision-making, political participation, and decision-making and power over economic resources." UNDP, Human Development Report 2009, P. 210. http://hdr.undp.org/sites/default/files/reports/269/hdr_2009_en_complete.pdf.

13. See Klasen (2004), Klasen and Wink (2002a,b), Nussbaum (2000), Sen (1990), Yount (2001, 2004), Yount et al. (2000), and World Bank (2014)

14. The World Bank (2014). World Development Indicators 2014. Last updated Septemebr 24, 2014. http://data.worldbank.org/data-catalog/world-development-indicators.

15. Sen (1990), Das Gupta (1999), Das Guptia et al. (2009), Guilmoto (2009), Klasen (2008), Yount (2001).

16. Recent research shows an improvement (a reduction) in the relative number of missing women that is associated, in part, with lower women's fertility rates in most countries (Klasen 2008: 16).

17. For example Saudi Arabia, in January 2013, King Abdulla appointed 30 women to the Consultative *Shura* (consultation or advising) council in Saudi Arabia for the first time in the history of Saudi Arabia, giving them twenty percent of the seats. However, the newly appointed female members must observe Islamic law and the proper Islamic veil (*hijab*), and be segregated with respect to having a separate entrance to the chamber and sitting in a special section apart from men (BBC 2013; U.S. DOSa: Saudi Arabia 2013).

18. Worldwide, 40–70 percent of homicides of women are committed by intimate partners. Studies also show that "women who are abused by their partners suffer more depression, anxiety, and phobias than women who have not been abused" (CHANGE 1999).

19. Honor killing is prevalent in similar cultures. For example, in Turkey, the government reported 1,806 honor killings and 5,375 female suicides between 2001

and 2006 (U.S. DOSa: Turkey 2008). The incidents of female suicides in Turkey increased after the Turkish government made the punishment against 'honor' killing more severe, such that concerned families stepped up their pressure on 'disgraced' women to commit suicide instead of deputizing a family member to commit the honor killing (US-DOSa: Turkey 2014). In Pakistan, The Aurat Foundation reported 2,773 honor killings in Pakistan between 2008 and 2012. Less than two percent of all honor killings were reported (U.S. DOSa: Pakistan 2014). In India, ten percent of all killings in India are related to honor killing (U.S. DOSa: India 2014).

2   Institutions and Gender Discrimination

1. Boulding classifies various types of images: the spatial image that refers to the individual's location in the space around her/him; the temporal image that refers to the stream of time and the person's place in it; the relational image that refers to the picture of the universe around the person as a system of regularities; the personal image that refers to the picture of the person in the midst of the universe of persons, roles, and organization; the value image that orders or ranks various parts of the image of better or worse; and the emotional image where various parts of the image are imbued with feeling. The image may also be classified according to its certainty or uncertainty, clarity or vagueness, and reality or unreality (1956). For more details, see Chapter Four in Boulding (1956).

2. Denzau and North define ideologies as "the shared framework of mental models that groups of individuals possess that provide both an interpretation of the environment and a prescription as to how that environment should be structured" (1993: para 3).

3. In the case of metanorms, one must punish not only the violators/dissenters of metanorms, but also the shirkers who do not punish the violators/dissenters (Akerlof 1976; Axelrod 1986; Basu 1986; Elster 1989; Horne 2001, 2007; Horne and Cutlip 2002). A detailed analysis of metanorms is covered in chapter 6.

4. For more details, see Dayan et al. (2001), Prietula and Conway (2009), Sedikides and Brewer (2001), Triandis and Trafimow (2001), Kishor and Subaiya (2008), and Coleman (1990).

5. Cultural capital consists of forms of knowledge, skills, and so on, that give a person a higher status in society. Women's lack of access to such knowledge and to social mobility, due to multiple constraints imposed on them, prevents them for acquiring a desired level or form of cultural capital (Bourdieu 1986). The collectivist society provides its preferred group with cultural capital by transmitting the attitude and knowledge needed to succeed in educational, social, legal, political, and economic systems.

6. It took England about 140 years (from 1830 to 1970) to prohibit child labor and raise the minimum working age to 16. Historical experience in the United States and Europe show that a mix of economic, technological, social, and legal factors acted together to eliminate child labor (Hasnat 1995). The same gradual changes took place in the USA, in the process of giving women the right to vote.

7. Islamic *shari'ah* refers to the core teachings, norms, and provisions in Islam. It consists mainly of the *Qur'an* and *sunna* which are *hadith* [narrations/sayings] of, or practices undertaken or approved by the Messenger (Prophet Muhammad) and established as legally binding precedents, followed by *ijma'* (consensus) of "*ulama*" (Islamic scholars), and finally, by *qias* (analogy) deduced from the *Qur'an* and

sunna. These too are considered valid in Islamic jurisprudence (Islamic Council 1981; Katulis 2004).

8. The Occupied Palestinian Territories, Somali, and Sudan have not signed as of November 13, 2014 (UN n.d.-b).

9. For more details see the articles regarding the followings aspects: *shari'ah* (Article XI in UIDHR), life (Article 1 in UIDHR and Article 2 in CDHRI), individual freedom (Article II in UIDHR), education (Articles 7 and 9 in CDHRI), free movement (Article 12 in CDHRI, and Article XXIII in UIDHR), inheritance (Article XX in UIDHR), legal rights (Article 19 in CDHRI), and freedom of expression (Article 22 in CDHRI, Article XII in UIDHR).

10. In July 2014, Mauritania withdrew it general rejection (UN n.d.-b).

11. Egypt withdrew its reservation to Article 9 (2) on January 4, 2008 (UN n.d.-b), following the reform of the national law of 2004 (UNFEM 2009).

4   The Capability Approach and Gender Discrimination

1. Hausman and McPherson defines the agency as other-regarding and altruistic preference, "the desire to do certain things rather than simply to enjoy the consequences of their being done" (1993: 687), in contrast to self-regarding or egoistic preference.

2. Effective participation emphasizes the role of practical reason, deliberate democracy, and public action influencing policies, inter alia. See Sen (1985b) and Clark (2005).

3. For a full list of the United Nations' international human rights conventions, declarations, and committees, see http://www2.ohchr.org/english/law/.

4. Most Egyptians, similar to other developing countries, underscore the provision of basic needs, such as food, housing, jobs, education, and healthcare as a definition of human rights. This reflects the crucial value of economic and rights in many developing countries. Few highlight political rights and civil liberties (Katulis 2004).

5. The 2004 Freedom House study in Egypt also shows that discrimination against men in hiring is due in part to women being more diligent, obedient, and are willing to accept lower salaries and benefits (Katulis 2004).

6. For critiques of Nussbaum's list of capabilities and functionings, see Clark (2005).

7. Observations show that people contribute effort to voluntary organizations, vote, do not cheat on taxes, and help the poor, in contrast to the zero contribution hypothesis that a non-self-interested person should contribute to the production of a public good (Ostrom 2000).

5   Norms in Collectivist versus Individualist Societies

1. See Ogilvie (2004a, 2004b) for detailed analysis of social capital, networks, closures, and multiplex relationships.

2. It is worth mentioning that even in one of the world most individualist countries, the United States, there is still certain exclusive practices. For example, the Augusta National Golf Club opened its exclusive membership to few celebrated women in for the first time in its 80-year history, in 2012 (Pearson 2012).

3. A study by Chesler (2010) shows that Muslims commit 91 percent of all honor killings in the world. In addition, 84 percent and 96 percent of the perpetrators of honor killings in the USA and Europe are Muslims.

4. The severe punishment of rape victims is partly based on the implicit assumption that rape victims play a role in seducing the perpetrators. Examples of this supposed role include wearing revealing clothes or makeup, not fighting the rapists, response to incest, the reduced value of women's testimonies or claims, and so on.

5. *Hisbah* is an institution in the Islamic state enjoined to monitor and facilitate the fulfillment of proper acts in the public sphere through public vigilance (Islamic Council 1981).

6. It is difficult to single out a common set of factors that contributed to the rise of conspiratorial thinking. Factors such as Western concern over Muslim terrorists, anti-Islamic activities by conservative groups in different Western countries on one hand, and heightened anti-Western propaganda by radical Muslim activists against the West may have played a role (Moaddel 2013).

7. In 2014, A Saudi court accused and sentenced human rights' activist, Ra'if Badawi, to a ten-year imprisonment, one thousand lashes, and a fine equivalent to $266,000. The accusation was that he had insulted Islam. He was accused of criticizing the virtue police in Saudi Arabia (BBC 2014a). Also, a Palestinian poet was imprisoned in Saudi Arabia in 2013 based on a claim that he promoted atheism in his 2008 Published poems *Al-Horreya* [freedom] (Kareem 2014).

6 Metanorms and Gender Discrimination

1. The terms "first and second-order free riders" are borrowed from Heckathorn (1989).

2. A m*ahram,* according to Islamic *shari'ah*, is a person who is prohibited from marrying certain people, usually close relatives. For example, a female is prohibited from marrying her father, grandfather, son, brother, uncle, or nephew (Al-Qaradawi 1997).

7 Cognitive Dissonance and Gender Discrimination

1. For further studies and examples on cognitive dissonance, see Brehm (1956), Festinger (1957), Festinger and Carlsmith (1959), and Herbert (2010), Knox and Inkster (1968), and Kunreuther et al. (1978).

2. This thought is similar to the one expressed by Akerlof and Dickens (1982), "people may want to believe that what they have just bought meets their needs. Advertising gives people some external justification for believing just that. People like to feel that they are attractive, socially adept, and intelligent. It makes them feel good to hold such beliefs—if the person buys the advertised product" (p. 317).

3. False consciousness was used by Karl Marx, in reference to the way of life where what is socially constructed seems natural and inevitable. Religion, for example, was an "opium" that prevented the formation of class consciousness (see Chapter 1 in Smith 2001).

8 Norms, Status, and Individualist Goods

1. Sahih Bukhari, Volume 4, Book 55, Number 623.

2. Sahih Bukhari, Volume 9, Book 88, Number 219.

3. In the 2004's Freedom House's study on women's freedom in Egypt, Christians were more open to the notion of women serving as judges, and other leadership positions (Katulis 2004: 20).

4. This simple model can be extended to include a subsidy on consuming collectivist goods. This should have the same substitution effect as increasing the cost of the individualist goods; however, it will cause a positive income effect, in contrast to the case of increasing the cost of individualist goods.

9 Measuring Gender Discrimination

1. Think of the simple model that for every unit of women's interest, the men can get $(1 + a)$ where $a > 0$. In the case of equal access, $a = 0$. As gender bias increases or intensifies, a will have a higher value and the collective decisions will reflect the men's position at the expense of women's positions.
2. A *hadith* narrated by Abu Huraira in Sahih Bukhari (volume7, book 62, number 121).
3. A *hadith* narrated by Abu Huraira in Sahih Bukhari (volume 7, book 62, number 120).
4. A *hadith* narrated by Abu Huraira in Sahih Bukhari (volume 7, book 62, number 123).
5. A *hadith* narrated by Abu Said Al-Khudri in Sahih Bukhari (volume 1, book 6, number 301).
6. "O ye who believe! The law of equality is prescribed to you in cases of murder: the free for the free, the slave for the slave, the woman for the woman. But if any remission is made by the brother of the slain, then grant any reasonable demand, and compensate him with handsome gratitude, this is a concession and a Mercy from your Lord." (The *Qur'an* 2:178).

10 Norms and Female Genital Mutilation/Cutting (FGM/C)

1. According to a 2011 report by the United Nations Population Funds, 97% of young girls in Hudeidah, Yemen, have undergone type II (excision) FGM/C (U.S. DOSa: Yemen 2014).
2. It is not uncommon for officials, especially in collectivist societies, to give foreign reporters different opinions than those held by local residents.
3. The law criminalizes FGM/C except in the case of 'medical necessity'. However, the law is not enforced effectively. Some organizations that advocated against FGM/C are no longer active (U.S. DOSa: Egypt 2014).
4. Al-Sheikh Mohammad Al-Barri is a former professor of Islamic studies at Al-Azhar University and chair of the Islamic Studies Center at Al-Azhar University.
5. *Sunan Abu Dawood,* Book 41, number 5251. The emphasis refers to the text in Arabic.
6. See, in Arabic, Muwta' Malik, book 2, number 2.19, 73, 74, 75 and 77, and book 20, number 20.46.161; Sahih Muslim, book 3, number 648; and in Tirmuthi, *hadith* 1.66.
7. Al-Azhar (Cairo, Egypt) is one of the one of the oldest and most respected Islamic universities and Islamic centers in the world.
8. Sheikh Jad Al-Haq Ali Jad Al-Haq (1917–1996), was appointed the Grand *Mufti* of Egypt in 1978, Minister of Religious Endowment in 1982, and the Grand Shaikh Al-Azhar (1982–1996), the highest Islamic position in Egypt.
9. The General Presidency of Scholar Research and Ifta'. Kingdom of Saudi Arabia. The following excerpts illustrate that view, 'Circumcision is an honor for women;

and it involves removing only a part of the clitoris without going to extremes in cutting it'. *'In addition, circumcision is one of the characteristics of Fitrah (unspoiled natural disposition)'. Fatwa* number 2613 part 5 Page 119. http://www.alifta.net/Default.aspx

10. An interview with Egyptian TV station Dream 2, (Good Words, *Kalaam Tayyeb* in Arabic), September 12, 2003.

11. It is worth mentioning that the former first lady of Egypt, Ms. Suzanne Mubarak was the sponsor of the 2003 Afro-Arab Expert Consultation on "legal roots for the prevention of Female Genital Mutilation' and the resulting Cairo Declaration for the Elimination of FGM (The National Council for Children and Motherhood, 2003), which may explain the political pressure imposed on Islamic leaders to change earlier religious decrees and *fatwas*. However such political pressure can be reversed with the change in political power, as is the case with Egypt and the shift of political power to the Islamists (especially the Muslim Brotherhood and *Salafists).*

12. For example, the 2002 UN Special Session on Children set a goal to end FGM/C by 2010, the 2003 Cairo Declaration to eliminate FGM, the 2003 Maputo Protocol adopted by 53 states of the African Union stipulated that FGM/C should be prohibited and condemned, the 2005 Sub-regional Conference in Djibouti against FGM/C, the 2012 UN General Assembly's resolution to intensify the global to eliminate FGM/C.

13. For more information, see The National Council for Children and Motherhood (2003), No Peace without Justice (2005), UN (2013).

14. Still under the new law, FGM/C remains allowable in cases of 'medical necessity' (Los Angeles Times 2008).

15. Some countries in the Arab world ban all signs of celebrating Valentine's Day since it is a non-Muslim celebration, for example, Saudi Arabia (CNN 2008).

16. A special class of members in collectivist societies that may still be subject to discriminating norms is the children, especially females, of collectivist members. These children are victims of discriminating norms, such as FGM/C and underage marriage, since adult collectivist members, mostly the children's parents, make these decisions.

11 Norms and Gender Violence

1. Lebanon is the only Arab country with a significant non-Muslim Population. Christians represent about 42% of Lebanon's population, with 54% Muslims, and 6.5% Druze. Lebanon is also the only Arab state that does not recognize Islam (or another religion) as the state religion. It also does not use the Islamic *shari'ah* as a source of constitutional law.

2. Sahih Bukhari, Book 62, Number 132. http://www.ishwar.com/islam/holy_hadith/book62/book62_03.html

3. Polygamy is prohibited among Christians since it is considered adultery in the Bible. Tunisia and Turkey are the only Muslim dominant countries to ban polygamy.

4. "Wealth and children are [but] adornment of the worldly life. But the enduring good deeds are better to your Lord for reward and better for [one's] hope" The *Qur'an* (18: 46). http://quran.com/18

5. A *Mahram,* according to Islamic *shari'ah*, is a person who is prohibited from marrying certain people, usually close relatives. For example, a female is prohibited from

marrying her father, grandfather, son, brother, uncle, or nephew. See Al-Qaradwi (1997)
6. In the Arab world (and other similar societies), marriages among cousins are allowed and even encouraged.
7. In January 2014, the Moroccan Parliament voted to amend the law that allowed the perpetrators of statutory rape to escape punishment if they marry the under-age rape victim (Alami 2014).
8. Narrated Aisha, "The Prophet engaged me when I was a girl of six (years).... Unexpectedly Allah's Apostle came to me in the forenoon and my mother handed me over to him, and at that time I was a girl of nine years of age." Sahih Bukhari (Volume 5, Book 58, Nmber 234). http://www.usc.edu/org/cmje/religious-texts/hadith/bukhari/058-sbt.php
9. The *Maliki* (one of four major Islamic schools of thought) laws give the last word over a women's marriage to a man.

12   Norms and Women's Economic Rights

1. "Allah instructs you concerning your children: for the male, what is equal to the share of two females. But if there are [only] daughters, two or more, for them is two thirds of one's estate. And if there is only one, for her is half. And for one's parents, to each one of them is a sixth of his estate if he left children. But if he had no children and the parents [alone] inherit from him, then for his mother is one third. And if he had brothers [or sisters], for his mother is a sixth, after any bequest he [may have] made or debt..." (The *Qur'an* 4:11)
2. Figart (2009) discussed the notion of considering racial identity as a type of pro-ductive property.

13   Norms and Women's Political and Legal Rights

1. Sahih Bukhari, Volume 9, Book 88, Number 219.
2. See Islam: Question and Answer (in Arabic). http://islamqa.info/en/20677 and Ahl Alhadeeth (in Arabic). http://www.ahlalhdeeth.com/vb/showthread.php?t=271481
3. Sahih Bukhari, Volume 4, Book 55, Number 623.
4. Lebanon is the exception to this norm and rule. Lebanon is the only country with is a significant Christian population minority at 40.5 percent. About 10 percent of the Egyptian and Syrian populations are Christians. In the rest of the Arab world, the Christian population represents a very small percentage of the total population. (U.S. Central Intelligence Agency 2015).

References

Abadeer, A. (2008). *The Entrapment of the Poor into Involuntary Labor: Understanding the Worldwide Practice of Modern-Day Slavery* (New York: The Edwin Mellon Press).

Abraham, A. and J.-P. Platteau (2001). "Participatory Development in the Presence of Endogenous Community Imperfections," http://siteresources.worldbank.org/DEC/Resources/84797-1251813753820/6415739-1251814028691/abraham.pdf

Abu-Lughod, L. (2002). "Do Muslim Women Really Need Saving? Anthropological Reflections on Cultural Relativism and Its Others," *American Anthropologist* 104(3), 783–790.

Afkhami, M. (1999). "Gender Apartheid and the Discourse of Relativity of Rights in Muslim Societies," in C. W. Howland (ed.), *Religious Fundamentalisms and the Human Rights of Women*, pp. 67–77 (New York: St. Martin's Press).

Ahmad, I. (2000). "Female Genital Mutilation: An Islamic perspective." *Minaret of Freedom Institute*. MFI Pamphlet #1. Accessed February 24, 2013. http://www.minaret.org/FGM/C-pamphlet.htm

Ahmed, Leila (1992). *Women and Gender in Islam: Historical Roots of a Modern Debate* (New Haven: Yale University Press).

Akerlof, G. (1976). "The Economics of Caste and of the Rat Race and Other Woeful Tale," *The Quarterly Journal of Economics* 90(4), 599–617.

Akerlof, G. and W. Dickens (1982). "The Economic Consequences of Cognitive Dissonance," *American Economic Review* 72(3), 307–319.

Akerlof, G. and R. Kranton (2000). "Economics and Identity," *Quarterly Journal of Economics* CXV(3), 715–753.

Al Banna, J. (2013). "The Enjoin What Is Just, and Forbid What Is Evil's Dilemma," in Arabic, *Al-Masry Al-Youm*, January 23, 2013.

Al Jazeera (2013). "Hamas Segregates Gaza Schools by Gender," April 11, 2013. http://m.aljazeera.com/story/20134711112489892

Al Marzouqi, W. (2011). "Fatal Traditions: Female Circumcision in the UAE," *The National*. July 23, 2011. http://www.thenational.ae/lifestyle/fatal-traditions-female-circumcision-in-the-uae

Al-arabyia (2008). *"Islamic Group Demands the Mufti of Egypt to Renege on 'the Prohibition of Circumcision',"* in Arabic, *Alarabiya.net*, July 6, 2007. http://www.alarabiya.net/articles/2007/07/26/36266.html

———. (2013). *Breakthrough in Saudi Arabia: Women Allowed in Parliament*, January 11, 2013. http://english.alarabiya.net/articles/2013/01/11/259881.html/

Al-Azizi, A. (2013). "Women's Rights Advocates: Secure Women's Rights through the Constitution'," *Yemen Times*, October 15, 2013. http://www.yementimes

.com/en/1720/report/3010/Women%E2%80%99s-rights-advocates-Secure-women%E2%80%99s-rights-through-the-constitution.htm

Al-Bayan. (2009). *Women May Practice Sports within the Framework of Islam*, in Arabic, May 22, 2009. http://www.albayan.ae/across-the-uae/1241101345078-2009-05-22-1.436340

———. (2013). *Women's Smoking Destroys Modesty*, in Arabic, February 18, 2012. http://www.albayan.ae/one-world/correspondents-suitcase/2012-02-18-1.1594574

Al-Ghanem, K. (2008). "Beating Your Maid is Normal in Qatar BUT also Beating Female Family Members Is Part of Being Qatari," *Gulf Times*, January 25, 2008.

Al-Liwa' Al-Islami (1996a). *Female Circumcision Is a Legitimate Demand*, in Arabic, *Egypt*, August 15, 1996.

———. (1996b). *Female Circumcision Is Sunna and It Is Not Permitted to Criminalize It*, in Arabic. *Egypt*, November 28, 1996.

Al Marzouqi, W. (2011). *"Fatal Traditions: Female Circumcision in the UAE"*. *The National*. July 23, 2011. http://www.thenational.ae/lifestyle/fatal-traditions-female-circumcision-in-the-uae

Al-Musnad, M. (1996). *Islamic Fatawa Regarding Women*, translated from Arabic by Jamaal Al-Din Zarabozo (Riyadh, Saudi Arabia: Darussalam Publications).

Al-Qaradawi, Y. (1987). *Fatawi Mu'asirah [Contemporary Fatwas]*, 3rd edn., in Arabic (Kuwait: Dar Al-Qalam).

———. (1997). *The Lawful and the Prohibited in Islam*, Al-Falah Foundation. https://thequranblog.files.wordpress.com/2010/06/the-lawful-and-the-prohibited-in-islam.pdf

Al-Sabbagh, M. (1996). "Islamic Ruling on Male and Female Circumcision," *World Health Organization*. Alexandria, Egypt, http://applications.emro.who.int/dsaf/dsa54.pdf. Accessed February 25, 2013.

Al-Sharq Al-Awsat (2010). *The Kurdistan Islamic Scholars Union: Female Circumcision Is Not a Legitimate Obligation*, in Arabic, July 7, 2010. http://www.aawsat.com/details.asp?section=4&article=577112&issueno=11544#.UTvDLhyW_Zc

Al-Talei, R. (2010). "Oman," in S. Kelly and J. Breslin (eds.), *Women's Rights in the Middle East and North Africa: Progress amid Resistance*, pp. 337–358 (New York: Freedom House/Rowman & Littlefield Publishers, Inc).

Aldeeb, S. (1994). "To Mutilate in the Name of Jehovah or Allah: Legitimization of Male and Female Circumcision," in Arabic (Translation by Frederick M. Hodges and D. Phil (Oxon).) *Medicine and Law* 13(7–8), 575–622. http://www.cirp.org/library/cultural/aldeeb1/

Alami, A. (2014). "A Loophole for Rapists Is Eliminated in Morocco," *The New York Times*, January 23, 2014. http://www.nytimes.com/2014/01/24/world/africa/after-debate-moroccan-government-amends-rape-law.html?emc=edit_tnt_20140123&tntemail0=y&_r=0

Alkire, Sabina (2002). *Valuing Freedoms: Sen's Capability Approach and Poverty Reduction* (Oxford: Oxford University Press).

Almosaed, N. (2008). "Money and Power in Saudi Family," *JKAU: Arts & Humanities*, 6(2), 61–87.

Amin, M. (2014). "Sudanese State TV Dictated Dress Code," *Daily Nation*, November 22, 2014. http://mobile.nation.co.ke/news/Sudan-state-TV-dictates-dress-code/-/1950946/2531758/-/format/xhtml/-/s3d7dqz/-/index.html

Amnesty International (2005a). *Gulf Cooperation Council (GCC) Countries: Women Deserve Dignity and Respect*, MDE 04/004/2005, May 11, 2005 <http://web.amnesty.org/library/Index/ENGMDE040042005>

————. (2005b). *Making Violence Against Women Count—Facts and Figures*, March 5, 2005. Accessed June 24, 2005 <http://web.amnesty.org/library/index/ENGACT770362004>

————. (2012). *"Culture of Discrimination: A Fact Sheet on 'Honor' Killings."*

An-Na'im, A. (1990). "Human Rights in the Muslim World: Socio-Political Conditions and Scriptural Imperatives," *Harvard Human Rights Journal*, 3, 13–52.

————. (2002). *Islamic Family Law in a Changing World: A Global Resource Book* (London: Zed Books Ltd).

Arab News (2014). *Woman Disguised as Man Caught in Stadium*, December 14, 2014. http://www.arabnews.com/news/674186

Asharqia Chamber (2012). *A Guide to Women Working in the Kingdom of Saudi Arabia*, in Arabic, http://www.chamber.org.sa

Awadallah, A, (2009). *Campaign against Summer's Marriages*, Al Ahram, in Arabic, August 25, 2009, http://www.ahram.org.eg/Archive/2009/8/25/WOMN1.HTM

Axelrod, R. A. (1986). "An Evolutionary Approach to Norms," *American Political Science Review*, 80(4), 1095–1111.

Azzouni, S. (2010). "Palestine," in S. Kelly and J. Breslin (eds.), *Women's Rights in the Middle East and North Africa: Progress amid Resistance*, pp. 359–395 (New York: Freedom House/Rowman & Littlefield Publishers, Inc).

Badawi, J. (1995). *Gender Equity in Islam: Basic principles*. Accessed January 23, 2004, http://www.jannah.org/genderequity/

Barsoum, G., N. Rifaat, O. El-Gibaly, N. Elwan, and N. Forcier (2011). "Poverty, Gender, and Youth: National Efforts toward FGM-Free Villages in Egypt: The Evidence of Impact," Working Paper 22, *Population Council* (New York: West Asia and North Africa Office).

Basem, W. (2012). "Female Circumcision in Iraq: Secret Operations Denied by Some," in Arabic, *Elaph*, April 17, 2012. http://www.elaph.com/Web/news/2012/4/730010.html

Basu, K. (1886) One Kind of Power. *Oxford Economic Papers*. New Series 38(2): 259–282

Basu, K. and J. E. Foster (1998). "Measuring Literacy," *The Economic Journal*, 108(451),1733–1734. http://onlinelibrary.wiley.com/doi/10.1111/1468-0297.00369/pdf

BBC (2002). *Saudi Police "Stopped" Fire Rescue*, March 13, 2002. http://news.bbc.co.uk/2/hi/middle_east/1874471.stm

————. (2012a). *Female Genital Mutilation Rife in Egypt despite Ban*, February 15, 2012. http://news.bbc.co.uk/2/hi/programmes/newsnight/9696353.stm

————. (2012b). *Uproar over Saudi Women's 'SMS Tracking*, November 23, 2013. http://www.bbc.com/news/world-middle-east-20469486

————. (2013a). *Saudi Arabia's King Appoints Women to Shura Council*, January 11, 2013. http://www.bbc.co.uk/news/world-middle-east-20986428

————. (2013b). *Gaza Marathon: UN Cancel Race over Hamas Ban on* Women, March 5, 2013. http://www.bbc.com/news/world-middle-east-21667883?print=true

————. (2014a). *Saudi Blogger Raif Badawi Gets 10 Year Jail Sentence*, May 7, 2014. http://www.bbc.com/news/world-middle-east-27318400

————. (2014b). The Consultative Council Recommends Allowing Saudi Women to Drive with Conditions, in Arabic, November 7, 2104. http://www.bbc.co.uk/arabic/middleeast/2014/11/141107_saudi_women_driving_council

————. (2014c) *FGM in Egypt: Doctor and Father Cleared in Landmark trial*, November 20, 2014. http://www.bbc.com/news/world-middle-east-30134078

Begum, R. (2013). "Give Saudi Women the Right to Drive," *CNN*, October 24, 2013. http://www.cnn.com/2013/10/24/opinion/begum-saudi-women-driving/index.html

Begum, R. and A. Coogle (2014). "Whether Princesses or Paupers, Long Road to Saudi Women's Rights," *Human Rights Watch*, March 28, 2014. http://www.hrw.org/news/2014/03/28/whether-princesses-or-paupers-long-road-saudi-women-s-rights

Ben Salem, L. (2010). "Tunisia," in S. Kelly and J. Breslin (eds.), *Women's Rights in the Middle East and North Africa: Progress amid Resistance*, pp. 487–515 (New York: Freedom House/Rowman & Littlefield Publishers, Inc).

Brems, E. (1997). "Enemies or Allies? Feminism and Cultural Relativism as Dissident Voices of Human Rights Discourse," *Human Rights Quarterly*, 19(1), 136–164.

Boulding, K. (1956). *The Image: Knowledge in Life and Society* (Ann Arbor: The University of Michigan Press).

Bourdieu, Pierre (1986). "The Forms of Culture," in J. E. Richardson (ed.), *Handbook on Theory of Research of the Sociology of Education*, pp. 241–258 (New York: Greenwood).

———. (1998). *Masculine Domination* trans. Richard Nice (Stanford, CA: Stanford University Press).

Bowles, S. (1998). "Endogenous Preferences: The Cultural Consequences of Market and Other Economic Institutions," *Journal of Economic Literature*, XXXVI, 75–111.

Brehm, J. (1956). "Postdecision Changes in the Desirability of Alternatives," *Journal of Abnormal Social Psychology* 52, 384–389.

Burch, Elizabeth Chamblee (2004). "Rhetoric or Rights? When Culture and Religion Bar Girls' Right to Education," *Virginia Journal of International Law* 44, 1073–1143. Available at SSRN: http://ssrn.com/abstract=812385

Butler, J. (2004). *Undoing Gender* (New York: Routledge).

CBS NEWS (2009). *Sudan Won't Flog Woman for Wearing Pants*, September 9, 2009. http://www.cbsnews.com/2100-202_162-5291738.html

CEWLA (Centre for Egyptian Women's Legal Assistance) (2005). "'Crimes of Honour' as Violence against Women in Egypt," in L. Welchman and S.Hossain (eds.), *"Honour" Crimes, Paradigms and Violence against Women*, pp.137–159 (New York: Zed Books).

CHANGE (1999). "Ending Violence against Women. Population Reports. The Center for Health and Gender Equity," *CHANGE*. Johns Hopkins University School of Public Health, Baltimore, Maryland. XXXVII (4). http://www.vawnet.org/Assoc_Files_VAWnet/PopulationReports.pdf

Charrad, M. (2007). "Unequal Citizenship: Issues of Gender Justice in the Middle East and North Africa," in M. Mukhopadhyay and N. Singh (eds.), *Gender Justice, Citizenship, and Development*, pp. 233–262 (New Delhi, India: Zubaan, an imprint of Kali for Women).

Chesler, P. (2010). "Worldwide Trends in Honor Killings," *The Middle East Quarterly* XVII(2), 3–11.

Chinkin, C. (1999). "Cultrual Relativism and International Law," in C. W. Howland (ed.), *Religious Fundamentalisms and the Human Rights of Women*, pp. 55–66 (New York: St. Martin's Press).

Chipper, R., E. El-Saleh, and J. El Harmi (2011). "Female Circumcision: Obstetrical and Psychological Sequelae Continues Unabated in the 21st Century," *Journal of Maternal-Fetal and Neonatal Medicine* 24(6), 833–836. doi:10.3109/14767058.2010.53 1318.

Clark, D. (2005). "The Capability Approach: Its Development, Critiques and Recent Advances," *Global Poverty Research Group*. GPRG-WPS-032. WWW.grpg.prg. Accessed November 17, 2012.

CNN (2008). *Saudi Arabia Bans All Things Red ahead of Valentine's Day*. February 12, 2008. http://www.cnn.com/2008/WORLD/meast/02/12/saudi.valentine/index .html?eref=rss_world

Coleman, J. (1987). "Norms as Social Capital," in Gerald Radnitzky and Pater Bernholz (eds.), *Economic Imperialism: The Economics Method Applied Outside the Field of Economics*, pp. 133–153 (New York: Paragon House Publishers).

———. (1990). *Foundation of Social Theory* (Cambridge, MA: Harvard University Press).

Comim, F., M. Qizilbash, and S. Alkire (eds.) (2008). *The Capability Approach: Concepts, Measures and Applications* (Cambridge: Cambridge University Press).

Commons, J. (1931). "Institutional Economics," *American Economic Review* 21(4), 648–657.

Cooper, B. C. Garcia-Peñalosa, and P. Funk (2001). "Status Effects and Negative Utility Growth," *Economic Journal*, Royal Economic Society 111(473), 642–665.

Corbett, S. (2008). "A Cutting Tradition," *The New York Times*, January 20, 2008. http://www.nytimes.com/2008/01/20/magazine/20circumcision-t.html

Cowell, A. (1989) "Egypt's Pain: Wives Killing Husbasnds," *The new York Times*, September 23, 1989. http://www.nytimes.com/1989/09/23/world/cairo-journal-egypt -s-pain-wives-killing-husbands.html

Crawford, S. and E. Ostrom (1995). "A Grammar of Institutions," *The American Political Science Review* 89(3), 582–600.

Crossette, B. (2000). "Culture, Gender, and Human Rights," in L. Harrison and S. Huntington (eds.), *Culture Matters: How Values Shape Human Progress*, pp. 178–188 (New York: Basic Book).

Cuthbert, V. (2012)."Focus on FGM," *The Week*, April 25, 2012. http://www.theweek .co.om/printCon.aspx?Cval=6181

Dar Al-'Ifta' Al-Masreyya, [The Egyptian Agency for 'Ifta'] (1994). In Arabic. Arab Republic of Egypt, Vol. 21.

Das Gupta, M. (1999). "Gender bias in China, South Korea and India, 1920–90: Effects of War, Famine and Fertility Decline," Policy research working paper 2140 (Washington, DC: World Bank).

Das Gupta, M., W. Chung, and L. Shuzhuo (2009). "Evidence for an Incipient Decline in the Numbers of Missing Girls in China and India," *Population and Development Review*, 35(2), 401–416.

Dayan, J., A. Doyle, and D. Markiewicz (2001). "Social Support Networks and Self-Esteem of Idiocentric and Allocentric Children and Adolescents," *Journal of Social and Personal Relationships*, 18(6), 767–784.

de Bary, T. (1998). *Asian Values and Human Rights: A Confucian Communitarian Perspective* (Cambridge, MA: Harvard University Press).

de Castella, T. (2013). "How Many Acid Attacks Are There?" *BBC News Magazine*, 9 August 2013,. http://www.bbc.com/news/magazine-23631395

Denzau, A. and D. North (1993). "Shared Mental Models: Ideologies and Institutions," *Economic History* 9309003, Econ WPA, http://128.118.178.162/eps /eh/papers/9309/9309003.pdf. Accessed February 24, 2014.

Doumato, E. A. (2010). "Saudi Arabia," In S. Kelly and J. Breslin (eds.), *Women's Rights in the Middle East and North Africa: Progress amid Resistance*, pp. 425–455 (New York: Freedom House/Rowman & Littlefield Publishers, Inc).

Drèze, J and A. Sen (2002). *India: Development and Participation* (Oxford: Oxford University Press).

Dugger, W. (1995). "Douglass C. North New Institutionalism," *Journal of Economic Issues* XXIX, 454–458.

Durkheim, E. 1984 (1893). *The Division of Labor in Society*, trans. W. D. Halls (New York: Free Press).

———. 1968 (1915). *The Elementary Forms of Religious Life* (London: Allen and Unwin).

The Egyptian Society of Medical Ethics (1994). *The Fatwas of Religious Institutions and Religious Clerics of the Legitimacy of Female Circumcision*, in Arabic. http://www.medethics.org.eg/esme/labia-minora-photos.htm

El Saadawi, N. (1980). *The Hidden Face of Eve*, trans. Sherif Hetata (London: Zed Press).

Elster, J. (1989). "Social Norms and Economic Theory," *Journal of Economic Perspectives* 3(4), 99–117.

El-Fagr (2014). *Al-Azhar Requires All Female Teachers and Staff to Wear Loose Clothes and Prohibits the Use of Makeup*, in Arabic, January 31, 2014, http://www.elfagr.org/514600

El-Zanaty, F. and A.Way (2001). *Egypt Demographic and Health Survey 2000* (Calverton, MD: Ministry of Health and Population [Egypt], National Population Council and ORC Macro) http://pdf.usaid.gov/pdf_docs/PNACL857.pdf

———. (2009). *Egypt Demographic and Health Survey 2008* (Cairo, Egypt: Ministry of Health, El-Zanaty and Associates, and Macro International) http://dhsprogram.com/pubs/pdf/FR220/FR220.pdf

Ennaji, M. and F. Sadiqi (eds.) (2011). *Gender and Violence in the Middle East* (New York: Routledge).

Evans, P. (2002). "Collective Capabilities, Culture, and Amartya Sen's 'Development as Freedom'," *Studies in Comparative International Development* 37(2), 54–60. http://culturability.org/wp-content/blogs.dir/1/files_mf/1271687823CollectiveCapabilitiescultureandamartyasendevelpomentasfreedom.pdf

Fafchamps, M. (2004). *Market Institutions in Sub Saharan Africa: Theory and Evidence* (Cambridge, MA: MIT Press).

Fawzi, M. (n.d.) *Female Circumcision: The Medical, Religious, Moral, and Social Facts*, in Arabic, School of Medicine, Ein-Shams University, Cairo, Egypt. http://www.medethics.org.eg/esme/labia_minora.htm

Fawzy, E. (2004). "Muslim Personal Status Law in Egypt: The Current Situations and Possibilities of Reform Through Internal Initiatives," in L. Welchman (ed.), *Women's Rights and Islamic Family Law: Perspectives on Reform*, pp.15–94 (New York: Zed Books).

Feldner, Y. (2000). "'Honor' Murders—Why the Perps Get off Easy," *Middle East Quarterly* 7(4), 41–50.

Festinger, L. (1957). *A Theory of Cognitive Dissonance* (Stanford, CA: Stanford University Press).

Festinger, L. and J. Carlsmith (1959). "Cognitive Dissonance of Forced Compliance," *Journal of Abnormal and Social Psychology* 58(2), 203–201.

Figart, D. (2009). "Discrimination," In J. Peil and I. van Staveren (eds.), *Handbook of Economics and Ethics*, pp. 91–98 (Northampton, MA: Edward Elgar).

Filmer, D., J. Friedman, and N. Schady (2008). "Development, Modernization, and Son Preference in Fertility Decisions," The World Bank, *Development Research Group*. Policy Research Working Paper 4716. https://openknowledge.worldbank.org/bitstream/handle/10986/6995/WPS4716.txt?sequence=2

Foster, J. and C. Handy (2008). "External Capabilities," *Oxford Poverty & Human Development Initiative*, Working Paper 08, http://www.ophi.org.uk/wp-content/uploads/OPHI-wp08.pdf

Foucault, M. (2002). "What is Critique?," in D. Ingram (ed.), *The Political: Readings in Continental Philosophy*, pp. 191–211 (London: Blackwell).

France 24 (2014a). *Saudi Police Release a Woman on Bail for Defying the Ban on Driving*, in Arabic, April 20, 2014.

———. (2014b). *Algerian Women Break In Football Stadiums*, in Arabic, May 30, 2014.

———. (2014c). *Why Moroccan Society Consider Virginity a Symbol of Chastity and Honor?*, in Arabic, August 18, 2014.

The General Presidency of Scholar Research and *Ifta* (n.d.). Kingdom of Saudi Arabia. http://www.alifta.net/Default.aspx

Ghanim, D.(2009). *Gender and Violence in the Middle East* (West Port, CT: Praeger).

Gibbard, A. (1985). "Moral Judgment and the Acceptance of Norms," *Ethics* 96(1), 5–21.

Global Gender Gap Report (2014). World Economic Forum. Geneva, Switzerland.

Goodwin, J. (1995). *Price of Honor: Muslim Women Lift the Veil of Silence on the Islamic World* (New York: Plume).

Gramsci, A. (1971). *Selections from the Prison Notebooks*, trans. Q. Hoare and G. Nowell-Smith (London: Lawrence & Wishart).

———. (2009). "Hegemony, Intellectuals, and the State," in J. Storey (ed.), *Cultural Theory and Popular Culture: a Reader*, 4th edn., pp. 75–80 (Harlow, UK: Pearson Education).

Guernbaum, E. (2001) *The Female Circumcission Controversy: An Anthropologicla Perspective* (Philadelphia, PA: University of Pennsylvania Press).

Guilmoto, C. (2009). "The Sex Ratio Transition in Asia," *Population and Development Review*, 35(3), 519–549.

Guinnane, T. (2005). "Trust: A Concept Too Many," Yale University *Economic Growth Center, Discussion Paper* 907. Available at http://ssrn.com/abstract=680744

Hamada, S. (2010). "The Hard Way Out: Divorce by Khula," *The WIP*, March 18, 2010, http://thewip.net/2010/03/18/the-hard-way-out-divorce-by-khula/

Harding, L. (2012). "Saudi Arabia Criticised over Text Alerts Tracking Women's Movements," *The Guardian*, November 23, 2012. http://www.theguardian.com /world/2012/nov/23/saudi-arabia-text-alerts-women

Harris, J., J. Hunter, and C. Lewis (eds.) (1998). *The New Institutional Economics and Third World Development* (New York: Routledge).

Hasnat, B. (1995) "International Trade and Child Labor." *Journal of Economic Issues*, XXIX: 419–426.

Hausman, D. and M. McPherson (1993). "Taking Ethics Seriously: Economics and Contemporary Moral Philosophy," *Journal of Economic Literatures* XXXI, 671–731.

———. (2006) *Economic Analysis, Moral Philosophy and Public Policy*, 2nd edn (Cambridge: Cambridge University Press).

Haworth, A. (2012). "The Day I Saw 248 Girls Suffering Genital Mutilation," *The Guardian*, November 17, 2012. http://www.guardian.co.uk/society/2012/nov/18 /female-genital-mutilation-circumcision-indonesia

Heise, L., J. Pitanguy, and A. Germaine (1994). "Violence against Women: The Hidden Health Burden," World Bank, *Discussion Paper* 225.

Heckathorn, D. (1989). "Collective Action and the Second Order Free Rider Problem," *Rationality and Society* 1, 78–100.

Hélie-Lucas, M. A. (1999). "What Is Your Tribe?: Women's Struggles and the Construction of Muslimness," in C. W. Howland (ed.), *Religious Fundamentalisms and the Human Rights of Women*, pp. 21–32 (New York: St. Martin's Press).

Herbert, W. (2010). "Cognitive Dissonance: Why We Rationalize Our Life Circumstances," *Huffington Post*, July 29, 2010, http://www.huffingtonpost.com /wray-herbert/cognitive-dissonance-why_b_642674.html. Accessed February 22, 2013.

Hirsch, F. (1976). *Social Limits to Growth* (Cambridge, MA: Harvard University Press).

Hirschman, A. (1970). *Exit, Voice, and Loyalty: Responses to Decline in Firms, Organizations, and States* (Cambridge, MA: Harvard University Press).

Qur'an, *The Holy*. http://corpus.quran.com/translation.jsp

Horne, C. (2001). "The Enforcement of Norms: Group Cohesion and Meta-norms," *Social Psychology Quarterly* 64(3), 253–266.

———. (2007). "Explaining Norm Enforcement," *Rationally and Society* 19(2), 139–170. Http://rss.sagepub.com. doi:10.1177/1043463107077386.

Horne, C. and A. Cutlip (2002). "Sanctioning Costs and Norms Enforcement," *Rationality and Society* 14(3), 285–307.

Howard-Hassmann, R. E. (1993). "Cultural Absolutism and the Nostalgia for Community". *Human Rights Quarterly* 15, 315–338.

Hoyek, D., R. Sidawi, and M. Abu Mrad (2005). "Murder of Women in Lebanon: "Crimes of Honour" between Reality and the Law," in L. Welchman and S. Hossain (eds.), *"Honour": Crimes, Paradigms and Violence against Women*, pp.111–136 (New York: Zed Books).

Human Rights Watch (2008). *Perpetual Minors: Human Rights Abuses Stemming from Male Guardianship and Sex Segregation in Saudi Arabia*, http://www.hrw.org /reports/2008/04/19/perpetual-minors

———. (2010). *They Took Me and Told Me Nothing: Female Genital Mutilation in Iraqi Kurdistan*, http://www.hrw.org/sites/default/files/reports/wrd0610webw cover.pdf

———. (2011). *How Come You Allow Little Girls to Get Married: Child Marriage in Yemen*, http://www.hrw.org/sites/default/files/reports/yemen1211ForUpload_0.pdf

———. (2012). *Iraqi Kurdistan: Law Banning FGM Not Being Enforced*, http://www .hrw.org/news/2012/08/29/iraqi-kurdistan-law-banning-fgm-not-being-enforced

———. (2013). *Saudi Arabia: End Driving Ban for Women. 24 October 2013,* http:// www.hrw.org/news/2013/10/24/saudi-arabia-end-driving-ban-women.

———. (2014a). *World Report 2014: Event of 2013*, http://www.hrw.org/sites/default/ files/reports/wr2014_web_0.pdf

———. (2014b) *UAE: Weak Protection Against Domestic Violence*, August 4, 2014, http:// www.hrw.org/news/2014/08/04/uae-weak-protection-against-domestic-violence

———. (2014c) *Saudi Arabia: Release Women Driving Activists*, December 2, 2014, http://www.hrw.org/news/2014/12/02/saudi-arabia-release-women-driving-activists

Husseini, R. (2010). "Jordan," in S. Kelly and J. Breslin (eds.), *Women's Rights in the Middle East and North Africa: Progress amid Resistance*, pp. 193–222 (New York: Freedom House/Rowman & Littlefield Publishers, Inc).

Inter-Parliamentary Union (2014). Women in National Parliaments. http://ipu.org /wmn-e/arc/world010914.htm.

Islamic Council (1981). *Universal Islamic Declaration of Human Rights*, adopted by the *Islamic* Council *of* Europe on September 19, 1981. http://www.alhewar.com /ISLAMDECL.html

Islamweb.net (2001). *Women's Practicing Sport in Public Clubs*, in Arabic, October 31, 2001. http://fatwa.islamweb.net/fatwa/index.php?page=showfatwa&Option=FatwaI d&Id=11213

IRIN (2005). *In Depth: Razor's Edge—The Controversy of Female Genital Mutilation. FGM/C Still Largely an Unknown Quantity in Arab World.* <http://www.irinnews.org/InDepthMain.aspx?InDepthId=15&ReportId=62474&Country=Yes>

———. IRIN (2010). *Indonesia: Female Genital Mutilation Persists Despite Ban.* http://www.irinnews.org/Report/90366/INDONESIA-Female-genital-mutilation-persists-despite-ban

The Islamic Awareness (2010). "Women Smoking as Social and Health Risks," in Arabic, September 3, 2010. No 532. http://alwaei.com/topics/current/article_new.php?sdd=882&issue=532

Jad Al-Haq, J. (1994). "Al-Khitaan," [Circumcision], in Arabic, *Mijallat Al-Azhar, Al-Azhar*. Cairo, Egypt.

Jamjoom, M. (2009). "Saudi Judge Refuses to Annul 8-Year-Old's Marriage," *CNN*, April 12, 2009. http://www.cnn.com/2009/WORLD/meast/04/12/saudi.child.marriage/index.html

Jensen, R. H. (2005). *Taking the Gender Apartheid Tour in Saudi Arabia.* Womensenews.org, March 7, 2005. http://womensenews.org/story/our-daily-lives/050307/taking-the-gender-apartheid-tour-in-saudi-arabia#.UwKD-fldWSo

Karayiannis, A. and A. Hatzis (2010). "Morality, Social Norms and the Rule of Law as Transaction Cost-Saving Devices: The Case of Ancient Athens," *European Journal of Law and Economics*. doi:10.1007/s10657-010-9150-6. http://users.uoa.gr/~ahatzis/Athens.pdf

Kareem, M. (2014). "Saudi Arabia Jails Palestinian Poet for 'Atheism and Long Hair'," *Global Voices*, January 19, 2014. http://globalvoicesonline.org/2014/01/19/saudi-arabia-palestinian-poet-jailed-for-atheism-and-long-hair/

Kassem, L., F. M. Ali, and T. S. Al-Malek (2012). "Domestic Violence Legislation and Reform Efforts in Qatar," *Perspectives* 4, 29–34.

Katulis, B. (2004). *Women's Rights in Focus: Egypt—Findings from May-June 2004 Focus Group With Egyptian Citizens on Women's Freedom*, Freedom House, October 19, 2004. Accessed July 2, 2014. http://www.freedomhouse.org/sites/default/files/inline_images/Women%27s%20Rights%20in%20Focus-%20Egypt%20.pdf

Kasper, W. and M. Streit (1998). *Institutional Economics: Social Order and Public Policy* (Northampton, MA: Edward Elgar Publishing Ltd).

Kelly, S. and J. Breslin (eds.) (2010). *Women's Rights in the Middle East and North Africa: Progress amid Resistance* (New York: Freedom House/Rowman & Littlefield Publishers, Inc).

Khalil, M. (2008). "The Story of Arwa.. A Female Child Who Was Married at the Age of Eight," in Arabic. *AlJazeera*. http://www.aljazeera.net/news/pages/5e3ec6ef-7a26-4f7f-b5b5-13405f09384b. September 7, 2008.

Kirdar, S. (2010). "United Arab Emirates," in S. Kelly and J. Breslin (eds.), *Women's Rights in the Middle East and North Africa: Progress amid Resistanc*, pp. 517–543 (New York: Freedom House/Rowman & Littlefield Publishers, Inc).

Kishor, S. and L. Subaiya (2008). "Understanding Women's Empowerment: A Comparative Analysis of Demographic and Health Surveys (DHS) Data," *DHS Comparative Reports* No. 20 (Calverton, MD: Macro International Inc). Accessed March 23, 2009 <http://www.measuredhs.com/pubs/pdf/CR20/CR20.pdf>

Klasen, S. and C. Wink (2002a). *Missing Women: A Review of the Debates and an Analysis of Recent Trends.* Available at SSRN: http://ssrn.com/abstract=321861 or doi:10.2139/ssrn.321861.

———. (2002b) "A Turning Point in Gender Bias Mortality? An Update on the Number of Missing Women," *Population and Development Review* 28(2), 283–312.

Klasen, S. (2004). "Gender Related Indicators of Well-being," *Ibero-America Institute for Economic Research.* http://wwwuser.gwdg.de/~fjohann/paper/DB102.pdf

———. (2008). "Missing Women: Some Recent Controversies on Levels and Trends in Gender Bias in Mortality," Discussion Papers. *Ibero America Institute for Economic Research*, No. 168, http://hdl.handle.net/10419/27458

Knight, J. (1992). *Institutions and Social Conflict* (New York: Cambridge University Press).

Knox, R. and J. Inkster (1968). "Post-decisions Dissonance at Post Time," *Journal of Personality and Social Psychology* 1(8), 319–23.

Konow, J. (2000). "Fair Shares: Accountability and Cognitive Dissonance in Allocation Decisions," *The American Economic Review* 90(4), 1072–1091.

Kroeber, A. and C. Kluckhohn (1952). *Culture: A Critical Review of Concepts and Definitions* (Cambridge, MA: Peabody Museum).

Kunreuther, H., R. Ginsberg, L. Miller, P. Sagi, P. Slovic, B. Borkan, and N. Katz (1978). *Disaster Insurance Protection: Public Policy Lessons* (New York: Jogn Wiley & Son, Inc.).

Lahamag.com (2014). *Will the Sexual Harassment Law in Saudi Arabia See the Light?,* October 19, 2014. http://www.lahamag.com/

Linden, J. (2014). "Asian Games: Women Sidelined as Saudi Arabia Selects All-Male Team," *Reuters*, September 8, 2014. http://www.reuters.com/article/2014/09/08/us-games-asian-saudi-women-idUSKBN0H31HI20140908

Los Angeles Times (2008). "Egypt: Parliament Criminalizes Female Circumcision," June 9, 2008. http://latimesblogs.latimes.com/babylonbeyond/2008/06/after-weeks-of.html

Lotfy, S., M. Fawzi, A. Hasan, A. El-Gendi and H. Shalabi (1996). "Female Circumcision Procedure," *The Journal of the Egyptian Society of Obstetrics & Gynecology* 22(10, 11, 12), 711–715.

MacFarquhar, N. (2011). "Saudi Monarch Grants Women Right to Vote," *The New York Time*, September 25, 2011. <http://www.nytimes.com/2011/09/26/world/middleeast/women-to-vote-in-saudi-arabia-king-says.html?pagewanted=all>

Mackinnon, C. (1987). *Feminism Unmodified: Discourses on Life and Law* (Cambridge, MA: Harvard University Press).

Malik, A. (2012). "Female Genital Mutilation: A Brutal Violation of Rights," *Gulfnews. com*, June 15, 2012. http://gulfnews.com/opinions/columnists/female-genital-mutilation-a-brutal-violation-of-rights-1.1036052

Manea, E. (2010). "Yemen," in S. Kelly and J. Breslin (eds.), *Women's Rights in the Middle East and North Africa: Progress amid Resistance*, pp. 545–575 (New York: Freedom House/Rowman & Littlefield Publishers, Inc).

Mansouri, B. (2013). "Underage Girls' Temporary Marriage in Egypt," in Arabic, *Al Hurra*, September 2, 2013. http://www.alhurra.com/content/egypt-underage-summer-marriages/233218.html

Marshall, G. (1983). "The Role of Rules," in D. Miller and L. Siedentop, (eds.), *The Nature of Political Theory* (Oxford: Oxford University Press).

Mathur, K. (2004). *Countering Gender Violence: Initiatives Towards Collective Action in Rajasthan* (New Delhi, India: Sage Publications).

Mayer, A. E. (n.d.) *Debating the Universality of Human Rights: A Plea for a Critical Perspective.*

———. (1995). "Cultural Particularism as a Bar to Women Rights: Reflections on the Middle Eastern Experience," in J. Peters and A. Wolper (eds.), *Women's Rights, Human Rights: International Feminist Perspectives*, pp. 176–187 (New York: Routledge).

———. (1999). *Islam and Human Rights. Tradition and Politics* (Boulder, CO: Westview Press).

———. (2000). "A 'Benign' Apartheid: How Gender Apartheid Has Been Rationalized," *UCLA Journal of International Law and Foreign Affairs* 237, 237–336.

Mayhew, A. (2009). "Institutions," in J. Peil and I. van Staveren (eds.), *Handbook of Economics and Ethics*, pp. 276–282 (Northampton, MA: Edward Elgar Publishing).

McGrath, C. (2013). "Underage Girls Are Egypt's Summer Rentals," *IPS* (Inter Press Service). August 5, 2013. http://www.ipsnews.net/2013/08/underage-girls-are-egypts-summer-rentals/

Mernissi, F. (1987). *Beyond the Veil: Male-Female Dynamics in Modem Muslim Society*, 2nd edn. (Bloomington: Indiana University Press).

———. (1991). *The Veil and the Male Elite: A Feminist Interpretation of Women's Rights in Islam* (Reading, MA: Addison-Wesley).

Ministère de la Santé, Maroc (2005). *ORC Macro, et Ligue des États Arabes. Enquête sur la Population et la Santé. Familiale (EPSF) 2003–2004* (Calverton, MD: Ministère de la Santé et ORC Macro).

Moaddel, M. (2013). *A Report: The Birthplace of the Arab Spring: Value and Perceptions of Tunisia and a Comparative Assessment of Egyptian, Iraqi, Lebanese, Pakistani, Saudi, Tunisian, and Turkish Publics.* University of Marylan, http://mevs.org/files/tmp /Tunisia_FinalReport.pdf

Myrdal, G. (1944). *An American Dilemma: The Negro Problem and Modern Democracy* (New York: Harper & Bros).

Nafisi, A. (2003a). "They the People," *New Republic*, March 3, 2003. http://www .newrepublic.com/article/muslim-allies-septmember-11-taliban-islam

———. (2003b) *Reading Lolita in Tehran: A Memoir in Books* (New York: Random House 2003).

The National Council for Children and Motherhood (2003). *Cairo Declaration for the Elimination of FGM. Afro-Arab Expert Consultation on "Legal Tools for the Prevention of Female Genital Mutilation."* Cairo, Egypt, http://www.childinfo.org/files/FGM /Cc_Cairodeclaration.pdf

Nayak, B. (2013). "Challenges of Cultural Relativism and the Future of Feminist Universalism," *Journal of Politics and Law* 6(2), 83–89.

NBC News (2009). "Sudanese Women Flogged for Wearing Pants," *NBCNEWS. com*, July 13, 2009. http://www.nbcnews.com/id/31897384/ns/world_news-africa/t /sudanese-women-flogged-wearing-pants/#.UYwbf7WW_Zc

Nomani, A. (2006). "Clothes Aren't the Issue," *Washington Post*, October 22, 2006. http://www.washingtonpost.com/wp-dyn/content/article/2006/10/20/AR200 6102001261.html

No Peace without Justice (2005). *Sub-regional Conference on Female Genital Mutilation, Toward a Political and Religious Consensus against FGM*. Djibouti, February, 2005 . http://www.npwj.org/FGM/Sub-Regional-Conference-Female-Genital-Mutilation -Towards-a-political-and-religious-consensus-a-1

North, D. (1990). *Institutions, Institutional Change and Economic Performance* (Cambridge: Cambridge University Press).

———. (1994). "Economic Performance through Time," *The American Economic Review* 84, 359–368.

———. (1998). "The New Institutional Economics and Third World Development," in H. John, J. Hunter, and C. Lewis (eds.), *The New Institutional Economics and Third World Development*, pp. 17–26 (New York: Routledge).

North, D. (2000). "Economic Institutions and Development: A View from the Bottom," in M. Olson and S. Kähkönen (eds.), *A Not-So-Dismal Science: A Broader View of Economics and Societies*, pp. 92–118 (New York: Oxford University Press).

———. (2002). *The New Institutional Economics and Development* (St. Louis: Washington University). Paper available at <http://www.econ.iastate.edu/tesfatsi /NewInstE.North.pdf>. Accessed February 24, 2014.

Nooteboom, B. (2009). "Trust," in J. Peil and I. van Staveren (eds.), *Handbook of Economics and Ethics*, pp. 547–554 (Northampton, MA: Edward Elgar Publishing).

Nussbaum, M. (1988). "Nature, Function, and Capability: Aristotle on Political Distribution," *Oxford Studies in Ancient Philosophy* (Supl.), 145–184.

———. (2000). *Women and Human Development: The Capabilities Approach* (Cambridge: Cambridge University Press).

———. (2003). "Capabilities as Fundamental Entitlements: Sen and Social Justice," *Feminist Economics* 9(2–3), 33–59.

———. (2011). *Creating Capabilities: The Human Development Approach* (Cambridge, MA: Belknap Press of Harvard University Press).

October Magazine (1994). In Arabic, October 16, 1994.

Ogilvie, S. (2004a) "How Does Social Capital Affect Women? Guilds and Communities in Early Modern Germany," *The American Historical Review* 109.2. http://www.history cooperative.org/journals/ahr/109.2/.html. Accessed February 13, 2006>.

———. (2004b) "The Use and Abuse of Trust: Social Capital and Its Deployment by Early Modern Guilds," *CESifo Working Paper Series* No. 1302, http://ssrn.com /abstract=614822. Accessed December 10, 2005.

OIC (Organization of Islamic Cooperation) (1990). *The Cairo Declaration on Human Rights in Islam*. http://www.oic-oci.org/english/article/human.htm

Okin, S. M. (1989). *Justice, Gender and the Family* (New York: Basic Books).

Oreibee, A. (2014). "The Summer Marriage," in Arabic, *Maseralarabia.com*, September 6, 2014. http://www.masralarabia.com/

Ostrom, E. (2000). "Collective Action and the Evolution of Social Norms," *The Journal of Economic Perspectives* 14(3), 137–158.

———. (2012). "Enhancing the Evolution of Institutions for Collective Action," *Social Evolution Forum*, March 24, 2012. http://socialevolutionforum.com/2012/03/26 /elinor-ostrom-enhancing-the-evolution-of-institutions-for-collective-action/

Pahl, J. (1983). "The Allocation of Money and the Structuring of Inequality Within Marriage," *Sociological Review* 13(2), 237–262.

Papanek, H. (1982). "Purdah in Pakistan: Seclusion and Modern Occupations for Women," in H. Papanek and G. Minault (eds.), *Separate Worlds: Studies of Purdah in South Asia*, pp. 190–216 (Columbia, MO: South Asia Book).

Parekh, B. (2004). "Putting Civil Society in Its Place," in M. Glasius, D. Lewis, and H. Seckinelgin (eds.), *Exploring Civil Society: Political and Cultural Context*, pp. 11–23 (New York: Routledge).

Pearson, M. (2012). "Augusta National Golf Club Admits First Female Members," *CNN*, August 21, 2012. <http://www.cnn.com/2012/08/20/us/augusta-female-mem-bers/index.html>. Accessed January 28, 2013.

Phillips, A. (2010). *Gender & Culture* (Cambridge, UK: Polity Press).

Platteau, J. (1994a) "Behind the Market Stage Where Real Societies Exist- Part I: The Role of Public and Private Institutions," *The Journal of Development Studies* 30(3), 533–577.

Platteau, J. (1994b) "Behind the Market Stage Where Real Societies Exist- Part II: The Role of Moral Norms," *The Journal of Development Studies* 30(3), 753–817.

Pilon, M. (2012). "Women May Compete for Saudi Arabia," *The News York Times*, June 25, 2012. <http://www.nytimes.com/2012/06/26/sports/olympics/saudi-arabia-to-allow-female-athletes-at-london-games.html?_r=3&emc=tnt&tntemail1=y&>

Poushter, J. (2014). *How People in Muslim Countries Prefer Women to Dress in Public*, Pew Research Center, January 8, 2014. http://www.pewresearch.org/fact-tank/2014/01/08/what-is-appropriate-attire-for-women-in-muslim-countries/

Prietula, M. and D. Conway (2009). "The Evolution of Metanorms: Quies Custodiet Ipsos Custodes?" *Computational & Mathematical Organization Theory* 15(3), 147–168. doi:10.1007/s10588–009–9056–4.

Qizilbash, M. (2009). *On Capability, Real Libertarianism and Paternalism* (UK: University of York). <http://www.happinesseconomics.net/ocs/index.php/heirs/markethappiness/paper/view/353/175>

Randerson, J. (2008. "Female Genital Mutilation Denies Sexual Pleasure to Millions of Women," *The Guardian*, November 13, 2008. http://www.guardian.co.uk/science/blog/2008/nov/13/female-genital-mutilation-sexual-dysfunction

Rasheed, S., A. Abd-Ellah, and F. Yousef (2011). "Female Genital Mutilation in Upper Egypt in the New Millennium," *International Journal of Gynecology and Obstetrics* 114(1), 47–50.

Rassam, A. (1980). "Women and Domestic Power in Morocco," *International Journal of Middle Eastern Studies* 12(2), 171–179.

Rawls, J. (1971). *A Theory of Justice* (Cambridge, MA: Belknap Press of Harvard University Press).

———. (1993). *Political Liberalism* (New York: Columbia University Press).

Ravindran, S. (1986). *Health Implications of Sex Discrimination in Childhood* (Geneva, Switzerland: World Health Organization).

Reuters (2007). "Egypt Mufti Says Female Circumcision Forbidden," June 24, 2007. http://www.reuters.com/article/2007/06/24/idUSL24694871

Riphenbrug, C. (1998). "Changing Gender Relations and the Development Process in Oman," in Y. Y. Haddad and J. Esposito (eds.), *Islam, Gender, and Social Change*, pp. 144–168 (New York: Oxford University Press).

Robeyns, I. (2003). "Sen's Capability Approach and Gender Inequality: Selecting Relevant Capabilities," *Feminist Economics* 9(2–3), 61–92. http://csde.washington.edu/~scurran/files/readings/April28/recommended/SelectingRelevantCapabilities.pdf. Accessed December 27, 2012.

———. (2005). "The Capability Approach: A Theoretical Survey," *Journal of Human Development* (6)1, 93–114.

———. (2011) "The Capability Apporach," in Edward N. Zalta (ed.), *The Stanford Encolpedia of Phiosophy* (Summer 2001 Edition). http://plato.stanford.edu/cgi-bin/encyclopedia/archinfo.cgi?entry=capability-approach

Roumani, R. (2006). "Study Reveals Domestic Abuse Is Widespread in Syria," *Christian Science Monitor*, April 25, 2006.

Rutherford, M. (1994). *Institutions in Economics: The Old and the New Institutionalism* (New York: Cambridge University Press).

———. (2001.) "Institutional Economics: Then and Now," *Journal of Economic Perspectives* 15(3), 173–194.

Sada El-Balad (2014). "El-Gendi:A Wife Is Not Permitted to File a Formal Complaint against Her Husband if He Beat Her," in Arabic, September 3, 2014. http://www.el-balad.com/1127170

Sadiqi, F. (2010). "Morocco," in S. Kelly and J. Breslin (eds.), *Women's Rights in the Middle East and North Africa: Progress amid Resistance*, pp. 311–336 (New York: Freedom House/Rowman & Littlefield Publishers, Inc)

Safilios-Rothschild, C. (1976). "A Macro and Micro-examination of Family Power and Love," *Journal of Marriage and the Family* (37), 355–362.

Sahih Bukhari. *Holy Hadith*. Translation by M. Mushin Khan. http://www.usc.edu /org/cmje/religious-texts/hadith/bukhari/

Saudi Gazette (2014). "Saudi Girl Detained for Attending Soccer Match Disguised as Man," December 14, 2014. http://www.saudigazette.com.sa/index.cfm?method =home.regcon&contentid=20141214227409

Sedikides, C. and M. Brewer (eds.) (2001). *Individual Self, Relational Self, Collective Self* (Philadelphia: Psychology Press).

Sen, A. (1985a). *Commodities and Capabilities* (Oxford: Elsevier Science Publishers).

———. (1985b). "Well-being, Agency and Freedom: The Dewey Lectures 1984," *Journal of Philosophy* 82(4), 169–221.

———. (1987). "The Standard of Living," in G. Hawthorn (ed.), *The Standard of Living: The Tanner Lectures on Human Values* (Cambridge: Cambridge University Press).

———. (1990). "More than 100 Million Women are Missing," *The New York Review of Books* 37(20). http://www.nybooks.com/articles/archives/1990/dec/20/more-than -100-million-women-are-missing/. Accessed February 22, 2013.

———. (1992). *Inequality Reexamined* (Cambridge, MA: Harvard University Press).

———. (1995). "Gender Inequality and Theories of Justice," in M. Nussbaum and J. Glover (eds.), *Women, Culture and Development*, pp. 259–273 (Oxford: Clarendon Press).

———. (1999). *Development as Freedom* (New York: Anchor Books).

———. (2002). *Rationality and Freedom* (Harvard: Harvard Belknap Press).

Sen, P. (2005). "'Crime of Honour': Value and Meaning," in L. Welchman and S. Hossain (eds.), *"Honour": Crimes, Paradigms and Violence against Women*, pp. 42–63 (New York: Zed Books).

Shelton, T. (2010). "Shocking Statistics on 'Female Genital Mutilation'," *Global Post*, June 21, 2010. http://www.globalpost.com/dispatch/iraq/100617/female-genital -mutilation-iraq-kurdistan

Sherif-Trask, B. (2004). "Muslim Families in the United States," in M. Coleman and L. Ganong (eds.), *Handbook of Contemporary Families: Considering the Past, Contemplating the Future*, pp. 394–408 (Thousand Oask, CA: Sage Publications).

Shihab-Eldin, A. (2012). "Saudi Arabia's Olympic Paradox: Insulting Women, Islam and 'Prostitutes'," *Huffington Post*, July 27, 2012. http://www.huffingtonpost.com /ahmed-shihabeldin/saudi-arabias-olympic-par_b_1709873.html

Singer, M. (1999). "Relativism, Culture, Religion, and Identity," in C. W. Howland (ed.), *Religious Fundamentalisms and the Human Rights of Women*, pp. 45–54 (New York: St. Martin's Press).

Smith, P. (2001). *Culture Theory: An Introduction* (Walden, MA: Blackwell Publishers).

Storey, J. (2009). *Cultural Theory and Popular Culture: An Introduction*, 5th edn. (Harlow, England: Pearson Longman).

Streeten, P., S. J. Burki, M. ul Haq, N. Hicks, and F. Stewart (1981). *First Things First, Meeting Basic Human Needs in Developing Countries* (New York: Oxford University Press).

Streeten, P. (1984). "Basic Needs: Some Unsettled Questions," *World Development* 12(9), 973–978.

Tadros, M. (2010). "Egypt," in S. Kelly and J. Breslin (eds.), *Women's Rights in the Middle East and North Africa: Progress amid Resistance*, pp. 89–120 (New York: Freedom House/Rowman & Littlefield Publishers, Inc).

————. (2012). "Mutilating Bodies: The Muslim Brotherhood's Gift to Egyptian Women," *Open Democracy*, May 24, 2012. http://www.opendemocracy.net/5050 /mariz-tadros/mutilating-bodies-muslim-brotherhood%E2%80%99s-gift-to -egyptian-women

Tandon, S. and R. Sharma (2006). "Female Foeticide and Infanticide in India: An Analysis of Crimes against Girl Children," *International Journal of Criminal Justice Sciences* 1(1). http://www.sascv.org/ijcjs/snehlata.pdf

Toh, S. M. and G. J. Leonardelli (2012). "Cultural Constraints on the Emergence of Women as Leaders," *Journal of World Business*. doi:10.1016/j.jwb.2012.01.013.

Triandis, H. and D. Trafimow (2001). "Cross-National Prevalence of Collectivism," in C. Sedikides and M. Brewer (eds.), *Individual Self, Relational Self, Collective* Self, pp. 259–276 (Philadelphia: Psychology Press).

Triandis, H. (1995). *Individualism & Collectivism* (Boulder, CO: Westview Press).

UN (n.d.-a) Division for the Advancement of Women. *Convention on the Elimination of All Forms of Discrimination against Women: Committee on the Elimination of Discrimination against Women.* http://www.un.org/womenwatch/daw/cedaw/com-mittee.htm

UN (n.d.-b) *Treaty Collection: Chapter IV. 8. Convention on the Elimination of All Forms of Discrimination against Women.* https://treaties.un.org/Pages/ViewDetails. aspx?src=TREATY&mtdsg_no=IV-8&chapter=4&lang=en. Accessed November 13, 2014.

————. (1948). *Universal Declaration of Human Rights.* Adopted and proclaimed by General Assembly resolution 217 A (III) of December 10, 1948. http://www.un.org /Overview/rights.html. Accessed February 10, 2013.

————. (1979). *Convention on the Elimination of All Forms of Discrimination against Women (CEDAW),* December 18, 1979. http://www.ohchr.org/en/ProfessionalInterest /pages/cedaw.aspx

————. (1993). *Declaration on the Elimination of Violence against Women. General Assembly.* http://www.un.org/documents/ga/res/48/a48r104.htm

————. (2003). *Integration of the Human Rights of Women and the Gender Perspective: Violence against Women. Amendment 1, United Nations' Commission on Human Rights.*

————. (2006). *Integration of the Human Rights of Women and the Gender Perspective: Violence against Women: The Due Diligence Standard as a Tool for the Elimination of Violence against Women. Addendum 1,* January 26, 2006.

————. (2009). *Convention on the Elimination of All Forms of Discrimination against Women: Reservations to CEDAW.* http://www.un.org/womenwatch/daw/cedaw/reser-vations.htm

————. (2010). *Convention on the Elimination of All Forms of Discrimination against Women (CEDAW): Declarations, Reservations, Objections and Notifications of Withdrawal of Reservations Relating to the Convention on the Elimination of All Forms of Discrimination against Women.* http://www2.ohchr.org/english/bodies/cedaw /docs/AdvanceVersions/CEDAW-SP-2010-2.pdf

————. (2013). *Resolution Adopted by the General Assembly on 20 December 2012: Intensifying Global Efforts for the Elimination of Female Genital Mutilation (67/146).* General Assembly. http://www.un.org/en/ga/search/view_doc.asp?symbol=A/RES /67/146

UN General Assembly (1993).*Vienna Declaration and Programme of Action,* World Conference on Human Rights.

UN General Assembly. (2014). *Global Violence against Women in the Name of "Honour,"* Human Rights Council. February 17, 2014. http://iheu.org/newsite/wp-content /uploads/2014/03/433_A_HRC_25_NGO_Sub_En_IHEU_Honour.pdf

UNDP (2008). *Human Development Report 2007/2008.* http://hdr.undp.org/en/media /HDR_20072008_EN_Complete.pdf

———. (2009). *Human Development Report 2009.* http://hdr.undp.org/en/media /HDR_2009_EN_Complete.pdf

———. (2011). *Human Development Report 2011.* http://hdr.undp.org/en/media /HDR_2011_EN_Complete.pdf

———. (2013). *Human Development Report 2013.* http://hdr.undp.org/en/media /HDR_2013_EN_complete.pdf

———. (2014). *Human Development Report 2014.* http://hdr.undp.org/sites/default /files/hdr14-report-en-1.pdf.

UNESCO (2009). *2009 UNESCO Framework for Cultural Statistics* (Montreal, Canada: UNESCO Institute for Statistics).

UNFEM (2009). *30th Anniversary of the United National Conventions on the Elimination of All Forms of Discrimination against Women.* http://www.unifem.org/cedaw30 /success_stories/

UNICEF (2011). "Early Marriage: Child Spouses," *Innoceti Digest.* No. 7, March 2011. http://www.unicef-irc.org/publications/pdf/digest7e.pdf

———. (2012). *Attitude towards Wife-Beating.* <http://www.childinfo.org/attitudes _data.php>. Last update: January 2012.

———. (2013a). *Female Genital Mutilation/Cutting: A Statistical Overview and Exploration of the Dynamics of Change,* http://www.childinfo.org/files/FGMC_Low _Sept2013.pdf. Last update: September 2013.

———. (2013b). *Percentage of Women Aged 15–49 Who Have Been Cut; Data for the 29 Countries Known to Practise FGM/C Widely.* Last Update: January 2013. http://www .childinfo.org/fgmc_prevalence.php

———. (2013c). *Percentage of Women Aged 20–24 Who Were First Married/in Union before the Age of 18.* Last Update January 2013. http://www.childinfo.org/marriage _countrydata.php

———. (2014). *A Statistical Snapshot of Violence against Adolescent Girls.* http:// www.unicef.org/publications/files/A_Statistical_Snapshot_of_Violence_Against _Adolescent_Girls.pdf.

USCIRF (United States Commission on International Religious Freedom) (2011). *Annual Report 2011.* May 2011. <http://www.uscirf.gov/images/book percent20with percent20cover percent20for percent20web.pdf>

USA Today (2009). *Taliban Threats Close Pakistan School,* January 7, 2009. <http:// www.usatoday.com/news/world/2009-01-17-pakistan-threat_N.htm>

———. (2013). *Egypt Constitution Will Be Bad News for Women, Activists Say,* January 13, 2013. http://www.usatoday.com/story/news/world/2013/01/11/egypt-constitution -women-rights/1784135/

U.S. Central Intelligence Agency (2015). The Worl Factbook. https://www.cia.gov /library/publications/resources/the-world-factbook/

U.S. DOSa (2006–2014). *Country Reports on Human Rights Practices.* U.S. Department of State. Various years and Countries' Reports. http://www.state.gov/j/drl/rls/hrrpt/

U.S. DOSb (2014). *Trafficking in Persons Repot 2014. U.S. Department of State* http:// www.state.gov/j/tip/rls/tiprpt/2014/index.htm

Von der Osten-Sacken, T. and T. Uwer (2007). "*Is Female Genital Mutilation an Islamic problem?,*" *Middle East Quarterly,* Winter 2007, pp. 29–36. <http://www.meforum .org/1629/is-female-genital-mutilation-an-islamic-problem>.

Washington Times (2013). "Muslim Brotherhood Condemns U.N. Declarations on Women's Rights," March 14, 2013. http://www.washingtontimes.com/news/2013 /mar/14/muslim-brotherhood-condemns-un-declaration-womens-/

Weiner, L. (2004). "Islam and Women: Choosing to Veil and Other Paradoxes," *Policy Review*, October and November 2004. http://www.hoover.org/research/islam-and -women

WHO, The World Health Organization (2002). *Facts: Intimate Partner Violence.* http://www.who.int/violence_injury_prevention/violence/world_report/factsheets /en/ipvfacts.pdf

———. (2008). *Eliminating Female Genital Mutilation: An Interagency Statement.* http://www.who.int/reproductivehealth/publications/FGM/C/9789241596442/en /index.html

———. (2012). *Female Genital Mutilation and Other Harmful Practices.* <http:// www.who.int/reproductivehealth/topics/FGM/C/FGM/C_trends/en/index.html> Accessed April 17, 2012.

———. (2013). *Female Genital Mutilation. Fact Sheet No. 241*, updated February 2013. http://www.who.int/mediacentre/factsheets/fs241/en/index.html

———. (2014). *Female Genital Mutilation and Other Harmful Practices: Prevalence of FGM.* http://www.who.int/reproductivehealth/topics/fgm/prevalence/en/

WHO,UNICEF, UNFPA (1997). *Female Genital Mutilation: A Joint WHO/ UNICEF/UNFPA Statement.* <http://www.childinfo.org/files/FGM/Cc_WHO UNICEFJointdeclaration1997.pdf>

Williams, R. (1976). *Keywords: Vocabulary of Culture and Society* (New York, Oxford University Press).

Williamson, O. (1993). "Calculativeness, Trust, and Economic Organization," *Journal of Law and Economics* 36(1), Part 2, 453–486.

———. (2000). "The New Institutional Economics: Taking Stock, Looking Ahead," *Journal of Economic Literature* XXXVIII, 595–613.

Willis, R. (2012). "Saudis Split on Female Olympians, Athletic Hijabs," *The Jerusalem Post.* 2 August 2012. http://www.jpost.com/Middle-East/Saudis-split-on-female -Olympians-athletic-hijabs

Wilson, R. (2009). "Islam," in J. Peil and I. van Staveren (eds.), *Handbook of Economics and Ethics*, pp. 283–290 (Northampton, MA: Edward Elgar).

Woodley, F. and J. Marshall (1994). "Measuring Inequality Within the Household," *Review of Income and Wealth* 40(4), 415–431.

The World Bank (2001). *Engendering Development: Through Gender Equality in Rights, Resources and Voice* (New York: Oxford University Press).

———. (2014). *World Development Indicators 2014.* http://data.worldbank.org/data -catalog/world-development-indicators

World Values Survey (2014). *World Value Survey 2010–2014: Crossing By Country.* Study #906-WVS201. v.2014.04.28.

Yoder, P. S., P. O. Camara, and B. Soumaoro (1999). *Female Genital Cutting and Coming of Age in Guinea* (Calverton, MD: Macro International Inc).

Yoder, P. S., N. Abderrahim, and A. Zhuzhuni (2004). *Female Genital Cutting in the Demographic and Health Surveys: A Critical and Comparative Analysis*, DHS Comparative Reports No. (Calverton, MD: ORC Macro).

Yount, K. (2001). "Excess Mortality of Girls in the Middle East in the 1970s and 1980s: Patterns, Correlates, and Gaps in Research," *Population Studies* 55(3), 291–308.

———. (2003). "Gender Bias in the Allocation of Curative Health Care in Minia," *Population Research and Policy Review* 22, 267–295. http://link.springer.com/article /10.1023%2FA%3A1026090207663#page-2

Yount, K. (2004). "Symbolic Gender Politics, Religious Group Identity, and the Decline in Female Genital Cutting in Minya, Egypt," *Social Forces* 82(3),1063–1090.

Yount, K., R. Langsten, and K. Hill (2000). "The Effect of Gender Preference on Contraceptive Use and Fertility in Rural Egypt," *Studies in Family Planning* 31(4), 290–300.

Zuckerhut, P. (2011). "Feminist Anthropological Perspective on Violence," in M. Ennaji and F. Sadiqi (eds.), *Gender and Violence in the Middle East*, pp. 14–25 (New York: Routledge).

Index

Printed and bound in the United States of America